He was the most thorough musician I've ever seen. Wonderful as a conductor, a performer. I never saw him make a mistake. Mr. Falcone make a mistake? Unheard of! It was a gift. His most important contribution was in developing one of the finest college bands in the country.

*~ Dr. Harry Begian*
*Director of Bands at Wayne State University (1964–1967), Michigan State University (1967–1970), and the University of Illinois (1970–1984)*

He was a musical icon. Though Professor Falcone never discussed with me anything like the meaning of life, religion, politics, or philosophy, by example, he always set the highest standard for honesty and personal integrity in all he did.

*~ Fritz Stansell*
*Founder and President, Blue Lake Fine Arts Camp*

Leonard Falcone was like a father to me. He was one of the warmest and most musical human beings I have ever known. I will never forget him, and the world shouldn't either! He was revered in the profession of band conducting as being one of its giants, not only as a conductor, but as an arranger, and his reputation nationally was unequalled as a euphonium soloist.

*~ Ken Bloomquist*
*Michigan State University Director of Bands (1970–1977) and College of Music Chair (1978–1988)*

I have been proud to be part of a university whose conductor of bands was so progressive in bringing his students into the music world of wind ensembles, wind orchestras, and various wind and chamber organizations. His incomparable musicianship elevated BANDS to higher levels.

*~ Dr. James Niblock*
*Michigan State University Distinguished Faculty Member (1948–1985) and College of Music Chair (1970–1985)*

Leonard Falcone made an enormous impact on the music world, and how he did it is both complex and simple. The sheer force of his dedication and his enormous talent play a large role, but perhaps most important of all, the lesson of his life is that he was a hero as a human being.

~ *Dr. Myron Welch*
*Director of Bands, University of Iowa (1980–2008)*

# SOLID BRASS

## *The Leonard Falcone Story*

**Rita Griffin Comstock**

Blue Lake Press
Twin Lake, Michigan

*Solid Brass: The Leonard Falcone Story*

Blue Lake Press
A Division of Blue Lake Fine Arts Camp
300 East Crystal Lake Road
Twin Lake, MI 49457
Phone: 231-894-1966
Toll-Free: 800-221-3796
Fax: 231-893-5120
www.bluelake.org



ISBN: 978-0-9835979-0-2

Design & Production: Richard Harris
Front Cover Photo: courtesy of Golden Crest Records
Back Cover Photo: courtesy of Michigan State University
Archives & Historical Collections

Printed in the United States of America

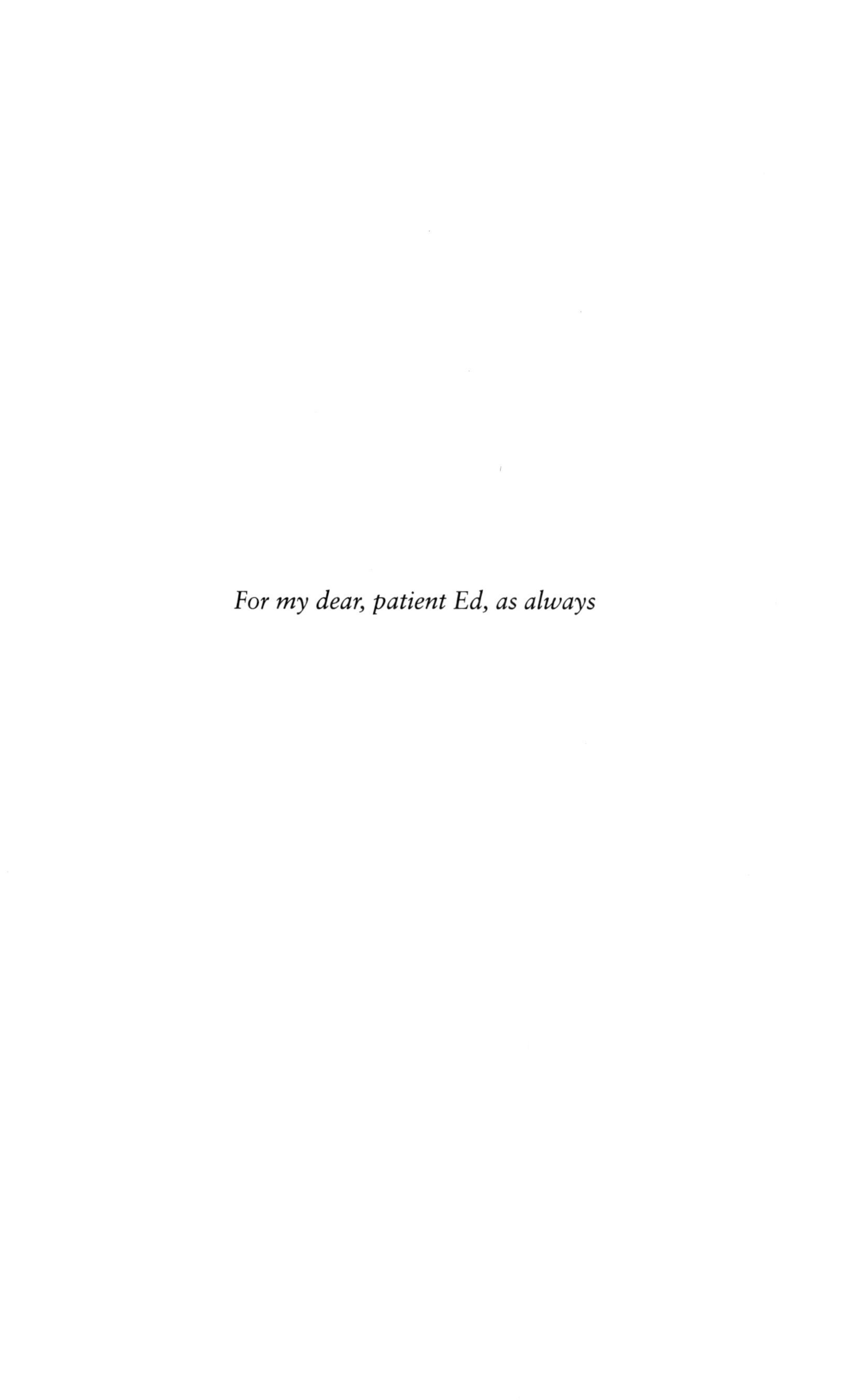

*For my dear, patient Ed, as always*

ACKNOWLEDGEMENTS

This book could not have come to pass without the "Falcone Five," a group of Leonard Falcone devotees which includes Myron Welch, Fritz Stansell, Tom Gillette, and, of course, Beryl and Cece Falcone. I owe them each a debt of gratitude, not only for their wonderful stories and insights, but also for the unfailing support I received from each of them in his or her own way. I would also like to thank Joe Dobos for his kindness in sharing his knowledge of the Falcone brothers, Bill McFarlin for his invaluable help during the publishing process, Sandy Sheroky for assisting me in typing some of the interview transcriptions, and Cesare Ruggiero for his translations from English to the Rosetan dialect.

## CONTENTS

CHAPTER 1

# THE SEARCH: JUNE 16, 1985

***"The past is never dead. It's not even past."***

**~ William Faulkner**
***Requiem for a Nun***

---

Leonard Falcone planned to take the Michigan State University Alumni Band on a concert tour of Italy in spring of 1985, which was to include a performance in his hometown, Roseto Valfortore. But one month before the tour began, Dr. Falcone passed away. The "Falcone Italian Band Tour" continued in the honor and memory of "a great pioneer in the band field."[1]

IT IS A WARM, DRY MID-JUNE AFTERNOON in 1985 in the Puglia region of Italy just outside the medieval city of Foggia, and the pilgrimage to Roseto Valfortore, the boyhood home of Leonard Falcone, has begun. Curious former students along with tagalong spouses and an interested Italian bus driver are headed there to play a concert and to search for traces of the slight, wiry boy who spent the first 16 years of his life on the other side of the Apennine mountain range, unknowingly preparing himself to be one of the greatest music educators of America's twentieth century. Nearly all are members of the Michigan State University Alumni Band, invited to entertain villagers for whom the name "Leonard Falcone," at least for today, is as well-known and as revered in Roseto as "Luciano Pavarotti" is in the rest of the country. In Roseto Valfortore, favorite son Leonard Falcone is a genuine celebrity.[2*]

Someone on board pulls out an early black and white photo of the venerated teacher and "Father of Michigan State Bands," a man they admire with a respect close to awe.[3*]

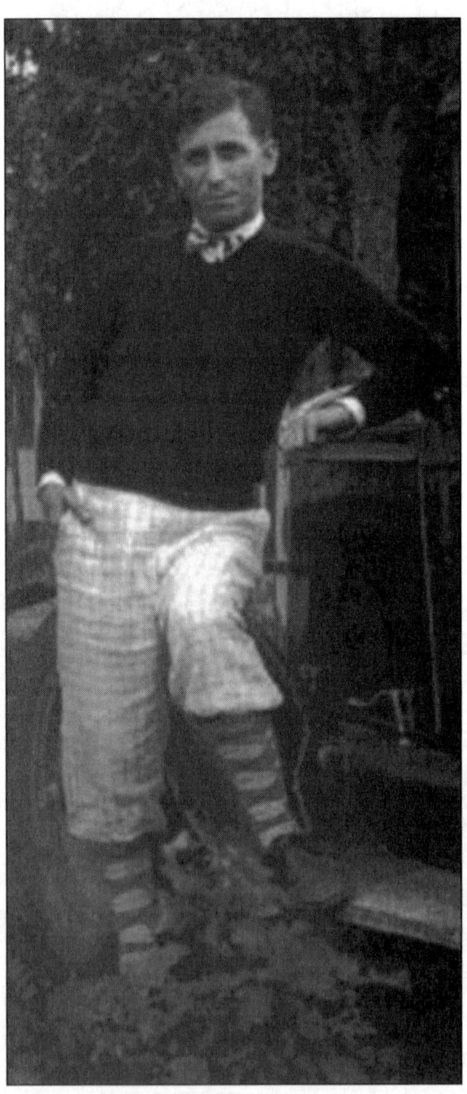

*Leonard Falcone, 1928*
*~ courtesy of the Falcone family*

Memory of him as frail and old is fresh, his death having occurred just a month before the trip began. But in this moment, as the picture is passed around, he is 29 and handsome, a young man on the fringes of adulthood, with the somber gaze of a conductor who takes his music seriously and expects others to do likewise. His lips are thin and pursed, but upturned, so that the set of his mouth projects hope, confidence, and anticipation. His dark, craggy skin is set off by a shock of brown hair neatly parted on the side, and by intelligent, deep-set eyes which contain both a twinkle and a hint of sadness. He is medium in stature, no more than 5'8", and nattily dressed in argyle socks, a striped bow tie, and windowpaned white knickers. One hand is in his pocket, thumb out, while the other makes a soft fist. An elbow leans against the doorframe of a Model T Ford, a foot rests on its running board, and taken all together, this makes for about as jaunty a stance as a young bachelor's stance could be. In time, his hair will gray, his eyes will fade, his posture will slacken and stoop. His memory, for nearly everything excepting his music, will diminish. But that time is not now.

The serpentine road touches several villages on its journey upward, offering varied views of the Tavoliere di Puglia before it finally crests the mountaintop. From there, the bus, a MSU FALCONE BAND TOUR banner affixed to its side, follows the Passo del Crocione down the mountain, down, down toward the village past a series of sprawling verdant vistas marked by luxuriant pine, oak, chestnut, and beech trees interspersed with arid patches of straw colored soil and coarse, stony ground. At 900 meters above sea level, it reaches a pass which affords a view of the entire Fortore valley with its soft outlines and rich vegetation; and then quite suddenly, from one of the many low, rolling hills sloping towards the river, the passengers catch their first glimpse of Roseto, cozily nestled on a small plateau against Mt. Stillo in the upper valley of the Fortore River, fronting the I Monti del Matese and the high, faraway Apennine peaks of Mt. Gran Sasso and Mt. Majella.[4]

The dog rose, a wildflower growing in pink and red profusion on the roadside, is pointed out by someone who thought to order a brochure from Roseto before leaving Michigan. Roseto Valfortore is a medieval town named during Roman times for this rose, she says, and for the Fortore River they can now see running through the valley below. Descending deeper, further into the vale, the bus traverses roads which on a map look like a tangle of spaghetti strands, and passes through foothills where for hundreds of years impoverished Rosetani worked the stone quarries. Here, the landscape changes color, offering rich hues according to the time of the year. In the autumn and winter seasons, the land is bare and brown, but at the first sign of spring, the valley takes on a deep green color. In summer, bald hills intersperse with patches of forest, sunflowers, and golden fields of durum wheat, a grain used to make breads and pastas, and present a pleasant, unspoiled landscape where the wolf, newt, and butterfly still survive, as in the old times.

Farther down the mountain, the stepped land a few miles below the village approaches, once a place of despair belonging to a few wealthy landowners to which desperately poor villagers walked five to ten miles daily with their mules and wooden tools. There, they spent grueling lifetimes eking out a meager living from the stingy soil, the importance of crop rotation being unknown.[5]

On a dusty part of the road, just before entering the north entrance to the town, the "contrada Piano dei morti" (Place of the Dead), an old burying ground, provides silent witness for the advancing bus. A steel cross monument marks the area where little is left except a few of the old farm houses and an ancient watering trough, filled to overflow with the Rosetani's strange folktales. It is a desolate place of gently folding hills where the first houses of Roseto once stood, farm homes inhabited by both people and animals and with *neveras*, or snow-filled holes in the ground, on their south sides. The *neveras*, plugged with snow in winter and covered with hay before first thaw, provided enterprising farmers the makings of *granita*, an ice dessert of snow and fruit or wine syrup, to sell during the summer months.[6*] And then, a surprise: on the wall of one of the still standing houses by the watering trough, there is a niche with a painting of the Madonna Incoronata.[7]

A quarter mile further down the road someone points out that a bumper sticker with "I Rosetani salutano la FALCONE BAND" has been stuck on a metal guard rail, the first of several they will see. From there, the bus enters the village itself, funneling up narrow streets to a spot a short walking distance from the main public square, the Piazza Castello, and comes to a halt on the one of only a handful of streets wide enough to hold it.

The village, situated on a very steep hill, beckons the disembarking pilgrims to walk up a rectangular-stoned, fan-patterned street and toward its heart, which they know as surely as they know the "MSU Fight Song" will be a central piazza (*Piazza Ranne*). They know this because if, as the brochure said, Roseto Valfortore is a 12th-century medieval town, then as with all medieval Italian villages it will have a central square where religious processions, celebrations, fairs, markets, and band concerts are held. And so they trek *en masse*, following their instincts to find the location of a place important not only because it is the cultural core of the village, but because they want to see a spot surely well known as a boy to Leonard Falcone, a man who, to them, has entered the pantheon of the immortal greats of music and of teaching.

When they reach Roseto's center, they are not disappointed. Closed to vehicle traffic but bustling with pedestrians, the Piazza Castello, sur-

*June, 1985, Falcone Alumni Band tour—Beryl, Cecilia, and Lisa in front of the tour bus in Roseto Valfortore*
*~ courtesy of the Falcone family*

rounded by attached two story buildings giving it the look of a walled city, rests proudly at the end of the Via Roma. It is dominated by a Rosetan stone memorial obelisk built to the village's fallen WWI and II soldiers, the *Monumento ai Caduti,* and the Palazzo Marchesale, the palace of the last of a long line of rulers of feudal Roseto, the aristocratic Saggese Marquis and his family.[8]*

At its end, they see workmen assembling a gazebo they know is for their concert that evening,[9]* a bandstand with a large electrified star hovering above its roof and the bright, colorful look of a very large carousel. It is a throwback. Once, Falcone described the region's early twentieth century bandstands as "round, covered structures of wood, complete with electric lights"[10]—just like this one. As they watch the construction, an electrician stands on a ladder and works on the lights, a man who a few hours later would astound and entertain them by shimmying up one of the gazebo's roof supports during the concert and, with his legs wrapped around a post, fix an electrical problem with the power on.[11] Once a site where justice was administered, the Piazza Castello now is a Rosetan reception room, a place planted with containers of the dog rose that gives the village its name and where one may welcome one's friends. Today, as most days, it is teeming with villagers: not only the workmen enlarging the gazebo to accommodate the band, but by village men promenading, stopping occasionally only to shoot the breeze with one another on a bench or at one of the café tables outside any one of a handful of bars near the square. It is great theatre. Clearly, a Rosetan bar, part pub and part coffee shop, is a gathering place the same way the Union on the MSU campus was in Falcone's day. People who know one another, and in the village of Roseto, where there are somewhere around 1,300 people, many with the same family names,[12] everyone knows everyone else, go there to discuss issues, exchange information, offer opinions, commiserate, brag, or show off an object of pride.

**Cecilia (Cece) Falcone, Leonard Falcone's daughter, French horn, WMU:** *On both my 1971 and 1985 band trips, the local villagers literally took me by both arms and dragged me around town from sidewalk bar to sidewalk bar as if I were a trophy. They*

> *spoke Italian and I didn't, so I just went along for the ride, letting them do their thing (as if I had a choice!). I remember in 1971, when I went to Roseto with a high school group my dad took there from Blue Lake,*[13*] *that when I was returned to the group mom said she had kind of been wondering where I was. She said she wasn't a bit worried for my safety, only concerned that the bus would soon be leaving. Thanks, mom. I didn't see much of dad, either, on that first trip—the mayor or some other biggie probably had him corralled somewhere.*
>
> *Of course dad died just before the MSU Alumni Band trip in 1985, so obviously he wouldn't have been around. Even though he wasn't there, there was a huge turnout at the concert. I'm sure that even the children would have been told that a band belonging to one of their own was returning. But mom was there, and once again, just as in 1971, I was abducted and shown off by the villagers and not returned for some time. Everyone else used the free time before the dinner the town hosted for us at the Miraville, the local hotel, to do some exploring . . . as for me, I was at the bars!*[14]

There are many narrow alleys (*strettole*), each less than six feet wide, each eventually channeling from the Piazza Castello to Roseto's Old Town Square, the Piazza Vecchia, and to the mother church, *la Chiesa Madre,* the *Santa Maria Assunta*. Though they can't know if this is the part of town where Leonard Falcone grew up, a small group decides that at very least, he had to have known these *strettole* well and that they are going to have a look. They splinter away, heading toward the ancient *Arco della Terra*, one of the archways which, unbeknownst to them, once had a door which was locked every sundown to keep out criminals and untrustworthy strangers or non-*campanilismo*— defined as anyone living outside the sound of the village church bell.[15] In other words, people like themselves.

They walk through the archway and follow the alley deeper into the village, up, up the narrow, steep pathway rising from the town square. It brings them to the Piazza Vecchia, the oldest part of town, which crosses rows of stair-like alleys and arches leading to the *sott I coste*, a street veranda ending in an expansive, sloping view of Roseto and of the *Bosco Vetruscelli,* the forest through which the Fortore River rushes down Monte Vento toward the town. Here, the majestic *Santa Maria Assunta* (*Chiesa Madre*), the Palace Marchesale facing its left side, rises to full view. It is the most important church in town. Bankrolled by Bartolomeo III Di Capua, one of Roseto's many feudal lords, and completed in 1507, it was constructed by Rosetani stonecutters who extracted its Stone Age carrara (*carattrizzata*) marble from a nearby quarry, and ornamented by village artisans who carved its intricate balustrade, among other pieces. An arc of land opposite its main door serves as a welcome mat for the group, and they enter.

When they leave the *Chiesa Madre*, they find themselves on streets no wider than six feet in the area of *Via Sottasanta* (under the saints). Flanked by huddled tan, gold, and white stone houses[16] skillfully worked long, long ago by local stonemasons, they choose a home at random to photograph, and to wonder: could this house, clinging so tightly to the hill, be a place Leonard Falcone knew well—perhaps the home of an aunt and uncle, a cousin, a grandparent? In a region where, at the turn of the century, more than half of marriages took place between men and women who lived within five miles of each other[17] and where even today a third of the population is named "Falcone" and more than a quarter of it is named "Finelli,"[18] the name of Leonard Falcone's maternal grandparents, this is not an absurd question. Is it possible, they muse, that this is the very house where he grew up and formed his talents and character? And even if it wasn't—what was there about living in a place like it that influenced him into becoming the person and great maestro he was? Its location in this village and this country? His parents? The village music teacher? What?

This house, like all the others, is a modest, two story stone home blanketed by a roof of alternating flat and round red tiles with an exterior staircase so steep the steps leading to the door above look like a ladder. On the second story, there is a shallow, wrought iron balcony sporting pots of basil and other herbs. They can see that the lower floor has a kitchen, a dining room, and a bedroom (which 100 years ago functioned as a storage area where livestock were kept) and so, they decide, the upper floor must contain more bedrooms.[19] And they are right.

As it turns out, this house is not, in fact, Leonard Falcone's boyhood home: but it is very much like it. If the little group were to head back toward the Arco del Terra and the Via Roma, they might eventually stumble across a wider and less steep street than those they have been exploring in the Piazza Vecchia area, a street running northeast of the main town plaza, the Piazza Castello, where tonight's concert will be played. Down that street, a quarter of a mile past its tall white file of houses, stands the Falcone house. If they were to find that house, they would discover that the only real difference between it and the house they photographed on the Via Sattosanti is in the location of the staircase. The Falcone's staircase is interior, they would note. It falls sharply from the upstairs landing directly down to the first floor, a fact they would have no way of knowing unless the tall, arched wooden door which empties directly onto the street were to open to reveal the inside of the home. Upstairs, they might see that there are two bedrooms. Downstairs, there is one. Over the years, perhaps hundreds of people

*Leonard Falcone in front of a place he believed to be one of his childhood homes in Roseto Valfortore*
*~ courtesy of the Falcone family*

have slept in those rooms. Among them, on the early morning of June 20, 1915, were seven of the nine members of the Falcone family. Missing were the eldest sons, Nicola,[20*] who had emigrated to America in 1912, and Carmelo, who had joined the Italian Army. Remaining were the parents, Maria and Domenico, and their youngest children, Leonardo, Guiseppina, Giovannina, Lucietta, and little Rosina—born 1914, a year before 16-year-old Leonardo, leaping out of one world and landing in another, left home. It is here, in this house, that the story really begins.[21*]

CHAPTER 2

# ROOTS: APRIL 5, 1899–JUNE 18, 1915

***"La Famiglia e la patria del cuore."***
***("Family is the homeland of the heart.")***

**~ Italian proverb**

---

*We are all denizens of a homeland constructed from the landscape of our youth, a place where, at the very core of our beings, we most authentically dwell. Recalled through the haze and hyperbole of memory, it is a world built by the influence of the most important people in our lives, by our nationalities and early experiences, and even by the shape and contour of the land. Look to your right in that place, young Leonardo. There, you will see your mother, your father, your teachers, Donato Antonio Donatelli and Filippo de Cesare. Now look to your left. Do you see the little village of Roseto Valfortore? It is the wellspring of your artistry, where you slept in your mother's arms as she walked to the town fountain to get the water to do the family's laundry and cook its dinners, where you played with your brothers while your parents worked, where its hills and valleys encompassed you and whispered their music to your heart. Everything that shaped you happened here. You learned important values in life here. You became a musician here. You last saw your parents here.*

There is little known about Leonard Falcone's mother, Maria Finelli Falcone, but it is certainly true that, as with all Rosetan women, she placed her family's welfare first. She was expected to,[1] and there is much evidence she did. Part of what is known about the framework of her life is that before Leonardo's birth, she and her husband agree to a move away from all she knows to Brazil,[2] a place so foreign to the young village girl she must have felt, like the Biblical Ruth, that even the corn seemed "alien." In a world that took kinship very seriously, leaving her family of origin had to have been wrenching. With her is her husband, two-year-old Nicola, and the baby, Carmelo, who will later, as a toddler, get lost in Sao Paulo during the Christmas season and have what was surely, at least to Maria, a dramatic police return.[3] Almost unquestionably this move was made in the hope of bettering her children's future. Four years afterward, she returns to Italy with her two little boys in tow,[4] and on April 5, 1899, soon after her arrival, gives birth in a small bedroom to a baby boy she and her husband name Leonardo Vincenzo Falcone.[5] And Dominico? Some eighty years later, Leonard would say that his father stayed on for two more years to work in Sao Paulo, not returning to the little family until 1900.[6] During this time, then, was Maria without her husband and, excepting the probable support of both sides of her family, the Finellis and the Falcones, largely on her own? It seems likely, and it seems, too, that she had a strength of character that allowed her the persistence to endure.

In all, Maria brings ten children into the world, only seven of whom survive to adolescence. In what had to have been crushing blows, one, a boy, dies at age six,[7] and two others die in infancy.[8] Alongside these losses, she calls on her courage to say goodbye to 20-year-old Nicola and 16-year-old Leonardo as they seek their fortunes in a place far from Roseto, and to Carmelo, as he faces an uncertain future in the Italian Army.

If family was at the center of Maria Falcone's life, no doubt homemaking came close to it. For the women of her generation, it was a measure of worth that the children be well behaved, the home clean and neat, the food tasty and well prepared.[9] All these goals and expectations, probably embraced cheerfully, translated into very hard work for her, and for all Rosetan women.

**Nick Ferrera, Leonard Falcone's third cousin:** *I can tell you that living conditions for the Falcones were hard and that keeping the house running was grueling and constant work. There was no running water, so there were, of course, no indoor toilets, either. Maria's job, which probably was assigned later to Leonard and his brothers, would have included tending to the chamber pots under the beds. She would have had to have gone regularly to the* funtana *to retrieve water for cooking, laundry, and a Saturday bath, and would have kept a large kettle boiling day and night every day of the year, replenishing it often. Like everyone else's, the Falcone household would have had a fireplace large enough to walk into, if you can picture it, with a sort of range made of tiles in the middle on which sat a kind of fire box. On it, Maria would build a fire of twigs or kindling and straw. When the tiles got red hot, she would put a brass* tripodi *(tripod) on them and place a cooking pot or frying pan on top. There were different sizes of pans and* tripodi. *Maria would have to cook for God knows how long just to make the family dinner. Naturally, she would not have been able to adjust the heat.*

*Another of her many jobs would have been to make dough for baking. Like every other family in town, the Falcones would have eaten bread every day. My mom's family, the Finellis, had a bakery (*forno*) in Roseto Valfortore, referred to as* u forn e Mamma Cia. *I believe it was on* Via Piazza Funtane. *The bakery was not what we now normally think of as a bakery, just as the Falcone barber shops weren't what we now normally think of as barber shops. Shops were usually located in people's homes, and this was true of* u forn e Mamma Cia. *It was in the middle of my grandparent's house, and it was virtually all ovens. If you looked at the house from the outside, you would see that on one side was an entry door, almost like a garage door, and on the other side were a of set stairs,* la scalinata. *The entry door on the street level led to the ovens in the main living space, while the stairs led to two or three rooms on the second floor, extending over the ovens located on the ground floor. I'm not sure if there was an inside stairway too.*

*Anyhow, the dough Maria Falcone would have made at home was called* massa. *My mother's occupation at 10 or 11 years old, which would have been around 1912 when Leonard was 13 and still living in the village, was to go out in the night carrying* a lunderna *(a lamp) and knock on doors and tell the people to bring her their massa. There was an actual name,* cumanna, *for going to wake the people to bring the dough. After all the customers brought their risen loaves to her (and as part of the Finelli family, unless there was a much closer bakery Maria or one of the Falcone boys was likely one of them) she would rush them back to the* forno *for her parents to bake them into bread, tarelli, biscotti, or whatever. It was important that my mother work quickly, because if she didn't, the night air would affect the rising.*

*Some people made a white bread dough, some people made* u pane nero, *or dark bread dough, some used potato flour, others corn, etc. My mother would have to keep track of each loaf, as no family wanted any surprises when their bread was returned. At the* forno, *my nonna had a special mark for each family that she would put on the loaves with her finger. She would make tiny designs on each loaf of bread so it wouldn't get mixed up with somebody else's. Of course there were some wealthier people who didn't massa their own dough. For them, my nonna would massa* her *dough, bake it, and sell the finished loaf to them.*

*On holidays the Falcones would have brought the capon, the lamb, or the* porchetta *(ham) to a bakery for their holiday feast, and there my relatives, if it came to* u forn e Mamma Cia, *would roast the meat. When the meat was returned to them, Maria would begin the preserving. Always, every family in the village slaughtered a pig on the Feast of Sant'Antonio Abate on Jan 19th, and then it was up to the women to cure the meats.*

*There were probably 10 or 12* forni *when my parents lived in Roseto Valfortore in the early 1900s, and there were 6,000 inhabitants. These numbers will give you an idea as to the amount of baking and roasting that was done.*

*Keeping warm in the winter months in Roseto was a challenge. My mother's family was always warm. Because of the ov-*

> *ens they were even cozy in winter, but of course they sweltered in the summer. But for the Falcones, in winter it was very cold. Roseto could get cold. No central heating. What the Falcones would have done was have a* u bracciere, *an iron circle with a pan in the middle. Now outside, Maria would have placed a bucket or container where she would have burned* carbone *(charcoal); she'd have gotten it real white and then taken it inside and put the coals in the pan on the floor so everyone could sit around it. The iron ring was made like a crown so that you could put your feet on it, most likely fully clothed. You moved what you had around the living space to warm it up a bit or, if you had money, you would use more than one. For Leonard to have been warm when he went to bed at night, Maria would have warmed* un mattone *(a brick) or even a couple of them, wrapped it in a towel, and run it over the sheets before he went to bed.*
>
> *My wonderful parents immigrated here in 1919 and 1920 and kept in their hearts 'til their dying day a love of Italy and Roseto Valfortore. My brother and sisters and I sometimes got tired of hearing their stories but they couldn't have cared less. They would say that we kids didn't elect them as our parents and our household wasn't a democracy. So dinner time, and especially Sundays before TV and everything else took over people's lives, we sat and listened to our parents and the* paesans *who were visiting and playing card games with them, and the talk usually reverted to* u Paese Roseto Valfortore.
>
> *I was blessed with a good memory and although I have forgotten a whole lot, what I say here is completely true to the stories I remember of what was typical in enduring life in Roseto in the early 1900s, and the life Leonard, his mother, Maria, and the rest of the Falcone family lived.*[10]

If Maria's life can be seen refracted through the shards of common memory of those who lived in Italy at the turn of the 20th century and later shared their experiences with others, then we can be sure that she, like all Italian women of the time, was raised to pamper the men in her family. In every household, the Italian father was an authority figure, catered to by his wife, "particularly in regard to food."[11] And so when her husband came home from the barber shop each night, it would have been Leonard's mother's job to see that his father was greeted by loving children and a hearty meal, most likely pizza or his favorite pasta with a tangy sauce, and/or bread, polenta, cheese, fruit (in season), a soup made from cabbage or cauliflower from the fields, beans or vegetables (primarily potatoes or peppers fried in lard), and wine.[12] Perhaps twice a month there would have been chicken, rabbit, or pork, but even in plentiful times she would not have served meat more than once a week.[13] While Dominico may have had a small garden that provided the dinner table with fruits and vegetables, it would have been Maria who canned them for the winter, made the pastas and sauces and the goat or sheep cheese, and bread. Family gatherings, large and small, would have counted for much with young Leonardo's mother. The nearly non-stop holidays, birthdays, christenings, funerals, and weddings would have been the best reasons to bring the Falcones and the Finellis together, and a way to combine the well known Italian love of cooking with love of family.

In addition to hostessing family gatherings, Maria would have to have found the time to cook and make bread dough, can and cure meats, keep the house clean, do the laundry, sew, knit, crochet, tat, embroider, mend the clothes, handle religious concerns, tend the animals, raise the children, attend mass, arrange marriages, keep the family warm and clean, and cater to her husband. Maria would have been the moral center of the family,[14] its heart.[15]

If she was like nearly every other Italian woman of the time, there was a duality to Maria's life. In public, she would have been expected to be submissive,[16*] but in the home, she could, and likely did, give her opinion boldly and as often as she liked: as long as it didn't challenge Dominico's authority.[17] It was her job to hold the family together, and as a good Italian wife, she would have taken it seriously. As the family's moral compass, she had the responsibility to instill in Leonardo the importance of kindness, hard work, respect to God, the saints, and all elders, especially parents.[18] It would seem, if Leonard was any measure, she was a success.

Some years later, when Leonardo had made the transformation to "Leonard," young American bachelor . . .

**Dave Wisner, clarinet, MSU 1959:** *. . .he never understood and often expressed dismay to his friends over how kids could misbehave. Leonard would say the equivalent of, 'Back in the old country, children knew their place.' The implication, of course, was that if he ever married and had children of his own, he would be a strict, no-nonsense father.* His *kids would tow the mark. But in later years, when he was married and Beryl (Leonard's wife) would bring their children with her to pick him up after rehearsals, we band members were astonished at how our stern, sometimes cross, and always serious leader would melt at the sight of his fun-loving, noisy, and not always well behaved little girls.*[19]

**Beryl Falcone:** *He was a good father. He was a soft touch, but they did what he said, even though he said it in a kind way.* [20]

Italian mothers spent their lives in self-sacrifice and total commitment to their families, especially their husbands and sons.[21] It's not too much of a stretch to assume that Leonard's patience and love for his children, his loyalty to his family, and his persistence and courage and penchant for hard work, were all values he learned at home in large part from his doting mother, Maria.

More can be known for certain about Leonard Falcone's father, Dominico, a barber who owned two or three shops in Roseto.[22]

**Nick Ferrera:** *My pop was also a barber in the village. I do not know how Dominico Falcone set up his business, but as for my father, grandfather, and great-grandfather, their* salone, *or barbershop, was in the front of their home on the Via Piazza Grande. Behind the shop was a large living area, and upstairs were two bedrooms. The Falcones probably had a similar arrangement. In those days, barbers also did leeching or sanguette.*[23]

**Beryl Falcone:** *(Dominico) got paid in chickens or eggs or products rather than money, because people around were mostly*

*Maria and Domenico Falcone, 1918*
*~ courtesy of the Falcone family*

> *farmers. A lot of the people around would go out and work in the fields and come home at night to sleep.*[24]
>
> **Nick Ferrera:** *One hundred years ago, Roseto was a barter economy, and it remained so up until about WWII. If a farmer made cheese, he struck a deal for so many rounds of pecorino or for so many baked loaves of bread or for ricotta or beans or a dress or suit from a tailor or for a haircut from Dominico Falcone, or from my pop. There wasn't any hard currency at that time, so all the trades and services did the same thing.*[25]

A professional picture of the patriarch of the Falcone family dated 1922 shows him seated surrounded by his daughters, his large workman's hands peacefully clasped together. He is immaculately groomed, dressed in his three piece suit and, most befitting a barber, is sporting a magnificent Jerry Cologna moustache. A watch fob hangs from his pants pocket.[26] The expression on his face is serious, stern, and in keeping with the nearly certain authoritarian role he played in the Falcone family as its undisputed head[27] and with the events of the era in which he spent most of the years of his life.

Some thirty years earlier than the moment of this picture, in the late 1800s when Dominico, then a young man, began bringing children into the world, there existed a bleak physical and emotional condition termed *la miseria* by Southern Italians. An onerous state of helplessness rested like a leaden pall on the shoulders of the people.[28] Everywhere, there were gloomy faces, and for good reason. By the 1890's, the proud villagers of Roseto were barely surviving and without hope of change. When Italy reunified in 1861 (the same year the first class at Michigan's "State Agricultural College" graduated and, without any commencement ceremony, marched off to fight in the Civil War), the political situation in the region remained chaotic as the inept administration of the Bourbons gave way to a northern Italian bureaucracy that drained from the south what little there was to be had. They levied a plague of taxes on tobacco, livestock, salt, and even on the grinding of wheat and corn—key ingredients in pasta and bread. Farmers remained trapped in a feudal land system with absentee landlords from the north, many of whom, as creditors, seized their properties.

Political upheavals and taxes aside, life became even more difficult when phylloxera epidemics destroyed thousands of acres of vineyards, so that France was able to drive Italy out of international wine sales. When a series of droughts in 1891 and 1892 ruined grain and citrus crops, America and Russia took over those markets and Italy lost still more exports. A lack of coal and iron ore severely hindered the growth of industry. There were deadly volcanic eruptions of Vesuvius and Etna, deforestation which ruined the soil and spread malarial swampland, problems with overpopulation, and then, in 1892, came famine. The list of sorrows seemed endless.

In the midst of *la miseria*, when word of the promise of good paying work in South America reached Roseto, Dominico Falcone didn't waste any time.[29]* Many had already immigrated to the United States, a known land of opportunity. But there was a financial risk involved in taking the journey since a trans-Atlantic ship passage was expensive and there was no guarantee of being able to remain in the country. So when in 1894 Brazil offered plots of land and subsidized steamship fares in return for working on one of Sao Paulo's booming coffee plantations,[30] many Rosetani, seeing little risk, left the village to take advantage of the opportunity. Dominico Falcone, then age 30,[31] was one of the first to go. He uprooted his young wife, two year old, and newborn son and, shortly after the Brazilian government made its offer, left behind his Italian homeland and headed for Sao Paulo.[32]

Though it is unknown if the lack of prospects in Roseto and the hope of good paying work in Brazil's coffee trade were the reasons why the Falcones emigrated, it seems highly probable. The possibility of the move having to do with the coffee plantations would certainly be consistent with the documented exodus of Southern Italians' relocation to Sao Paulo in the mid-1890s; at very least, it would be a striking coincidence that the Falcones' travel coincided with Brazilian economic fortunes, arriving as they did in 1894 when the plantations were thriving, in need of workers, and the government was offering free passage, and returning to Roseto in 1898 (Maria and children) and 1900 (Dominico)[33]* as world coffee prices fell and the economy floundered and worsened.[34] One way or another, the move had to have been made to improve the family's fortunes, as no one during this period, and certainly not a family man like Dominico Falcone, would displace his wife and little ones lightly.

Dominico's decisiveness and forward thinking were personal attributes which surely came into play again years later when another life-changing decision, this time for his third son, Leonardo, was made. In Italy, then as now, very few young people were granted the autonomy to make decisions about their lives. All important decisions were made by a watchful father, ideally, though not always, with the consent of the son or daughter for whom they were being made. Fathers demanded total respect from their families which, in their eyes, meant 100-percent adherence to their wishes.[35] So it was almost certainly Dominico, in a move which unsurprisingly came down on the side of assuring his dreams of a better future for his children, who decided that when the time was right Leonardo would leave Roseto and emigrate to America.

**Beryl Falcone:** *I think Leonard wanted to come to the United States—but whether he did or not, his father said he was going, and that was that.*[36]

As it turns out, this is one decision which wouldn't have received much, if any, opposition from his ambitious son.

> **Leonard Falcone:** *Back then, everyone wanted to go to the United States. It was expected that people would leave Roseto, live in America for 5–6 years, make their fortune, and return home. Several people had gone to America and returned with stories of wealth and grandeur. They claimed that, in America, all one had to do was dig a hole and find gold. In Roseto, there were not many prospects.*[37]

And then, in August, 1914, Leonardo was thrust into a situation mirroring his father's 1894 crisis both in its threat to his dreams for a better life and the opportunity it presented to fulfill them. One day during that month he picked up a newspaper and read that World War I was beginning in Europe, and he knew immediately: if he stayed in Italy, he'd be conscripted into the Italian Army. And soon.[38]

> **Leonard Falcone:** *I was only 15 years old. My older brother Carmen was already in the service, and my father was hoping to keep me out of it.*[39]

America was an appealing place to a young man who had been taught to think of his future, and the reasons for Leonardo to go there as soon as his father could secure him passage and travel money were adding up with a convergence of force. Because in Roseto profession and class were passed on within the family, there was little chance for a boy to do anything much more in life than his father had done or to move up the social ladder.[40]

Emigration was the progressive thing to do, Leonardo thought at the time, much as learning to play an instrument in the band or learning a trade had been[41]—both skills he had already accomplished. What's more, his older brother, Nicolas, had already emigrated to Ann Arbor in the United States, and would be able to support him financially for a while and help him settle there.[42] Now that the situation in Europe was dire, it seemed that America, land of opportunity and wealth for those who would work for it, wasn't merely speaking his name, it was shouting it.

Clearly, Dominico decided that the "right time" for Leonardo to emigrate wasn't at some future date, it was now. And so he amended the original plan for the best moment for his son's departure,[43*] and on June 23, 1915, Leonardo left Italy for America.[44] The timing proved to be auspicious. Two months after he set foot on American shores, Leonardo Falcone's fifteen Roseto Band classmates were called into the Army.[45] He had battled with the fortunes of life, and won.

With him, young Leonardo brought gifts, most likely given him by his father, of ambition and confidence. . . and something more important. All Rosetani fathers knew that ambition and confidence won't take a boy far without a solid work ethic, and taught their sons by words and example that earning a living by working hard and working well is as intrinsic to a man's identity as his eye color or family name.[46] While we can't know precisely all the kinds of work Dominico expected Leonardo to do, we do know that he had him lather men's faces in his barber shops when he wasn't in school or with the town band,[47] and that by age nine, the age at which mandatory education ended and at which most Rosetani fathers expected their sons to begin to provide for themselves,[48] his third son was earning his own living.[49] We know, too, that somewhere around 1909 when he was "ten or twelve," he began learning a practical trade that would assure him a dependable income. Figuring it was the work his brother, Nicola, had chosen before him, that it was respected as an art form, and that it was ". . . a convenient trade to combine with music" because he could easily arrange his (future) store hours to fit being in the band, he chose to be a tailor. In his dreams, little Leonardo was already imagining himself a musician. Tailoring, he hoped, would only serve as a safety net.[50]

> **Leonard Falcone:** *It was natural that all youngsters learn a trade. You had to have a trade, unless you were very wealthy and could go to university. And so I learned to be a tailor, starting around 10 or 12. I was an apprentice. No pay. I learned the trade gradually. There was a dignity about it, and it was appreciated. I never wanted to be a tailor for the rest of my life, but there was a security about it.*[51]

He must have learned well, as many years later, he would uncharacteristically boast, "I can make a suit from scratch!"[52]

> **Tom Gillette, baritone, MSU band 1975-1979:** *I was at his home once doing some work, and watched him get out an ironing board, an iron, and some supplies. He took a tape measure and a piece of tailor's chalk and expertly marked the proper leg length on a pair of cuffed trousers. I made some comment and he reminded me that in his younger days he had apprenticed as a tailor. I don't recall the details, but I do remember him walking me through the process, as if he were the master teaching the apprentice. He worked quickly, assuredly, and deftly, and it wasn't long until at least one leg was hemmed. I suppose I went back to my work before the whole job was finished, but it was something that stuck with me—how workmanlike and "in his element" he was in doing that task.*
>
> *I think he could have had them done at Twitchell's on the way home from MSU for less than $4.00, but he did them himself. By the way—his clothes, while not always "new" and "stylish" (by 1970s standards!) always fit well.*[53]

According to Leonard, Dominico also knew the thrills of music, though unlike his sons he had never played a musical instrument. But he loved melody, had once sung in the church choir, and knew many of the great Italian arias. It's easy to imagine him charming his family and barber shop customers with his rendition of a lump-in–the-throat aria, though we can't know for certain if he ever did. Yet Leonardo surely heard him sing from time to time and sensed his father's delight. At very least, he knew he took pride in his three sons' musical accomplishments, as he always "encouraged (them) to participate in music"[54] and was proud of them to the extent that he would argue with Roseto's band conductor about their musical value and proficiency: when members of Roseto's Band received an annual stipend (handed over to the fathers), varying in amount according to the importance of the player, Dominico would grouse that his sons were not getting enough and negotiate harder.[55] Plainly a perfectionist, he pushed his sons musically even to the extent of placing astonishing pressure on Leonardo, for one, to play to precision.

**Leonard Falcone:** *My father couldn't read music, but he had a very fine ear, very sensitive. He knew the arias well and could sense if I was out of tune or played a wrong note. He understood pitch, key relationships. Whenever I made a mistake in my practice, he would know, and he would correct me, even though he didn't have training. Once he became exasperated because I was having trouble changing from quarter to eighth notes. I had trouble speeding up the notes from one to the beat to two to the beat. I suppose I finally got over the problem. One time he became very upset with me. He kept telling me that I was making a mistake. . . and I kept making that same mistake over again. He finally came over and twisted my ears and said, "That's the last time you'll play that wrong note!"*

*He had a very good ear.*[56]

When it came to music, and perhaps other things as well, "getting it right" was important to Dominico Falcone. Italian fathers taught their sons to be just like them.[57] Little wonder, with a father like this as a role model, as an adult Leonard had a great ". . . self-assurance, and never doubted himself as introspective people do."[58] Yet inner thinker or not, he was surely at least vaguely aware that his father had taught him many quiet lessons about success. Ambition, confidence, courage, vision, adventure, hard work, responsibility, perfectionism, and a love of music: these were values and traits they shared.

So it was that along with his trombone, Leonardo carried with him to America lessons taught him by his parents, Maria and Dominico. But there was one lesson, a lesson given him by his father, that was more precious than the others because it spoke directly to his heart, and it was this: that the sweetest joy of being Italian comes from a love of music. *La musica*. It resided in every molecule of Leonardo's mind, body, and soul, and already it was flowing through his veins as naturally as the waters of the Fortore run through the valley of Roseto.

CHAPTER 3

# LESSONS: APRIL 5, 1899–JUNE 18, 1915

*"Oh, this learning, what a thing it is!"*

~ Shakespeare
*The Taming of the Shrew*

---

**Saturday**

Morning: Walk to the host village.
Afternoon: "March" to the town's main square.
Evening: Play a concert in the town's band gazebo.
Night: Sleep in a local building on a straw mat or, if lucky, a cot.

**Sunday Feast Day**

7:30 a.m.: Parade through village to wake up townsfolk.
8:00 a.m.: Eat breakfast.
8:30 a.m.: Perform around the village in small groups of 6-8.
10:30 a.m.: Perform at the church service.
12:30 p.m.: Parade of the Saints
2:00 p.m.: Sunday dinner in a village home
3:30 p.m.: Siesta
5:30 p.m.: Parade briefly through village once again.
9:00 p.m.: Perform another concert in the town's band gazebo.
Night: Sleep in a local building on a straw mat or, if lucky, a cot.

**Monday**

| | |
|---|---|
| Morning: | Walk back home to Roseto |
| Afternoon: | Time to relax at home with family[1] |

THERE WERE INFLUENCES OTHER THAN HIS FAMILY, of course, which inspired Leonard Falcone to be the virtuoso he became. Most important among them, Falcone once said, was the "rich musical heritage of the country and city of his birth" and playing in Roseto Valfortore's municipal band.[2] The two were inextricably intertwined. That the Italy of Leonard Falcone's time had a "rich musical heritage" goes almost without explanation. The 19th century exploded in lyrical melody written by the likes of operatic giants such as Rossini, Donizetti, Bellini, Verdi, and Puccini. Their operas were everywhere, not just in great opera houses, but also on village streets.

Everywhere, too, were the ubiquitous and popular Italian wind bands, which played not only for public events, but also led religious processions and funerals through the streets of Italy's cities and villages. By the end of the nineteenth century, almost 5,000 of these bands, most sponsored by a local merchant or businessman, were in existence, representing nearly every commune and military unit in Italy.[3] One of the best, perhaps *the* best, of the community bands was located in Leonard's village, Roseto Valfortore.[4]*

What music might it have played in the early 20th century when Leonardo was 5 or 10 or 15 years old? No account shows, and in the end it hardly matters. What counts is that something of its power seized his imagination in a way that marked the young boy forever.

> **Leonard Falcone:** *In programming and performance, you might say that the Italian heritage is with me. When I think of it, it's there. But it isn't conscious. I don't think, "Now, that's what we did in Italy!" No. Not that. But if I were to analyze, shall we say, my musical feelings. . . they have been influenced by the training and experience I received in Italy before I came here. Very much so. The clarity, the lightness of technique, and the sparkling*

> *style that you hear in Rossini, for instance, well, that influenced me. When teaching, I sometimes think students' performances are too heavy, too thick. That idea stems from my training and experience in Italy. Yes.*[5]

Roseto took pride in its band[6]* even to the extent that the village itself hired a top conductor— Donato Antonio Donatelli, grandson of its founder Domenico Egidio Donatelli, the man who in 1790 organized the village's first band[7]—and then made sure he made a good living. In a town with many poor, his home was a comfortable place complete with servants. His job was simply this: to offer beginning instrumental instruction to the village boys free of charge, and to build a good musical unit to be made available for municipal festivals and events, which sometimes included service to the king and other royals.[8] Donatelli's career is interesting for a number of reasons, not least of all for its magical qualities. When he was merely seventeen, his music director took ill just before the band he played in at the time was to give a concert at the San Carlo di Napoli exhibition in honor of King Umberto Primo and Queen Margherita of Savoy. He was called upon to fill in as conductor. The performance was so successful that the royals personally "congratulated him with a handshake" and released "400 pounds," a handsome amount of money, to him as a reward.[9] Later, in 1878 when Donatelli was the director of Roseto's band, King Umberto Primo and the queen crossed his path again when the band gave an impressive performance after walking all the way to Foggia, some nine hours from Roseto on foot, to play at a banquet given in honor of the royal couple's visit there. The king and his queen, in true fairy tale fashion (and in a in a gesture not unlike that of Oldsmobile's "Black Jack" Wolfram's to MSU's John Hannah forty years later), summoned the conductor and asked if they could grant him a wish. Maestro Donatelli didn't hesitate. He requested that his son, Michangelo, the group's principal clarinet player, be sent to the Conservatory San Pietro Majella in Naples so he could study to become a conductor like his father. The wish was granted. The latter story so took hold of Leonard Falcone's imagination that he told it many times in interviews,[10] including during his final interview, ninety six years after its occurrence. Perhaps it had also fascinated him as a young boy as he hoped against hope to someday be in one of the two service bands in Foggia, the principal city in the region, or like his teacher and his teacher's son before him, become a music student at the Naples Conservatory.[11] The first of the two goals was within his reach. But as for the second, realistically, he knew along with everyone else, that a conservatory education was only for the rich or the very lucky— like Michelangelo Donatelli, the boy whose dream came true when he was favored by a king.

Donato Donatelli's influence on Leonardo's musicianship was nothing less than profound. Superbly trained at the Conservatory of San Pietro Majella in clarinet, piano, harmony, theory, and arranging, he also had more than a working knowledge of brass instruments, though he didn't play them. Leonardo began his lessons with Donatelli on the upright alto horn, a non-melodic rhythm instrument. He was only eight years old, and the youngest or one of the youngest of a beginning class of fifteen boys who from October 1907 to March 1908 received fifteen-minute, five-day-a-week private lessons, which included brief daily assignments. Though he tried, not everything came easily to the nascent musical genius. For one thing, apparently he had rhythm problems.[12]

> **Leonard Falcone:** *I remember I had trouble with time changes, especially changing from 2/4 to 3/4 time. I could not play 3/4 time. During one of the lessons, Maestro Donatelli became so exasperated that he took ahold of my right foot and forced it up and down to beat the time said, "This is one on this side! The second beat is the foot to the right! The third is up!" I finally got over the problem.*[13]

Troubles with time signatures or no, Leonardo must have mastered his beginner's skills quickly, as at the end of the first few months of lessons he was one of just a few in his class to pass his band entrance examination. He was surely delighted. The chance to join his older brothers Nicholas, who played clarinet, and Carmen, who played tuba, in the band, parade around town in front of his friends (all of whom, according to him, admired village musicians they way young American boys admired sports heroes and so naturally aspired to become band members themselves),[14] and please his family had to have been heady stuff for the youngster. Selected to work his way up to playing fourth alto horn, he was to begin rehearsals immediately in preparation for his first spring band tour, a gig that paid. As if it weren't enough to receive the adulation of peers and the pride of his family, his selection meant that "at the age of (barely) nine, he was earning his own living,"[15*] a feat which would also allow him to pay for his music lessons. Now that he was a member of the band, he was no longer entitled to the free basic instruction provided by the city.[16]

So it was that shortly after Christmas of 1907, Leonardo began attending rehearsals in preparation for his first April through August concert season with the band.

> **Leonard Falcone:** *Following policy, I was first instructed in the simpler instruments. I crashed the cymbals in my first appearance with the band.*[17]

In no time, he was playing the alto horn, followed by instruction in other brass instruments.[18]

Practices, which lasted two hours, five evenings per week, brought about magnificent outcomes—but were tiresome affairs. Donatelli's deliberate, section by section rehearsal technique would have left little Leonardo waiting in silence and inactivity for long periods of time which must have, at least at first, bored the little boy nearly to distraction. And while this method no doubt taught him persistence and musical perfection, it also caused him a bit of problem when he first came to the United States: under Donatelli's tutelage, he never learned to sight read,[19] a skill particularly necessary to his future work as a theater musician.

> **Leonard Falcone:** *(Donatelli was) very methodical, note by note. Every note had to be correct. It was a very thorough training, and no distractions were allowed. The band was the main thing. (Rehearsals) were tedious, meticulous, slow—but the results were absolutely perfect in technique, expression, and style.*[20]

Each year the 40-member band's repertoire was wide-ranging, and included approximately a dozen new marches, many written by Donatelli himself, fifteen or so selections extracted by him from opera scores, and numerous lighter numbers, such as mazurkas, polkas, and potpourris. One of the band's flutists hand copied all the parts in manuscript form during the off season, a daunting task which also included copying the daily lessons and etude books. Years later, after immigrating to the United States, Leonardo saw his first printed music in Ann Arbor and, unaccustomed to it, found it difficult to read.[21]

The Roseto Banda Municipale was in demand all over the Apulia region for spring and summer religious celebrations, but most especially during the month of August, when it was so popular it had nearly daily performances. Leonardo and the other bandsmen walked the pathways over the tawny, green dappled hills of Apulia to these concerts, sometimes as much as twenty miles away,[22] each carrying his own instrument, some bread, cheese, fruit, bacon, or prosciutto (or the equivalent), and a small suitcase of clothes. One donkey in the strange menagerie would carry Donatelli, while others, carefully negotiating the rutted, bumpy cart paths, carried trunks of music, uniforms, and music stands.[23]

Feast days were always on a Sunday, but celebrations began on Saturday afternoons. On arriving in a host village on Saturday morning, the band followed much the same routine.

> **Leonard Falcone:** *Usually we had a schedule. The festivities would start the day before the fiesta, on a Saturday. After we walked to the village in the morning, we'd march (a kind of slow meandering) through the streets to the town's band shell, a wooden structure, where we stood in a circle with the conductor in the middle. We carried our own stands, they were metal stands, especially made, you know, and we never sat down. No complaints. That was the way it was done. Afterwards, there would be a break, a 3 hour siesta.*
>
> *For the evening concerts (on Saturday and Sunday) we played purely symphonic pieces, except at the end, there would be some popular songs. They were very well attended. The concert se-*

*lections, by the way, were very long. They would last anywhere from 15 to 25 minutes or 30 minutes. We might play the entire second act of Rigoletto, and then there would be a break, an intermission, and the people would promenade for 10 to 15 minutes, and maybe take some refreshment. And then the drummer would roll the drum to call the people back for the next selection. Very relaxed. We'd play 3–4 big selections and then a few shorter popular things. It would be 11:30 or 12 o'clock before it was over. These were big events.*

*The next day, (Sunday) morning, there would be a parade from 7:30 or 8 o'clock to get the people up, you see.*[24]

Then, after the band leisurely paraded through the town and had breakfast, it would break into small groups of six to eight, and visit every villager's home.

**Leonard Falcone:** *These groups would cover various sections of the city, playing folk songs, polkas, waltzes, and other music. It was in this way that I, and many others, made our first solo appearances.*[25]

Accompanying them was a committee person from the village in charge of collecting money to defray the costs of the fiesta. As for the band, its remuneration was that it got a portion of the proceeds, along with lodging (often straw strewn on the floor of the local school) and one free meal in a villager's home.

**Leonard Falcone:** *Afterwards, there would be the church service, a high mass. Usually there would be an important speaker, a well known priest, and he would talk about an hour so. The sermon would be extra long. You can imagine—we were sitting most of the time up in the loft, so we all would sleep during the sermon. Toward the end of it, the conductor would wake us up and we would play the "Ave Maria" or something of that nature.*

*Following the church service, we'd have the procession with all the statues of the various saints through the main streets of the community, and the band would play various slow marches.*

> *Every so often they'd stop the parade and the people would offer a 1,000 lira bill. (The parade) would take about 2 hours.*
>
> *Then, at about 2 o'clock in the afternoon—well, that was the time to eat! Most of the time, we'd eat in homes—the people in the community would invite the members of the band as their guests. After that there was a siesta for 3 hours, and then from about 5:30–6 o'clock, the band would play again briefly before the concert that evening.*[26]

After playing the three hours of music (again, all this in less than 24 hours), the band would lead the crowd in a parade to the city park to witness a spectacular ending to the feast: a dazzling display of fireworks.[27]

> **Beryl Falcone:** *We were in (Roseto) Italy, in 1963, (it was the year Mary, our first daughter, had her thirteenth birthday) for this particular holiday, I don't know which one . . . and at night they had fireworks—and you never saw such fireworks like they have over there. Their fireworks are completely different than ours—much more elaborate. This particular trip we also went to Venice, and we saw fireworks there, too, but from a boat, and they were fabulous. They are much bigger, more colorful, the shapes are different, they are louder than ours, and they go on forever—maybe a whole hour of fireworks.*[28]

Being in the Roseto band had to have brought a lot of enjoyment and pride to young Leonardo, as it also provided him a model of musical performance excellence. Part of that modeling came from the number of outstanding solo players in the band that he could hear and emulate.

> **Leonard Falcone:** *The band was very good, I thought. It had some outstanding soloists. I remember that all the players who started the same time I did, we were very much impressed by soloists' performances and we would try to imitate their styles and play their parts— sometimes even during concerts, to the dismay*

*of the conductor, who didn't approve. But we were so taken up by their beautiful style that we would try to imitate them. The first cornetist, for tone and style, I believe was one of the very finest I've ever heard. He was quite a musician and performer. His name was Filippo de Cesare. I studied with the conductor, but I also studied with de Cesare. He aided me in becoming a better musician in terms of my understanding of musical style.*[29]

During the first three years of Leonardo's private study of the alto horn with de Cesare, he tried the various brass instruments, and finally settled in 1911 on the melodic Italian *trombone de canto*,[30] a valved instrument which performs the tenor aria parts in the vast Italian operatic concert repertoire. His lessons with the master cornetist continued for eight years,[31] until, barely sixteen years old, Leonardo left Roseto for America, toting his trombone along with him.[32]

Leonard's study with Donatelli and de Caesare and his years with the Roseto Banda Municipale were invaluable, teaching him during the most impressionable period of his life that a love of musical instruments is as powerful and as Italian as the love of music itself. These two men and the band they built not only gave him high standards of performance and style, but something more exquisite . . . and more important. The sheer magic of the sounds they created captured the young boy forever, and fashioned in him a very Italian musical mystique so that when he played, it "was like hearing a tenor from an Italian opera; his vibrato, intense tone, and lyricism, created a brilliant sound, unequaled today."[33] They gave him the precious ability to hear melody calling to him from a place and dimension outside the boundaries of mundane human awareness, to answer that call, seek its source, and, following blissfully past all limits of reality, to lose himself in it and vanish altogether.

CHAPTER 4

# SUNRISE: JUNE 20, 1915

***"In every conceivable manner, the family is link to our past, bridge to our future."***

**~ Alex Haley**

---

**10 Rules For a Good Family Life: Italian Proverbs**

1. Fear God and respect the saints or else you will really repent it.
2. The father is the father and he is experienced. The son will never fail if he imitates him.
3. The elders are prudent and experienced. Do as they do and you will learn and prosper.
4. Always honor and obey your parents; then even the stones will love you.
5. If you don't listen to your helpful mother, everything will turn into shit right in your pants.
6. Father is master.
7. Experience is power.
8. Work hard, work always, and you will never know hunger.
9. Work honestly and don't think of the rest.
10. Whoever doesn't want to work, dies like a dog.[1]

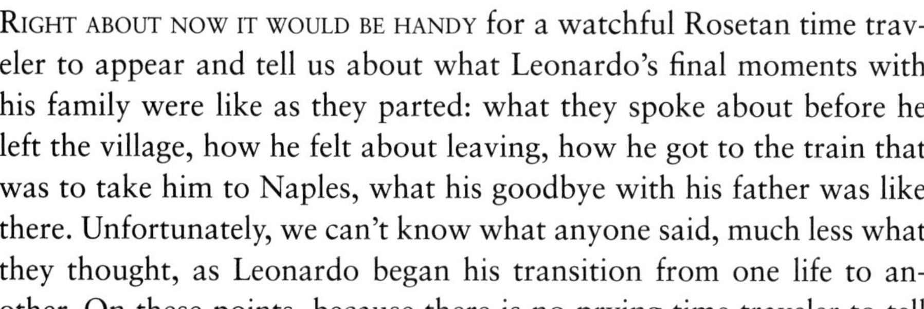

Right about now it would be handy for a watchful Rosetan time traveler to appear and tell us about what Leonardo's final moments with his family were like as they parted: what they spoke about before he left the village, how he felt about leaving, how he got to the train that was to take him to Naples, what his goodbye with his father was like there. Unfortunately, we can't know what anyone said, much less what they thought, as Leonardo began his transition from one life to another. On these points, because there is no prying time traveler to tell us, we are left to conjecture.

> *A young boy awakens on an early June morning in 1915 to hear his mother's voice swim into his fitful sleep like a melody floating up from his childhood. "Leonardo, Leonardo," it whispers. His eyes flutter open. By the shadowy glow of a flickering oil lamp, he can see from her partially lit, swollen face, that she has been weeping.* "E' ora di andare in piazza ad incontrate Antonio," *she says, a note of false cheer in her voice.*[2]*
>
> *He knows. He has thought of little else for almost a year and for most of the long week, his mind teeming with images of hope and anticipation.*
>
> *It is still hours from dawn and the precise moment has come for him to rise from his comfortable cornhusk*[3]* *mattress for the last time and get dressed for the long journey to America, and he is ready. He is ready to walk downstairs to the kitchen for a final breakfast of warm milk and pane cotto with his father*[4] *and go to the piazza with his family to meet twenty-seven-year-old Antonio Romano, an old acquaintance who will be his chaperone.*[5] *He is ready to see his older brother, Nicola, who will be waiting for him in Ann Arbor, and he is ready to begin a new life. A better life. A life where he can support himself, perhaps as a farm laborer or better yet, a tailor, and still send some of his earnings home to his family, a life where perhaps he can even play his valve trombone, his most precious belonging, alongside his brother in a theater or a local city band.*[6]* *In 1894, the year his own family*

*left Italy for Brazil, some twelve hundred Rosetans had applied for passports to America, leaving the narrow village streets so abandoned that they were nicknamed* vie degli Americani *(streets of the Americans).*[7] *He has heard the improbable rumors spread by the steamship companies that the streets in America are paved with gold, but more important, he has seen returning Rosetani welcomed home as heroes and wearing store bought clothes and shoes and telling stories about jobs and plentiful meat and about single family houses to buy if only a person works long and hard enough.*[8] *America, he knows, is a place where he has a chance to better himself.*

*And so, his vision firmly focused on the future, he is ready to leave a village thick with the past, a place nearly emptied of its lifeblood, a village of old men, women, and children,*[9] *his beloved village nevertheless, his Roseto.*

*Although it is hours before first light, Leonardo sees by the dim glow of the dying lamp flame that his mother has packed his open satchel with bread, sopressate, a block of hard cheese, and some homemade wine, and placed it near him as he slept. His new trousers and crisp white shirt, clothes he made himself for this journey, are laid out neatly on the floor where he placed them the evening before, next to his suitcase.*[10*] *He rises.* "Tuo padre si e alzato, e sta' preparandosi per la giornata," *his mother says, her voice trembling. But he is ahead of her, having heard the familiar scuffing sounds on the red kitchen tiles downstairs, and so he knows, too, that his father is up and readying himself for the day. He looks at her kind, rumpled face and is mildly surprised to see that she doesn't even try to hide the tears coursing down her cheeks. When he reaches to hug her tiny body, she gasps.* "Non ti preoccupare mama," *he says confidently, his blue eyes burning.* "Tornero' a casa presto!"[11*]

*He is wrong about this, though he doesn't yet know it. He won't be back home soon at all, and he won't be seeing her before long, either. In actuality, it will be 1931*[12] *before he returns, after she has died and a world war has been fought on Italian soil. By then, everything— his family, himself, Italy—will have changed.*[13*]

*After breakfast, he walks with his mother, father, and little sisters to the piazza where a group of his and Antonio's relatives, though it is still dark, have gathered for final farewells. There, his valve trombone, suitcase, and satchel, the one containing clothing and the other with the food packed by his mother for the long trip to Naples, are added to Antonio's belongings in a donkey cart loaned by a neighbor who bartered the ride for a haircut from Dominico. There, though he has already said goodbye to his extended family many times, he says it again. Suddenly, his mother breaks down into a silent weeping, her tears wetting little Rosina who is clinging to her neck and sobbing, though she doesn't know why; unexpectedly his other sisters, Guiseppina, Giovannina, and Lucietta, begin wailing, their eyes streaming. Leonardo tries to say something, but chokes. He looks at them all heartbreakingly for a moment and then, his mouth and chin trembling, hangs his head and climbs into the cart. Antonio settles in behind him with his luggage as Dominico takes his place next to his son in the driver's seat, picks up the reins, and urges the donkey forward.*[14]*

*The countryside on this day looks much the same as it did when the MSU Alumni Band (the "Falcone Band") saw it on their way to play a concert in Roseto in 1985. A moonlit, star salted sky reveals a landscape which offers a sweeping view of the dark, broad shoulders of Monte Stillo and Serra Montanara, and in the far distance, a Petrera. A tremolo of breeze softly ripples the stillness of the air above the open cultivated land, and though daybreak is hours away, Leonardo can see the dog rose growing bountifully in the meadow. Soon enough, in a pleasant duet of sight and sound, a pair of red kites will enter the scene, circling and swooping at their invisible prey in the languid morning air, their rapidly mewing "weoo-weoo-weoo" cadenzas as ancient as the land itself.*[15]*

*Shortly after the road begins, they all say goodbye yet again, this time being the very last time, and Leonardo joins the group of over 2 million Italians who, between 1906 and 1915, leave their villages and all they have ever known with hope in their hearts for a chance at a better life in America.*[16] *From afar, the little congregation would have presented a colorful picture as Antonio and Leonardo's families, their mothers and sisters weeping as they walked slowly beside the cart funneling through the cobble stoned streets*[17*] *to the newly improved Roseto-Castlefranco road, once a red brown clay path, rutted and uneven from the hundreds of horse, donkey, and mule-drawn wagons used over the course of years in the mass exodus from Roseto.*[18*]

Nothing about this scene distinguishes it from others of young Rosetan boys leaving their families to seek a new beginning in a new country, nor is there anything to outwardly mark the young man as special in any way. The morning might have been any early summer morning from any one of the 50 or so years of the Italian diaspora, and the boy any young boy leaving any Southern Italian village for America. Dressed in his new black pants and white shirt and filled with dreams and adventure, he is nearly interchangeable with tens of thousands of other emigrant boys departing Italy, except for one thing: this boy is a musical genius.

From Roseto to Naples is a distance of nearly 125 miles, by car something under three hours; but for travelers making the journey in 1915, the trip would have taken the entire day. The slow walk or donkey or horse cart ride from Roseto over the hills of Apulia to the train station in the province of Benevento which served as the primary outlet to Napoli for Rosetani emigrants[19*] would have accounted for perhaps ten hours. Once at the station, more time would have passed in wait for the arrival of the locomotive that was to take the boy and the young man westward. Then, once aboard, at least two or three more hours would be spent as the train, groaning and shrieking against the force of its brakes, stopped in village after village to collect passengers as they made their final, tearful goodbyes.

When he arrived at the train station young Leonardo would have seen unforgettable scenes of farewell, some probably even more painful than his own in Roseto that morning. Partings were occasions of high drama to families who knew that they might never see one another again, and the train platform, crowded with friends and relatives of emigrating loved ones, would have been filled with a cacophony of sobs and piercing wails which sounded even after the hissing iron beast that held the mourners' nearest and dearest lumbered out of sight. As the train crawled away, the anguished crowd would have clutched at its sides, waved handkerchiefs, and kissed loved ones' hands through open windows. These same wrenching tableaus would be repeated as the train, rattling and thumping its way to Naples, stopped at other stations to board more passengers.[20]

We can't know how Leonardo and his father said goodbye to one another as they broke the corporeal thread connecting them, but it can be guessed that for them, a father and a son who had prepared themselves well for this day, theirs was a less agonizing display of emotion than others'. Some freeze frames: a final word of advice from Dominico to Leonardo to be careful of thieves; a handoff of the precious money that had been saved for the journey, along with a passport, train tickets, and other papers; an assurance of a return to Roseto in a few years; goodbye kisses on the cheeks; an embrace, perhaps a tear. This is likely what the farewell between the two was like.

As for what Leonardo might have said to Antonio as the train's cars jiggled and curved around bends to reveal new, unfamiliar sights and landscapes—we can't know that for sure, either. But we can presume that worries about the looming war or the possibility of never seeing his village or his parents and sisters again or of passing health inspections in both Italy and the US or if there were strikes or anarchy in Naples[21]*or if he was going to be able to find a job in Ann Arbor or how he was going to travel alone across the United States from New York to Michigan without being able to speak a word of English barely, if at all, entered Leonardo's head. More likely, his thoughts were consumed by the excitement of what was no doubt his first train ride (though far from his last), by the newness of the countryside as it rolled by his window, by happy images of seeing his brother, Nicola, whom he hadn't been with in three years, of the ship voyage ahead, and of the vivid, lively, charming, passionate, gritty city of Naples, towered over by an ominous and erupting Mt. Vesuvius. "*Vedi Napoli e poi mori:*" "See Naples and Die." It was a phrase he had most certainly heard his entire life, the suggestion being that once the beauty of Naples is beheld, there is nothing in this world to surpass it, nothing else worth living to see. Well, now he was going to see Naples, the playground of Virgil, Luculius, and Augustus, the most Italian city of them all. From there, he was going to board his ship, the *Stampalia*, emigrate to the United States, and begin a new life.

For an impossibly young Italian boy, the adventure didn't get much better than that.

## CHAPTER 5

# "VEDI NAPOLI E POI MORI": JUNE 21–23, 1915

*"Italia! O Italia! Thou who hast/ the fatal gift of beauty!"*

~ Lord Byron
*Childe Harold*

---

*LIST OR MANIFEST OF ALIEN PASSENGERS*
*FOR THE UNITED STATES IMMIGRATION OFFICER*
*AT PORT OF ARRIVAL*

*SS Stampalia sailing from Naples 23 June 1915*
*Arriving at Port of New York 7 July 1915*

*This White sheet is for the listing of*
*STEERAGE PASSENGERS ONLY*

*Name in full:* Falcone, Leonardo
*Age:* 16
*Sex:* M
*Married or single:* S
*Calling or occupation:* Farm laborer
*Able to read and write:* Yes
*Nationality:* Italy
*Race:* Italian South
*Last residence:* Italy

*Name and complete address of relative or friend in country whence alien came:* father Dominico, Roseto
*Number on list:* 30
*Final destination in United States:* Michigan, Ann Arbor
*Whether having ticket to such destination:* Yes
*By whom was passage paid?:* Self
*Whether in possession of $50, and if less, how much?* $46
*Whether ever before in the United States, and if so, when and where.* No
*Whether going to join a relative, and if so, what relative—their name and address:* Brother Nicola Dominico, Ann Arbor, Mich.
*Ever in prison, or almshouse, or supported by charity? If yes, state which:* No
*Whether a polygamist:* No
*Whether an anarchist:* No
*Whether under contract, express or implied, to labor in the United States:* No
*Condition of health— mental and physical:* Good
*Deformed or crippled—nature and cause:* No
*Height, feet and inches:* 4' 9"
*Complexion:* Regular
*Color of hair and eyes:* Brown, brown
*Marks of identification:* None
*Place of birth, country, city or town:* Italy, Roseto Valfortore[1]

EIGHT YEARS BEFORE 1915, workable housing and health procedures were in place for emigrants from Italian ports, and in Naples, the ship companies ran eighty *locande* (hostels), emigrant stations under the supervision of the United States Government constructed to augment the company supported hotels. Basic, overcrowded, many not situated very close to the port, they offered a necessary 2,157 beds and 745 dormitory accommodations and the required medical examinations by sanitary and emigration officials which included two lice treatments—one upon arrival and one just before embarkation. One meal a day,[2] as a stipulation of the $25 third-class ticket,[3] was also provided by the ship company.

Leonardo and Antonio, arriving as they did at their lodgings in the late day after at least fourteen hours of travel, would have been tired nearly to death. Legs weary, backs aching with the weight of carrying their luggage, they most likely would have fallen onto their beds as though shot—if they'd been allowed to. But first, after traveling to their hotel or hostel on foot or by horse cab from the train station, they would have met the desk clerk, and been shown their room.

> **Broughton Brandenburg, Port of Naples steerage passenger, 1904:** *The host, a short, unshaven, bibulous-looking person appeared, and we were conducted to the second and third floors, and allowed to sort ourselves out into three large rooms, filled with single beds. All of the women and children were given a front room with light and air, and the men took the others . . . It was not ten minutes after we were indoors, before every member of the party was stretched out and sound asleep. . . .*
>
> *[Soon], the host roused everybody to tell them that if they wished to take advantage of the one meal a day the steamship broker was paying for, they should be going to the trattoria. It was a subdued party that arrayed itself, filed down the stairs, and went to its first substantial meal since noon the day before . . .*
>
> *At the restaurant we found some hundreds of emigrants coming and going, and others seated at the tables. For a half hour we waited until those eating made room enough for us, and then we gathered around one of the large tables arranged about the long room, and soon were served by unkempt waiters with soup made with tomatoes and paste, and a stew of meat and vegetables, the meat being from the portions of the goat not the most savory, melons, and wine.* [4]

Like most of the emigrants in Naples, Brandenburg and his family took a walk through the city after they had some rest and a meal. Leonardo and Antonio likely did the same.

The grandeur of the " City of Sirens"[5]* is legendary. If the two Rosetans had the chance to look down on Naples from one of its heights, they would have seen a majestic amphitheater of adjoining hills, each one a proud monarch in its own right holding court above the largest city in the kingdom. The domes of the city's nearly 300 cathedrals, the hazy gray green tiles of its pointed roofs, its fountains with their draping, watery plumage outlined against the dark backdrops of buildings, its twisting, deep-cleft streets, and its horse-pulled trolleys navigating the thoroughfares, all would have figured into the scene. Further down, beneath the city, the obeisant, sparkling waters of the sapphire blue Bay of Naples stretched as far as the eye could see. If the day were clear, there would have been magnificent views of the isle of Capri across the bay to the south, and of the lovely villas, vineyards, and orange groves of the hamlets clinging to the crescent shaped eastern shoreline.[6] Towering over all with an alarming grandeur was the great monster Vesuvius, a place of legend where Spartacus and his band of gladiators and slaves were said to have taken a stand against Rome in 73 BC. Its May, 1913, eruption was so intense it had been felt in San Francisco.[7] By June of 1915, when Leonardo and Antonio saw it, it was a powerful cyclops, angrily belching smoke and ash from its bellyful of molten rock, sending shockwaves from its frequent earthquakes, and streaming glowing rivers of lava at night from its crimson red eye.[8] It was a remarkable vision, to be sure, and one can easily imagine young Leonardo's wonder of it.

No record shows how long the two travelers were in Naples, but at a time when train schedules were not coordinated with ship schedules and the task of securing a US visa had to be completed upon arrival in the city, it's likely they were at their hostel or hotel for several days. Even if during that time the two did not climb one of the broad shouldered hills of Naples to view the lovely panorama of the city and its bay from above, from street level they most decidedly saw Vesuvius, the surrounding wave of hilltops, and the bay, as they made their way from the train station to their hostel, and later, from their hostel to the port. This experience surely caused any fanciful notions they may have had about Naples and its transcendent beauty to die a little—and not in the promised aesthetic bliss, either, but in disillusionment. The streets of the city had become so overcrowded, unsanitary, and filthy by 1915 that, according to one visitor, "The south Italian shore that curves around the Bay of Naples would be an earthly paradise—if we could but leave Naples out."[9] Though some Neapolitans lived in clean, large, tastefully decorated rooms overlooking the water, the great majority lived in squalid, "unsanitary piles of flats (facing) without shame the lovely panorama of the Bay of Naples, and other flats, even less habitable, (facing) one another at stiflingly close quarters in the long, deep, narrow streets."[10] The families who lived in these flats, with their "frightful flights of steps,"[11] commonly left their doors open so that passersby could see directly into their dark, dilapidated bedrooms, nearly all of which had tables set with paper flowers flanking a statue or lithograph of the Virgin, and ground floor beds "so near to the pavement that the bed linen (would) come fluttering through, while . . . passing dogs (would) turn into these chambers and look around."[12] Inside these airless low ceilinged maws could be glimpsed domestic scenes of families with an average of 8 to 12 children[13] going about their daily routines in rooms which, when the doors were closed at night, were transformed into oppressively stifling sealed boxes. Walking down these alleys, Leonardo and Antonio, if they were recognized as emigrants, would have been asked by people on balconies above or coming out of rooms below to carry messages to loved ones in America in a indecipherable Napoletano vernacular called by one writer "a barbarous, scolding dialect that fearfully offends the true Italian ear."[14]

Incredibly, the appalling state of the health and living conditions in Naples, then the most densely populated city of Europe,[15] was ignored. A 1906 *New York Times* news article even went so far as to assure readers that though the sanitary conditions of Naples' slum tenements were dreadful, there was nothing to worry about as "the masses are germ proof and epidemics pass by them. . ."[16] Such ignorance concerning "the masses" (euphemism alert: "the masses" = "the desperately poor") had its price when in 1911–1912, cholera, a disease largely caused by infected food and drinking water, stalked the city and killed hundreds. The official reaction was to cover it up out of fear of a negative economic impact (Naples, after all, had a thriving port and emigration business to consider!) equal to that which occurred during the city's 1884 cholera epidemic, when over 14,000 men, women, and children died. Though the contagion had passed when Leonardo and Antonio saw Naples in 1915, health and sanitary conditions still hadn't much improved.

Disease wasn't the only concern in the city. Though "see Naples and Die" was a celebrated and well known adage throughout the kingdom, another, just as famous, was less flattering. The city was also known as "The City of Thieves," a place teeming with the dregs of Italian society, small armies of peddlers selling useless wares at inflated prices, of thieves and con men. They were everywhere, circulating freely looking for a pocket to pick or an item of value to snatch, but they were most densely congregated at the port. Before boarding, confused emigrants, surrounded by troops of demanding liars and robbers, needed all their wits about them to battle the fraud and deceit that threatened to swallow them whole.

Yet in spite of squalid living conditions and unremitting poverty, Naples had charm: the near deafening din of shouting and howling vendors selling everything from newspapers and pencils to ice cream, fish, and roasted chestnuts, organ grinders grinding out strains from well known operas as *Norma* or *La Traviata,* and young men setting off fireworks and watching gleefully as the shooting display threatened the tattered, freshly scrubbed laundry hanging from plant decorated balconies above. And there was the unusual sight of dairymen and goatmen plying their trade by milking their animals on the spot under the watchful eyes of customers who supplied them with container jugs and specific instructions.[17] Tied to doors (sometimes even in upstairs hallways), the cows and goats lined alleys every morning and evening so that buyers, who spent the equivalent of a costly 10 cents a pint for milk, could check out the animal they were getting it from.[18] There were *corni*, or good luck charms, that were carried by nearly everyone in hopes of warding off evil spirits and winning the Saturday "Lotto," a numbers game sponsored by the state, and of course there were the churches, whose beautiful interior mosaics and statues reminded one and all of a better life coming.

Away from the teeming alleyways and on the broad thoroughfares of Naples, home to the city's lively festivals and processions, were even brighter and more animated scenes of vendors, traffic, and people. In the poorer part of town on the Santa Lucia, the center of noisy street life, were "women (engaging) in domestic duties, naked children, and peddlers of all sorts. . .a unique spectacle."[19] Most came from the largest "hotel" in Naples, the *Albergo dei Poveri* (the poor house), the tenement flats, or lived on the street itself. For entertainment, many working Neopolitans frequented the *Villa del Popolo* ("People's Park), near the Custom House, where every day at four o'clock, speakers would read passages from Tasso, Ariosto, and other poets "to an audience made up of longshoremen, rag pickers, and porters who (paid) two centimes for the privilege of listening." At no cost at all, onlookers could watch as Popolo's quack "dentists" harangued the crowd with medical jargon and then pulled the teeth of people desperate enough to do whatever had to be done to rid themselves of toothaches. And near the Popolo was a spot, "a veritable rag fair," where old clothes could be exchanged by their owners, who "in a short time and without spending a penny, were able to leave in an entirely different costume from which they just wore."[20]

On the Toledo, another principal street (now called the *Strada Roma*), the young, wide-eyed Leonardo might have marveled at the sight of bustling carriages, one horse cabs, and automobiles rushing here and there with little to no traffic order. A bewildering array of thriving people, including lemonade and water salesmen with their ancient, round earthenware vessels, brightly dressed girls from nearby villages selling fruits and flowers and urging young lovers to buy a little something for their sweethearts, mandolin playing minstrels singing such identifiably Neopolitan tunes as "*O Sole Mio*," ("*Che bella cosa e' na giornata 'e sole, n'aria serena doppo na tempesta!, Pe' ll'aria fresca pare già na festa, Che bella cosa e' na giornata 'e sole*". . .[21]* the player misses a note and tries to recover . . . does Leonardo scowl in alarm? Does he wonder, "*How could anyone play a note that isn't there? How would he know what note to play?*") and colorful street performers re-enacting entire wars in front of painted backdrops are among those glutting the way. There are also new streets to be explored, some cutting through old dilapidated districts, their fine businesses and department stores screening much of the city's heaving slums.[22]

Clearly, the Naples of Leonardo's day, had a character all its own, made even more interesting by the Neopolitans themselves. It was the kind of city whose inhabitants could live in the worst kind of poverty but who were again and again characterized by tourists of the time as a "good natured people,"[23] "dirty and happy,"[24] even "cheery"[25]—and with "fire and passion, with minstrels who can and do still sing love songs and such a well remembered barcarolle as 'Santa Lucia,' sweet and pathetic as it is, as no other people can."[26] It was a city that claimed Ferdinand as its son, a man who, at the medieval Church of St. Maria la Nuova near the Toledo, erected two large chapel monuments and dedicated them to his most vicious and vindictive enemies in order to carry out the Christian teaching to "do good to them that hate you."

It was a unique place, no doubt about it, and Leonardo, who almost certainly had never seen a big city before, must have already felt the fear and exhilaration of a foreign exchange student in a new land.

By 1915, the time Leonardo left Roseto for the United States, the US and Italian governments had in place a multi-stepped emigration procedure as partial safeguard against transporting diseased or mentally unfit passengers, and as protection from rejection at Ellis Island for the immigrants themselves, many of them poor villagers who had spent a near lifetime's savings for the journey. Leonardo probably came into contact with the process first in Roseto, when an agent of the ship company (who, while serving 20 to 30 municipalities, traveled from village to village) gave him and his family information about the United States, sold him a ticket, and told him how to get a passport from local officials and a visa from the US consular office at the port. In Naples, a committee of officials would have provided the same service when he and Antonio arrived, and may even have guided them on their journey.[27]

During their days at the hostel or hotel, the two travelers would have submitted to frequent health check-ups for any number of maladies, check-ups which culminated in their being sent to a square concrete hive of activity, the *Capitaneria del Porto,* Naples' customs and emigration building, on the day of sailing. Here, in this large soulless structure on the Bay of Naples near the quay and point of embarkation, US Marine surgeons and a coterie of American and Italian officials oversaw or conducted the Mother of all Examination procedures to ensure that the law requiring foreign ships to have an officially signed clean bill of health before sailing to the US be fulfilled.

Most likely, when Leonardo went to the *Capitaneria del Porto* on the day of embarkation he saw the emigrant steamship *Stampalia* for the first time, docked at the long, 42-foot-wide pier on the Strada del Molo, a colorful promenade ending in a lighthouse with spiral marble steps leading to a gallery with good views of the bay. Bathed in bright bursts of limoncello sunlight, Neopolitans, countrymen, and foreigners, would have been walking the pier's length, some, their photo op smiles and duke and duchess postures signifying their pleasure both in seeing and being seen, others, unsavory characters hoping to relieve poor emigrants of what little money and belongings they had.

Did the leviathan that was to take him to America spark Leonardo's imagination? It's doubtful that he had ever before seen anything even a fraction its size. It can be guessed that the *Stampalia* was an extraordinary sight to an unworldly village boy who, though he had walked the narrow mountain paths of the Foggia region with the Roseto Band, had never been so far from home, had never seen such a huge and exotic vessel. Surely he was in awe of it, and of the journey ahead—a journey which was far from risk free. Eight Rosetani had drowned in the Straits of Gibraltar in 1891 when their passenger ship went down, a fact that both Leonardo and Antonio had to have known. And they knew, too, that Italy had joined in the growing war in Europe just a month earlier, on May 23, 1915, and that it was possible that they could meet with a disaster at sea in an encounter with a submarine—a concern that led to two three inch guns being mounted as defense on the *Stampalia*'s stern just a few months later.[28]*

Originally named *Oceania*, the steamship *Stampalia* weighed nearly 9,000 tons, measured 476 feet by 56 feet, and traveled at a speed of 16 knots. Outfitted with two funnels, two masts, and twin screws, she could carry a total of 2,650 passengers.[29] Poised closer to function than to poetry, on the day Leonardo boarded her, she was in seaworthy state and ready to do her duty to Italy's emigrants.

When our two travelers arrived at the *Capitaneria* on the day of embarkation, they were probably led to an outside iron enclosure where the *Stampalia*'s steerage passengers were strewing containers of all sizes and shapes over the ground, their contents in various stages of exposure. They would have seen chests, kegs, bundles, and cardboard luggage tied with grass ropes, all carefully sealed or secured just three or four days before, laying in the bald morning sun. There, like the others, they would have sorted their bags into "carry-on" and "cargo," opened their bundles, and stood silently until the American consular agent and the port health authorities inspected, numbered, listed, and tagged everything headed for the ship's hold.

Meanwhile, on the south side of the building, a small steamer waited, impatient to take luggage headed for the hold to the fumigation plant near the breakwater a half mile across the harbor where an inspector and several assistants were steaming bags to kill insects and attaching important yellow inspection labels from the US consular service to belongings.

Sometime after midday, the fumigation process complete, Leonardo entered a dreary room in the *Capitaneria,* where the floodgates of examinations were opened and in the deluge he and Antonio and all the other of the *Stampalia*'s third class passengers fought to survive the ordeal with dignity intact.[30*] Few, if any, of those in that room that day had ever had a shot or private medical examination, much less a public one, and to parade openly in a line before two United States Marine surgeons, receive a vaccination, be searched by inspectors for signs of tuberculosis, insanity, feeblemindedness, and favus,[31 *] have their heads rubbed, suspicious parts of their bodies felt, possibly be sent to bathe or fumigated for lice, and asked a myriad of questions to complete the manifest, all under the watchful eyes of the nearby Italian Immigration Commissioner, representatives of the police department, a detail of *carabinieri* (military police), the ship's doctor, and often, too, the doctor of the port, an Italian Navy surgeon representing the Italian government, and/or an inspector of emigration, was intimidating, to say the least.

"*Occupazione*?" asked one of the officials of Leonardo (and we hope gently, and not in the manner of an inflamed prosecuting attorney). And though he had the grander dream of playing his trombone in a theater orchestra in Ann Arbor with his brother, he responded, "*bracciante agricolo*." Farm laborer.[32] That he'd never been a farm la-

*The Stampalia*

borer and had no aspiration to be one is a certainty.[33]* Smart boy to offer authorities a practical skill that all but assured his admission to the United States in the weeks before the outbreak of WWI, as all that was available to *adult* Italian immigrants were unskilled laborers' jobs, the skilled and semi-skilled jobs having already been filled by earlier immigrant groups—the Irish, Germans, and British. As a young, non-English-speaking Italian *boy*, to have claimed anything grander might have caused suspicious inspectors to think "What's going on here? Has he illegally lined up a job. . . or is he just crazy?" and drawn unwelcome attention.

Somewhere in the long battery of examinations, Leonardo and Antonio underwent the most feared of them all, the one the mere thought of which put many in a frantic state of mind. It occurred when the "eye men" checked for symptoms of cataracts, conjunctivitis, and the dreaded infectious eye disease trachoma, said to have been "brought into Italy from Egypt and Napoleon's army."[34] Taking a button hook or the back of a hairpin, the "eye men" were doctors who turned eyelids inside out in a frightening and painful procedure which could, and often, did lead to refusal at the Port of Naples and, later on, at Ellis

Island. Failing the eye test was the number-one cause of rejection, the kiss of death to dreams of a better life in the United States.

It would seem that Leonardo, who was, after all, a young, very bright boy in good health, sailed through this first gauntlet of examinations to the steamship company's satisfaction and so, after he showed an agent his money and counted it and the agent recorded it and returned it, after he passed before a police officer who examined his passport for its legality, he was finally awarded his US railway tickets, information about when it was necessary to be aboard, and a card with his name and the letter and number of the group of thirty to which he was assigned.[35*] "Keep this card at Quarantine and on Railroads in the United States," he would have been told, and frightened that the card not be lost, he, like the others, would have put it on a string around his neck or tied it to his shirt so he would be sure to have it at Ellis Island and beyond to Ann Arbor.[36]

Incredibly, when Leonardo and Antonio were finally sent to board the waiting *Stampalia* and were at the ship's gangway, they found that the inspections still were not over. There, the two Rosetans were met by police officers and a representative of the United States medical team, whose job it was to see that their inspection cards were stamped properly and their baggage labeled as having passed sanitary inspection. Only then, after their cards were given their last stamp, a seal of the US Public Health and Marine Hospital Service, were they allowed to move on to the gangplank, where they were inspected again for trachoma and favus by the ship's doctor.[37*] Finally, they boarded, as on deck bewildered steerage passengers hauling children, trunks, knapsacks, bedding, cooking utensils, cardboard suitcases, and prized possessions (who is that little boy[38*] carrying a trombone?) tried to make out what agents and officials were shouting under the full decibel noise of firing steam boilers preparing for their long labor. Even then, after all examinations were carried out and all passengers were approved and boarded, the ship did not sail until all papers were in order and inspectors declared it in lawful condition.[39]

"Chi non e paseggero a terra!" *"All ashore that's going ashore!" The ship's whistle blows, and the crowd on deck quiets. Excite-*

*ment is palpable; still, the women cry, and in sorrow, the men turn their faces seaward. Some flutter handkerchiefs as others hold babies high for relatives on shore to see one last time. Balls of yarn, their ends gripped tightly by passengers on board and relatives on the dock, begin to unwind as the ship pulls away until, finally, those on land and those at sea lose sight of one another and the colorful strings float high on the wind.*[40]

*Naples' enchanting coast, studded with a succession of dazzling views, is seen now from the departing ship as it steams westerly to Ischia,*[41]* *"one of the most beautiful places in the bay," with "Monte Epomco rising blue and pink above the morning mist" and a view that becomes more and more charming as looking back the passengers see the Bay of Naples, dominated by Vesuvius and surrounded by mountains, with Capri lying to the south "like a gem on the blue waters."*[42]

One wonders what thoughts Leonardo might have had as he saw that view unribboning in the wake of the ship that was to transport him to an uncertain future, its path shrouded in mysterious haze. What might he have felt that day when he was young and free and the world was filled with anticipation and joy? How did the sea breeze feel on his cheek, the briny air in his nostrils, the gentle motion of the rolling deck under his feet? Did he marvel at the glorious crescent of hills surrounding Naples Bay? "*Vedi Napoli e poi mori.*" Well, by the time he boarded the *Stampalia,* he had seen Naples. But for him it was a beginning, not an end—a bridge that spanned the chasm between the little village of Roseto Valfortore and the New World.

Next stop: the land of milk and honey.

## CHAPTER 6

# THE LEAP: JUNE 23–JULY 7, 1915

***"Music and rhythm find their way into the secret places of the soul."***

**~ Plato**

**carved above the main entrance to the Michigan State University Music Building**

---

**Leonard Falcone:** *I played valve trombone in the (Roseto Valfortore) band from 1911 to 1915, and came to the United States carrying it with me.*[1]

IF, ON APPROACHING THE SHIP, Leonardo had asked where they would be bunking, Antonio would have gestured toward the *Stampalia's* belly. Steerage, so named because of its location near the rudder, was a low-ceilinged space beneath the main deck where nearly 90 percent of the steamer's passengers, including Leonardo and his chaperone, would live for the two week Atlantic crossing.

Though by 1915 immigration laws had the effect of improving steerage conditions on some lines, these improvements were found entirely on ships carrying emigrants from the north of Europe, a small percentage of the flood of passengers to Ellis Island. Southern European ships such as the La Veloce line's *Stampalia*, had what was termed "old type" steerage conditions, as described in 1911 in a report for President Taft from the US Immigration Commission:

> *From the stacks and the odors from the hold and galleys . . . the only provisions for eating are frequently shelves or benches along the sides or in the passages of sleeping compartments. Dining rooms are rare and, if found, are often shared with berths installed along the walls. Toilets and washrooms are completely inadequate; saltwater only is available.*
>
> *The ventilation is almost always inadequate, and the air soon becomes foul. The unattended vomit of the seasick, the odors of not too clean bodies, the reek of food and the awful stench of the nearby toilet rooms make the atmosphere of the steerage such that it is a marvel that human flesh can endure it... Most immigrants lie in their berths for most of the voyage, in a stupor caused by the foul air. The food often repels them... It is almost impossible to keep personally clean. All of these conditions are naturally aggravated by the crowding.*[2]

Yet in spite of the stifling, stinking, miserable third class conditions, in spite of scurvy and seasickness, in spite of continual fear that the ship would sink,[3] "seventy-five percent of the emigrants lived better on board ship than they did at home."[4] As bad as it was in the bowels of the ship, for many, living in Italy, with its frequent disasters, disease, abject poverty, and looming war, was worse.

*Down steep stairways to the lower deck, squeezing through a passageway past the ship's machinery, Leonardo and Antonio find their way to steerage and search for available berths amongst the several large compartments designated for single men on the ship's deck. The least noisy compartments, like others accommodating as many as 300 passengers or more, are reserved for families and unaccompanied women; the noisiest are set aside for single men such as themselves.*

*When they find a suitable space, each claims a berth, 6 feet long, 2 feet wide, just a slot, really, one of many crammed to the* *ceiling with a mere 2.5 feet of space above it. On its iron frame is a straw filled burlap covered mattress, a life preserver, and a blanket. Because there is no space for hand baggage, not even hooks for clothing, Leonardo hangs a fresh shirt and cap to wear on arrival at Ellis Island on the bed's framework, and, concerned that one or the other might tour America without him, places his carry-on below*[5]* *and trombone at the end of his bunk where he can keep an eye on them. Then he takes off his shoes, puts them at the end of his already crowded berth,*[6] *and stretches out, taking the size of the mattress. He is luckier than most, and he knows it. At only 4 feet 9 inches, he will not be nearly as cramped in this space as some.*

*Leonardo and Antonio are barely situated on their bunks when the stewards come around. "Divide into groups of six," they bark from the corridor, and minutes later, as the task is completed from compartment to compartment, they hand each passenger a crude plate, a cup, and some cutlery.*[7]* *One of the six in Leonardo's group, as with each of the others, is appointed the "leader," and given a meal ticket, a large tin pan, a ladle, and a one gallon pail that looks disturbingly like a slop bucket. His job, he is told, is to get his group's food from the twenty-five gallon tanks sitting on deck.*[8] *Though tonight's dinner, soup and pasta, is one they will have again, on some nights, they will receive instead bread, potatoes, and a gristled, low quality meat, or leftovers from the first and second class passengers.*[9]

*When Leonardo receives his portion, he drags his spoon through the gummy pasta, and plops it back onto his plate. There is plenty enough of it, but it is prepared by a kitchen whose unspoken motto is, "Who cares? It just has to be done all over again in a couple hours."*[10]* *Later in the journey, on days when the weather is bad, he is relegated to eating wherever he can find a space in the compartment. But because it is a nice evening, and because there are no tables below, he and Antonio and some of the other boys and men decide to try to find some room on the open deck, though they must sit under a skunk's tail of sooty black and white smoke and listen to the bullish snorting of the* *smokestack as they dine.*[11]* *Here, at least, the air is less stifling and the smell less overbearing than in any other place they are allowed. Below, where there is no cross draft, and where sweat, urine, and vomit will by morning brutally assault their nostrils, it will soon enough become unbearable. There, no sick cans are furnished for the ill, and the vomit of the seasick is permitted to remain a long time before it is removed.*[12]*

*But tonight, the first night at sea, is pleasant enough, and they take their time after dinner to lean on the rail and, staring westward at the gently undulating horizon, to watch as the last of the sun smolders its fiery reds and oranges and finally sinks into the dark Mediterranean. "And so they melt, and make no noise, no tear-floods nor sigh-tempests move" and from their homeland "endure not yet a breach, but an expansion, like gold to airy thinness beat."*[13]*

*The following day, and on most days thereafter, Leonardo and the other steerage passengers are initiated into a tedious ceremony involving a required, but superficial, two minute medical inspection conducted by the ship's doctor. On certain random days it won't be conducted at all, and when at last it is, everyone will have his or her health card punched for the missing inspections anyway.*[14] *It will take hours to commence, as the passengers stand crowded together in the heat of the white hot summer sun awaiting the ship doctor's pleasure. Babies, tired, hot, and hungry, wail for mercy as the women complain and the men curse until finally the doctor deems it the right moment to bless the assemblage with his appearance and briefly glance into each passenger's eyes before passing on. At a farther point each health card will be punched or stamped as a detective sharply scans the exhausted travelers, and at last, the ordeal will crawl to its miserable end.*[15]

*Equally wearisome are the questions posed by agents who are anxious that each immigrant pass through American customs and not become the responsibility of the ship company. Prompting passengers in how to conduct themselves upon reaching Ellis Island, often on days of high seas or rainy weather when they are confined to their compartments (and though we can't know whether the Stampalia on this journey encountered stormy weather, it probably did at least once), they interrogate their charges over the reverberating and alarming sounds of the groaning and creaking ship.*

*"Leonardo, are your papers in order? Where is your vaccination certificate?" BOOM! A screech of terror cuts through the room. "Do you have the card indicating your name, destination, and letter and number of the group of thirty to which you are assigned?" Roiling seas pound the shuddering hull plates. "Where is it? How about train tickets to Michigan from New York? Do you have them now or are you buying them when you arrive?"*[16]

*Because they are first time passengers who are likely to find the Ellis Island legal exam exceedingly intimidating, they are also practiced in responding to questions from the ship's manifest, a log previously completed in Naples, until they can recite their answers without qualm.*

*"Name? Age? City of residence? Race?*[17]* *Occupation?" A mountain of water licks the ship's frame as a vibration strikes a note as clear as a tuning fork. "F#," one aboard thinks to himself. "Prison record? Name of the person paying for your ticket? Amount of money on hand? Is it in a safe place? Is it in dollars? If not, do you know how to exchange it at Ellis Island?" They continue down the list of questions, oblivious to cries of the passengers that they are unquestionably headed toward a certain and watery death.*

*"Can you read? Write? What is the name of the person with whom you will be staying in the US? Do you understand that contract labor laws forbid prior employment arrangements and that you must say that you have no work waiting for you in the United States?"*[18]

And so it goes.

**Edward Hemmer, Italian immigrant, 1925:** . . . *we had ten days of maximum storms. Just unbelievable. Looked like Everest*

> *mountain in the sea . . . It's hard today for people to understand what it was like to be on a boat then in a storm like that. Tremendous noise. It sounded as if the boat was heading for rocks. The great waves would smash, the noise tremendous, and I thought we would founder at any moment. They posted "Captain's Messages" up. At that time, it was Morse code received from other ships in the ocean saying, "SOS—We are foundering! Help!"*[19]

Certainly, not everything that occurred below decks was so tedious or frightening. On those days when Leonardo had to remain in his bunk because of unruly winds or foul weather, he and his fellow passengers surely relieved the monotony and dread by doing what all New York bound Italian steerage passengers of the day did: play card games, sing, purchase food at the canteen, and play musical instruments. One can imagine the plink-plinking of mandolins and the pulsing tremolos of harmonicas, the most common shipboard instruments, filling the corridors of the third class compartments with musical sounds that soothed the bored, frightened, and seasick passengers, and made their journeys more bearable. But on the June 21st, 1915, sailing of the *Stampalia*, there was assuredly another instrument added to the usual mix: that of a valve trombone, played with such effortless grace and nimble purity every note, melody, and accompaniment formed a memory of transcendent beauty in the minds of those who heard it, as the ship rose and fell on the swells, her speed swallowing the waves from first light, through the day, and on into darkness.

July 7, 1915, and the *Stampalia* at last approaches New York harbor. Throughout the day her warm decks are a study in theme and variation, the women, all with scarves tied around their heads, blouses reaching high on the neck, and in long skirts with aprons, some black and white and others checks or calicos, and the men, each in a single or double breasted jacket and wearing a head covering—a felt hat, cap, straw boater, or fedora. Hoping for the first glimpse of the Statue of Liberty and the New York skyline with its Woolworth Building and Metropolitan Life Tower, the world's tallest buildings, they lined the rails and stared ahead. And then, suddenly, a billow of joyful sound, as first one and then another points, laughs, cheers, and cries in relief and happiness as they see Lady Liberty and the Promised Land coming into view, and thanking God for the safe end of their voyage and the opportunity to work and thrive in this new country, some fall to their knees. They had arrived.

> **Angelina Palmiero, Italian immigrant, 1923:** *Somebody yelled, "The Statue of Liberty, the Statue of Liberty!" We all ran to the railing to see, and everybody was praying and kissing and happy.*[20]

> **Nina Hemmer, Italian immigrant, 1925:** *The ladies were not allowed on the deck at all. Then, one day, the captain announced we were entering the harbor of New York City and that there was a marvelous statue there that would greet us, and they invited us to come up to the deck. That was one of the happiest days of my life.*[21]

Yet as physically and emotionally exhausted as they were, their journey still was not over. While passengers who could afford first or second class tickets are processed and given health inspections in their cabins before being sent on their way, they, because they were third class, had to undergo still another medical nightmare, the "six second physical," as it was called,[22] before being released from the island.[23*] Wearing a large nametag including not just his own name, but also the ship's manifest numbers and name, Leonardo and Antonio would have joined their designated group of 30, disembarked the *Stampalia* (most likely at a Manhattan pier), and crowded aboard a barge for transfer to Ellis Island.[24*]

In the first excitement of setting foot on land, and not just any land, but the United States of America, the cavernous main building, a beautiful French Renaissance structure of red brick with limestone trim and four cupola-style towers, would have seemed a bright and thrilling place to Leonardo and the others.

> **Rosanne Welch, granddaughter of Guiseppe Italiano, Italian immigrant, 1904:** *I remember my grandfather always telling me how he knew he could be rich in America because he saw riches*

> *in the architecture of Ellis Island. He felt that if they let the poor in such a gorgeous hall then life in this country was just.*[25]

Swarming with thousands of immigrants, doctors, and customs officials, its organized chaos was exhilarating, especially after two stuffy weeks at sea. But then, as an interpreter[26]* leads the group up the front stairs to the second floor, past doctors who, holding pieces of chalk, were closely watching them and, using a system of shorthand, marking the clothing of anyone with a suspected medical or mental condition—B for back problems, C for conjunctivitis, L for lameness, H for heart conditions, X for a mental condition, Pg for pregnancy, and so forth—like other groups before them, fear would have descended like a fog, and they would have become quiet.[27] Mute with worry, many wondered, "What if I am marked and sent back to Italy?[28]* What if someone notices that my child isn't feeling well?[29]* Which one of us will return home with him? How will we manage if we have to split up the family?" These uncertainties, and more, would have crowded their minds, as one in every five[30] passengers received a chalk mark on his or her back or shoulder and, wretched and fearful, was sent to a special examination room to be checked for a suspected illness, given a brief physical, and sent on to a screened cage-like detention pen in full view of all the other immigrants to await further examination. Luckier aliens, such as Leonardo and Antonio and most of the others in their group, were passed on unmarked to the "eye men" and, once again, to the most feared examination of them all.

Afterward, the nearly processed group would have been sent to wait in line for a summons to the inspector's desk for the legal exam of papers and identification tags, an examination they had practiced for on board the *Stampalia* and the only thing standing between them and their landing cards. Conducted by a primary line inspector who, well armed with medical certificates, telegrams from family or friends, and, most importantly, the ship's manifest, asked questions to determine signs of inadmissibility, it probably lasted about two minutes. Most of the questions were drawn from the manifest. But sometimes, particularly when the inspector was uncertain about a particular immigrant, he would ask an additional, unexpected question, which sometimes brought an unexpected answer.

> **Pauline Notkoff, immigrant, 1917:** *They asked us questions. "How much is one and one? How much is two and two?" But the next young girl, . . . they asked her, "How do you wash stairs, from the top or from the bottom?" She says, "I don't come to America to wash stairs."*[31]

A cheeky response, particularly considering the threat of detention, which could last hours, days, or even months.

And sometimes during the questioning, the inspector might make an unusual request, which sometimes might cause an unexpected moment:

> **Joe Dobos, University of Michigan Band, Leonard Falcone interviewer:** *At Ellis Island, while being questioned in Italian by the immigration officer, Leonard had his trombone with him. The officer asked him to play a tune.*[32]

Why was he asked to play his instrument? Perhaps, as steerage class immigrants were required to have a token $50 on them and Leonardo had only $46 (and possibly less at this point), there was a concern about his ability to support himself and not be a burden on the country. More likely, since the inspector knew that Leonardo was being sponsored by his brother, Nicola,[33] he merely wanted to break the tedium of routine and hear a boy play his trombone. Whatever the reason, Leonardo passed through this final test as smoothly as a glissando, and the inspector, satisfied by what he heard, issued him his landing card and sent him on his way.

While most left the legal exam for the money exchange or the rail ticket office, Leonardo was an exception: he already had US money, and he already had a rail ticket.[34] His next stop was the railroad ticket office waiting room on the first floor, a place marked for each rail line served by the ferry terminal; there, nearby, he bought himself a $1 box lunch[35] of salami, bread, and fruit for the journey ahead.[36]

If while he waited for the others he thought to wonder if Americans were obsessed with pins, badges, cards, and markings, as everywhere he looked there were people wearing pins, badges, cards, and markings, it wouldn't be surprising. The line inspectors were sporting nautical insignias. Hours earlier, a man wearing gold eagles had given him a badge with numbers corresponding to his place on the ship's manifest. And now, as he observed others loaded with tickets and vaccination cards in caps, or hats, or teeth, to free hands for carrying baggage or babies, he and they were to be marked again, this time with a card prominently attached to his hat or jacket informing railroad conductors of his name, the rail lines he would be traveling, the connections he needed to make, and his final destination.

Properly processed and tagged, Leonardo was finally sent with his group to the Baggage Room to forward luggage that had been in the ship's hold and, joining the 2/3 of all immigrants who left Ellis Island for places other than New York City,[37] followed an official through the door labeled "Push—To New York,"[38] to the train ferry dock and the boat to the New York Central Railway station.[39]*

> **Theodore Lubik, immigrant:** *There was a group of young inspectors, young fellows only, who knew all kinds of languages. One of these young men was the leader of a bunch of immigrants. He would slip a button on you and say, "Watch me." You watched him, you followed him, and he took you to New York on the dock. From there, if you were going to Chicago or someplace, you went on. . . a boat (to the train station) . . . (Another) inspector put the immigrants on the train. He knew already which cars would take them. The immigrant already had the tickets and so on paid and everything, and everyone had a place or some address where they were going. They stayed on the train until the conductor told them to get off.*[40]

It was probably at some point during the journey from the baggage room to the train that Leonardo bade farewell to Antonio, a man who mysteriously had his final destination listed on the ship manifest as both Ann Arbor, Michigan, and Roseto, Pennsylvania,[41] the former entry more than likely made by a confused official in Naples when Antonio, acting as chaperone, mentioned where Leonardo was headed. Regardless, the fact remains that from here on, Leonardo was likely largely on his own, no longer escorted by Antonio or under the protection of the United States Government, thrust into an environment of people waiting to either help, take advantage of, or condemn a young, defenseless immigrant boy who was unable to speak or understand the English language, and whose only desire was simply to earn a living in a country that all too often viewed Italians as a criminal class because of appalling crime accounts written by the yellow journalists of the times. It would take *compari*, the kindness of strangers, and his own wits for him to get to Ann Arbor and his waiting brother without incident.[42*]

> **Beryl Falcone:** *Leonard didn't know the language and so they pinned tags on him at Ellis Island with his final destination and so on. It was set up that he would buy a box lunch and take the train; it went up the Hudson River and somewhere crossed over and came down by Ann Arbor. There are lots of Italians working the mines in the U.P., and if some were headed on his same train in that direction, they may have helped him.*[43]

*A railroad employee leads Leonardo's group from the Ellis Island ferry to a New York Central line.*[44*] *Train smoke rising like warm breath on a cold morning, a confusion of languages, babies crying, disembodied voices barking orders, scarfed and hatted heads bobbing and funneling toward train doors, baggage, porters, children scrambling up silver steps, faces looking out windows. The train jerks and starts. Leonardo holds on to the back of a seat. The city's scenery unwinds empty lots, brown brick factories, long warehouses, smokestacks exhaling filth into a putrid gray-yellow sky. And then, in time, views of the broad Hudson River's stunning palisades, high cliffs running perpendicular to the clear water, and to the mansions of America's wealthiest captains of industry, literary giants, and political bosses. The train rackets toward the Mohawk Valley's forest woodlands and gently rolling hills, where the sun showers its white gold glitter on farmhouses, barns, apple trees, cows, horses, farmers perched*

*atop their red and green Mogul tractors. A sea of corn and wheat spills from the horizon in a flood of maize and tan. Farm smells, doubly pungent in the day's heat, fill passengers' nostrils. From Albany, a chain of cities and towns, and intermittent views of the Erie Canal, one of America's greatest public works, all the way to the great city of Buffalo where, on the Canal's banks, Leonardo and others disembark where the tracks dead end, and walk a few blocks to another station to board the Great Western Railway of Canada and continue their journey westward. Leonardo tips a helpful porter two pennies, a generous amount of money in Italy, as he steps aboard this new train. The porter takes the coins into his pink palm, has a second thought about accepting them from this slight, wide-eyed boy, and hands them back.*[45]* *The train snorts and lumbers out of the station, its linked cars bouncing and bending around curves all the way to Niagara Falls, where it halts to allow passengers to view the roar that struck Tchaikovsky himself mute when he saw it in 1891, declaring the beauty of the Falls too difficult to express in words.*[46] *From there, it crawls through Canada's small farm settlements, where clothes floating in the breeze from back yard clothes lines and a gently undulating haze blurring the horizon lend the flat corn- drenched landscape the elusive feeling of a fading dream. Finally, an arrival in Detroit, and Leonardo boards the interurban to Ypsilanti. And then a surprise.*

*At the Ypsilanti stop, as he glances out the window, Leonardo sees him at once, towering above the crowd and working his way forward through the people on the platform. The first thing he thinks is that it can't be his brother. He isn't supposed to be here. But it is Nicola, all right, though he looks different, not the teenager who left Roseto just three years ago for New York to find a job, unsuccessfully, at least in that city, as a musician. For one thing, by the yellowish glow from the train station's gaslights, he seems a dark, mysterious figure, a grown man, actually, and not the person he was when Leonardo last saw him. For another, he is much taller, a full six feet.*[47] *Excited, Leonardo calls his name through the crack in the window. "Nicola!" he shouts. Suddenly,*

*Nicola's eyes find him, and Leonardo sees their blank, level gaze change to a shock of recognition. They beam at one other through the twenty feet of chaos separating them, and then across the divide Nick comes, and then down the aisle, toting his baggage and his trombone, Leonardo goes to meet him.*

**Leonard Falcone:** *I sent Nick a telegram from New York that I was arriving on a certain day in Ann Arbor, and so feeling that he wouldn't be there when I arrived, that he'd still be in Ypsilanti playing at the theater, he asked a friend of ours to go to the Ann Arbor station to meet me. When I changed trains in Detroit I went downstairs and I had quite a time trying to get on the right train, and I remember this clearly: I was on the train all by myself, and the only stop on the way between Detroit and Ann Arbor was Ypsilanti, and I saw my brother there.*[48]

**Joe Dobos:** *After Leonard and Nick met at the train station, they took a streetcar together to Ann Arbor. It was nighttime, and Nick had just finished playing a show at the Martha Washington Theater in Ypsilanti.*[49]

A pair of taciturn Germans might have shaken hands and ridden the Ypsi-Ann down Packard Street, side by side, in silence.[50]* But Leonard and Nick were Italian. One can imagine them talking to one another all eight or so miles to Ann Arbor, and long into the night.

CHAPTER 7

# SUMMER YEARS: ANN ARBOR, JULY 19, 1915–AUGUST 1927

***"You have navigated with raging soul far from the paternal home, passing beyond the seas' double rocks, and now you inhabit a foreign land."***

~ Euripedes
*Medea*

---

*Monday, July 19, was the beginning of a stifling Ann Arbor summer week,*[1]* *the thick, heat filled air over campus filling with light long after Hill Auditorium, Tappen Hall, and the other great buildings on campus lay in shadow. The young man, newly arrived from Italy, had spent the day walking around town getting the lay of the land, thinking about how he could get a job, and settling in his brother's apartment. Now, as the sun was disappearing on the western horizon, its burning image fading into the neon colors of the evening sky, he thought of the day's stroll on shaded and paved sidewalks past the university's impressive buildings, of the scents emitted by the aromatic plants and trees on central campus and from the fruits and vegetables on peddlers' pushcarts, and of the "diag," dotted with young men reading or talking with friends as they lazed on the grass, intoxicated by the heat and the thought of a good movie and a cool beer come Friday night. Much of what he had seen was confusing, but he had recognized and understood the diag immediately. It was "una piazza," a place for him to relax, make friends, and get the news of the day: if only he could speak English.*

In 1915, Ann Arbor, Michigan, was a vibrant little town of 15,000, not including the 5,000 university students who attended school there from late August to May.[2] During the summer, when there were fewer students, it was slower paced. Its magnificent university, trolley system, and broad, level streets lined in brilliant electric lights were the marvels of south east Michigan, along with its great theaters and growing German population— both of which were proving to be fertile ground for an increasing and extraordinarily gifted musical community.

Nick, of course, was the reason Leonard was there. In the days before radio and record players, there were few opportunities to hear music. After the Civil War, returning soldiers, having been exposed to the sounds of rousing military bands, hungered for more—and touring bands, military bands, and community bands became all the rage. But since there were few music conservatories and music schools in the US, the country had to turn to European trained immigrants, (who because of Europe's patronage system were both numerous and accomplished) to get it. Of these, Italians were the favored source of musical talent, not only because of their skill and dazzling concert repertoire, but also because their conductors were entertaining and flamboyant showmen on the podium. The famous Guiseppe Creatore, an Italian American bandsman who was described in the Broadway musical *Music Man* as the musician rivaling March King John Phillip Sousa, was one example of such an entertaining showman who, with his long black hair and big moustache, pleased crowds by flailing his arms as he conducted, and descending the podium to egg on his musicians as they played.[3]

By the time Nick arrived in New York City in 1912, Italian musical influence was valued, and was everywhere.[4]* From the late 1800's to 1920, popular Italian touring bands, the most famous led by Creatore and Alessandro Liberati, and other well known groups, led by Gregory, Corrado, Gallo, Vesella, Phillipi, Tommasino, Ferulla, Satriano, Cassaassa, Ruzzi, Francisco Creatore, and from Roseto Valfortore, Michangelo Donatelli,[5]* the great maestro Domenico Donatelli's son, were drawing large audiences all across the country. European musicians became so popular that John Phillip Sousa grew a beard to appear more foreign, had many Italians play in his band, and included Italian *bel canto* in his programming. In fact, approximately one third of his programs consisted of Italian music. In addition to business bands, Italian immigrants joined military bands in large numbers, thus providing them a way to remain in the US and earn a living as well as retain their Italian heritage. As early as the 1700s, Thomas Jefferson suggested that Italian musicians be hired to save the floundering Marine Corps bands: they were, and they did. Later, after the Civil War, military band conductors, eager to enlarge their groups, greeted newly arrived ships at Ellis Island, looking for prospects. Soon, Italian music had an impact at the community level, as in small and large American towns across the nation, local bands sprang up, playing not just marches, but Italian operas and light pieces, thus spreading the popularity both of European musicians and Italian music. So it was that Italian immigrants, figuring into many of these bands, brought opera to America. Rossini, for one, became a part of nearly every band's repertoire.[6]

Still, when Nicola came to New York in 1912, hoping for a job in one of that city's huge theater pit orchestras,[7*] he wasn't able to find one.[8] It seems he had made a tactical error. Union jobs were posted every September, and because he'd arrived on American soil in November, he was told he would have to wait 10 months before the next posting. He waited four, and then, out of money, contacted his childhood friend, cornetist Mike Converso, who was working as a tailor and teaching wind instruments in Ann Arbor at the University School of Music, a private school not a part of the University of Michigan,[9] a place that was later to have great impact on Leonard's life. He urged Nick to come to Ann Arbor, and in March of 1913, Nick did, and with Converso's help, soon found a job tailoring and playing clarinet at the Majestic Theater on Maynard Street.[10]

Most important to Ann Arbor's development as an intellectual and cultural hub was, of course, the university. No surprise there. But beyond that, its reputation as a cultivated and refined place rested nearly as firmly on its menagerie of local German bands,[11*] the University Musical Society, and, most important of all, its numerous extraordinary movie and vaudeville theaters. In early 1900's Ann Arbor, the Majestic, the Arcade, the Orpheum, the Wuerth, the Whitney, and the Rae were among the most popular, while in nearby Ypsilanti, the Martha Washington, and the Opera House held court. What *was* a surprise, especially to big city folk, was that many of these theaters boasted orchestras that played with a control, precision, and style several notches above those found in the nation's largest metropolitan hubs—places like Detroit, Chicago, New York, and San Francisco.

Autumn now, October, 1915, and sixteen year old Leonard already established as a tailor's assistant, a job he was to hold for over three years.[12] But because Nick was conducting and managing the orchestra at the Opera House (later the Wuerth) in Ypsilanti, he was able to arrange for his young brother to play his valve trombone in the group. It was Leonard's first American musical gig.

> **Leonard Falcone:** *I had a job assisting as a tailor, and I also played at the Opera House in Ypsilanti. In those days the farmers would come in with their horses and buggies on a Saturday night, you know, and tie up their horses on the hitching post and come in to see a show. They were all, of course, silent movies then, you see. We added mood.*[13] *(For example), when the shooting ended and the marriage took place in the movie, well, then we'd play the "Wedding March."*[14]

> **Addie Murray, wife of Opera House Theater owner "Smiling Al Renne":** *My husband purchased the "Old Opry House." . . . The sign in the box office read "Mutual Movies, Make Time Fly." The admission for all— ten cents. Keystone Cops. Fatty Arbuckle, Mary Pickford in "Tess of the Storm Country." Margaret Clark, Mary Miles Minter, Valentino, William S. Hart, Wallace Reed. Then the old time vaudeville acts, some very good and some pretty awful. And every fall several weeks of dramatic stock, playing such things as "Tempest and Sunshine" and 'East Lynne.' Then there were one night stands of large dramatic shows who would break the jump between Detroit and Chicago at Ypsilanti with such plays as "The Lion and the Mouse," "Paid in Full," also musicals like "The Cat and the Fiddle." . . . The well known Falcone brothers played in our old orchestra.*[15]

**Leonard Falcone:** *We had a seven piece combination of violin, cello, clarinet, cornet, trombone, piano, and drums. It was a very fine experience for me because it was the time I learned to sight-read well. It was important. We had a rehearsal before each show and I couldn't read fast enough. I was in trouble (laughs)!*

*After 2 or 3 months, with help, I improved. It was a matter of concentration, and being able to recognize pitches and rhythms quickly . . . Recognition is what bothered me—I had to learn to recognize quickly. I met some nice people (at the Opera Theater). One was the pianist. She was a lady.*[16]

**Addie Murray:** *Old Joe Wilcox supplied the props from his second-hand store and then there was Bill Morey, who took the tickets at the door. I remember that fine big moustache.*[17]

**Leonard Falcone:** *The pianist, she took pity on me and during intermissions when others would go outside and have a smoke, we would stand there and she would teach me words I didn't understand. She tried to teach me English.*[18]

Learning English was a problem Leonard tackled without delay, and he mined every opportunity to learn it that came his way. There were plenty of Italian newspapers available at the Blue Front and other places, but newspaper news wasn't all he wanted. Within weeks and perhaps even days of being in America, he understood this truth: that language is more than a tool to communicate facts, it's the best and sometimes *only* way of establishing a social identity. Without knowing English, how would he understand what the girls on the interurban were saying to one another? How could he talk with the pretty English professor he had seen engrossed in a book, without knowing how to read it himself and how to discuss it with her?[19*] How would he be able to progress as a tailor or even as a musician?

**Leonard Falcone:** *I had a terrible time learning the English language. I knew that it was quite different from the Italian, but didn't realize how different it could be. It made me shy and of a* *silent nature. It soon became my objective to learn it. I acquired the habit of carrying a pencil and pad of paper with me. Every time I heard a word and understood its meaning clearly, I jotted it down. Thus, I acquired my English vocabulary. I thought I got to first base when I overheard a joke and understood its meaning. From then on, English seemed to be a bit easier.*[20]

**Donato Bracco, Italian immigrant,1956:** *When you don't understand, you feel stupid. If they are saying something important, or friendly, or if they are being disrespectful, you never really know. All you've got to go on is body language, and that's not enough. It's terrible.*[21]

**Leonard Falcone:** *It's a lonely life (when you don't speak the language) but when you're young, you don't feel the hardship so much.*[22]

He would listen to war news every day to learn the language, and kind people reached out to help him, not only the pianist at the Opera Theater who wrote down words and phrases for him to practice and gave him English lessons during intermissions, but also the tailor he worked for, who took a special interest in trying to help him learn. But in the end, such halfway measures proved inadequate, and realizing he needed a more formal training, he enrolled in a university night school language course in the fall.[23] It was a powerful decision, a beginning step in the journey of remaking himself as an American, a process that would place him squarely between *la via vecchia ed i sogni americani* (the old way and the American Dream), and start him down a path that would separate him from his mother tongue,[24]* minimize his gestures,[25]* require him to accept American institutions and traditions, and affect nearly every aspect of his life right down to his appearance and what he ate. It was a courageous thing to do, as it meant that, to some extent, he had to lose that which made him Italian.

Winter came and went, then spring, and daylight lengthened, melting the remaining snow as crocus popped on the diag lawn and miniature bouquets of yellow forsythia burst on twiggy bushes around town;

soon, there were the hot close days followed by apple crisp football weekends, and then suddenly it was winter and spring all over again. And throughout those first years, Leonard and Nick played in the theater orchestra and began to make names for themselves and kept up their tailoring and were able to send money home to the family, as planned.[26*] And so it went.

And then one day in 1917 at an Ann Arbor street fair there came a serendipitous stroke of luck that changed the trajectory of Leonard's life.

> **Leonard Falcone:** *There was a raffle for a violin somewhere, and I bought a ticket for $2.50. . . and I won! It sounds silly (laughs) but that's the way it is.*
>
> *I never won a thing since then.*[27]

Violins had fascinated him for some time. Orchestras were unusual in Italy in his day, and the few that did exist were located in large far away cities. The only time he'd ever even seen a violin in Italy was when a traveling group of blind musicians and singers had passed through Roseto. The instrument captured his childish imagination.[28]

> **Beryl Falcone:** *Later, when he came to the United States, he saw a well known violinist play with the Chicago Symphony in a concert at Hill Auditorium. He just couldn't understand this instrument called the "violin." He wasn't acquainted with it, and he was intrigued. It didn't have any frets on it – he was used to guitars.*[29]

> **Leonard Falcone:** *I took the violin home after I won it, and I began to play on the thing. I recall I was playing by ear, not by any positions, the melodic violin part of the "Cavalleria Rusticana"—it goes up to high "E" at the end (sings); how I got up there, I don't know—and I began to realize I had to study with some expert. Until then, I had no intention of going to school. But shortly after I acquired that instrument, I began taking violin lessons from Tony Whitmire, a very, very old, blind, very fine person and violinist from Germany. Well, between him, my brother, and*

*Young Leonard hanging out in Ann Arbor*
*~ courtesy of the Falcone family*

*other friends, they began to influence me to go to school. "Why don't you take a full course and graduate as a musician?" they asked. I didn't hesitate. The war was still on, so this was about 1917, I think.*[30]

And so he entered the University School of Music,[31]* and with the thought of earning his musician's diploma dancing tantalizingly at the center of his imagination, attended his first class, an important theory course. It was a near disaster. In spite of English having been relatively easy for him to learn at night school two years earlier, he found himself barely holding on, and in less than a week, he decided to quit school.[32]

**Leonard Falcone:** *Dr. Earl Moore, the theory teacher, lectured so fast that I could only jot down a semblance of what he was talking about. I wasn't proficient enough to write, so my notes were*

> *abbreviated . . . and when I got home I couldn't understand. After three or four days in this class, a very important class, I decided I couldn't go on. I just didn't know the language well enough. And so my brother said, "Why don't you go see him?" And so I went to talk to him. "Oh, I'm sorry," he said. "I don't want you to quit. I'll slow down." He did, but I still had quite a time.*[33]

Though Dr. Moore was true to his word, the language barrier still had Leonard in white water. He could not think rapidly in English, and time didn't allow the translation of everything into Italian. When he resorted to his own brand of English shorthand and attempted to transcribe the lessons at home, he couldn't—they didn't make sense. Classmates to the rescue. Realizing his plight and also his great musical genius,[34]* students banned together to help the struggling Italian boy. Leading the cavalry charge to save Leonard were Arnold Berndt, supervisor of music for the Birmingham, Michigan Public Schools, a man who remained a close, life -long friend, and Miss Helen Snyder, a flutist in both the University and Wuerth Theatre Orchestras. Leonard hit the lucky trifecta when he met Helen Snyder, and he knew it. In addition to being a musician and kind, she also taught British Literature at U of M at a time when University School of Music students were required to take literature courses there.[35] Perfect: Leonard took her class. A grace note before the downbeat of his life, the young and pretty Miss Snyder played an important role in teaching him the language and helping him graduate from music school. She kindled in him an interest in reading which not only helped him with all his studies, but also led him to be (his words) "intensely interested" with the great works of the English language.[36]

1917, a seminal year for Leonard, was the year he left the Opera House, began playing at Ypsilanti's Martha Washington Theater, and quit tailoring, which gave him time to practice his violin and to study theory, orchestration, composition, arranging, instrumentation, and conducting, along with other coursework. It was also the year he decided to remain in the United States and not return to Roseto after the war as originally planned. "No one expected the war would last as long as it did,"[37] he said in a statement that implied he had put down roots in his adopted country. He had learned the lesson of America: he had learned to hope for a better future.

His studies progressed slowly, not only because he had to learn to read textbooks in a second language, but also because of his long work hours at various Ann Arbor theaters and his three night a week job playing valve trombone at dances at the Detroit Golf Club on East Hamilton and the Detroit Yacht Club on Belle Isle.[38] It was a back-breaking schedule.

> **Leonard Falcone:** *I'd drive back and forth to Detroit in an old Ford jalopy. It was a good experience. At the yacht club we had a group of 2 saxophones, a violin, a piano, and me. All good musicians, and it paid well . . . I even had extra to help support my family at home.*[39]

At school, Leonard's first training in conducting came from David Mattern, head of the Music Education Department, and in just a year he had progressed to a conducting and instrumentation class taught by the pioneering music educator Joseph Maddy, who was to form the National Music Camp now known as the Interlochen Center for the Arts. Maddy, a man who would figure into his future as a bandsman, allowed Leonard and a few select others to conduct a student orchestra, even during concerts. The class also focused on musical instruments, and while Leonard was successful on every other instrument he played, he never quite got the hang of the piano, and all his life played it the same way he typed: with two fingers.[40]

Meantime, Leonard made such quick progress on the violin that in three years or so he had begun advanced study under Professor Samuel Lockwood, head of the violin department and conductor of the University Symphony Orchestra. It was Lockwood who also taught him the basics of transcribing solo piano music for orchestra, and showed him techniques he later used to transcribe music for band.

Then, while still a student, Leonard landed an important audition.

> **Leonard Falcone:** *I had no definite aims in life. Things just sort of happened. In 1924 or '25, I auditioned for the Detroit Symphony*

*Orchestra, and I was accepted. At that time, I was thinking of making a professional career of playing in an orchestra. In the course of conversation, the man who auditioned me asked me what I was doing—and when I told him, he said, "You're about to make a mistake. You don't want to join an orchestra. Do you know what this means? You're traveling constantly. You're never sure of a job from one year to the next. It's terrifically competitive. You're in school now, and you're interested in your schoolwork. Seems to me you'd be happier getting your degree and teaching than in joining an orchestra. I know you'd get satisfaction playing, but you'd get just as much or more satisfaction from teaching." Well, I thought it over and talked with the people in Ann Arbor, and they said the same thing: "Orchestra is wonderful, but it's so uncertain," they said. So I was discouraged from it, and I continued with school and I continued playing.*[41]

By his final year at the University School of Music, Leonard Falcone, a man whom most of his future students never knew as string player at all, was the University Symphony Orchestra's concertmaster.[42]

**Erik W. Nielsen, MD, trombone, MSU band, 1969–1973:** *In the spring of 1972 during a break in a trombone lesson with Mr. Falcone, I noted a picture of a U of M orchestra on his wall and finally built up the courage to ask what it was doing there. He proceeded to take me over to the picture and point to the principal violin. "That's me," he said. He then began to name about 5 more members of the section who were seated below him, and the major symphony orchestras they played in. I was in awe. The most talented brass soloist I had ever heard was also a string virtuoso! I still remember that day, and the feeling I was in the company of true greatness, imbued in this quiet, humble man.*[43]

And so it was that in May of 1926, nine years after beginning his studies at the University School of Music, Leonard Falcone played his graduation recital on the violin,[44]* and in June, was awarded an Artist's Diploma.[45]*To make the achievement sweeter, sitting in the audience was not just one Falcone brother, but two. Carmelo had arrived.

> *On a clear, sunny day in May, 1925, the ship Columbo steamed past the Statue of Liberty and into New York harbor from Naples, Italy, after a calm two weeks at sea. On deck was second class passenger Carmelo Falcone, age 31, a WWI veteran of the Italian Army. Like his brothers Nicola and Leonardo, he proved himself to authorities to be literate in Italian, but unable to speak, read, or write English. Unlike them, he claimed his profession as "musicista," a claim which both declared an expectation for the future and represented the prosperity of the times. As with many of this generation of immigrants, he hadn't felt it necessary to state his occupation as "laborer" or "field hand." He had in mind making a professional living playing tuba or trombone in one of the Ann Arbor area's local bands or orchestras, and he knew he would get it: his two brothers had already paved the way.*
>
> "Si," *Carmelo responded, when asked if he had paid for his own ticket.* "Andro a raggiungere mio fratello Nicola ad Ann Arbor, Michigan, negli Stati Uniti, e sara' la mia residenza permanente." *"I will be joining my brother Nicola in Ann Arbor, Michigan, and the United States will be my permanent home." The official dutifully recorded this, along with his "race" as "S. Italian," his complexion as "regular," his height as "5'5" and his hair as "brown." "Nearest living relative?" he asked in Italian, passively looking up from the form.* "Carmela. Lei è la mia moglie ed e' a casa a Roseto," *he answered. "Carmela," the official wrote. "Wife." "Roseto Valfortore."*[46]
>
> *This immigrant, he may have noted, as with most Italian male immigrants, had left his wife at home, no doubt intending her to join him at a later time.*

Carmelo Falcone was one of 6,203 Italians to enter the US in 1925, and the 3rd of Dominico and Maria Falcone's sons to leave their household forever.[47] The brothers had been separated for thirteen years. Now, though the Falcones as a family continued to be irrevocably split, Dominico and Maria's three boys were to be together once again.

> **Susan Falcone, Leonard's great niece:** *Carmelo, my grandfather, played trombone and tuba, and he, Leonard and Nicholas all played in the local bands and orchestras plus in the Wuerth Theater Orchestra (Ann Arbor). He was also a cobbler and barber. Since Leonard and Nicholas were his brothers, they were my great uncles.*[48]

As for Carmela, by the time she arrived in New York on May 12, 1928, on board the steamship Roma, she had not seen her husband for three full years.[49]

During these same years, 1917 to 1926, Leonard continued to make a reputation for himself as a theater musician. In 1917, when both he and Nick left the Old Opera House to play at the Martha Washington in Ypsilanti, he substituted violin for trombone in his theater work, a shift that soon allowed him not only to play, but also, one year later, to conduct.

> **Joe Dobos:** *Sometimes in these scores when Leonard was playing violin and Nick a clarinet—they would play like a duet—it was played as one, you could not tell one from the other. It was years later when Leonard reflected on this—how similar they were in everything they did musically. They agreed about how to do things.*[50]

In 1918, the year WWI came to an end, Nicholas was asked by Ann Arbor theater manager Gerald Hoag to form and manage the orchestra at the new Wuerth Theater on Main Street.[51*] Leonard, still a teenager, was appointed the orchestra's conductor, while Nicholas played clarinet and supervised the group.[52*]

After two years at the Wuerth, Leonard, 21, accepted the job of violinist, manager, and conductor of Ann Arbor's Arcade Theater, located at 715 N. University.[53*] The Arcade, with its box seats, balcony, and forty-three rows of floor seats, was situated at the end of a passage that ran along the north side of a tailor shop where a "motion picture machine" reeled out movies from the shop's second floor, outside the theater itself.[54] Because it wasn't until the 1930s that the practice of composing original scores for films took hold, during his time as conductor at the Arcade (and previously at the Wuerth) it was Leonard who was responsible for compiling a musical score to fit each film's scenes, moods, and themes. To do it, he referred to lengthy cue sheets provided by the film maker, which included detailed notes about any rapidly changing effects. Then, according to the notes, he would choose appropriate pieces from the theater's music library, perusing light classics for stock situations, agitatos for action scenes, and so forth. This was no easy job: a single film might require over 35 separate pieces[55] of music to describe the character, location, emotion, or action being seen on the screen, such as when in "Down to the Sea in Ships" (1922) Clara Bow falls hard for Jimmy, a cabin boy on a whaler. For that film, he would had to have selected music to express the 19th century whaling community of New Bedford, Massachusetts, Quaker family music, strict father music, good daughter music, son lost at sea music, found baby music, tomboy granddaughter music (Bow), neighbor returning from college music, falling in love music, disapproval music, bad guy music, kidnap music, stowaway music, whaling music, wagon train music, mutiny music, rescue music, and happy ending music. And it was important to find just the right piece to create an effect that moved or entertained the audience. The success of the film, the act, or even of the theater itself, depended upon it.

> **Robert Sherwood, playwright, editor, screenwriter, film critic:** *I once saw* The Cabinet of Dr. Caligari *in a projection room with no musical accompaniment, and while it excited and impressed me profoundly, it didn't quite scare me out of my skin. I later saw it in a crowded substantial theater. At the moment when the heroine woke up suddenly and gazed into the fiendish countenance of the maniacal somnambulist, the clarinet player in the theater orchestra emitted a wild, piercing shriek. Fear came through my ear then, all right. In fact, the gruesome sound of that clarinet terrifies me to this day.*[56]

It's easy to imagine such a reaction being savored and shared, and after their musical scare, the "substantial theater" Sherwood refers to would have been one he, and others, would have wanted to return to.

Because a typical two to three hour evening of theater entertainment might include a stage show as well as a movie, Leonard, as conductor, was also responsible for the rest of the music program at the Arcade. Most likely he would have opened with an overture by Rossini or Tchaikovsky, and followed it with music supporting a twenty minute live presentation, shorts (including a cartoon), a two reel comedy, newsreels, and then finally, with the music for the feature film.[57*]

It took a good deal of energy and concentration for an orchestra to emotionally manipulate an audience watching a silent film. For one thing, there were no quiet moments—the music was continuous. As director, Leonard would have followed the movie's action and kept precise track of the cue sheet in order to begin the right piece at the right moment, depressed a pedal that flashed lights on each player's stand to signal a new tune, and, while skillfully playing his violin, indicated musical attacks, phrases, releases, times, and tempos with slight gestures from its neck and bow. The orchestra's job, beyond playing their instruments, was to pay very close attention to him, an exhausting job in itself.[58]

In 1923, after three years at the Arcade, Leonard moved to the Majestic on Maynard Street, directly across the street from the University School of Music to become its violinist-manager-conductor.[59] It was still "new and proud," having opened in 1920, and farmers drove their buggies from miles around just to see it, especially at night when Gerald Hoag, the manager, turned lights on and off for the visitors.[60] Once a skating rink, "The Maj" was a huge, 1,100-seat theater, with a large stage, box seats, balcony, confectionery, dressing rooms, ladies' waiting room, and manager's office. It was the major entertainment source for Ann Arbor area, and affordable: a ticket to a "Complete DeLuxe Show" with director Leonard Falcone's "New Majestic Orchestra" cost a mere 10, 30, or 40 cents, depending on the seat or the show.[61]

> **Gerald Hoag, Majestic Theater manager, 1919-1928:** *We usually had a western such as Dorothy Ralston in "Red Butte" or a Tom Mix or William Hart picture. Then on Sunday we would start the feature, such as Wallie Reid in "Valley of the Giants," which was the first big picture after I arrived.*[62]

While working as a full time orchestra leader and manager at the Arcade and then the Majestic, Leonard was also working toward his graduation from the University School of Music, practicing his instruments, preparing for his final graduation concert, accepting help from Helen Snyder, Arnold Berndt, and others, on his English and his school work (including British literature) and American citizenship coursework,[63]* playing occasional dance band gigs, and successfully auditioning for a spot as a violinist for the Detroit Symphony Orchestra. It was not a schedule for the faint of heart, the "part time" theater job alone most likely requiring not only numerous performances, but also rehearsals twice a week for 3½ hours each[64] in addition to the program selection work. Clearly, with all the work on his plate, he had very little time for personal enjoyment. But then he probably would not have seen it that way.

**Kenneth G Bloomquist, MSU Director of Bands 1970-1977, Director of the School of Music, 1978 –'88:** *Music was always uppermost in Leonard's mind. When an MSU colleague once asked,*

*After a Cap Night ceremony, the nearly all-male audience seen here rushed to Ann Arbor's Majestic Theater to demand a free movie.*
*~ courtesy of the Bentley Historical Library, University of Michigan*

*Leonard's Majestic Theater Orchestra, 1926*
*~ courtesy of the Falcone family*

> *"Leonard, what do you do for fun?" he answered, "I do a little conducting, a little arranging, a little writing, a little playing ." "No, Leonard," the colleague said, "What I'm asking is what you do for fun." Leonard smiled. "I do a little conducting, a little arranging, a little writing, a little playing," he repeated. Everyone who knew Leonard Falcone can recognize him in this response. He lived his musical life to the fullest.*[65]

Though his school work at the University School of Music, his orchestra work in the various theaters in Ann Arbor, and his English and naturalization classes took up nearly all his time, it would be going too far to say that Leonard's early life was *all* music and study. In fact, though clearly hard work in one form or another dominated his young life, it's certain that he did have social fun, at very least as he studied and worked with new friends at school and the theater or hung out with *paisani*. As his early experiences in Italy bumped up against

American behaviors and attitudes, his observations about American life surely became the basis of amusing conversations with his brothers Nicholas, and later, Carmen, and with other newly arrived Italians, as Nick's friend and fellow Rosetan, Michael Converso. Without a doubt, they had found themselves in a Wonderland of confusion and human comedy. "Nothing looked like Italy or Italians," commented one immigrant, describing the experience. "I couldn't make heads or tails out of anything."[66] Only other immigrants could understand how steep the learning curve was, and only other immigrants could laugh, probably heartily, at what passed for "normal" in American life.

Take the centers of student social life in Ann Arbor, the theaters, for example. Among their cultural traditions was the "Frosh Bible," the 1919 version of which outlining in graphic form the horrors that would be visited upon any first year man (identified by his required freshman beanie, called a "pot"[67*]) who even tried sitting in the first six rows of "The Maj,"[68] and the sometimes astounding behavior of student patrons—such as their frequent theater rushes. Gerald Hoag, manager of the Majestic the entire time Leonard was there, faced the challenge of handling these rushes, which were usually made after the pep rallies at the Michigan Union the night before a football game. Thousands would amass on Maynard, ready to charge the theater if Hoag didn't offer free admission. In time, when the student rushes became very large, Hoag finally moved the theater's reels of film and projectors to Hill Auditorium for its Friday night shows.[69*]

> **Gerald Hoag, Majestic Theater Manager:** *The only time one (a rush) actually happened after a game was when the team came in from a successful game with Wisconsin. It was on a Sunday, and at about 4 o'clock they came trooping down.*[70*] *Small riots broke out, bricks and stones were thrown, and students were wrestled and hauled to the police station. And finally, the students got their way . . . Rushes on the theater didn't really bring the results they wanted. There was no confrontation—they were allowed to see the picture, and that was it. This took away half the fun.*[71]

> **Bob Hall, 1920s Majestic rush participant:** *They'd holler and yell and demand a free movie. They always got in. I was scared stiff—I was afraid I'd get squashed—but I wanted to see a free movie. My mother didn't like it. She castigated me when I got home.*[72]

Some of the people Leonard worked with at the theater were character studies, too, and had to have been the source of interesting discussions. At the Majestic, a short, stocky, red-faced German immigrant named Conrad Van Hofe, who had just entered the country after serving four years on the Western front in the German army, served as a bouncer. His customary solution for a rowdiness problem usually ended in his rolling around on the theater's linoleum floor with the miscreant, the two of them exiting the building in ground level rotation into the gravel alley outside through a pair of freshly opened double doors. After these episodes, "Van" would always return to the theater alone, brushing himself off and readying himself for more action.[73*]

Clearly, Leonard wasn't in Roseto any more.

Of a less peculiar nature, Ann Arbor and the university itself had to have held a fascination for the young man. Among other new sights, it was there, in the fall of 1915, twelve years before the newly constructed Michigan Stadium was dedicated, that he saw an intriguing spectacle, something very different from anything he was accustomed to in Italy:

> **Leonard Falcone:** *My first recollection of a college band is at a football game between Michigan State College and the University of Michigan in Ann Arbor. I had just arrived in this country in June, 1915, and the following fall the first game was (between the two schools). It was my first football game, and the first time I had seen college bands in a halftime performance. At that time I had no idea that twelve years later I would be Director of Bands at Michigan State. The bands at football games then just marched in a straight formation, did a few letters, and played the school songs. The emphasis was on straight marching with a few turns and some countermarches.*
>
> *I can still see the MAC band marching down the field with*

*straight lines and precise footwork (enhanced by the clean cut look of the leather puttees) at a steady 120 cadence. This was the first good marching band I had ever seen.*[74]

Leonard's friendships with members of the Majestic orchestra, whom he praised as "a very fine group—good fellows!" must have provided him with entertaining diversions as well.[75*] And for more conventional fun, there were the movies and stage acts he most certainly saw while working at the various theaters.[76*]

There's no doubt that Leonard's years in Ann Arbor had a profound influence on his assimilation into American society as well as on his musical thinking, both important factors in what occurred next. In Ann Arbor, he mastered the English language, became a naturalized citizen, made friends and learned to be comfortable with his new country's customs, and discovered that he could be a good American without abandoning his Italian heritage. Musically, while a student at the University School of Music and a violinist in its orchestra, he became an expert on his instruments (including valve trombone and baritone, which he sometimes played in the theaters and dance bands),[77] formed his concept of band sound based on his understanding of a nuanced orchestral string style, and developed a flexible approach to articulation, which he learned from violin bowing practices.[78*] The skills he gained as a theatre orchestra conductor and member of an area dance band are no less impressive. In these groups, he learned sight-reading, broadened stylistic concepts he had learned in Italy, was introduced to countless musical scores, became a leader and conductor, gained performance experience, and developed his sense of timing and showmanship. [79]

His massive talents honed to a fine point, he was now ready to move on to bigger and better things—and none too soon. Across America, sound was beginning to come to the movies.

**Jack Caldwell, organist, Palace Theater, Dallas:** *We had 40 men, good musicians. And they said, "Aw, it won't ever happen." Well, it did happen! "That's just a fad!" they said. "It'll be good to be off 2 weeks and then we'll be right back in the pit."*

> **Gaylord Carter, organist, Paramount Theater, Los Angeles:** *As soon as sound was definitely in, all the theater orchestras were let go immediately. I recall a headline in the* Los Angeles Times*: "Sound Drives Organists from Theaters, Managers Rejoice." They hated to pay us, you see. I was making $100 a week.*[80]

By 1926, Leonard's days as a theater musician were numbered. But because word had long been out that "good music" of considerable sophistication was being played in Ann Arbor's theaters by the Falcone brothers, important people from the University of Michigan and the School of Music, including Joe Maddy, had come to listen.[81] What happened next was a surprise to nearly everyone, most of all, most likely, to Leonard himself.

CHAPTER 8

# NEW BEGINNINGS: 1926–1927

*"What nobler employment, or more valuable to the state, than that of the man who instructs the rising generation."*

~ **Marcus Cicero**

---

Michigan State College
of Agriculture and Applied Science
Office of the Secretary
East Lansing, Mich.

Herman H. Halladay

August 9, 1927

Mr. Leonard Falcone
515 S. Fifth Ave.
Ann Arbor, Michigan

My dear Mr. Falcone:

Referring to our conversation relative to the band, I wish to state that it is my understanding that you are willing to take charge of the two bands and render such instructions as may be necessary to carry them along in good shape and that you are willing to accept the position at a salary of $200 per month for ten months beginning September 1st. Also that this in no way will interfere with your giving private lessons, providing it does not interfere with your college work.

Of course, all details in connection with the handling of the band and matters pertaining to the reorganization will have to be worked out with Mr. Richards when he comes to campus, September 1st.

Will you kindly acknowledge receipt of this letter?

Very sincerely yours,
H. H. Halladay
Secretary

HHH:EM

---

Michigan State College
Of Agriculture and Applied Science
Office of the Secretary
East Lansing, Mich.

Herman H. Halladay

August 15, 1927

Mr. Leonard Falcone
515 S. Fifth Ave.
Ann Arbor, Michigan

My dear Mr. Falcone:

This will acknowledge receipt of your letter of August 12th, accepting the appointment as Director of the Band.

I am delighted to think that you have accepted and assure you of every cooperation to make your stay here both pleasant and successful.

Very sincerely yours,

H. H. Halladay
Secretary[1]

HHH:EM[1]

When in 1926 Nicholas Falcone was appointed assistant director to Director of Bands Norman Larson at the University of Michigan, he was asked to organize and direct the new "University Reserve Band," a group of freshmen and some sophomores who were unable to make the top group. He formed the second string Reserve Band in October of that year[2] and early the following spring asked his brother to guest conduct and play a solo. Leonard did, and on March 24, 1927, the day after the concert, the student newspaper *The Michigan Daily,* published this review:

***The Varsity Band and Soloist Astound Concert Audience***
***Falcone and Men Give High Class Program***

*The band being composed of freshmen, Mr. (Nicholas) Falcone nevertheless has succeeded in whipping together a band which responded instantly to his finished conducting . . . Leonard Falcone, brother of the director, playing a trombone solo, the 'Rondo Caprice' by Herbert L. Clarke, astounded the large audience with the richness and depth of his tone, and marvelous technique he has at his command. The band setting of the three Michigan songs. . . were Leonard Falcone arrangements for tenor with band accompaniment. The songs were well sung by Frank Ryan, tenor, with Leonard Falcone conducting.*

**Joe Dobos:** *Nick knew all the best players in town and all students in School of Music. He had a nice little band. When they had the concert, that so-called "second band," the Reserve Band, outplayed the U of M band—which was well noted by newspapers. In one of the numbers, Nicholas took a march that he wrote for the students who regularly attended shows at the Wuerth Theater and made a band arrangement out of it. It was written for 7 instruments originally, but he expanded it for band. He had Leonard write the baritone part and he called it "M Men March"and he dedicated it to Robert Campbell, at the time the mayor of Ann Arbor, University of Michigan's treasurer, and also the faculty advisor or business manager of University of Michigan bands. He was in the audience that night and was impressed with the band's playing a piece of music dedicated to him—and of course at heart he was a politician, and it had a favorable review from the newspaper.*[3]

Neither the concert nor the review could have hurt either man's chances for a bright future, and as fate would have it, some few months after Leonard's appearance with his brother's band, Herman Halladay, secretary of Michigan State College, called Robert Campbell ("Uncle Bob," to the men of the Varsity and Reserve Bands) to ask him for a recommendation for an important position that had just opened up at State: Director of Bands. Ironically, Norman Larson had just left his position as the Varsity Band Director at U of M, and Campbell himself had been considering candidates to succeed him. He had seen and heard enough of the Falcone brothers to know who to recommend, all right.

An August 6, 1927, *Ann Arbor News* article about the selections tells what happened next, and suggests that though the appointments for the top band positions at the two schools came separately, they were publically announced simultaneously—or nearly so. Nicholas, it states, "was officially named last June[4*] to succeed Norman Larson as head of the local Varsity band, (though) the appointment was not made public until today. Leonard Falcone, however, was not appointed to lead the Michigan State band until recently."[5]

So it was that in an indelible moment that defines a life, Leonard, 28 years old, accepted the job as Director of Bands at Michigan State College, and with his future unreeling before him as dramatically as a D.W. Griffith movie, began preparing to throw a very large rock into the rising pond of the small regional agricultural school.[6*]

Before Leonard Falcone arrived on the Michigan State campus, he must have been aware that great things were in the works. By 1928, the new science and arts curriculum that had been introduced in 1921 had resulted in nearly doubling the school's enrollment to 2,813 in less than a decade, and the off campus extension service had increased its budget seven times over and grown from 4 to 55 agents. More, 1,375 acres of new off-campus lands had been acquired, and the college farm had doubled in size thanks to the annexation of six adjacent farms and the three hours' daily manual labor students were expected to contribute to the school in garden or field work—labor which for many years translated into clearing forested areas so that the gardens and fields could be planted in the first place.[7] Another change came to the school in the form of college President Kenyon Butterfield, whose term lasted a mere four years (1924–1928). A native of a small farming community of Lapeer, Michigan, his deep interest in the sociological problems of the farmer led him to devote much of his life's work to helping them adjust to the economic, social, and religious trends of the times. Under his leadership, MAC offered an increasing number of courses to uplift and enhance mankind, and in short order was able to develop entire departments geared toward the various disciplines of the humanities.

This focus resulted in some very good news for teachers and students of music, who learned in 1928 that the board of trustees had agreed that MSC should distinguish itself as a place where young men of talent could come to study music. One of America's finest harpsichordists, Lewis Richards, who had studied piano at the Royal Conservatory in Brussels, and later played at the White House for President Hoover and his guests (among whom was the UK's Prime Minister Ramsay MacDonald) was chosen to create a top caliber music conservatory to train students in music as an avocation, preparation for teaching, or concert stage; to do it, Richards joined with the Lansing Conservatory to form the Michigan State Institute of Music and Allied

Arts and selected as faculty twenty one world class musicians, including Leonard Falcone, Michael Press, chair of the violin department at the Moscow Imperial Conservatory of Music, Alexander Schuster, formerly assistant conductor and principal cellist of the Schlesischen Orchestra of Breslau, and Arthur Farwell,[8]* noted Indianist composer and well known conductor of massed choral performances such as the "Canticle of Praise," played across America on Armistice Sundays. It was a renowned staff in which the Lansing community took genuine pride, comprised of virtuoso teachers who were to offer unprecedented opportunities to both college and non-college local area students. To encourage these outstanding musicians to join the staff, State allowed them to use campus buildings to teach private lessons to the Institute students, and supplement their faculty salaries with a share of the private lesson fees these pupils brought in.[9] It was a decision that would come to haunt them in the future.

Yet other than perhaps these few facts, by his own admission Leonard knew very little about the school he had just agreed to work for as "Teacher of Wind Instruments" and "Director of the Michigan State College Military Band."[10] In fact, it's possible that the first time he saw the newly named (in 1925) "Michigan State College of Agriculture and Applied Science" was when, in late August, 1927, he traveled on the rutted gravel roads leading to campus, past bucolic cow-dotted pastures and fields of sun drenched Michigan corn marching unceasingly to the horizon. Nearly there, he crossed over the Red Cedar at the vibrating steel bridge at Farm Lane, passed the dairies and barnyards north of the river, and reported for work at the Armory, a place that up until his arrival had served the combined functions of drill hall, gymnasium, and ballroom, and whose pool in the adjoining Bath House had been floored over to make a band practice room.[11] Though the familiar sight of young men in raccoon coats or yellow slickers or plus-fours, and bob- haired coed "flappers" in short skirts and four-buckled shoes would have been recognizable enough to him,[12] the MSC campus was surely something of a surprise the first time he laid eyes on it. It was less developed, its facilities less utilizable, and in a setting considerably more rural than the sophisticated University of Michigan's in Ann Arbor. What he saw then, of course, was much different from what the university grounds look like today. The president and the deans lived in wood houses, and the only structures on the south side of the Red Cedar (a location previously forbidden to female students because it was considered too wild and dangerous)[13] were the stadium, which had been built in 1923, just four years before his arrival, and Demonstration Hall, which was under construction. Then, as now, buildings clustered around Circle Drive, which was a dirt road, but a street car track looped the place where Campbell Hall was later to stand, and picnic grounds were spread invitingly on the spot claimed in 1931 by Mary Mayo Hall. There were barns and fields on a slope just south of Kedzie Hall, which were replaced in 1938 by a band shell, where for twenty one years the young Leonard Falcone would conduct enormously popular open air concerts—until the shell met its demise in 1959, a sacrifice to its replacements, Ernst Bessey Hall and a parking ramp. The occasional bare bulbs hanging from campus trees served then as outdoor electrical lighting,[14] but they would soon enough make way for streetlamps. Even the Armory (1886) and Bath House (1902), the site of his own rehearsal and office space near the newly built Beaumont Tower,[15*] would be eventually demolished in 1939 and replaced by the music building so well known to his future students.

> **Leonard Falcone:** *There was no auditorium on campus when I first came. The only place to play was a little theater, which no longer exists, located on the third floor of the Home Economics Building. And that served for recitals and concerts. Back then, the band had to play in the women's gym or the ROTC building— the Armory. It (the Armory) was later torn down, you see, and then the music building was built on top of it. A very small place. And they played basketball there, everything. It held about 400 people at the very most. When the women's gym was built (1918), they moved the concerts over there. Then Demonstration Hall was finished the year I came here (1927), and so we played our concerts in Demonstration Hall . . . There was a terrific echo in there . . . At that time, they had a sawdust floor for the horses to prance around. They built a temporary wooden platform for the band, and we played there . . . especially for the*

> *yearly Farmer's Week, which was a big thing in those days. And then occasionally we would go over to the People's Church. We would have the stage extended. We played two or three concerts in there.*
>
> *So you see, we had no place. When they built the auditorium (begun in 1937), it was a lifesaver for us.*[16]

It wasn't just the campus that was new to him when he arrived in September of 1927; the school's culture and traditions were new, too, and many of them were in a state of flux. A MAC cow named Belle Sarcastic, who had held the world record for eleven years for producing 23,190 pounds of milk and 722 pounds of fat in 1897 and had borne a St. Louis Exposition Grand Champion steer, Sarcastic Lad, remained the college's unofficial mascot, but the school's name had been changed from "Michigan Agricultural College" (MAC) to "Michigan State College" (MSC) just the year before. The athletic teams, "The Spartans," were just settling into being called that name after a contest to change it from "The Aggies" ended with the winning name "The Michigan Staters" being chosen, and then overturned a week later by sportswriter George Alderton of the *Lansing State Journal*, who thought it too long and, on his own volition, selected "Spartans" from the losing entries. People liked it, and it stuck. With the new names for the school and its sports teams came other changes, among them the adoption of "Block-S" as the athletic award letter, and an edit of the words to the school song from "Their specialty is farming/But those farmers play football," to 'Their specialty is winning/ And those Spartans play football."[17]* The new ritual of "Lantern Night," a procession of coeds meandering through campus on a mild May evening and passing their lanterns to members of the junior, sophomore, or freshman class below them[18] had begun in 1926, and then, of course, there were the traditions of the band, a group that unbeknownst to the young Leonard Falcone was soon to give him the most worrisome challenge of his young life.

It's generally agreed that the genesis of the Michigan State University Band was a small group of ten brass players brought together in 1870 by a student and Civil War veteran named Ransom McDonough

Brooks, class of 1874. The group provided music for the military drills required of students by the Morrill Act,[19*] and appeared occasionally at community parades and events. From 1874–1878, the then 15 member band was led by R.H. Gulley, '78, who had it play from a four-horse bandwagon at the Lansing Fair, present a fall concert which included such pieces as "Midnight Val Polka," "Serenade," and "Joy of Life Gallop" during his first year of leadership. Their "band room" consisted of "the flat roof of Williams Hall, except when rain drove it into the tower."[20] When in 1885 the college established a permanent military department, the band became a Cadet Corps unit and received its first uniforms—gray with a black braid trim.[21] Throughout these years and on into the early 1900s, the band was conducted by students and military officers. But then, in 1907, 37 years after its beginnings, there was an embarrassing event involving US President Theodore Roosevelt that precipitated a change. In June of that year during the college's semi-centennial celebration, twenty thousand people showed up to hear Roosevelt deliver a commencement address which paid tribute to "the first agricultural college in America." On graduation morning, crowds lined Michigan Avenue to watch him and other tuxedoed and top-hatted dignitaries ride from the Capitol to the campus in an open Reo, driven by its manufacturer, R.E. Olds.[22] But the parade suffered a lengthy delay when four or five of the 24-piece college band's best musicians went on strike.

Because the student body had stopped supporting their concerts, they reasoned that it was only fair they should stop their free support of MAC.[23] Furthering their logic, they decided that since members of the Milwaukee Symphony Orchestra had been paid for playing a concert when they visited campus, they, too, should receive remuneration.[24] As time dragged on, the decision ultimately was made that the band would lead the parade, all right—but without the rebellious students. Though instrumentation (and no doubt quality) suffered, the remaining bandsmen pulled together and managed to get the president to the campus in style. Later, after a meeting of the disciplinary committee, two ringleaders were asked to leave the college,[25] all the strikers were dismissed from the band, and it was decided that a faculty member should take charge of the group.[26] That faculty member was A. J.

*MSC's young Director of Bands, Leonard Falcone*
*~ courtesy of the Falcone family*

Clark, a chemistry teacher and proficient cornetist who enhanced the band's activities to include a broad range of school events, from athletic contests to sacred concerts on Sunday afternoons, outdoor performances in East Circle, "promenade concerts" which combined concert music with social dancing at the Armory, and "away" concerts that featured dramatic readings by professor E. Sylvester King, who taught public speaking classes at State.[27] Across his 10 years of on again/off again leadership, from 1907–1925, the band grew from 24 to 60 musicians and, at its peak, accepted only approximately 60% of those who auditioned in the fall for a position.[28]

Because the band was a unit in the military department, one perk for its members was that they were allowed to waive both military drill and physical training during their four years at MAC. In 1910, when Sergeant Patrick J. Cross joined the military department, the "MAC Touch-down Band"[29] gained a drill sergeant to teach it maneuvers. The result was that the band's reputation was enhanced further, enough so that by the time of the Ohio State game in 1912, the 50 member group so impressed one Columbus news reporter that he wrote "never has there been a band on the Ohio Field that can compare with the Michigan Aggie." Prof. Frank Kedzie, who later was to become president of the college (1916–1921), took notice as well, and praised Clark by saying that he had developed "the best military band the college had ever had."[30]

Fred Abel of Detroit assumed command of the group for the following two years, but Professor Clark returned to lead the band for the 1918–1919 school year. In 1919, Clark turned over the 60 piece group to music professor J.S. Taylor, a well known march composer who initially spoke enthusiastically and confidently of the band's future.

> **J.S. Taylor:** *They were splendidly equipped with uniforms and instruments . . . [They] had fifty three members, and [were] looking ahead to a better band next year.*[31]

A year later, the spigot of reality open and flowing, he declared that the band needed a larger building and more equipment. Yet despite whatever was lacking in this regard, Taylor did build a "better band."

For one thing, when in 1921 he arranged for members to receive music lessons without charge, 65 percent of the group took him up on the offer and (no bombshell revelation here) the band improved greatly.[32] In 1922, Taylor resigned and A.J. Clark resumed directorship of the group. Clark was replaced for the last time in 1925 by Carl Kuhlman, a well liked man who was released for incompetency, just before 28 year old Leonard Falcone came on board in 1927.[33]

Though he didn't know precisely what he had let himself in for, Leonard was eager to take charge of the band at MSC and began preparing for the job right away.

> **Leonard Falcone:** *I looked forward to it and thought of the possibilities of what to do with it. The very first thing I did was to go through catalogs and find music and order . . . a repertoire of marches to play that fall.*[34]

But whatever he had in mind, hope collided with reality when he first heard the group. He told the story of his initial rehearsals with the MSC band many times over the years, remembrances that were to stay with him for a lifetime.

> **Leonard Falcone:** *The level of performance of the band was so low that I was completely flabbergasted and felt helpless. And the fact that we were going to Ann Arbor to play at the annual football game there just floored me. I thought "I just cannot go down there with this kind of a band and play." I was very, very discouraged. Extremely discouraged. I think about the second or third week I decided I would go to Mr. Halladay, the secretary of the university who hired me, to tell him I wanted to quit. I said, "I'm very sorry, I appreciate it and all, but I cannot put up with the level of musicianship around here."*
>
> *Of course, he knew that I was a youngster. He listened carefully, like a father, and said, "Leonard, I'm going to tell you something. I appreciate what you're saying, and know exactly how you feel. But I must tell you this: Michigan State is still a small school, but it is well-known, and if you quit now you won't be*

> *able to get a job anywhere because you are a quitter. The unwritten rule is that anybody has to stay on the job for at least two years. If anyone quits before they give a job a good chance, no one will put any confidence in you."*[35]
>
> *I said, "My God, two years! How can I possibly live through two years of this sort of thing?"*[36]
>
> *Secretary Halladay then went on to say: "Secondly, that is why we brought you here—because we want this band to improve. Otherwise, we would have brought in anybody. So I don't care how badly they play. Everybody understands this. But I know from your attitude that it won't be this way all the time—that you are going to do something about it. So, don't give up. As a matter of fact, I don't think I would accept your resignation. Stay at least two years; then, if you still feel unsatisfied, you can go."*
>
> *And so finally I agreed to stay the two years. Well, I can tell you what happened—I'm still here, after 45 years!"*[37]

"To me," he said speaking of the memory many years later, "it wasn't a (workable) challenge. Now days, I'd just know how to deal with it."[38]

Marching Band weighed heavily on Leonard's mind that first fall. Concert Band activities were minimal, but the Marching Band made appearances at military drills and parades and also entertained crowds at home and away sports contests as well as at local community events. It was a highly visible group,[39*] and its quickly approaching debut where it would perform aside his brother's fine band at the University of Michigan loomed large. If there was one silver lining to the approaching storm cloud, it was this: even though "the band didn't sound too well musically, it was a good marching band."[40] At least when it came to marching around a football field, the MSC bandsmen, Leonard saw, could be easily trained.

Whoops! If only he knew how to train them. That was another worry. Though he'd seen marching bands when he'd attended a few football games in Ann Arbor, Leonard had never been in charge of a military unit, which was what the MSC band was then, and he didn't know how one drilled.[41*]

> **Leonard Falcone:** *I didn't know a thing about it. Fortunately, they didn't do any formations for the first 2 or 3 games back then. We marched up and down the field for pregame, played the "Star Spangled Banner" for the raising of the flag. We played the school song. We played on the side of the field, and when we marched it was straight forward. In those days, they didn't do more than just the letters of the school, and that was quite a task in itself. When we made the "Block S" at the third game—it was quite an accomplishment!*[42]

As it turned out, he needn't have worried about the game show at Michigan as much, as in spite of its faults the first presentation of his band in Ann Arbor turned out to be a crowd pleaser after all. "If there was any thrilling moment in the afternoon's performance it was not during the game (State 0, University of Michigan 21) but between the two bands, ingeniously interlocked in the first strains of the 'Star Spangled Banner,'" asserted the October, 1927, issue of the *Michigan Daily*. "Never before has Michigan State played in Michigan's new stadium—or with such a band as Michigan State had yesterday." The

*1927–1928, Leonard Falcone's first band*
*~ courtesy of Michigan State University Museum*

*Detroit News* named the band show a "brother act rarely seen on any stage or in any area," and went on to claim that though sartorially, Michigan's colorful blue uniform trimmed with maize made a better appearance on the field than State's utilitarian army khakis, musically, the two bands were a draw.[43]

Bullet dodged.

That first game behind him, one might think that MSC's new band director might have relaxed a little. But no. Leonard was just beginning to fathom the difficulties that lay ahead, the most serious of which was to test his mettle and push him into battle against his own bandsmen. At issue was a popular tradition that threatened the quality and dignity of the band, and by extension, of the Michigan State College itself. It was raw meat stuff, a time of discord, a watershed moment that revealed that when it came to principles of musical excellence, leadership, and control, Falcone was as firm as a slab of Italian carrera marble. He was not about to lose.[44*]

> **Leonard Falcone:** *When I came here I found this opposition, even from the top players. And so the situation was quite tense for 3 or 4 full years . . . it was a bad situation.*[45]

A lot of the problem occurred because Leonard could not have been more different from his predecessor, the popular Carl H. Kuhlman, than if one of them had feathers and chirped. Under Kuhlman, band membership was a laid back affair. His relationship with his students was friendly and loose, so much so that he allowed them special privileges even when they compromised the band's musical integrity. When he was fired for incompetency, his students were frustrated and angry.[46]

Enter Falcone. Only seven to ten years older than most of the band's members, many of whom must have seen him as a peer of sorts, he was a strict, goal-oriented disciplinarian, focused on producing the best musical outfit he could. An experienced musician and conductor who could expertly play several instruments, he was ready to play his role in leading the MSC's band to greater heights.

> **Leonard Falcone:** *I felt confident; I had a good background to carry on the work.*[47]

But the all important question was, would the MSC band follow him? Like a steamship navigating a sharp turn in roiling seas, the Kuhlman/Falcone turnabout caused an enormous wake and more than a few cases of queasiness. Most bandsmen much preferred the band's original heading and didn't care how gifted or proficient their new captain was. They wanted Kuhlman back, and more—they wanted the privileges he had handed out like Halloween candy, especially those involving the "Swartz Creek Band," a costumed clown group named for a mythical school where one of the campus barbers claimed he'd earned a degree.

The "Swartz Creek Band" was a huge hit on campus, rivaling the popularity of the official band[48] and comprised of all of Falcone's top players as well as several non-students from the local area. At pep rallies, baseball, and basketball games, "Swartz Creek" provided comedy entertainment by wearing bizarre costumes and playing eccentric music, such when they had appeared as a "Chinese Band" wearing "the shrouds of the Orient" at an MSC – U of M baseball game that spring;[49] this all might have been well and good if none of it had interfered with "the official band" that represented MSC: Falcone's Varsity Band. But since Kuhlman had loaned the Swartz Creek Band college-owned instruments and allowed its members to miss regularly scheduled rehearsals (and even concerts) if they had a gig, it did.

Though he recognized that the Swartz Creek Band was providing good fun, Leonard wouldn't tolerate its intrusion on the official Varsity Band's rehearsals and concert attendance, or its inferior music, which he felt was detracting from both the school's and the band department's prestige. Tone deaf to the criticism he was receiving, and not just from his bandsmen but from students all over campus, he got Richards and Halliday to agree with him that MSC should have one director in charge of all band activities and, while swimming in a shark tank of opposition, made it policy that regular attendance at all rehearsals and public concerts be an obligatory feature of band membership. Then, he forbade Swartz Creek Band members from rehearsing in the band room or removing college owned instruments for unauthorized performances. After a collective intake of breath, his students, angered and rebellious, struck back by attempting to break in the band room at night to steal the instruments they thought were rightly theirs to use.[50] But with Hemingwayesque grace under pressure, Leonard stood firm in his resolve for what became a four year siege, and by 1930, his position had gained enough popular support that the fall issue of *Michigan State News* noted that though "much dissention has been voiced about the campus" concerning the Swartz Creek policy, it "appears to be wholly unjustified." There is little enough space for the college sanctioned Varsity Band to use, the article explains, and though both the Varsity Band and the Swartz Creek Band are a part of the college,

> *. . . at present the Swartz Creek Band is not a truly college organization. The college has no jurisdiction over the band, its personnel, is not confined to college students, nor is its scope entirely within the bounds of the college. . . as far as (it) being entirely 100% of the college, for the college, and by the college—it just isn't. When Swartz Creek confines its personnel to MSC students, when it submits to college jurisdiction, and when its scope becomes entirely that of the college, then Swartz Creek can truly expect the privileges now accorded the Varsity Band.*[51]

Precisely.

A year later, the group dissolved, and though the long conflict (1927–1931) significantly strained relations between Falcone and his students,[52] the memories of Kuhlman's tenure and the drama of the Swartz Creek Band fiasco were all but forgotten.

Scene Ends. Fade to Black.

Throughout it all, Leonard focused on the work of forming the band into a proud unit that carried his imprimatur, highlighting that first difficult year with several notable events. Farmer's Week,[53*] initiated in March of 1914, had grown rapidly in the 1920s as scores of livestock associations and other agricultural groups came to campus for lectures, discussions, and demonstrations. Six thousand people jammed the newly completed Demonstration Hall during Farmer's Week of 1928 to watch a greased pig catching contest, a horse pulling demonstration, a parade of MSC's prize winning livestock, a handicap race by track Coach Ralph Young's relay team, and to hear Leonard Falcone direct the MSC band in a half hour concert which began with a Sousa march and ended with Verdi.[54]

Also that spring, Leonard and his brother Nicholas collaborated in a concert event that combined their two bands, with MSC and the University of Michigan playing both individually and together at Ann Arbor's Hill Auditorium on May 4, and again on the following weekend, May 12, at State. And then a mere three days later, on May 15th, Leonard's band was again in the spotlight as it cut a record in East Lansing with the Brunswick Company of New York, shortly after the Minneapolis Symphony Orchestra finished a recording session with the same company in Chicago. At the time, State was one of the first college bands to record for a corporation of such magnitude. The record of Spartan songs (including the "Alma Mater" and the "Fight Song") along with a classical selection, sold for $1, and as it was distributed throughout the Midwest, was not only a good PR move for the college and the band, but since proceeds were used for new instruments and other band department needs (in addition to the new Union Memorial Building), was also good for the music program itself.[55]

Perhaps as the year drew to a close 29-year-old Leonard was reminded of the old Italian immigrant's lament, "I came to America because I heard the streets were paved with gold. When I got here, I found out three things: first, the streets weren't paved with gold; second, they weren't paved at all; and third, I was expected to pave them." At MSC in 1927–1928, after encountering a band department whose musical avenues had fallen into serious disrepair, Leonard began the labor of paving them for the long uphill journey that would lead the group from being a little-known, regional agricultural college band to one that, 27 years later, would stand at the apex of college band notoriety and capture the imagination and respect of an entire nation.

* * *

When Falcone's first year at MSC ended in 1928, an extraordinary opportunity arose for him not only to relax and regroup for the upcoming year, but also to participate in a historic event in music education. In the 1920s, few high schools had music programs. When Leonard's Ann Arbor friend, Joseph Maddy, saw a need, he convinced the Music Educators' National Association to bring talented young people together to participate in a student honors orchestra. From 1926–1928, more than 200 student high school musicians traveled from all across the country to form the National High School Orchestra, a group which made appearances at conventions for school administrators and music teachers. Not only were they a hit, but because the experience turned out to be so intense for everyone involved, Maddy and Thaddeus Giddings, another music educator, determined to do even more for talented high school students—something that would allow them to play together in a more habitual and conventional way.

The solution came in the form of a failing summer camp named Camp Pennington, and $15,000 in borrowed money. With these meager beginnings, the nation's first orchestra camp and one of its first first coeducational camps, the National High School Orchestra Camp (Interlochen Center for the Arts), was incorporated July 6, 1927, at a time when "a lot of eyebrows were raised at the idea of boys and girls spending the summer together for 'culture.'"[56]* Nearly a year later it welcomed 115 students and a faculty of some of the best music teachers and performers of the day: among them Leonard and Nicholas Falcone, the former there to supervise violin sectionals, conduct the National High School Band in its August 5th concert, and appear as a baritone horn soloist, very likely his stage debut on that instrument.[57]

And so in the opening public event, when thousands of concert goers packed the bowl to witness an occasion that was a first of its kind—a high school group that could play like a professional orchestra[58]—they were privileged to hear Leonard Falcone play his euphonium with the effortless grace and pure crystalline sound that inspired camp founder Maddy to say, "There isn't a better baritone player in the country."[59] As for Leonard's feelings about the occasion, of all his many solo appearances across his lifetime, his Interlochen concerts, beginning with this one, were among his most memorable.[60]* "I was well received," he said, "every time I appeared there"[61]

By fall, 1928, though Falcone had had the previous year's experience directing a marching unit, it would seem that he was still on a learning curve. A *Michigan State News* article snidely entitled "A Military Band?" notes that the thrill of traditional college music and the crisp maneuvers of the "crack organization" of past years were now gone, replaced by "ragged lines," and "indifferent or badly trained marching." The article allows that time to train the band had been short, but that "according to our information little stress is being placed" on marching because of an emphasis on concert work. "As yet," it charges, "the musicians have not begun work on the formation of the traditional MSC which it has been the custom to form during the half." Even the kind of music being played on the gridiron came under fire. "We do not understand why the band doesn't play the fight song or other typical college music pieces," the article's writer grumbles. "Perhaps they are simple and of little real musical value, but nevertheless they do materially aid in boosting up that Spartan spirit . . ."[62]

Undaunted, 29-year-old Leonard cut the article out of the newspaper, pasted it neatly in his scrapbook, and kept working on the band's field presentation: a job harder than most anyone ever could have thought. Unbeknownst to most on campus, he had merged Michigan State's varsity and second bands into one large 75-piece group to make a bigger and hopefully, in time, a better band. It was a risky move. The new combined band was comprised of over 50 percent rookie freshmen[63] who, without hours of training, could and undoubtedly sometimes did march like ivy wandering through a trellis. The result of his efforts can be found on the next page of that same scrapbook, where there appears a follow-up article entitled "An Improved Band." In it, an effusive writer, presumably the same person who wrote "A Military Band?" just two weeks earlier, comments that as the seventy five piece band marched down the gridiron on Homecoming Day, "the old grads were thrilled and the students reassured. The band had again achieved that difficult combination of military precision and fine musicianship." Not only were the lines straight, the marching crisp, the turns snappy, but Falcone had astounded them with a "very well executed" forma-

*The traditional MSC letter formation*
*~ courtesy of the Michigan State University Archives & Historical Collections*

tion of the letter "S" as a climax to their performance, a surprise because of the change from the former 'MSC.' And as if that weren't enough, there had been a costume change as well. In place of the "red decoration" in the drum major's shako was a prominent green "S." [64]Falcone and his band had won the hearts of the crowd, and remarkably had made the turn around in a mere two weeks.

After Michigan State's Marching Band had risen to national prominence many years later, one bandsman had this to say about the man who, from the beginning, bore the mark of greatness:

> **Robert Sack, clarinet, MSC, 1950–1954:** *From the very start, Leonard Falcone had everything to do with the Marching Band's success. Everything. He was always out there, climbing the high*

*ladder they had for him, directing things, and making sure everything was working right. He worked hard, and he always got the results he wanted.*[65]

1928–1929, Falcone's second year at MSC, was a year of growth for him for a number of reasons other than the Marching Band's *coup de grace.* When the Michigan State Institute of Music and Arts opened its doors that school year, Falcone was given new job titles: in addition to being Director of Bands, with the dissolution of the Reserve Band he became an Italian language instructor and teacher of wind instruments. Also that year, with Detroit Symphony members contracted to offer music instruction on campus one day a week, he was left to teach the six to seven remaining brass students. And it was then, during this second year at Michigan State, that Falcone began a budding association with two other great bandsmen, John Phillip Sousa and Edwin Franko Goldman.

In an effort to encourage a greater interest in bands, Falcone arranged for Sousa, a man whose band he had heard on two other occasions, to direct the MSC band along with some invited talented area high school musicians. Since the visit occurred on the Friday of Sousa's last tour, December 7th, 1928, the famous band had the time to play two concerts, one that afternoon at Prudden Auditorium, and one later in the evening. Not only did the MSC band have the opportunity to perform in the afternoon during the Sousa Band welcoming ceremony and attend the evening concert as honored guests, but Falcone also had the privilege of hosting Sousa and showing him around town.[66] He recalled Sousa's visit in a letter years later.

**Leonard Falcone:** *. . . I had my Michigan State Band meet him and his band at the train depot and escort him to his hotel. Before the concert that evening, I drove Mr. Sousa from his hotel to the theater where the concert was to be played. On the way to the concert Mr. Sousa asked several questions and was quite friendly. I noticed (he) had a rather high voice and spoke softly.*[67]

The next time the two musicians crossed paths in any significant way was during the finale of the National High School Band Contest of 1929, held in Flint, Michigan, when Falcone performed Boccalari's clarinet solo "Fantasia di Concerto" on baritone horn, accompanied by Flint's Central High School Band. Along with his Interlochen performances, this solo appearance at the National High School Band Contest of 1929 was one of Falcone's most unforgettable.

> **Leonard Falcone:** *It was my first big one. I was invited to be a guest soloist in the evening. All these bands were waiting to see who won the contest.*[68]

It was midnight before he mounted the stage, and contest judges John Phillip Sousa, A. Austin Harding, Director of Bands at the University of Illinois, Urbana, Dr. Edwin Franko Goldman, professional bandmaster of New York City, Capt. Taylor Bronson, conductor of the US Marine Band, and Harold Bachman, director of Chicago's "Million Dollar Band," had to roust themselves "from a long sleep" to hear him play. They weren't disappointed. When he was finished, the enthusiastic judges met with him[69] and among other compliments, John Phillip Sousa remarked that he had had many fine baritone players in his band, but this one, this Leonard Falcone, surpassed them all.[70]

But Sousa wasn't the only judge moved and astounded by Falcone's performance. As a result of hearing him play, Dr. Harding invited Falcone to solo with his famed University of Illinois Concert Band, and the internationally known Goldman, the "Dean of Bandmasters of the World," originator of New York City's free summer concerts in Central and Prospect Parks, and composer of over 100 marches, including the still famous "On the Mall," asked him if he would be willing to live in New York and play in his band. In the end, Leonard took them both up on their offers. In the summer of 1930 he headed for New York to play in Goldman's band, the "best known band in the world."[71] But because he wasn't a New York Musician's Union member and because Goldman was unable to waive the six month's residency requirement for Leonard's membership, he was not able to perform.[72] Nevertheless, this was not the end of the Falcone/Goldman relationship, for the two men belonged to a mutual admiration society that didn't fade as time passed. Years later, on the occasion of Leonard Falcone's Twenty-Fifth

Anniversary Testimonial Dinner on January 17, 1953, Goldman sent this note:

> **Edwin Franko Goldman, conductor, composer:** *You have rendered valuable service in the cause of bands and band music, and you have set a high standard and maintained it through these many years. Your contribution has been a very valuable one indeed.*[73]

And two years after that, on March 6, 1955, Falcone welcomed Goldman, whom he considered the best professional band leader in the United States, as guest conductor for Michigan State's Centennial Concert. The famed white haired maestro, warmly greeted by a near capacity audience, inspiringly conducted his own "Grand March, International Accord," followed by a number of classical pieces including "Finlandia," "The New World Symphony," Rachmaninoff's "Polka," and a quintet of his march compositions.[74]*

One of the marches, "On the Mall," was added to the program after the audience demanded to hear it; in turn, Goldman, in a trademark move, insisted that everyone sing and whistle along. He ended the concert offering praises of the Michigan State Band as "one of the best three or four bands in the country " and of Falcone as a "great conductor, a wonderful organizer, and a virtuoso in his field."[75] Goldman's March 6 concert was the musical highlight of 1955, and marked the first time Falcone had invited anyone to guest conduct.

Later that day, Dr. Goldman joined the Falcone family for one of Leonard's famous spaghetti dinners, lightly seasoned with pride and remembrance, as always. It was to Beryl one of the most memorable of all the dinners they hosted over the years.

> **Beryl Falcone:** *When Dr. Goldman was here, Cecilia . . . was about 3 and we had a comfortable chair with wide arms on it. She had gotten one of her books and was sitting on the chair arm asking him to read it to her. And he did. His grandson was four at that time and he was used to these little ones. I got my camera and got a picture of it. One of my favorites.*[76]

Commencement week activities at the close of the 1928–1929 school year included a performances at the dedication of Beaumont Tower on June 22, and again at commencement exercises on June 24. The *Wolverine*, Michigan State's yearbook (ironic, eh?), skipping over the Beaumont Tower dedication, noted that Falcone had produced "a fine concert band (which had been) honored by being asked to play for the state convention in Lansing, the Knights Templar conclave at Benton Harbor, the Potato show at Greenville, the Horse Show at East Lansing, and commencement."[77]

During the summer, Falcone returned to Interlochen where, among other performances, he played his baritone at the Lyric Theater in Traverse City with the "Little Old German Band."[78] By then, he had completed two years at Michigan State and, according to what Secretary Halliday had told him, could resign from the college without forever being labeled a "quitter." But with no better position available and both the sound of the band and his relations with students improving, he chose to remain.

It was a prudent decision. The stock market crash just months later, in the fall of '29, made nearly everyone's job uncertain, and though like every other college Michigan State was affected by it, it was still a financially secure institution. At State, though several upper-level administrative posts were eliminated, supplies were scarce, spending was thoroughly scrutinized, and trips sponsored by the Athletic Council were eliminated, the college never missed a salary payment. Reductions in faculty salaries came, however, the first occurring in 1931, when Leonard's annual $2,100 pay was reduced to $1,955, and then again in 1933, when it was cut back to $1,855. Tight finances also affected the operation of the Institute. The well known Marius Fossenkemper, future director of the Lansing Symphony Orchestra (1936–1939), was the only woodwind teacher retained, and Falcone undertook all brass instruction as well as teaching a new course listed in the 1929 course catalog as *Orchestral Instruments: A preparation for conducting school orchestras and bands as well as an individual study in various instruments.*[79]

That fall, too, the military department began cooperating in helping the band better their field appearance at football games in order to leave "Mr. Falcone free to handle the musical end of the partnership."[80]

*Edwin Franko Goldman reads a story to Cecilia Falcone*
*~ courtesy of the Falcone family*

*Interlochen, 1930*
*~ courtesy of the Falcone family*

> **Leonard Falcone:** *When I first came to East Lansing, the department was very small. I had to teach all the brass instruments besides conducting the marching and concert bands and administering the department of bands: I was very busy.* [81]

But in fact, the arrangement brought him little workload relief: in addition to creating shows, he now had the job of teaching them, along with band management, to his appointed military "helper."[82]

CHAPTER 9

# DEPRESSION YEARS: THE 1930s

*"Sempre piu avanti. . . sempre piu in avanti"*

---

**Michigan State College President:**

Robert S. Shaw, 1928–1941

**Money, 1930–1933**

$1 in 1930 = $15 in 2011

Average cost of student tuition in 1933 = $238[1]

Average annual income: = $1,300

**Life Expectancy:**

Male, 58.1; Female, 61.6[2]

**Entertainment, 1930–1939:**

*The Wizard of Oz, Snow White, Gone with the Wind, Mutiny on the Bounty, Scarface, All Quiet on the Western Front, Modern Times, City Lights, King Kong, Top Hat,* Fred and Ginger, Will Rogers, Charlie Chaplin, W.C. Fields, Clark Gable, Greta Garbo, Laurel and Hardy, The Marx Brothers, Mae West, Errol Flynn, Cary Grant, Duke Ellington, Benny Goodman, Glen Miller, Tommy Dorsey, Louis Armstrong

**Headlines:**

The Great Depression

> *"Say, don't you remember, they called me Al;*
> *it was Al all the time.*
> *Say, don't you remember, I'm your pal?*
> *Buddy, can you spare a dime?"*
>
> ~ from "Buddy, Can You Spare a Dime?"
> by Jay Gorney (music) and Yip Harburg (lyrics), 1931

The Dust Bowl, 1930-1936

MSC Band plays on the White House lawn for President Hoover, October 1930

President Hoover opens the Empire State Building in May, 1931

"The Star Spangled Banner" becomes the national anthem, 1931

President Roosevelt elected 1932 and 1936

> *"Happy days are here again,*
> *The skies above are clear again*
> *Let us sing a song of cheer again*
> *Happy days are here again."*
>
> ~ from "Happy Days are Here Again"
> by Milton Ager (music) and Jack Yellen (lyrics), popularized in 1932

Hindenburg air ship burns, 1937

MSC band shell dedicated on the banks of the Red Cedar, May, 1938

1930 WAS A SIGNIFICANT YEAR for Leonard Falcone in establishing himself and the MSC band as an important influence, and not only on the MSC campus—but beyond that to the American College Band Movement itself, a movement in the midst of a dramatic and spectacular rise of bands from small groups playing summer concerts in village gazebos just twenty years prior, to highly skilled college bands that were playing an ever widening role in entertainment, education, and American culture. During the winter months of 1930, the Spartan band continued to be an important feature of basketball and baseball games as well as other large campus affairs. Trips to play at the Benton Harbor Blossom Festival, the Armistice Day ceremony in Grand Rapids, and to Flint to represent the Lansing Commandery of the Knights Templar[3] not only continued to present an image of MSC as an active and exciting school, but also resulted in the band's being singled out from others for praise in newspaper accounts.[4]* And later that spring, the band proved to be a popular attraction at military reviews and with the crowds attending Farmer's Week at Demonstration Hall. During one of its four concerts there, when a great roar of approval greeted the last note of Wagner's "Rienzi Overture," bandsmen weren't sure if the ovation was for them or for the prize cows that had accidentally been brought early into the arena ("Cue the cows!") for judging just as Falcone was finishing the piece.[5]

But perhaps most far reaching in its effect in the development of the band program was Falcone's inauguration that year of open air spring concerts, a campus custom discontinued after Professor Clark left the band in 1925. It was an important renewal to him for a number of reasons. Like all Rosetani, he loved the outdoors and open air concerts. And so, in part because of his boyhood experiences, he looked forward to reinstituting them on the MSC campus at a time of year when he and his audiences and bandsmen could enjoy the mild weather of spring after being cooped up all winter. Musically, he appreciated outdoor acoustics as compared to the annoying echoes of the Armory, Demonstration Hall, Women's Gymnasium, and People's Church, where his regular band concerts were presented, and perhaps best of all, he was happy for the chance of getting away from the endless programs of marches the band was tasked with playing at campus athletic and military events.[6] And so expecting to draw upon the crowds that came to Michigan State's "Founder's Day," he initiated the popular four week series at 7:30 p.m. on Founder's Day Eve, May 14th, from a canvas topped portable platform erected at the foot of Beaumont Tower.[7] Chairs and programs were provided for the audience of 500,[8] who braved the hour long concert in threatening weather to hear marches, classical pieces and light opera numbers from "The Fortune Teller" and the "Prince of Pilsen." The crowd that showed up the following week in the Forest of Arden in front of the museum was double the size of the first, and by the end of the concert series, one paper noted that Lansing and East Lansing residents had so enjoyed the music that "when rain swept down upon two concerts before the programs were finished, the audience made no great dash for dryer places until they were certain the band would stop;" ". . . it is amazing what Leonard Falcone has done with the material at hand and the small amount of time," stated the May 22 edition of the *Lansing State Journal* after the first two of the four concerts were completed. What might have amazed them even more, had they been able to see into the future just two short years, was that the open air concerts would become so popular that by the end of spring, 1931, the band was performing on its wooden canvas-covered stand before "large and enthusiastic audiences numbering at the peak on exceptionally fine evenings at around 3,000."[9] But there was more—much more—to come in the years ahead. Months later, when MSC opened its doors for the start of the 1930–31 school year, the second year the music department offered a Bachelor of Music degree, the band had only 40 returning members. That meant that Leonard, now age 31, was faced with the daunting task of auditioning and training 35 freshmen bandsmen in short order[10*] and, in a hauntingly familiar scenario, with no time to spare before their appearance at the October 4th MSC – U of M game in Ann Arbor;[11*] it was a game that meant much to not only the team and the fans, but also to the Spartan band and Falcone, who would be pitting his "cow college" musicians against his brother's "gentlemen musicians" on the gridiron. Two hours each day were dedicated to drills and practice to ready the MSC band, and in the end, according to the *State Journal*, "they made a big hit." For his part, noting that he liked the American spirit that made such quick, intensive, and successful work possible, Leonard, in an interesting metonymy, told the newspapers that "Europe (and quite possibly Leonard himself) would never believe that such a thing could be done."[12]

That fall, the *Michigan State News* began a campaign for the band to "stress the 'fight song.'" "Realizing the necessity for a college song that truly emphasizes the tradition and spirit of MSC athletic teams," the article stated, "the *Michigan State News* this week fired the opening guns in a campaign to re-popularize MSC's 15-year-old 'fight song.'" The emphasis on State's 'Alma Mater,' it complained, "has overshadowed the more peppy and rhythmical marching song of the Fighting Spartans."[13] It was a short "campaign," and it seems that firing guns were unnecessary. Falcone wholeheartedly agreed to the request and henceforth led the band in playing the march not only at the opening of every football game, but also at the start of the third quarter.

The band made 54 public appearances during the 1930-1931 school year. Undoubtedly the highlight—and one of the highlights of Falcone's long career—occurred shortly following the MSC – U of M game, and after generous local businessmen added $2,000 (this, less than one year after the stock market crash) to the $1,500 already in the band's treasury, enough to allow it to accompany the Spartan football team to Georgetown University in Washington, D.C. and perform on the White House lawn for President Hoover.[14] And so on Thursday, October 30, 1930, the "Spartan Special," an eleven coach train loaded with football players, musicians, and fans, rolled into Washington D.C., greeted by cheering MSC alumni who helped load the group with all its luggage and equipment into waiting cars for the trip to the hotel. Almost immediately the entire entourage embarked on a half day tour of Mt. Vernon, followed by free time to explore Washington in the evening, minus the football team, which headed for Griffith Field for practice drills.

They all arose the following sunup, a Friday, to greet the day. That morning, the band paid its respects to the war dead at Arlington National Cemetery, where it played the "Star Spangled Banner" while Secretary H. H. Halladay, Professor Lewis Richards, and other college officials placed a wreath at the Tomb of the Unknown Soldier.[15] Soon after, the delegation went directly to the White House where Richards, who had a personal acquaintance with President Herbert Hoover because of their work together on Belgian Relief after the WWI Armistice, had arranged for the President to receive both them and the Spartan football team. As Hoover strode toward the group down a dirt path on the south lawn, Falcone struck up "Hail to the Chief" and, after everyone had said what they wanted to say and with camera and "movie men" recording it all for posterity, finished the event with the newly written alma mater, the "MSC Shadows"[16]*

A picture from that day shows Hoover, hat in hand, in a three piece suit and well shined shoes. He stands alone on the path which cuts through college dignitaries and the band, and which stretches all the way to a White House seemingly floating above the assemblage in the background. Placed proudly in the forefront on the leaf strewn lawn, next to the path and just a few feet to Hoover's right, is the young Falcone, his baton firmly clasped in his right hand.

Years later, one of Falcone's "band boys," one of a cadre of bandsmen whom Falcone and his wife welcomed to their home over the years to help with cleaning and handyman jobs, had this to say:

> **Tom Gillette:** *He (Falcone) treasured a picture of the MSU band with Herbert Hoover; this was one of the things in his bedroom that I remember seeing.* [17]

Though it turned out that State lost to Georgetown by a single point that afternoon (State 13, Georgetown 14), it was an important day for the band. Newspapers reported that "with its military snap and precision (Falcone's MSC band) took the spectators at the Griffith stadium by storm. Their marching feats, including an alphabet-juggling drill between halves, was (sic) the talk of the crowd."[18]

After the game, the entire delegation returned to the hotel where 100 alumni enjoyed lunch, and where, that evening, the hotel management sponsored a dance for the entire MSC delegation. Led by varsity yellmaster Howard Mitchell ('32), the crowd "rocked the corridors of the hotel with Michigan State yells, cheers, and songs" into the night.[19]

The spring and summer of '31 were important for Falcone personally. In March, he enhanced his reputation as an euphonium artist by accepting Dr. Harding's invitation to play in Urbana, Illinois, with his

*At the White House October 31, 1930*
*~ courtesy of Michigan State University Museum*

excellent band. There, he played "Flower Song" from Carmen, and "Fantasia de Concerto,"[20] and liking what he saw and heard from the group, held them as a standard when working with his own band.[21*]

> **Leonard Falcone:** *I remember my performance with the University of Illinois concert band the first time, which was in '31 or '32. I was impressed by the excellence of the band—the technique, and the fluency, the musicianship, the accuracy. And of course when you hear something like that, then you release it to your own group.*[22]

When on June 24th he sailed on the *Vulcania*[23*] (this time a bit more in style—he went as a second class passenger) back to Roseto, it was his first time home since he'd emigrated to America in 1915.[24] Though his sisters and father were there to greet him, Maria, his mother, who had passed away before he had a chance to see her again, was not.[25*] Little else is known about his visit to Roseto, excepting what can be discerned from two newspaper articles about the trip. In the first, Leonard notes that while in the village of his birth "the tempo is the same and old customs prevail," Italy's cities had changed significantly and were materially better off than previously. Their "magnificent highways" and "improved railroads, 90 percent of which were electric," had clearly impressed him.[26]

The second article, a glowing report about the returned son in the Italian language newspaper *La Stella*, offers more insight. After a few cursory statements concerning Leonard's staying in town with his father for several days, reuniting with friends, attending the Feast of Madonna del Carmine, and planning his return to the US in August, the article moves on to praise Leonard for his "study and sacrifice," his "deserved honors," and his "raised social status." And then a shift in focus. The journalist imagines what it must have been like for Dominico to welcome home Leonardo at a time when many of Roseto's children left their families of origin and became "wealthy in America," only to "forget the parents." Dominico, it is noted, is "overjoyed," and is lucky, too—for his sons have risen to become gentlemen. "*Sempre piu avanti. . . sempre piu in avanti,*" the article ends in benediction. "More and more forward. More and more forward."[27]

Other stops on his journey that summer were made in Rome, Naples, Venice, Florence, and Milan, as well as several cities in England, Austria, Switzerland (where in Lausanne he attended the Anglo-American Music Conference),[28] and France, where, according to one article, Falcone, at the Colonial Exposition in Paris, noted something "only a musician," would have noticed. At the "supposed replica of Mt. Vernon . . . there was no flute lying on the harpsichord as there is in the music room at Mt. Vernon."[29] What he learned along the journey about the state of music in Europe both surprised and distressed him.

To his surprise, he found that because of political and economic influences the quality of the great orchestras and the critical attitude of the listening public had declined during the 16 years he'd been away, and the best musical organizations were now in the United States. In the US, he noted, good orchestral men were selected primarily for their ability to play well. But in Italy and the rest of Europe, nationality was taking precedence over skill. And many of Europe's best players and conductors had left their countries for the better pay offered by American orchestras; those who stayed behind found that a lack of rehearsals was prohibiting their organizations from progressing musically —rehearsals cost money, and money was short. Finally, he was surprised to see that Europe's concert going audiences had changed, and for the worse. He watched, perplexed, as "salvos of applause" honored conductors for flawed performances— performances, he claimed, that would have been received coldly in the US. The lowered appreciation and taste on the part of the public saddened him. For centuries, European audiences had maintained high standards of music criticism and always demanded the best. But this, he noted bleakly, was no longer the case.[30]

Despite the Great Depression, the music department at Michigan State was growing. It moved out of the floored-over pool room in the Armory's adjoining bath house and into old Abbott Hall (the Music Practice Building), which contained both a rehearsal room for the band and an office for Falcone. With increased student enrollment (817 students, which included non-enrolled conservatory students) came expanded course offerings, such as Orchestra Ensemble and Management, Band Instruments, Brass and Woodwind Instruction, Instrumental Methods, Cornet (Class Instruction), Advanced Cornet, Horn, and Trombone—all of which were added to Leonard's already full teaching load.[31]

The final spring concert of 1932 included two Falcone transcriptions: "Bolero," by Ravel, and the Borghi harpsichord "Concerto in D Major," (transcribed for piano and band) featuring Richards as soloist. Tchaikowsky's "1812 Overture" brought the program to a dramatic close: as band instruments were quieted, the pealing bells of the Beaumont Carillon rang out at the hands of Jack Daubert, and bursts of concealed artillery and rifle fire came from the vicinity of Abbott Hall.[32]

> **Leonard Falcone:** *Since the concert was outdoors, I thought it would be appropriate to follow tradition and add some sound effect to the "Finale" of the" 1812 Overture" . . . so I arranged for a gentleman to assist us with the bell tower, and the ROTC Department . . . (placed a) 75 mm cannon . . . in the depressed area near the Music Practice Building. So, when the time arrived*

*in the overture, I pressed the electric button and the bells began to ring and the cannons began to boom and the kids that usually go to band concerts had a lot of fun; they began to run around the stands to find where the cannons were shooting from. There was a lot of bedlam, but nevertheless I thought it was very effective. Hundreds of people came up and offered their congratulations for a fine concert and the use of sound effects.*

*The next day, Mr. Halladay, who lived in the home where President Hannah now lives, came over and said, "Leonard, I'm terribly sorry that your concert was spoiled. I was sitting on my porch enjoying it when those cannons started to fire. But I just couldn't stop them in time. I went there and told those boys, "Just what in the devil are you doing? Don't you know there's a band concert going on? Now, I want you to stop right now!"*

*I said, "Mr. Halladay, I appreciate this, but it's one of those things you have no control over."*[33]

Also that spring, Leonard was guest conductor at a Southwestern Michigan Band Festival held in Kalamazoo in March, and also (at the invitation of his brother, Nick) at the University of Michigan's Spring Homecoming Concert on May 7. Life for him at Michigan State was good and seemed to be getting better—until the new school year rolled around, and with it, an unprecedented situation.

In August of 1932, five Ingham county citizens prompted a grand jury investigation of financial irregularities at Michigan State. A fountain of scandalous accusations rained down in many directions, the most sensational of which were aimed directly at Michigan State's Institute of Music and Allied Arts. Among the charges eventually produced were that the Institute's faculty was using campus buildings for private teaching, receiving fees from the college for student lessons, profiting in numerous ways from its connection with the music department, and making salary payments to tenor Louis Graveure up to three months after his resignation.

In the end, Circuit Judge Leland Carr, acting as a one man grand jury investigating the charges, and Assistant Attorney General Joseph A. Baldwin, who at the request of the board conducted a separate examination for the college, came to the same inescapable conclusion: there had been no illegal or unethical activity, though there had indeed been wrongdoing—and not by the Institute. In Carr's words, the charges were unwarranted and rooted in remarks "distorted by repetition;" Baldwin more pointedly wrote that "a certain few members of the staff. . . by continued loose talk and destructive criticism, (have) endangered the morale of the college as a whole."[34]

The two determined that though the music Institute's faculty had been permitted to use campus buildings (under terrible working conditions, it should be noted) for the private lessons of non-enrolled students, it was an entirely legal arrangement justified by the quality of the faculty the arrangement had attracted. As to the more serious charges that the College collected only $35 a term in tuition from each student but was paying up to $50 to the Institute for each student's private music lessons, and that the college's enrolled students were paying a lower fee for lessons than the Institute's students ($50 for college students, while a 40-minute weekly violin lesson with Michael Press, for example, cost $120),[35] it was further explained that local patrons had been making up the difference. And though it was true that the college had paid student fees to encourage the Institute project in its first years, beginning fall of 1932 students had been paying for private lessons themselves. The storm, once a Category 5, had been effectively downgraded to a 1.

Still, though the investigation revealed nothing illegal, it stung, and changes in how the music department did business were made as a result. Its relationship with the Institute was forever dissolved,[36*] the costs of all music department activities were absorbed by the college, and lesson and practice room fees were paid directly to the college's general fund.[37]

At an administrative level, some changes were made as well. Acting on the implications of Baldwin's "loose talk and destructive criticism" statement, the Board in November 1932 dismissed three men: Professors Cox (author, dean of Agriculture), Hasselman (pioneer sports announcer and head of Journalism and Publications), and Kedzie (ex-President of MSC, former head of Chemistry, ex-Dean of Applied Science, College Historian, staff member for 52 years).[38]

On the whole, the incident ended well from a music department perspective, with none of the resultant changes curtailing any if its activities. Its budget, previously in the top 5 of all the college's departments, remained there. As for Leonard, though the charges against the Institute had eventually swelled to 35,[39] and though he was connected with the Institute, he was never mentioned in any of the many articles printed on the scandal.[40]

Also in 1932, Falcone became a published author, writing "How to Choose a Solo for the Baritone" for the *Educational Music Journal*, the first of ten articles he wrote during his lifetime on bands and band instruments, the later ones appearing in the *School Musician, Instrumentalist*, and the *Music Educator's Journal.*[41]* Though he certainly must have been proud of this accomplishment, the year had to have been a rough one. That fall, in addition to the stresses of the investigation of his colleagues and his department, band membership decreased to an even lower level than fall of 1930.

> ***State News*, October 6, 1932:** *With only 30 veterans back, Leonard Falcone. . . is working hard to build up an organization composed largely of inexperienced men. Forty five musicians were chosen this fall from a group of 60 (freshmen) who tried out. This brings the total membership to 75, a number slightly less than last year.*[42]

Though the previous winter term of 1932 had been opened with a formal party at the Olds Hotel for band members and their guests, and an annual band smoker was initiated that fall, and there was an active "Band Club" for upperclassmen, and he and everyone else was making a sincere effort to promote a camaraderie between the new and old members not only for the fun of it but as a way to retain members throughout their four collegiate years, all efforts had failed. And Falcone understood. For one thing, since two years of band satisfied the two year ROTC requirement, there was no incentive for juniors to continue in band. For another, these were the Depression years, and economic problems were forcing many students to find part–time and even full time jobs and drop their campus activities.

But understanding the situation isn't the same as accepting it. Falcone knew that if there was a way to stem junior year dropout for the good of the band and the college it represented as well as to reward students for staying on, then he was going to have to find it. Never a man to place his fate in luck, he took matters into his own hands and came up with this idea: "*What if*," he proposed, "*band members were to receive the usual 1½ credits per term for band for freshman and sophomore years, but were able to earn 3 credits per term during their junior and senior years? Doubling the upperclassmen's credits might offer sufficient inducement to retain the juniors and seniors, especially if they had to take six terms of band before they can receive their three credits.*"

President Shaw approved the recommendation.[43]

That spring, as Michigan State gave its final concert for the season on May 31st, 1933, to an audience of over 3,000. Nicholas conducted the band as Leonard played the "Fantasia di Concerto" for baritone horn by Boccalari, the same selection he had played two years earlier when Nicholas conducted the University of Michigan band in Detroit. The *State Journal* dubbed Leonard a "supreme master of the instrument" who "gave to his audience the rare gift of beautiful and perfect tone." It was a "priceless experience, " the article swooned, referring to the solo, and "the delicacy and accuracy of the trills and runs, the floriture of the brilliant passages written to display the technical prowess of the performer, the range of the instrument for the skilled soloist" left the audience with a "memory of . . .an ethereal sort of loveliness." When Leonard was cheered back to the stage to play an encore, he answered with a "tremendously appealing voicing of 'O Sole Mio' as the sun set in the West, after which he took the baton back from his brother's hands and, as the evening slipped into starry darkness, conducted the Michigan State band in the first and third movements of Tchaikovsky's 'Pathetique Symphony'."[44]

There has always been a rivalry between the Michigan State and the University of Michigan bands, and no doubt there always will be. But during the Leonard and Nicholas Falcone years, it was surely at its friendliest, a win-win situation beginning with the brothers encouraging one another and their respective bands to reach greater and greater heights of musical expression, and ending in a spaghetti dinner at the home team band director's home. The night of Wednesday, May 31, 1933, wasn't the first time, nor would it be the last, that the titanic duet of conductors exchanged services in a spirit of cooperation and love of music. But unbeknownst to either of them on that balmy spring night, the final and most important and dramatic of their musical co-operations was drawing close, occurring as it did when for Nicholas, the bottom suddenly gave way and put him in free fall. Soon, it would be as though he had been plunged from reality and dropped into an Edward Albee play. Nothing would make any sense. Nothing would be predictable.

When the school year beginning fall of 1933 rolled around, the band was still undermanned, and worse, in spite of earlier efforts, its numbers were further depleted. Attempts to remedy the situation continued, as Falcone sent a notice to all Michigan high schools requesting lists of prospective bandsmen, and the Band Club made elaborate plans for a picture booklet the basis for a publicity drive to rebuild membership back to its former level. Even so, Leonard's goal wasn't just numbers. It was selectivity. And he had neither.

Still, Leonard worked to make his band the best it could be, and the fall 1933 Marching Band season went well enough, but with one stunning exception: the entire band was nearly lost at sea. High winds and a violent torrent of rain had already pounded the Midwest for two days when the marching Spartans traveled to Muskegon to board the Milwaukee Ferry, cross Lake Michigan, and perform at Marquette in what was to be one of the strangest football contests ever played by any college team anywhere. On the way to the game, the ferry, with Leonard and the entire Michigan State band in it, nearly went down. When they finally made it to the playing field, Falcone took one look and sent the band buses back to the hotel. Anticipated attendance at the game had been 5,000, but at start of play, there were ten people in the stands and, wading through the ankle deep water on the sidelines with the MSC team, the stalwart John Hannah. In the end, State, after letting Marquette do all the work with the slippery ball and punting 20 times (usually on the first down) won the game (State 6/Marquette 0).[45]

On a better day (at least one with no threat of the band's drowning) just two weeks earlier, at the MSC–Michigan game, Leonard and his brother Nick met on the gridiron in a friendly rivalry that according to the *Michigan Daily* had "become a leading feature of the traditional Michigan–MSC game and (was) known all over the country." "The outcome of (the game) may be uncertain," stated the article, "but one thing is sure—whichever band is triumphant, it will be because its director's name is Falcone."[46] The final game score was State 6, Michigan 20 (oh, whatever), but the school winning the battle of the bands, though not known, may well have been MSC. Although the Spartan football team consistently performed poorly during Leonard's early years at State, the band, under his leadership, and in spite of its membership problems, was steadily building a strong reputation.

Nevertheless, Leonard Falcone, age 34, was clearly discouraged in his job, and couldn't help but hear the siren song of opportunities at other colleges trilling his name. Finally, he answered the call some weeks later by registering with the Lutton Teacher Employment Agency (though Lutton felt Michigan State had a bright future and that more advantageous situations were not available) and typing this letter, found by a future student, Myron Welch (MSU Class of '66), in Dr. Harding's files some 40 years later:

*Prof. A, A, Harding* *December 10, 1933*
*Director of Bands*
*University of Ill.*
*Urbana, Illinois*

*Dear Mr. Harding:*

*I have taken the liberty of submitting your name for reference to a Chicago teacher's agency. I hope it will not cause you any inconveniences.*

*No, I am not out in the cold. In fact, my job here is quite secure, but I want to be on the lookout for a better position—one that would give me better material than I have here to work with. In order that my present position may not be jeopardized I wish that the matter be kept strictly confidential. In the event you should personally hear of an opening in some large university and wish to recommend my name, I would appreciate it greatly, only, please do not intimate that I wish to leave here.*

*Wishing you and Mrs. Harding a very Merry Christmas and best wishes for the New Year, I am,*

*Cordially yours,*
*Leonard Falcone*[47]

But then a month later, in January of 1934, there came a cascade of events that altered the Falcone brothers' center of gravity as Nicholas was suddenly kidnapped from normalcy, and plunged into a drama as gripping as any in an Italian opera; any thought Leonard might have had about moving on was put on hold. Speaking in third person, Nicholas reported what happened.

**Nicholas Falcone:** *(at the end) of WWI, Mr. Falcone was stricken with influenza as so many were. On Armistice Day, November 11, 1918, Mr. Falcone was asked to play in a band; eager to aid in celebrating the victory of the Allies and in spite of having a high temperature he arose from his bed and played in the band that marched during the day in both Ann Arbor and Ypsilanti. He returned to bed and the next day felt ringing in his left ear, followed by partial deafness . . .*

An unpleasant event to be sure, but apparently once he was over the flu, the symptom completely disappeared and he resumed playing and conducting without further incident. Until sixteen years later.

**Nicholas Falcone:** *In January, 1934, while directing the Varsity Band at the Field House during a basketball game with Northwestern, Mr. Falcone raised his baton, glanced over at the University of Michigan Band, which was alert and watching him, and gave the downbeat. The band launched into a routine performance of a familiar march. But nothing routine or familiar was happening to* *the popular conductor. His band began to sound to him as though it had been whisked away as far as the football stadium. This was Professor Falcone's first warning of the difficulties slated to hamper his musical activities—the musician's dread, deafness.*

*The next day Mrs. Falcone called his brother Leonard from East Lansing to come to Ann Arbor. Mr. Falcone had prepared several concert programs to be given. . . and asked Leonard if it was possible for him to take charge of the U of M band and the lessons to his private students. Leonard said he could . . .*

And he did.

**Nicholas Falcone:** *The university granted Mr. Falcone six months' leave of absence. The U of M band played a band concert at Hill Auditorium on April 2, 1934. The band also played three out of town concerts, in Flint, Saginaw, and Detroit (all conducted by Leonard) . . .*

*Mr. Falcone returned to Ann Arbor from New York (in) June. He could hear some if he was close enough to the person. After a few days he could hear so much better that he was able to rehearse two band concert programs and (appear with the band) at the Michigan . . . Commencement Day.*[48]

That spring, in a stunning news flash in the campus paper, it was disclosed in excruciating detail the amount of work it took to be in the MSC band: 41 miles of "intensive marching" during the eight week "grid season"! "trudg(ing) up and down football fields"! "practic(ing) at the old armory no less than five hours per week"! "One evening practice of two hours' endurance weekly"![49] Ironically, the same paper made no mention of the herculean work load Leonard had been carrying since the onset of his brother's hearing problems.

**Leonard Falcone:** *. . . when my brother was ill, I directed the band down there ( in Ann Arbor) for half a year and I did some of his teaching then. He was in New York being treated for his illness and I took over his band and I went on several concerts on and off campus. It was a terrific undertaking.*[50]

In addition to traveling back and forth to Ann Arbor during the Michigan winter (no small feat) and on into spring to conduct the University of Michigan band and present concerts with them there and in cities around Michigan, at MSC. he appeared with State's band at Farmer's Week, prepared for the annual series of spring concerts in the Forest of Arden[51]* (daily rehearsals!), played at baseball games, military reviews, and at convocation. In time, the *State News* picked up on all he was doing and referred to him as "performing the well-known 'iron-man' stunt. . . (for) directing both organizations and conducting some instrumental classes at the Ann Arbor school."[52]

What causes a man to work himself the way Leonard did for the six months he was a band director at two colleges? Certainly, his love for his brother and his desire to "hold his spot" for him at Michigan was a factor. But it goes much deeper than that. Years later, he would say that his drive and perfectionism came from personal pride—that he wanted always for Michigan State and its students to be proud of the band and of him, and accordingly, he always performed every musical task to the best of his ability.[53] It would seem that he didn't know any other way to do things but to do them the right way, and he simply couldn't understand those who chose a different path.

Years later, in a telling story, he would reminisce about an encounter he had with an administrator.

> **Leonard Falcone:** . . . *some time after the war when Mr. Underwood was head of the department here, I used to go in to tell him about shortcomings, and what the band could do to increase the reputation of the school. He said, "You know, I don't think we have to have the best band in the country. It's good enough the way it is."*
>
> *Amazing! Those were his* exact *words (raps table with fist). "I-don't-think-we-have-to-have-the-best-band-in-the-country!" . . . To me, that's a defeatist attitude . . . My aim was always to make the group the best possible, as musical as possible.*[54]

Addendum: "Iron man" Falcone's aim was to make not just State's band the "best possible, as musical as possible," it was to bring musical excellence to every group he conducted; it was one of his guiding principles, one to which he adhered throughout his lifetime.

After the ordeal he'd been through, Nick decided to take a week at the end of summer school to go "up North" (Michigan-speak for the Upper Peninsula) with his family on a long vacation and rest up before the new fall term. There, he fell down the rabbit hole.

> **Nicholas Falcone:** *Mr. Falcone and his family went to Charlevoix for this purpose. For about a week there the weather was nice and warm. Then suddenly it started to rain and get chilly. After a few days, Mr. Falcone became deaf again. He returned to Ann Arbor (to tell administrators) that (he) would be unable to take charge of the band in the fall . . . (There were no) mechanical aids that Mr. Falcone could use . . . mechanical aids are of no avail for people afflicted with nerve deafness.*[55]

Sucked into a vortex of silence, Mr. Falcone would never hear again.

> **Joe Dobos:** *There was no pension for Nick from University of Michigan. Earl Moore who was Dean of School of Music and Nicholas' former boss was in charge of the Roosevelt Administration WPA where they would put artists to work, and Nick got a job writing band arrangements. Most of these are in the Library of Congress.*[56]

> **Beryl Falcone:** *Yes, he couldn't hear a thing, and from then on Leonard had to write everything for Nick. He wrote pages and pages of notes to him in conversations they carried on—and I think Nick reached a certain point where he was lip reading from Leonard. They had certain gestures between them and Nick would talk to Leonard in English—but because of his Italian accent and his losing his hearing, his English was hard to understand. But we would go to concerts and Nick would sit there like he was holding his clarinet and play the notes. If he knew the music, he could tell where they were by the way they were fingering and the vibrations, but if the music was new to him, he couldn't do this. Eventually he went to work in a factory in Ann*

*Arbor—it was a very noisy facility, a good place for Nick because he couldn't hear anything.*[57]

In September, 1934, Leonard received a promotion to assistant professor. It was after his "Iron Man" months, and Michigan State was clearly worried about losing him to another school, as well they should have been.

**Leonard Falcone:** *There were a few occasions (when I thought seriously about leaving MSU). The 1st time it was an offer that came indirectly from University of Minnesota. Their director had retired, and they made inquiries at different music departments, and they inquired at the U. of M. and Dr. L. Moore, the Dean of Music there, he recommended me for the position. That didn't turn out very well; when they contacted Mr. Richards over here, he told Minnesota, "Leave him alone." Mr. Richards stopped it.*

*Another time (I was approached by) the University of Wisconsin, and another time the University of Missouri was interested in me. I notified the head of the department here (that I would be leaving), and they recommended that I stay and gave me a promotion. That's the first time I was promoted as assistant professor. Promotions at that time were very, very slow.*[58]

Though there would be one more important job offer that, at the time, he fully expected to get (and didn't) the offer from Missouri was his last.[59]

The promotion meant that he would no longer have to teach instrumental methods courses, and would soon be able to drop orchestra ensemble and management to confine his instruction to band, applied brass instruments, and beginning and advanced brass classes. Also that fall, because an increasing number of woodwind students created a need for a full-time, on-campus woodwind teacher, Falcone suggested that State hire Keith Stein, the only teacher of applied instruments he ever recommended to a department head. Stein, a young man who had been solo clarinetist with Nick's Michigan Band and who was completing his Master's degree at Eastman School of Music, was approved by Lewis Richards, who liked the idea that he had been a member of the Chicago Symphony Orchestra after graduating from Michigan—a credential consistent with his conservatory philosophy. Falcone was pleased, as he knew the young clarinetist would be a great asset to State not only as an excellent teacher, but also because he attracted fine talent to the college and encouraged students to participate in the band.[60]

Though the *State News* had printed this plea before the fall term to the entire male student body, the year began as it had in the past: with a struggle for band recruits.

> *Some men who are actually fine musicians have failed through some reason or other to try out for membership in the band. It is these men as well as prospective students that can do much to keep up the high standards of the organization.*
>
> *The band at this time is rather small and the amount of work to be done is constantly increasing. There are many fine instruments now unused which are available for players with some degree of talent. Students can be of much assistance by boosting the band in their home schools.*[61]

The struggle for band members was getting to be old news, and Leonard, now accustomed to the scramble, built his instrumentation as best he could, discharged his duties with his usual dedication, and in the end the band received its usual compliments and State played its usual game with Michigan, losing as usual (0–16), and nothing particularly noteworthy occurred band-wise until November when, in the one and only time in Falcone's 40 year long history with Michigan State, he missed a band event. Illness kept him from traveling to the football game at Syracuse University (State 0, Syracuse 10), but no worries. College Treasurer Charles C. Wilkins, affectionately called the "Godfather" of the College by Falcone, filled in as chaperone, and George Cochrane, the band's principal clarinetist, led the performance.[62] And the beat went on.

The following year, fall term of 1935, one young man who answered the call for new members showed up for auditions and had this recollection of the experience:

**Jack Bates, flute, 1935-1937:** *I remember Leonard Falcone very well having first met him in the fall of '35 when I auditioned for the State Marching Band. I graduated from a very small (high) school where there was no band, thus I never had seen any marching music until he put a sheet on a music stand in front of me and said, "Play!" There must have been a great shortage of piccolo-flute players as what a great surprise when I saw my name showing up in a few days to report for practice.*[63]

What occurred during his years in band remains clear, even after more than 75 years:

**Jack Bates:** *We had to wear green caps or "pots" while drilling to identify us as beginners and the old timers would jump on us should we march out of line. Another man taught us our positions while forming the letters. During the performances and practices we 'toed' the mark with no fooling around.*

*At the time ('35–'36), the State Band was the official band for the Detroit Lions. It was the custom for the Lions to play football in Detroit on Thanksgiving Day afternoon and we performed for the game. Following the game we were bused to the Hotel Statler, one of the two largest hotels in Detroit, for a big T-day dinner with all the trimmings. Afterwards, the police escorted our bus out of town!!!!*

*One time during one of those fall seasons while we were playing on the sidelines (always on the 50 yard line) at a State football game, I recall that Mr. Falcone left us to go to a nearby radio and listen to our playing. When he returned, he had the piccolos all move to the back of the band and out of the front line. Either we were out of tune, made too many mistakes, or were creating too much noise!*[64]

In February of 1936, Nicholas Falcone, after several efforts to cure his deafness including a visit to St. Anne's in Canada for faith healing,[65] sent his resignation to Dr. Charles A. Sink, President of the University School of Music. He had been Director of University of Michigan Bands for six years. Soon after Nicholas' resignation, Sink invited

Leonard to his home to discuss the possibility of succeeding his brother at the University of Michigan.

Michigan's resources and facilities far surpassed those of Michigan State, and since Nick and his wife Thelma lived in Ann Arbor and he was well acquainted with the town, according to Leonard himself it's likely he would have accepted the position had it been formally offered. But it wasn't.

> **Leonard Falcone:** . . . *you might not know this, I was considered for the University of Michigan, you see. As a matter of fact I was told, you see, that if they ever let me go from here (Michigan State) . . . they didn't want to do anything to create hard feelings, but if they let me go from here . . .*
>
> *I was never contacted after I was told that very likely, a 90% chance, that I would succeed my brother there (U of M) . . . I had directed the band there for half a year and I did some of his teaching then . . . Yes. Of course, yes! I would have considered that move!*[66]

Perhaps the only reason Leonard wasn't tapped to succeed his brother was that officials at both Michigan and Michigan State didn't want to strain relations between the two schools by making such an appointment. It's a likely explanation, but we'll never know for sure. According to one source, when Charles Sink, director of the University Musical Society, sought the advice of Edwin Franko Goldman, Goldman recommended that William D. Revelli be selected. He may not have known that Leonard was interested in the position, or that he could make the move from State. Whatever the case, he said of the young Revelli, "Give him your whole-hearted support, and Michigan's band will be the finest of its kind in the world."[67] Subsequently, 33-year-old Colorado native William D. Revelli, a respected supervisor of music for Hobart Public Schools in Indiana and proud son of Italian immigrants from a small village outside Turin, was the one who got the job. As for Leonard Falcone, he remained at State another thirty one years— and more—and built one of the most, if not *the* most, dynamic, respected, and innovative bands in the nation.

During this time, Nick's situation undoubtedly weighed on Leonard's mind, and it showed. Bates had this to say about Leonard's mindset during the two years' time bracketing Nick's resignation:

> **Jack Bates:** *I was in the last chair of the four flute/piccolo players so I was seated directly in front of him when we were practicing. I never recall him smiling. He impressed me as always being very serious, and I wondered if he had many friends.*[68]

> **Beryl Falcone:** *His closest friend was Nick. We went over there to see him quite a bit, and they came here now and then. He had a lot of professional friends he worked with, but I wouldn't say he had a lot of close friends.*[69]

In 1936, for a number of reasons, the battle for selectivity and band members came to an end. Social Security laws and Roosevelt's New Deal seemed to be weakening the Great Depression, and then there were also a number of changes that improved the band program that year. For one, Falcone was able to offer 10 scholarships of $30 (the amount of the course fee) per term for one year to new band students based upon their musical and scholastic abilities, a move that he proposed in order for MSC to keep up with Wayne State University's (Detroit) tuition rebates to its band members and to keep ahead of the University of Michigan's band scholarship ideas. The result was that four years later, because he was able to give 10 scholarships each year, nearly half of the band was receiving assistance. The "10 scholarship sneeze" went viral as public school band directors and MSC's applied teachers spread the word in their classrooms, clinics, and concerts, and since the award also covered out-of-state tuition, recruiting improved such that the band's quality and size grew. Another change occurred when, because authorities had adopted a policy in 1935 of providing funds for one out-of-state trip each year, the now 80-member band, in addition to taking trips to Ann Arbor and three Detroit Lions' games that fall, was able to travel to Philadelphia's Temple University. With the largest and most complete instrumentation in its history, the papers reported that it made a halftime hit with the Philadelphia crowd, who had never seen anything quite like it. "Those guys could do a manual of arms with a trombone and keep it snorting all the time!" claimed one fan. "The half-time event was certainly won by the Spartan band."[70]

Another innovation that occurred during the fall of 1936 was the marching band clinic, which Falcone initiated as yet another way of attracting students and teachers to Michigan State and serving Michigan's high school band directors. Presented for members of the Michigan School Band and Orchestra Association at their fall meeting at East Lansing, it consisted of a marching demonstration narrated by Captain H. J. Golightly, a member of the military department and band drillmaster, and a discussion on marching techniques. The clinics were an annual event until 1945. Also that fall, the Michigan State Band had the honor of performing for its third President and 25,000 locals when Franklin D. Roosevelt's election campaign train stopped for a half hour at the Grand Trunk Station in Lansing.[71] And there was more: 1936 ended with a pleasant surprise for Leonard, as he was named in the *Italian-American Who's Who*, a list of prominent Italian-Americans compiled by Vittorio De Fiori.

The band was on a roll. Three more surefire morale boosters came by the end of the 1936–1937 school year, as the band's name was changed from the "Michigan State College Military Band" to the "Michigan State College Band," it got its own practice field, and it received new uniforms.

> **Jack Bates:** *The band was part of the ROTC (thus the uniforms were military in appearance). My first two years the band members all had to wear Sam Brown belts and leather puttees. In May of the'36-'37 school year, I was issued a very attractive coat and long pants, which I never got to enjoy as I had left State and enrolled at the U of M. I had to return the uniform unworn.*
>
> *The band wore them for the first time in fall of '37 and I was not there. I was very disappointed.*[72]

And so the old General Pershing-style officer's uniforms were retired, exchanged for a uniform which consisted of trousers, a shirt, a green and white lined overcoat cape, an olive drab cap, a Sam Brown belt, and a braided fourragere, and the "Michigan State College Band" began marching practice on its own football field. No more "trooping down to College Field nearly every afternoon in the autumn" and getting "in the way of the football players." No more occasional "prancing halfback. . .coming perilously close to having a tuba in his lap when the play was finished."[73]

January now, 1938. Leonard heads for Florida for six months' leave of absence to enjoy the mild weather, transcribe orchestral compositions for his band,[74*] and visit several large universities. In his absence Keith Stein takes over as conductor and Albert Mancini, first trumpeter of the Detroit Symphony Orchestra, assumes his other teaching duties. That is, until May, when he returns to campus to conduct the annual spring concerts, this time in the new Michigan State campus band shell.

After thousands had been attracted to Leonard's outdoor concerts each year, there began a push to build a permanent concrete shell which could "give resonance necessary for a truly fine performance." Leading the charge was the class of 1937, which presented a gift of $2,500 for it to be constructed. When the State Board of Agriculture augmented that amount by $22,500, it was a done deal. The structure, located on the south side of Kedzie Hall, was modeled as per Leonard's suggestion after Chicago's Jackson Park shell, and was completed within the year.[75] At the dedication ceremony and concert on May 11, 1938, only four days after completion, over 3,000 spectators sat in temporary seats or stood shivering in the cool night air to witness the ceremonies and to hear Falcone conduct the first concert in the shell. But before Leonard thanked everyone involved in the project and took the podium, two important College administrators had this to say:

> **John Hannah, College Secretary 1934–1941, future college president:** *(This shell is) the culmination of a dream that envisioned an outdoor stage for the presentation of cultural programs.*

> **Robert S. Shaw, College President 1928–1941:** *The structure symbolizes many things. Because of its strength, beauty, and durability we hope it stands here forever, saying to the world "we here understand and appreciate the importance of cultural pursuits."*[76]

The new band shell was a triumph for Leonard, and was for many years a symbol of his success in popularizing the concert band medium.[77]*

After the May concerts, Keith Stein conducted the June concert and commencement exercises while Leonard continued his leave, traveling this time to Europe and visiting France and Italy to look for new concepts in band rehearsal and performance techniques, literature, and arranging. While in Italy, he was able to spend time with his father and four sisters in Roseto as well as travel to Rome to attend the open air concerts set up by Mussolini's Ministerial Culture at the *Terme di Caracalla*—the ancient baths built by Caesar, where crumbling columns formed a stage for the nation's greatest orchestras and opera singers, and at the Roman forum where Caesar was killed and the laws of civilized nations were born. In Milano, he sat under mellow skies with 20,000 others to hear opera in a courtyard once owned by the Sforza family, and in France he was permitted to roam around the famed Garde Republicaine Band of Paris's rehearsal, where he was amazed to note that the clarinetists at the end of the section were almost as accomplished as the principal, and that the entire section played as beautifully and as delicately as strings. The relationship between orchestra and band instrument sounds was one he thought about a great deal.[78]

> **Leonard Falcone:** *They (European bands) have a wider range of instruments, hence of expression. The contra bass reed is there giving an effect of strings; flugel horns, little used here, fill in between clarinets and trombones.*[79]

Though he felt that the Garde Republicaine Band of Paris, the Italian Royal Carabinieri (police) Band, and the Italian Financiers (customs police) Band military bands were the greatest military bands in Europe, he noted that in United States, "There are more bands than any other nation in the world. Once this was not so, but no other nation has developed public school music as America has."[80] What he didn't say was this: public school music was developing successfully because high school music directors were being skillfully trained by top notch musicians in some of the nation's colleges, particularly Midwestern colleges such as Michigan, the University of Illinois, and most particularly, Micchigan State College in East Lansing, Michigan.

*Carmelo, Nick, and Leonard, June, 1938*
*~ courtesy of the Falcone family*

*The band playing for graduation day at the shell*
*~ courtesy of the Falcone family*

*Leonard relaxing on board the Conte Di Savoia in 1938*
*~ courtesy of the Falcone family*

CHAPTER 10

# WAR YEARS: THE 1940s

***"Always to be best, and to be distinguished above the rest."***

~ **Homer**
***The Iliad***

---

*Tired musicians sat in band practice yesterday listening to their maestro, Leonard Falcone, attempt to get that last cornet note located . . . Suddenly the chimes of Beaumont tower broke the calm of the class. They were unusually loud and everyone could distinctly hear them bong out the hour.*

*"My gosh," said Maestro Falcone, apparently stunned by the lateness of the hour. "Can it be 6:00 already?"*

*There was a deathly stillness as all browners continued their silent worship. Suddenly from the back of the room came a quick voice in agreement.*

*"Yep," said the wag.*

*There was no argument. Two heads are better than one, and the class was dismissed—but only* after *the selection had been ironed out once more.*[1]

By 1939–1940, not only had the marching band gained in stature, the 100 piece concert band was gaining as well. In a word, this ensemble, for the first time in State's musical history, achieved what Leonard had been striving for: excellence.[2] It didn't come without long hours of hard work, and at times, Leonard's drive to "get it right" was leading to extra long rehearsals.

But the idea of producing a mediocre group had never made the in-box of the Falcone psyche. His uncomplicated philosophy was to work for perfection, and that philosophy was paying off in every aspect of the band program.

> **Leonard Falcone:** *The role of the college band as I see it is very simply stated. Primarily, it is to develop a group to the highest degree of proficiency, constantly striving to improve the standards of band performance and match the performance to the level of professional orchestras. Also, its role is to train teachers who are going into the field of public school music as conductors. That's very important, but it's secondary, though the two are related. If the caliber of the band is mediocre, you have mediocre students with mediocre training. But if the band is first class, then the students get a first class training in turn, and after graduation they go on to train their own students well.*
>
> *I think in terms of the band itself: as a performing group, but at the same time, as educational. But the term "educational" as interpreted by some people in the education field has some unsatisfactory connotations. When they say "educational" they don't mean "professional." They mean an "experience," an "exposure." I don't think of education from that standpoint. I think of education as a very closed application of what you are doing. In other words, education is based on excellence."*[3]

The accomplishment of excellence in the bandroom at MSC at the start of the war decade was integral to the college's having a band that was accepted as a serious musical medium, and beyond that, to the American Band Movement itself. The key to Leonard's attaining it, and then being able to sustain it for years to come, was both easy and difficult to achieve: over and over again, his students asserted that what inspired them to work and reach and do their best was his great "talent, caring, determination, graciousness, helpfulness, persistence, practicality, and professionalism," in the words of Thomas Broka, euphonium, MSU, late '70s.[4]

Decide for yourself which part of that is the easy part.

School year 1939–1940, and several changes have affected the band. For one, because of the increase in enrollment and the band's formidable schedule of activities to both the military and athletic departments, a second band is formed to lighten the burden. For another, in addition to the new shell, a new music building financed by applied music fees is opened,[5*] and in early 1940 a million-dollar auditorium is completed. The music building, containing as it did (and does) an excellent rehearsal room[6*] large enough for State's growing ensembles, and the multi-purpose auditorium, though far from being a music hall wonder, is still a huge improvement over the temporary staging and impossible acoustics of the Armory, the Women's Gymnasium, Demonstration Hall, and People's Church. The band's first performances in the new auditorium are unscheduled spring concerts intended for the shell, but driven inside because of the weather.

Then, in 1941, John Hannah becomes president of Michigan State College and begins the largest expansion of the school's history. Shortly after Leonard arrived, in 1928, the college's enrollment had been 2,813. By 1940, just prior to Hannah's appointment, 6,776 students called themselves "Spartans,"[7] and ten years later, helped by the returning flood of servicemen, the GI Bill, and Hannah's leadership, Michigan State College boasted 15,000 students. By 1965, Hannah had enlarged the university to 48,000 students, over three times its 1950 enrollment number.[8] In 37 years, from 1928 until 1965, Leonard would see the school grow seventeen times over. It was a growth that obviously would have a great effect on the band, giving him still more "selectivity" and opportunity for excellence. At Falcone's insistence and at the encouragement of colleagues in southeast Michigan who had just formed a group that was later to become the Michigan School Band and Orchestra Association, in April of 1941 MSC hosted the MSBOA's State Festival, an event which had for several years been held at the

University of Michigan. More than 5,000 students arrived on campus for the solo and ensemble contest on Friday and the band concert on Saturday, the first to be scheduled in the new auditorium.[9]* Leonard, as chairman, was responsible for it all. The following month the band's annual series of spring concerts, "the largest number of spring concerts in its history" (there were nine) began on campus on May 21, along with preparation for the Holland Tulip Festival. Amongst Michiganders, the consensus was that these concerts would be the best for a long time to come.

> **Lansing State Journal:** *The band will be heard this year with enhanced interest . . . throughout the community there is a definite feeling that before another concert season arrives, draft regulations will take their toll of this ensemble of more than 90 musicians. New and younger musicians will undoubtedly be filling posts in all divisions-making a change of personnel considerably greater than the turnover which Mr. Falcone meets every year.*[10]

There would be a "change in personnel," all right, but not one that anyone could have predicted: women, long barred, would soon be coming to the MSC band.

> **Keith Stein, clarinet professor, 1932-1973:** *There were girls that studied music (in the early years). But there were none in the band. That's for sure.*[11]

From September, 1941, to September, 1942, Leonard was granted a leave without pay. Sunday's August 16, 1942, *State Journal* noted that "His heavy schedule during the spring months, together with his intensive work with the State band, forced him to take a leave of absence."[12] In September, the same paper wrote that "fatigue induced by his intensive efforts" had caused him to spend several months resting in California before his return to Michigan, where he was ending his year long convalescence in Ann Arbor."[13] Clearly, his work ethic and high expectations were extraordinary, and they were taking their toll on his health. Yet it would seem that he knew no other way of doing things.

**Walter Hodgson, Music Department Chairman, 1958–1963:** *Leonard . . . works all day Saturday, thinks about it all day Sunday, and expects you to put in 16 hours a day, too. And if you don't, well then you just aren't doing your job.*[14]

In his absence, the Spartan Band was directed by Dale C. Harris (1941–42), director of music in the Pontiac schools and past president of the Michigan School Band and Orchestra Association. As expected, with the United States's entry into World War II on December 7, 1941, Harris saw membership decline from a 110 member marching band in the fall to just 80 men by spring. Nationalistic themes dominated activities that year, and Harris's final outdoor concert on May 27, 1942, included a speech on the American flag and patriotic songs by the combined chorus and band. Leonard, who had recently returned to Michigan, appeared on stage at the end of the concert to lead the singing of the "Alma Mater"[15] and re-introduce himself as State's returning band director, as he had fully expected to return to campus for the 1942–43 school year. But Uncle Sam was cooking up other plans for him, and so rather than waiting to be drafted mid-term, he enlisted in the US Army Air Corps on September 23, 1942, serving for eight months as a member of the Air Force Band at Maxwell Field, Alabama, and later in Stuttgart, Arkansas, where he organized and led the 388th Air Force Band.[16]*

**Beryl Falcone:** *It was not a happy assignment.*[17]* *The post band in Arkansas nearly killed him it was so awful. If anyone came in and could play an instrument, they were assigned to him."*[18]

During his absence, Edward D. Cooley, an outstanding percussionist and member of Falcone's band for four years, took charge of the marching band, and Roy L. Underwood, who had assumed the music department chairmanship after Lewis Richards' death in August, 1940, led the concert band. It was then, during the 1942–43 school year, that a second band called the "Varsity Band" was formed in addition to the regular Concert Band to accommodate the "less gifted students and women of the institution." This group, conducted by band alumnus Arthur Best of Pontiac, was well enrolled and well received during its winter term appearances at a newly created and popular series of weekly Sunday concerts, which alternated appearances of it and the Concert Band and included semi popular music and familiar melodies in addition to a community sing along. Enrollment in the Concert Band continued to dwindle. Between December 1, 1942, and April 1, 1943, the concert band lost 65 men to the armed services. But when thirty-five new members enrolled for the spring term, the concert band was able to retain a membership of around 70 men.[19]

In spite of the popularity of the winter series program, Underwood wanted Leonard back on campus, and soon. MSC was being used for Air Corps Cadet training, and the group of 1,500 men had their own band of 60 who had the college's blessing to use its band equipment and facilities. Not surprisingly, the student directed organization managed to damage and lose several instruments, prompting Underwood to request that Falcone do what he could to hasten his return. Because the Army was approving discharges to those working in essential employment, Leonard was able to request a release from duty using the argument that he could be of greater use to the nation as an educator at MSC. When the Army agreed, he returned to State in the summer of 1943 and organized the school's first summer band, which was to last the full 11 weeks of the term.

And then a surprise, Army style. A memorandum suddenly appeared on his desk from the 6th Service Command in Chicago, ordering him to report to a munitions factory, the Buhr Machine Tool Company in Ann Arbor, within five days, or be recalled to active duty. And so for the remainder of the summer, Keith Stein once again assumed leadership of the band. Even though Leonard was still engaged in factory work that summer his release from Buhr was pending, and he continued to make plans for the coming school year hoping that the factory would release him so he could resume his position at State. It did. And though after several weeks of factory work, on October 1, 1943, he returned for good to the college, it wasn't before an unexpected decision had to be made—a decision which, for Underwood, was a nail biter. In a letter dated August 23, written while he was still working at Buhr, Leonard explained the situation.

**Leonard Falcone:** *Casey Lutton has written me to say that the University of Missouri is looking for a man to head their band department this fall. Lutton would like to nominate me for the position and wants to know if I am interested. . . .Naturally I want to talk the matter over with you before it goes any further. Please give me a ring . . .*[20]

Underwood, anxious to convince Leonard to stay at State, acted quickly and promised him not only an associate professorship upon his reinstatement, but a promotion to full professorial rank in the very near future. Leonard declined the Missouri offer, and never considered leaving Michigan State again.

It was during this time, fall of 1943, that the Varsity Band was forced to disband and the Concert Band, as it continued to lose male members, began to accept women. Change was in the winds, and by spring of 1944, 22 of the 44 students in the Concert Band were female, and Falcone, who had no reservations about allowing women into the all male organization and wasn't in any position to act on them if he had, was happy to discover an immense untapped resource of talent. Never again were women kept from playing in the Concert Band.[21]

**Leonard Falcone:** *When I returned from my short army service, the bulk of the students from the male student body had gone to the service. In order to keep the band going at all, we had to use the girls. And that was a good thing, because we found some very fine players on campus.*[22]

Though WWII brought a reduction in the number of Falcone's applied brass students and a discontinuation of most athletic activities, Leonard's schedule was still arduous. For one thing, two new classes had been added to his schedule: Band Arranging and the directorship of a new band of fifty or so men from the Army Specialized Training Program (A.S.T.P.) for engineers, which had come to campus in the fall of 1943.[23] But one year later, fall of 1944, the ASTP was discontinued and athletics were restored to boost sagging student morale. Though the 51 member band, nearly half of which were women, played at athletic events, marching down the field was discontinued. The drop in male enrollment continued throughout the school year so that by spring, there were fewer than 1,000 men on campus, with women outnumbering them three to one.[24]

Also that spring, on June 9, 1945, just weeks after the European end of WWII, a *terra cotta* statue titled "The Spartan," claimed by some at the time to be the tallest free-standing ceramic sculpture in the world, was unveiled at a campus traffic intersection to a delighted crowd. It soon was to be known as "Sparty."

Because marching was still curtailed in the fall of 1945, high school bands were invited to perform at Spartan football halftime shows. But gradually, the troops were coming home and by December, returning GIs helped to create a greater male majority in the band. A few months later, in the spring of 1946, college applications flooded the admissions office with many of the returning servicemen taking an interest in public school music. The result was that band enrollment soared, a varsity band was added, and Leonard got an assistant.[25]* Even so, he had a bit of a problem manning the Marching Band that fall: only 38 members of the previous MSC band had returned.[26] And so with only five days left before the opening Sept. 28th football game (MSC 42, Wayne State 0), he was forced to pick up 50 players from the freshmen ranks, train them, and parade them on the football field the coming Saturday. Even the drum major's job posed a problem, with the only applicant being a young man with no musical experience. "I don't know how we'll do it," Leonard said, "but we'll be ready."[27] The reason for the crisis?

> ***Stars and Stripes*, September 21, 1946:** *The Michigan State College band is in a hard way, all because former GIs have had all the marching they want. Even with a student body of 10,000 to draw from, director Leonard Falcone is having a tough time organizing a 100-piece band in time to play for the MSC football opener Sept. 28.*
>
> *"Ex GIs don't want to spend an hour a day for the next three months marching up and down a drill field," moaned Falcone.*

Though in 1946 he had wanted to bring his military band back to its former 100-man membership, not only was he unable to do so, he was also unable to teach the freshmen recruits enough marching fundamentals in five days to get them through the first game performance. And so he settled for an 85-piece band which did not perform halftime during the first game, and instead made its first appearance on Macklin Field during the second game on October 5 (MSC 20, Boston 34).[28] One of his players recalls that band, and recalls, too, having a very tense personal experience at game three (MSC 0, Mississippi State 6) that lasted several hours—one that made Falcone chuckle several years later when he heard about it.[29]

> **A. Roger Welton, flute and piccolo, MSC, 1945-1950:** *In my second year of band, the third home game, I left my piccolo at home on top of the piano. There was no time to go back for it, and I couldn't find another one to use. I was afraid I would lose my scholarship if Mr. Falcone found out. What to do? There seemed to be only one solution: I told the other three piccolo players to play as loudly as they could while I played the hell out of a flute cleaning rod. To get away with it, I was going to have to play it in Mr. Falcone's full view during the rehearsal, the march to the stadium, the pregame, while seated in chairs on the field during the game, at the halftime show, and during the march back to the music building. And it worked! Mr. Falcone never said a word!*
>
> *When I graduated in 1950, I told Mr. Falcone about it and we had a good laugh.*[30]

1946 was the year, too, that the Concert and Marching Bands became separate units. Though women had saved the Concert Band from near extinction during the war, Leonard objected to their marching.[31]

> **Leonard Falcone:** *[in 1946, women could] be part of the concert band, but not the marching band . . . it wasn't even considered . . . the band [was] an all male organization. It just wasn't done, and the girls didn't even ask. It was like the football team: it was an all male group.*[32]

It wasn't until 1972, five years after Leonard retired, that Beth Mlynarek (baton twirler) and Lynne Charbonneau (saxophonist) were allowed to enter the Spartan Marching Band as the doors, closed for so long, were finally inched opened to all competent musicians, regardless of sex.

And so it was that from 1946 until 1972, the Marching Band was a men's club whose membership came from the Concert Band, the Varsity Band, and some who played in neither group, while the Concert Band which didn't play engagements until after football season, became a very select group of both highly talented men and women. In 1946, its first year as a separate ensemble, it boasted 90 skilled players, the largest in the history of the college. Chosen from an enlarged student body containing capable women and experienced returned GIs, many of whom had played extensively in the army,[33] it created a lot of excitement as the spring concert series grew near.

> ***Lansing State Journal***: *It is estimated that 3,500 has been the all-time high in outdoor attendance to date. With State's student enrollment greatly increased and with more and more band directors bringing in their ensembles from adjoining areas, it is thought that 5,000 will be a conservative (concert attendance) number this spring.*[34]

By the 1947–1948 school year, both the Marching and Concert Bands had surpassed pre-war ensembles in quantity and quality.[35*] Late registration and an early game forced the Marching Band to miss its appearance in Ann Arbor at the gridiron opener with the University of Michigan on September 27 (State 0, Michigan 55),[36*] though soon enough, with Falcone shouting commands like a carnival barker from his megaphone atop his new 20-foot tower, it was making a good showing.

The following school year, fall of 1948, Leonard was determined that the band not again miss the opening game on September 25, again with the University of Michigan (State 0, Michigan 13). The problem, especially since his assistant was on a one year leave of absence,[37*] was how to train his men in time. And then he figured it out. The football team met during the summer to train for its first of the season games . . . why not the band? And so one week before registration and two weeks before the game, 90 bandsmen, 81 of them returning players, lived and ate with the football squad in Quonset Village, and readied themselves for the home field showdown with Michigan (State 7, Michigan 13). It was a first, and it produced a marching unit that put on exciting crowd pleasers such as the game four Homecoming show (State 61, Arizona 7. . . yes, you read that correctly). Then, to the delight of the 36,616 fans seated at the Macklin Field gridiron, the band staged a clever and well received campaign skit lampooning the candidates "Druman" and "Tooley." As the band formed an elephant and donkey, the donkey wiggled its ears as Druman promised all freshmen 50 yard line seats and blamed the Republican 80th Congress for overcast skies; Tooley's speech, culminating in a pledge to bring all the best football talent in the country to Michigan State, ended with the band striking up "Happy Days Are Here Again."[38]

The postwar years had to have been an exciting time for Leonard, and not just because now that World War II was over there would be a flood of new band talent. Before the decade was to end, State would be admitted to the Western Conference (the Big Ten),[39*] it would have a new Alma Mater that would forever be associated with him,[40*] he

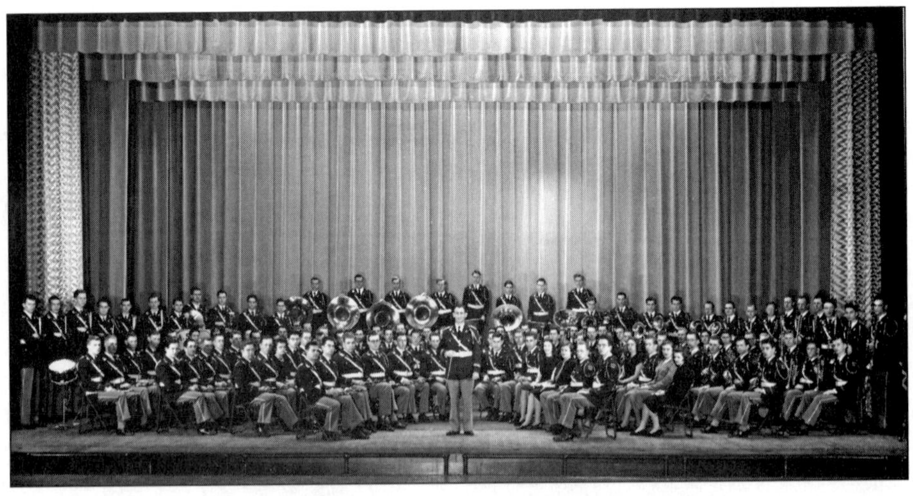

*Women join the Concert Band in the 1940s*
*~courtesy of Michigan State University Archives & Historical Collections*

would be promoted to professor of music and Director of Bands and relieved of all applied upper brass teaching,[41*] and, best of all, romance was in the air in the person of a beautiful young French horn player named Betty Beryl Cromer.

*Betty Beryl Cromer, 1940*
*~ courtesy of the Falcone family*

CHAPTER 11

# WEDDINGS: ROSETO VALFORTORE, ITALY, 1910 HOWE, INDIANA, DECEMBER 19, 1948

***"We will have rings, and things, and fine array."***
**~ William Shakespeare, *The Taming of the Shrew***

---

**Nick Ferrera:** *In Leonard's time at the turn of the twentieth century in Roseto, couples usually got engaged* (fa la promessa) *on Palm Sunday. Then, a day or two before the wedding, there was a wedding tradition called* curedde *(no doubt symbolic of the bride's purity and of the wedding night). The female side of the bride's family would gather at the bride's house, but beforehand, they would have assembled the* biancheria, *which is a collection of whites—the sheets, pillow cases, towels, etc. The whites were tied with red ribbons,* ziaredda, *to ward off the evil eye, the* malocchio. *The women, the bride's mother, the bride, the sisters, aunts, cousins, etc., would walk through the streets to the groom's house, each carrying some of the bedding and towels in a public procession witnessed by neighbors—everybody. When they got there, the mother-in-law would be waiting, and would take something from the* biancheria*—a sheet, pillow, scarf, or whatever—hold it up, and sort of snap it. That was the signal that the* biancheria *was accepted.*

*I believe the groom's family provided the mattress, because after the acceptance, everyone went inside the mother-in-law's home to make the marriage bed, and have some wine, tarelle, and other treats.* [1]

IT IS A COLD SUNDAY AFTERNOON, nearly 1 o'clock, the day of their wedding, December 19, 1948. A large group of 320 family and friends are seated in the sanctuary of the Lima Presbyterian Church in the little town of Howe, Indiana, where the bride, Betty Beryl Cromer, has been a music teacher for the past three years. Twin candelabras decking either side of the church altar are flanked by Christmas trees and brilliant red poinsettia plants graduating in a slant from the altar's center, providing a colorful and festive holiday background for the service. Two ministers stand in front of the altar, waiting for the groom and his best man to enter from the side door, leading to the sacristy.

The bride, waiting with her brother and bridesmaid in the church foyer for their entry cue, is lovely in a street length frock of iridescent bronze taffeta, styled with a heart neckline and short sleeves. Her gloves are of a matching color, as are her shoes, and her small Dutch cap is handmade of bronze metal thread. A cameo lavaliere, worn by her maternal grandmother at her wedding, is suspended from a tiny gold chain around her neck. She carries a bouquet of white roses and gardenias (she loves roses and is fond of the smell of gardenias, and thinks they will make a pretty keepsake when pressed).

As her father passed away some time ago, it is her brother, David, who will give her away in marriage. Her only attendant is costumed in a street length dress in forest green, fashioned with a high neckline, short sleeves, and a bustle back. She carries an arm bouquet of bronze colored baby mums.[2]

In the sacristy, the groom, Leonardo Vincenzo Falcone, the son of the late Maria and Domenico Falcone of Roseto Valfortore, Italy, is becoming anxious. His brother, Nicola, the best man, does what he can to calm him.

That this particular bride and groom would end up together comes as a surprise to many sitting in the congregation. Her deep interest in music and pedigree as the daughter of a musician are right. But her age, 28, and his, 49, have taken many off guard. And there's more: for her part, when she told her friends about the impending nuptials, she was met with astonishment. "We had no idea!" they exclaimed. "We didn't think he was the marrying kind!" For his, when after marching practice one day the band manager unexpectedly brought everyone to attention and then suddenly screamed, "The 'Old Man' is getting married!" everybody cheered. But they were caught as unawares as Beryl's friends. They thought him a somber bachelor who, if he married at all, would wed a staid, older lady[3]—not a beautiful, petite, lively young woman. But one among them, one who knew the maestro's softer side, wasn't a bit surprised. His name is Eldon Rosegart.

**Tammy Tellenger, daughter of Eldon Rosegart, MSC '41, drum major:** *My father says he recalls Leonard opening the door of the band room one day and "crooking a finger at Beryl to come with him to his office." That's when he began to think there was more than just a student/band director relationship going on!*[4]

**Beryl Falcone:** *I had graduated from Western Michigan University and was teaching in Indiana when I decided I'd go to summer school and work on an advanced degree–so I came to MSC. That summer Leonard decided to have a summer band, and I auditioned for it. Right in the middle of the audition a string broke*[5]**—I had strings on my horn where they ran from where the valves were put together–they do it differently now. He sent me to a repairman downtown and when it was fixed I told him, and said "Do you want me to play for you again? He said, "No, just come to rehearsal." Well, we had just one rehearsal and the summer band idea ended because we had only 2 clarinets, 10 trumpets and probably 4 horns. It was all lopsided. Later I would talk with him in the hall, I wasn't a MSU grad and so I didn't know I was supposed to be half afraid of him as everyone else seemed to be, and he would say he hoped I was still playing my horn. Then one day he asked me if I would like to go out to dinner. I thought, "Yeah!" So that's how I met Leonard—with that old French horn.*

*When we got engaged, he looked younger than he really was. We were sitting in a car—probably nighttime or dusk—when Leonard actually proposed. We used to ride around Lansing a lot in the evening, often to an amusement park out by one of the lakes. I sort of sensed that a proposal was in the works, but when it finally came there was a problem. I had just found a position outside of Chicago—a wonderful position—went for an interview, signed the contract, the whole thing.*

*I didn't know when I accepted that job that our romance was going to get more intense. When he proposed, because of our jobs, we decided that we would get married in June, after the school year was over. But then when I came down that fall for a couple of football games, we looked at each other and said, "What are we waiting for?" We decided right then and there to get married at Christmas time.*

*We decided to go back to this little town in Indiana to this little church and have the wedding there. I had been teaching there and had the church choir. The town was so small I had all the music, K-12, and was allowed to do anything I wanted to do musically. We had a little orchestra, and we had a choir in the high school group. I had some good singers—there are always 1 or 2 or 3 that can carry it!*

*Nick stood up with Leonard, and they were Catholic, of course. My maid of honor was Jewish, and at the church we had one pastor who was Methodist and one who was Presbyterian. So we had all these religions involved, and somebody said what we needed was a Muslim and a Hindu to round things out.*

*I grew up a Methodist, but at the time we were married I offered to turn Catholic. Leonard said "no." I never really knew why he didn't take me up on the offer. The agreement was that any daughters we had would go to church with me and any sons would go to church with him. I have to say he wasn't – he didn't go to church every Sunday. He went at Christmas and Easter, and he would play a New Year's service. But in his heart he was Catholic, and of course his memorial was Catholic.*

*After we were married, there was a reception for everyone in the church parlor, and then later there was a sit down dinner for 40 family and close friends at the local hotel, which had a restaurant. Everybody was keeping an eye on the weather because it was snowing, and it looked like it might get worse. On a Midwestern night on the 19th of December in the year 1948 anything could happen—the weather forecasting was not like now. As I recall the dinner was—not exactly eat and run, but we didn't linger around, either.*

*After dinner we left for a two week wedding trip to New York. I carried my little white bridal bouquet all the way there and I put it on the hotel windowsill to keep it fresh – and it blew away! I don't even have one flower! But we had a lot of fun. We went to the opera and all the concerts you could think of at that time. It was wonderful.*

*When we returned to East Lansing, we found out that we had no wedding pictures because the guy we hired to take the pictures forgot to put film in the camera. Now, Leonard was not an angry man. He could get upset with people, but he didn't blow his top very often. But when he did, get out of the way! If you ever wanted to see him really mad, this was the time. His blue eyes turned to ice. I thought he would explode. He had wanted something to send back to the family in Italy, and he had nothing. I think he told the photographer off. I think he laid into him. He couldn't understand how someone could say they were doing a job and yet not have the necessary equipment. It was typical of him that he just couldn't understand when somebody didn't do their job right—and this guy hadn't done his job right, and so we had no wedding pictures. There was the 13-year-old son of a friend of Leonard's who had his camera and he took a picture of us coming down the aisle, and that is the only picture of our wedding.*

*We weren't married long at all before I started to think that Leonard might be important professionally. I didn't realize it at first. I got my first tiny glimmer when he said to me on the way back from our wedding trip, "You have to remember you are not a student, you are a faculty wife." And I kind of looked at him and I thought about it and decided, "Oh, he means I have to act differently than I do in the summertime when I talk in the halls with other grad students." I don't know what he thought I was going to do—but I thought it was an interesting remark.*

*I became a good faculty wife. I joined Faculty Folk, an organization of faculty wives, and was active in it until I went back to school. Then I was invited to join the East Lansing Woman's Club, an organization started on campus by faculty wives in the 1890s. I became their president until I went back to school and finished my masters in education at MSU when the girls were in junior high. After graduation, I went back to teaching and taught in Lansing elementary schools from 1968 until I retired in 1987. The summer I retired I went to a Past President's Luncheon and someone said, "Come back!" I did, and I became president again—and I still belong. I'm now one of the club's oldest members.*[6]

Another club Beryl joined after getting married, this one with her husband, was the "Newcomers Club," a Michigan State faculty group. From this group evolved a supper club of about eight couples which met once a month for a potluck supper and an evening of cards. Falcone, a fine bridge player, enjoyed getting to know professors from other departments of the University.

**Leonard Falcone:** *If you do nothing else except go to work at 7 a.m., have your lunch at noon, come home and have your dinner at 6 p.m., go to bed, and then the next morning go to work with no relaxation whatever, that becomes drudgery, whereas if you have the possibility of a little social life, that makes it a lot more enjoyable, a lot more full, more relaxing. I think if you understand that colleagues—the people you are dealing with—are warm human beings interested in what you are doing, and if you are interested in what they are doing, it makes your living much more pleasant.*[7]

Nearly twenty months after marrying, Falcone became the father of a baby girl with the birth of Mary Beryl[8]* on August 6, 1950; just two years later, the little family welcomed a sister for Mary, Cecilia Yolanda,[9*] born on May 25, 1952. In fewer than three and a half years, 53-year-old Leonard had transitioned from bachelor, to married man, to father of two.

**Walter Hodgson:** *I think his family was a great joy to him . . . it just really was something that he wanted.*[10]

**Beryl Falcone:** *He was thrilled about having children. And he was very handy, much more handy than I was. I had never been around babies. He would do diapers and get up at night.*[11]

(Four months after the wedding, on April 12, 1949, Leonard's brother, Carmelo, passed away.)[12]

*Newlyweds, 1949*
*~ courtesy of the Falcone family*

CHAPTER 12

# THE FABULOUS FIFTIES

***"There is music wherever there is harmony, order, or proportion."***

**~ Browne**

**carved above the entrance to the**

**Michigan State University Music Building**

---

*Oh, for the band trips of times past! Crammed into passenger seats was a brotherhood there for the having, swapping apples and peanut butter sandwiches for cookies and pop and passing the time playing games, sometimes, even, with Leonard's girls, Mary and Cece (who were just little tykes then), or sleeping or singing silly songs made up on the way to every Big 10 game MSC ever played. Even now, in moments of quiet, many still hear the echo of voices filling those buses and train cars with harmonies while the sun rose and the rattling ker-thunk-thunk-thunk of the roadbed marked a steady beat through the softness of an early Michigan morning.*

*Minn a so tah, where is your team?*
*Nowhere on the field to be seen.*
*Minn a so tah, hang up your shoes.*
*You're all done, and you're all through,*
*We will beat you next year too!*
*Three cheers for MSU!*

—to the tune of the "Minnesota Rouser" (see Appendix I)

THE 1950S WERE SURELY FALCONE'S GREATEST YEARS at Michigan State. For one thing, after WWII, the number of students tripled as the school became a major university. This translated into a similar growth in the music department and a higher percentage of music majors in the band. Though Leonard predicted that a leveling-off in the bands' growth would follow, it did not, and the band continued to expand as the college's enrollment grew.[1]

In spite of the annual winter concert on March 5, 1950, having a discouragingly small audience, especially considering it was the musical highlight of the year, 3,500 concert goers showed up for the first spring concert, and the band's reputation continued to develop. State's Marching Band had been impressing national football audiences for years, and now annual out -of -state trips and televised games were spreading its recognition well beyond state and local acknowledgment.[2]

A performance of the Concert Band at the North Central Division of the Music Educators' National Conference at Fort Wayne, Indiana, on April 7, 1951, for an audience of 5,000 musicians, was the first of several of its significant appearances, and occurring as it did just one month after the nation's leading bandmasters unanimously elected Falcone to lifetime membership in the American Bandmaster's Association, it confirmed his national stature as a conductor, teacher, and musician.[3]* The acclaim given the Band at the North Central meeting reinforced Falcone's own growing opinion that the Concert Band, a group he recognized as "the heart of the music department," was no longer merely an equal of the Marching Band, it was slowly but surely surpassing it.[4]

The band's excellence was due to a number of things, of course, but certainly one of them was the respect Leonard inspired in his students—a respect which caused them no little fear in their quest to do better.

> **Keith Stein:** *You bet he was demanding. I've had kids call me up and say, "I've overslept! I can't go on back (to Leonard's office)!" And I would say, "Yes, you go on back. You face him. You'll be all right. Don't worry." But they were* that *frightened. He never*

*was rough to anybody. But they learned a lot of discipline out of that, for living, for life.*[5]

**Burton Bronson, tuba, 1946–1950, 1952–1953:** *You learned out of respect for him. I was always afraid to go to a lesson. Not afraid of him as a man, but of not doing well enough to please him.*[6]

**Robert Sack:** *He strove for perfection, and didn't accept any excuses for not playing awfully darn good. I sat in the front row of the clarinet section, and I always thought, "Boy, you know, if I ever squeak, I'll be sure to not look up!" One thing you'd never want to do is look up, because you'd get those laser blue eyes coming down right at you.*

*He demanded great things from the band. He was in no way a mean person, just highly professional. Top notch all the way around. We all respected him so much because of his professionalism, his integrity, his honesty. He had a furiousness, but not a meanness.*[7]

A "furiousness, but not a meanness," with something of the volcanic fire of Vesuvius glowing in his heart. Yes.

In 1952, the band did its part in welcoming Gen. Douglas MacArthur to Lansing. MacArthur, fired during the Korean War for insubordination, returned to America to a hero's welcome. When he gave his "old soldiers never die, they just fade away" speech to Congress, he received massive public adulation, which aroused expectations that he would make a run for the presidency in the 1952 election. Though he in fact endorsed Sen. Robert Taft of Ohio and never wanted to be a candidate himself, it seemed the nomination was his for the asking. He was so wildly popular he looked like a shoo-in.

**Fritz Stansell, 1950-1954, baritone:** *He decided to conduct a national tour of appearances, and Lansing was on the list. When he arrived at MSC, the band was lined up at the main entrance* *on Grand River. MacArthur followed us in an open convertible as we marched all the way to the State Capitol steps, where he gave a very hawkish speech. I remember we played the "US Field Artillery March" by Sousa over and over and that there were crowds all the way along both sides of Michigan Ave . . . probably a distance of 2 or 3 miles.*

*Leonard was for Eisenhower in 1952, (when I went into his office for lessons that fall, he always wore his "I Like Ike" button) so undoubtedly he was also supportive of MacArthur's visit.*[8]* *Not that he let his political views influence his response to requests for the MSU band to perform. The marching band also played for Harry Truman at the train station when he came through on a whistle stop tour campaigning for Adlai Stevenson in fall of 1952, some months after the MacArthur parade and speech.*[9]

On January 17, 1953, a banquet held in the Union Ballroom at Michigan State honored Falcone "Not only for his 25 years of service here but for his courage and persistent goal in the American way up the musical ladder."[10] Knowing his great modesty, the committee, headed by James Pino ('40) and Richard Snook ('46) kept the event a secret until three weeks prior to the occasion, as they knew Leonard would have tried talking them out of holding it. The state's musical leaders, representatives of the MSC music and athletic departments, administrative staff, and former "band boys," as Falcone affectionately called his players, spoke in his honor and presented gifts which, among others, included a new Baldwin spinet piano (positioned behind stage curtains and dramatically revealed during the banquet) and a tape recording of the evening's events.[11] The recording, which includes the extemporaneous speech closing the banquet, is interesting to listen to if for no other reason than that it clearly reveals Leonard's much imitated idiosyncratic pronunciation—clear, but delightfully somewhat "off," as though he'd learned English from an ancient sequestered Florentine academic or nobleman. His vocal nuances mirror who he was as a man: sincere, proper, measured, unique, at once both gentle and authoritative. And so do the words of his speech, which clearly reveal his humility and sense of humor.

> **Leonard Falcone:** *I have been told by a good many people at different times that I have a very expressive face. If my face has been showing the feelings I have been experiencing for the past half hour, then I don't need to tell you that I have been very embarrassed, fidgety, and very uncomfortable. In fact, I have been feeling quite uncomfortable for quite some time, since I first began to hear rumors that this event was being organized. You see, most of my life I have been on the other side of the fence. By that I mean that I have always helped pay tribute to other people. So to be on the receiving end is a new experience for me, an uncomfortable one. Nevertheless, I would not be honest with you if I did not admit that I'm very grateful and I certainly appreciate the tribute that you people are so kind to pay toward me this evening.*
>
> *Being in one place for 25 years has many advantages, but I can think of at least one disadvantage: people will remind you of that fact. And they'll ask you about it in a very peculiar way, as if asking, "How old are you anyway?"*[12]

He went on to relate amusing stories about his experience at Michigan State, and in a closing remark had this to say: "Whatever advancement the band has made in size, music, and attainment, the credit belongs to the players."[13]

Though more than 800 invitations had been sent and 200 reservations were confirmed for the evening, a near blizzard kept all but 120 from attending. But dozens of former students and giants in the music field had sent congratulations by telegram or letter. His old friend Edwin Franko Goldman honored his valuable contribution to bands and band music, and Clarence Sawhill, President of the College Band Directors National Association noted that "The loyalty which prompted this occasion is evidence of the high regard in which you are held by your students. In the teaching field, no man can ask for a higher recommendation than that his students respect him."[14]

Appropriately, the banquet honoring Leonard's courage and 25 years of service was held during what was to be a perfect storm of events that occurred from 1950–1954 that was to revolutionize how the country viewed the band and Michigan State, what programs the band presented at half time, the way the band felt about itself, the level of recognition it received—everything. The outward symbol of the thrilling realization sweeping campus that there was "a whole lot of shakin' goin' on" at MSC was personified by the football team.

> **Robert Sack:** *Early in my freshman year (1950) after winning the first two games we lost badly to Maryland (7–34), and we thought "Oh, dear. Things are bad. The team isn't going to be any good." But then we went on to win 28 games in a row. We were unbeaten for the rest of the year and for the two and a half years after that.*[15*] *It was an exciting time.*[16]

Unfortunately, while State's football team was winning glory for the College on the field, the Marching Band, though it sounded exceptionally good, looked about the same.

> **Fritz Stansell:** *At the time, the MSC Band still dressed as a military band because of campus-wide required ROTC. The entire male student body was required to take it for the first two years at MSC. The band played for reviews, held on Old College Field, in spring term (every Tuesday?), involving perhaps as many as 4,000 uniform clad ROTC members. It was quite a sight to see all these students in uniform marching from Demonstration Hall to the large area behind the Field House. At any rate, our band uniforms were fashioned after army officer's uniforms of WWII with Sam Brown belts. They were drab. The only thing dressy about them were the white gloves and spats. In contrast, the U of M uniforms, with the cross belts, capes, epaulets, etc. were flashy.*[17]

And so it was that in the fall of 1950, the *State News* began a campaign for the band to have new uniforms, uniforms that "everyone will be proud of." But at least one very important person was not supportive of the idea—at least not initially.

> **Earle Louder, euphonium, MSU 1955:** *We'd been wearing an army tan with a regular style army hat. The overcoat was a*

*trench coat. A "horse blanket" we called it. It was okay in the cold weather sometimes. When there was a push for the band to update the uniforms, Mr. Falcone originally resisted it.*

*Tradition was important to him. He liked the military look, like that at the University of Illinois.* [18]

**James Niblock:** *Leonard was adamant that such items were irrelevant to the band's performance.* [19]

**Leonard Franke, MSC Band 1940-1941:** *He used to tell us, "I don't care what you look like. . . but we're going to sound good!"*[20]

**James Niblock:** *After I spoke to him and suggested he give this some thought at leisure, Leonard came back to me with his decision that this was "a good idea." He was most amenable to changing his mind after he had thought things through.*[21]

So it was that beginning early 1951, polls were conducted, design contests were sponsored, and contributions were solicited from various organizations. Finally, after the Board of Agriculture appropriated funds to cover the complete cost of the new outfits, a "new uniform" committee was composed of the head of the music department, the director of athletics, the comptroller of the college, the secretary of the State Board of Agriculture, the college purchasing agent, a professor of military science and tactics, a student representative, and Falcone. But all did not go well.[22]

**Leonard Falcone:** *We had quite a time agreeing on the uniform. I had proposed a certain style, and we had a lot of discussions and a lot of proposals and two members of the committee were quite set in their opinion of what the uniforms should be. And then, of course, there was the military (who suggested minimal changes such as a pouch to carry music and white canvas puttees) . . . Mr. Underwood suggested we adopt Spartan helmets—and I wouldn't hear of it from the first, from the beginning. And so we*

> *had all these ideas. I said my idea is to have a uniform in the colors of the school, green and white, and have a regular band uniform and get away from these other things. From the point of the ROTC, we'll play ball, but there's no reason we have to be in the same uniform as the other ROTC regiments. Finally (pounds table) they began to find faults with (the uniform I wanted). They claimed that the stitching wouldn't hold, and so forth and so on, and I'll tell you I have had some experience myself in tailoring! I was an assistant tailor in Ann Arbor when I was there. We had samples of the uniforms sent to the Home Economics Department and I stuck to my ideas and said it basically has to be a band uniform . . .*[23]

It surely helped Falcone's position that students were complaining about military style uniforms, but apparently not enough to move the committee along toward making a final decision. Frustrated with the procrastination and in need of new uniforms by fall, Leonard, with solid brass conviction, took matters into his own hands.

> **Leonard Falcone:** *We couldn't come to a clear decision and so I went to the president (John Hannah) and he said, "Leonard, what do* you *want?" I said, "This is what I want." And the president said, "If that's what you want, go ahead. You're the director of the band."*
>
> *After all that! And then they criticized us for being dogmatic and so forth. (Raps table) But if you have a position, make it! I had to have them (the uniforms) for the next fall! The next time we got new uniforms (in 1964) no committee, no problem—nothing.*[24]

> **Beryl Falcone:** *Leonard always had a good relationship with John. A professional, warm friendship. John's wife, Sarah, was the daughter of his predecessor, President Shaw, and Leonard had been close to President Shaw's family. They always came to all the concerts.*[25]

New uniforms had a larger importance to the band than the public would ever know. In addition to being morale boosters, new uniforms meant that the band could provide more contemporary halftime shows. Since World War II, some bands across the nation had replaced their usual gridiron performances of stagnant pictures and simple block-letter formations with clever scripts, movements, and themes. Several schools, among them the University of Michigan, even had been offering their audiences dance routines as early as the late 1940s. But the military uniforms of the MSC band required military-type maneuvers which, out of respect, could not include dancing or loose movements. Even the military cap was a problem that prevented a more modern show: it fell to the ground if its wearer bowed to the audience.

Not that State's band committees hadn't tried to modernize by following pop music trends. They had—whether their director "got it," or not.

> **Ted Thompson, clarinet, MSC Band 1949-1953, 1956-'57:** *One of my friends from the 1945- 1950 marching band told me a story that demonstrates how Leonard didn't always "get" things. This may be partly because he had spent his youth in Italy and so didn't quite understand American culture, but I also think it was just in his nature.*
>
> *In the late '40s, those in the jazz community used the term "hep-cat" for anyone who was really "cool." This was soon shortened to just "cat" for anyone of the male persuasion. During that time, a small group of band members often met with Leonard in his office to come up with ideas and plan half-time shows. The shows back then were basically picture formations with a story of some sort to connect them. At one of these brainstorming sessions, the students' ideas were taking shape when one of them said, "At this point, we can have a "cat" walk in from the end zone and join the formation."*
>
> *When the ideas for the show seemed complete, Leonard, totally perplexed, said, "I like this show. But I don't understand why would we have a cat come onto the field. . . and how are we going to train a cat to join the band formation?"*[26]

**John Underwood, clarinet, MSC 1946-1950:** *During the 1946-'50 period, as I recall, a short be-bop jazz number was a part of a football half-time show. Dr. Falcone, during an inside rehearsal, innocently asked the band to play the "Bo Peep!"*[27]

But a new day dawned on September 2, 1952, when at the Michigan State-Michigan game (State 27, Michigan 13!) the 120-member band, the largest ever, appeared for the first time on the field in magnificent new kelly green uniforms with white trim, cross belts, shoulder knots, trouser stripes, arm bands, spats, and a hat with a green and white plume.

**Fritz Stansell:** *When we ripped out onto the field at Ann Arbor with flashy new uniforms, a fast tempo, updated arrangements, kick turns, high steps, etc., etc., the MSU fans gave us a terrific reception. The attitude that the band was out of date changed*

*Charting a show*
*~ courtesy of Michigan State University Archives & Historical Collections*

*overnight. But the U of M student body groaned and laughed derisively, assuming that MSC was stealing the U of M band brand. Of course, what they didn't know was that Revelli, a few years earlier, had hired Jack Lee, his assistant band director for marching, away from OSU, where the fast tempos, high steps, and eight to five had first begun.*[28]

**Joe Dobos:** *Revelli created this aura that Michigan was the first to do something, when actually they weren't the first. . . though they did it very well.*[29]

Meanwhile, over at the Oldsmobile plant in Lansing, new leadership was being ushered in as Jack Wolfram took over as general manager in December, 1950. Wolfram, a friend of the gregarious John Hannah, had earned the nickname "Black Jack." And not without cause. An authoritarian, died in the wool engineer, "Mr. Wolfram," as he was addressed by subordinates, was not only a taskmaster but also something of a character. In 1949, when famous Indy winner Wilbur Shaw drove a Rocket 88 convertible pace car at the Indianapolis 500, it was Olds' then chief engineer, "Black Jack" Wolfram, who rode shotgun. Perhaps this experience developed a taste for speed in the new general manager, as he went on to test Rocket V-8 refinements by using the streets of Lansing as his proving ground. Wolfram would pair with the new chief engineer, Harold Metzel, in one prototype, while former general manager Sherrod Steele and assistant chief engineer Lowell Kintigh rode in a second. As the two cars roared down South Logan Street side-by-side, Wolfram's remained safely (all things being relative) on the right, leaving Steele and Kintigh's in the left lane to dodge oncoming traffic. Wolfram got a big kick out of it all, but Steele anxiously recalled a few near misses.[30]

One Saturday when Wolfram attended a State football game as Hannah's guest in his press box, he posed a question to the university president.

**Beryl Falcone:** *Wolfram became interested in the band at halftime and asked John what he could do for the university.*[31]

**Leonard Falcone:** . . . *and President Hannah said, "What would you say if I asked you to sponsor the band on some of its trips?"*[32*] *Suddenly, I was approached by the president and Oldsmobile with the idea, and we agreed. We accepted their proposal.*[33]

Arrangements were quickly made, and on June 11, 1953, it was announced that the Michigan State Band would appear at the Minnesota and Ohio State games the following fall, courtesy of Oldsmobile. That same month, Excalibur, a senior men's honorary, gave its annual award to "the faculty member who has contributed most in the interest of the students during the past year" to Leonard.[34]

**Leonard Falcone:** *The next thing that happened was that (Olds) felt the band should play the Oldsmobile song at games. There was some sort of printed edition of (it) for dance band, but I wanted one special for our band and so I contracted to have an arrangement made. We played it, tried it out during the summer. The officials from Oldsmobile came to hear, and they were just delighted with it. And so they paid for the trips we made out of town, even to Ann Arbor. We played the song sometimes during time outs. That's the only request they ever made. They were very considerate, very, very, cooperative, and they were a tremendous help.*[35]

Not only had the annual search for financial assistance and the last minute scheduling of trips ended, but more importantly, because of post WW2 enrollments, new uniforms, and Oldsmobile funding, the band was poised and ready to play a significant role in MSC's long climb to the apex of countrywide recognition.[36*]

All it needed now was opportunity, and that opportunity presented itself that fall 1953, when MSC started competing in the Big Ten Athletic Conference.

**Fritz Stansell:** *It was the first football season MSC was eligible for the Rose Bowl, and when the team came through with a series of wins and tied for the Big Ten football title, it was chosen (on a Sunday night, November 22) to go to Pasadena.*[37]

**Leonard Falcone:** *The trip we made to the Rose Bowl the first time—I don't know how many meetings we had, but there were 10 or 15 people, the top people at Oldsmobile. In many instances they would simply pick up the telephone and contact someone in San Francisco or Denver and say, "We need this or that, will you arrange for so many buses and trucks to meet the band at this time and have a police escort and food for everyone?" It was just amazing. And dependable. No question about it. It was done.*[38]

**Fritz Stansell:** *The band traveled West by special train, all paid for by Oldsmobile.*[39]

The train, bearing banners marked "Michigan State Marching Band Enroute to Rose Bowl," was a 12-car Rock Island special with 7 Pullmans, 2 lounge cars (one with a glass vistadome), two diners, and a baggage car painted green for the occasion. As it pulled out of Lansing's Grand Trunk station on Saturday, December 26, at 11:55 p.m., it carried 120 band members, 10 alternates, one drum major, three baton twirlers, six cheerleaders, one "Sparty" mascot, and several managers and officials.

**Robert Sack:** *(It) was an exciting experience. We slept and ate in style, and the food was wonderful. It was just an awful lot of fun—a neat trip. I remember a lot of nights playing cards on the train. There was wonderful camaraderie.*[40]

**Ted Thompson:** *With the exception of two nights at Occidental College in Pasadena, we lived nearly two weeks on that train. The cars converted into sleeper cars at night, and the meals in the dining car were outstanding.*[41]

As the relatively unknown, often mockingly labeled "cow college" or "Moo U"[42*] band pioneered across America over plains, mountains, and deserts on its way to the West Coast, tens of thousands heard them play as they stopped in big city centers, and were calling them "great." When a silly rumor had it that State's "horntooters" must be paid professionals and that "the Spartan Foundation" (whatever that was) was being investigated by the Big Ten for "proselytizing and subsidizing" bandsmen who had obviously been "as carefully picked as halfbacks," there was this to say:

> **Leonard Falcone:** *I know of no one who got a Cadillac for playing in our band.*

> **Jim Marugg, reporter, *Pasadena Star News*:** *That may be true, Professor Falcone, but how about Oldsmobiles?*[43]

But the acclaim was just beginning: the 1954 Rose Bowl band trip was to be a Michigan State College media coup of immense proportions.

> **Fritz Stansell:** *We stopped in Kansas City, El Paso, and other cities along the way (Oklahoma City and Tucson) playing "The Michigan State Fight Song," "In My Merry Oldsmobile," and*

*All Aboard!*
*~ courtesy of the Falcone family*

> *"California, Here I Come" in parades in each location. The local Oldsmobile dealer had convertibles, of course, with the local beauty queens on board as part of the promotion.*[44]

And leading the parades were the Falcones and the Olds officials, followed by a papier-mâché-headed Sparty, a drum major, 3 twirlers, and finally, the band itself. In Kansas City, after the band played a 7 p.m. Sunday concert in the station plaza, Leonard received a gold key to the city. In Oklahoma City, the band paraded through the town before thousands of locals with "prancing, dancing steps," and "lilting, brassy music,"[45] and was presented by city mayor Allen Street with a commendation which named it "ambassadors of goodwill" and recommended it to "people of other cities and stations and of the nations beyond the borders of the US." And when it came to El Paso, it awoke to a special treat, one especially sweet to flatlander Michiganders: mountains!

> **Dick Goodrow, 1954–1955 band manager, publicity:** *Most of our members (had) never been west of Kansas City. They were really excited. . .when they saw mountains. Only a few had ever seen (them) before. They rushed off the train to buy souvenirs, and some of them came back with 10 gallon hats.*[46]

Afterward, the band strutted a mile through the city in front of 5,000 spectators, instruments swinging to a lively cadence, and then played a concert in front of the Hotel Cortez. There, they were given miniature cowboy hats with pin attachments as mementos of their visit. On its stop further west, in Tucson, Leonard was lassoed by a cowboy (but "freed" before the big parade), "tried" in a mock trial in front of a horde of Arizonians, and nearly strung up by the crowd. For real.[47]

> **Leonard Falcone:** *As our special train pulled into the station at Tucson we were greeted in a regular Western style by the shouting and gun-shooting local Vigilantes. A quartet of tough-looking gents from the Vigilantes quickly surrounded and escorted me to a small wooden plank in front of the railroad station for a mock*

*lynching ceremony. There was a large crowd gathered to watch the spectacle. Just when the rope was being adjusted around my neck, someone in the crowd accidentally kicked the wooden plank from under my feet. Fortunately, two of the Vigilantes had their hands under my arms and caught my fall. Nevertheless . . . the sharp pull of the rope around my neck caused my head to suddenly veer to one side and made my face cringe. At that moment there was a roar of laughter from the crowd and the members of my band. Evidently the grimace on my face looked like the real stuff because afterward many people remarked about my acting ability. Perhaps the kicking of the wooden plank from under my feet was part of the show and not accidental. But believe me, I was grateful for those strong hands of the Vigilantes who held me up when the rope tightened around my neck—otherwise, there might have been a real lynching party at my expense!*[48]

In addition to receiving a sombrero, for being a good sport Falcone was made an honorary vigilante of the 50-member posse, which then led MSC's band and the omnipresent "Sparty" in a march through the city in front of several thousand cheering spectators.

One city at a time, as they crossed the country, their reputation grew,[49] until at last, under the national media spotlight in Pasadena, the band simply took the nation by storm.

Getting to that point had not been easy. Earlier that fall, Falcone's plan to hover over the band in a helicopter (for perspective) while shouting drill instructions through a loudspeaker was mercifully aborted when there were no helicopters available for the job[50] and he had to train his band from his usual perch atop a ladder. An idea to keep "the boys" on campus for four extra days over Christmas break to prepare for the trip worked out better, though it was not without challenges: there was the "Winter Wonderland's" brittle 20-degree weather to contend with.

**Leonard Falcone:** *Preparing the band for an outdoor performance in frigid weather, snow, and sleet is a tremendous handicap. The other Big Ten band directors told me that (there) would be a lot of work, but I really didn't expect (that) to happen.*[51]

It had been cold, all right. The snow and slippery ground had driven the band off the field and to the Auditorium to practice, which was, at half the size, so small that all movements had to be shrunk down and then re-inflated in California. But it had worked, and Leonard, along with C. Oscar Stover ("Oscar the Charter"),[52]* the drillmaster, and Gene Hickman, the drum major, were confident that the band with its 174 steps a minute "hat tip," "double to the rear," "hesitation step," and other sharp maneuvers, was ready to wow the crowds on the trail west to the Rose Bowl show.[53]

> **Gene Hickson, drum major 1951–1954, civil engineering major:** *All told, the men spent over 34 hours to practice for a 12-minute show, plus the uncountable hours spent in the charting room. It (added) up to the hardest show (we'd ever) done.*[54]

*It's all smiles after the Vigilante mock hanging in Tucson on the way to the 1954 Rose Bowl.*
*~ courtesy of Michigan State University Archives & Historical Collections*

But the band's marching skills were just the half of it. There had also been 25 musical numbers for the band to memorize and prepare.

> **Earle Louder:** *Mr. Falcone always had us, since the first time I went in 1950 to band camp, memorize music to be played at a moment's call. He would call the name and we would play it.*[55]

> **Leonard Falcone:** *It's not enough to get a band together and have its members merely go through marching formations. Musicianship is equally important. The sound of a band is half of its reputation. Sure, you can plan a show full of fancy footwork and formations, but if a band doesn't have the sound it should, it's only a marching unit.*[56]

After the band marched and played a concert upon arrival in Pasadena on December 30 for the crowd gathered at the Alhambra Station, it pitched camp at Occidental College and rehearsed there in the warm California sun, putting the finishing touches on routines.

Before game day, a march up Wilshire Boulevard to the Ambassador Hotel ended in a concert and marching exhibition on the lawn. Meanwhile, newspapers were predicting an extraordinary parade and half time show from the Spartan Band, one even having forecasted before their arrival that "Michigan State's band (will) defeat UCLA's musical marchers by three tubas and an extra glockenspiel."[57] And the band didn't disappoint. In the three hour 6.5-mile-long 65th Annual Tournament of Roses Parade, the lively group strutted behind the leading unit from the local junior college, impressing crowds at every turn with its cockiness and flair.

> **Leonard Falcone:** *The band (had) remarkable spirit. I think that's what pulled them through, especially in the parade when in every block people on all sides were clamoring for them to play. Only three times. . .were the band members at rest, and then only for a few seconds were they able to relax under the burden of their instruments . . . Tubas weigh 60 pounds each!*[58]

**Ted Thompson:** *The Rose Bowl parade was a 6.5 mile long parade. There was so much marching I remember the balls of my feet being really sore at the end.*[59]

**Robert Sack:** *We had to get up really early in the morning, about 5 a.m. We did a lot of waiting around before we marched those 6.5 miles, but it was worth the wait. I still remember the newspapers. They couldn't say enough good things about us.*[60]

**Seth Whitmore, reporter, *Lansing State Journal*:** *All along the route of the Rose parade, the Spartan band received a thunderous ovation from the 1,500,000 spectators. No other unit in the parade was so well received.*[61]

*Leonard with Oscar Stover and 1956 co-drum-majors Archie Patton Jr. and Richard R. Morsches*
*~ courtesy of Michigan State University Archives & Historical Collections*

Directly behind State's band was Michigan's Rose Bowl parade float, with 20,000 live flowers (100 dozen of which were tulips) depicting books titled "Agriculture," "Vacationland," and "Industry," flanked by two 17 foot tall bronze Spartan statues serving as bookends; adjacent was a factory, sailboat, barn and silo made entirely of flowers, and at the very front of the float rode Michigan State's own Dee Means, "Miss Big Ten" of 1954, sitting in sea of green maidenhair fern in a white dress (Get it? Those are State's school colors), under a fruit tree in bloom.[62]

> **Robert Sack:** *After the parade, we had boxed lunches and boarded a bus for the stadium, where we played at the football game. . . we had developed the kick step where we would raise our left knee on a couple of beats. Anyway, I still remember that the UCLA band put on their performance first in the pre-game, and then MSC's band burst from the tunnel in double file doing the kick step—and the stadium just erupted. They had never seen a band with that kind of step and cadence.*[63]

Newsmen covering the game had apparently never seen anything like it, either.

> **Ken Lewis, reporter, *Pasadena Star News*:** *What . . .about the 1954 spectacle will live the longest in the memory of those who saw it?. . . the "out of this world" marching of the Michigan State Band. If the Bruins were impressive (and they were) the Spartans were sensational. From the moment they pranced onto the field in double time, using their famous "hesitation step," you knew why they've been acclaimed the nation's best.*[64]

Exploding onto the field in the brash manner that was making it famous, it took only seconds for the band to form ranks and files so straight they could be used as wallpaper plumb lines. With their unique power to create a musical tension of order and excitement, they immediately challenged the Bruins with the "The Michigan State Fight Song" and then, before forming "UCLA." and playing "Sing UCLA." and joining the

UCLA band in "The Star Spangled Banner," they presented an intricate Mexican dance routine to the tune of "The Peanut Vendor."

> **Fritz Stansell:** *Dr. Owen Reed's student, Jack Kimmel, wrote some fine arrangements especially for that trip, and "Peanut Vendor" was one of them.*[65]

> **H. Owen Reed:** *It was a great forward looking jazz related arrangement that was far removed from the usual transcription for band. Shortly after the Rose Bowl I flew to L.A. for a performance of a work of mine, and I was visiting with my seatmate when the subject of MSC's band came up. "What a great band!" he said. "After that game, half the band conductors in California were fired!" I told him that Jack's arrangement was a large part of that.*[66]

The "Peanut Vendor" along with "The Gandy Dancer's Ball," became one of the two most popular tunes of the trip.

Staged below a backdrop of hazy mountains, the halftime entertainment theme featured the band's "Visit to California," with a formation of a San Francisco cable car moving to the tune of "Clang, Clang, Clang Went the Trolley," a Hollywood meeting with Bugs Bunny, and a giant electric sign spelling out "Rose Bowl." The show ended with the block MSC formation and State's Alma Mater. It was thrilling pageantry of the first order, and the Michigan State Band "got the biggest hand of the afternoon."[67] It was well deserved.

> **Alan Ward, reporter, *Oakland Tribune*:** *There probably is no other college band in the country to compare with the Michigan Staters. They play well, march with the precision of West Pointers (if not with the same stately dignity) and engage in midfield precision stunts which would make the Rockettes turn green with envy. UCLA has a clever band, and almost as large as the one from Michigan State, but while the Spartans were trouncing the Bruins on the football field yesterday, the Spartan musicians were playing musical rings around the Uclan tooters and drum beaters.*[68]

High praise, but ironically, the band's best moment came after the game ended.

> **Seth Whitmore, reporter, *Lansing State Journal*:** *Everyone was impressed over the great pep the Spartan musicians possessed after the game was over. The band took the field immediately after the final gun sounded, and for nearly an hour they played and went through their snappy drills. They were immediately surrounded by thousands. . .*[69]

> **Leonard Falcone:** *The most thrilling part of it all was the crowds which surrounded the band after the Rose Bowl game . . . They listened and cried, "More! More!" That's when we really put on a show—with plenty of time, and feeling pretty happy of course.*[70]

In all, the mob called for nine encores.

January 1, 1954, was to go down in history as the day a volcanic green earthquake shook the Rose Bowl. Not only did the band rock the stadium, but the team did, too. Coming back from 14–0, in a dramatic second half eruption of touchdowns and a last minute field goal, it ended the contest with a score of 28–20. It was a terrific game, and it was famed Coach Biggie Munn's last.[71*]

Following the Rose Bowl, the band boarded their special train and headed for San Francisco and the East-West Shrine Bowl game, where their smart high stepping march up Market St. and later at the pregame and halftime festivities at Kezar Stadium dazzled thousands of San Franciscans and game spectators. That evening, some of the bandsmen headed for one of the clubs in town to hear Woody Herman play.[72]

After sightseeing on the 3rd, they departed the West Coast for parade dates in both Salt Lake City, where they toured the Mormon Tabernacle, and Denver, where Leonard received another Stetson, this time from Gov. Dan Thorton on the statehouse grounds. Finally, they arrived in Lansing—tired, but none the worse for wear, and in time for classes to begin.

All told, tens of thousands had seen the Michigan State Band march in cities across America, 1,500,00 had seen them in the Tournament of Roses parade, over 101,000 spectators had watched them perform at the Rose Bowl, 62,000 had enjoyed their show at Kezar stadium,[73] and perhaps millions had viewed them on television. Falcone estimated that the band had played "The Michigan State Fight Song" 120 times before the Rose Bowl had even begun,[74] and countless times afterward. By the time the band's 12-day adventure ended and it returned to cheering well-wishers at the Grand Trunk Railroad Station in Lansing on January 6, 1954, the words "On the banks of the Red Cedar, there's a school that's known to all" were no longer an empty boast. They were fact.

The following fall term brought with it the introduction of a humorous student newsletter, the *Spartan Bandsman*, which highlighted the week's rehearsal trials and poked fun of clueless marchers or the opposing band. Published prior to each game by the band officers and a special committee, it has continued, although sporadically, to this day *(see Appendix J)*. The season also brought high school bandsmen from around Michigan to perform and observe State's crack marching unit for themselves at MSC's first annual Band Day on November 7, 1954, when twenty-one bands were invited to participate in a salute to the Sousa Centennial (1854-1954) and the upcoming Michigan State College Centennial in 1955. In the musical highlight of the 1954–1955 school year, the winter concert on March 6, 1955 (the Centennial Concert), the band welcomed as its first guest conductor, Falcone's friend and one of the world's most famous band conductors and composers, the energetic maestro Edwin Franko Goldman.[75]* Later, at the end of the summer, Falcone originated a Marching Band Clinic in conjunction with the Continuing Education Department, and invited Manley Whitcomb of Florida State and Clarence Sawhill of UCLA as guest clinicians.

Another exciting 1955 centennial year event was that the State of Michigan officially made the school a university. MSC thus became the "Michigan State University of Agriculture and Applied Science," a name it kept until 1964 when it was changed simply to "Michigan State University." To add to the celebration, the team and band were again invited to represent the Big Ten at the Rose Bowl for the second time in three years, with Oldsmobile once more footing the bill at a cost of $100,000.[76]

As an advance guard of 1,225 headed for the Union Pacific East Los Angeles train station in what was the start of "the largest non-military mass movement across the nation in memory,"[77] the Spartan band was close behind, stopping only to sightsee or march in parades such as the event-packed one in Las Vegas—where they were herded onto buses, taken on a guided tour of Boulder Dam, and brought back to their train for dinner, where they changed into their uniforms so they could march down the strip, perform a concert, and pack onto buses again for a nighttime tour. By the time they arrived at the Union Pacific train station in East L.A., thousands there roared in welcome, including MSU alumni groups, representatives of UCLA, MSU beauty queen Rhosan Dobben, and Big Ten Clubs. In addition to appearing in the 67th Annual Tournament of Roses Parade and performing with extraordinary synchronization at the pregame and halftime shows (theme: "The Story of the American Dance Band") at the Bowl game on January 2, 1956, the 130 member band, 35 of whom had previously appeared in the 1954 Rose Bowl, marched not only the streets of Las Vegas, but also Denver, Los Angeles, Tucson, Dallas, and St. Louis en route to and from Pasadena, and even appeared on The Bob Crosby CBS television show. The '56 Rose Bowl was another media coup for Leonard and the Michigan State Marching Band, one which brought the school great honor and placed Leonard on the Mt. Rushmore of college music world giants. Though he was never pleased with personal attention, he was delighted by the spotlight that had been placed on the band.

> **Earl C. Boitel, Jr., trumpet/cornet, MSU 1956:** *I recall Professor Falcone once saying, "1952 through 1956 were my most exciting years, what with our new green and white band uniforms and the introduction of the "kick step" and our performing in two Rose Bowls."*[78]

The Rose Bowl attention had triggered a cascade of superlatives for the Spartan Marching Band—brilliant, extraordinary, outstanding—

and had placed it at a wheel hub of public awareness with the Concert Band relegated to the rim. But that was about to change, as the Concert Band, too, was catapulted to national fame.

> **Leonard Falcone:** *It wasn't until Oldsmobile began sponsoring our band on trips that we began to get exposure. That was the first it came about. And the next thing, we were invited to play in Ann Arbor for the first time for the Midwest. And that really broke the wall, so to speak, as far as the (concert) band was concerned. People couldn't believe it! . . . (They) began to hear our band. . . and they said, "Where have you been all this time?" . . . And about the same time we were invited to perform for the MENC (Music*

*President Hannah, Leonard Falcone, Jack Wolfram. The "Oh-h-h!" band formation is in tribute to Oldsmobile's plan to send the 125 piece MSU Marching Band to the 1956 Rose Bowl.*
*~ courtesy of Michigan State University Archives & Historical Collections*

*Leonard on high*
*~ courtesy of Michigan State University Archives & Historical Collections*

*Las Vegas 1956 Rose Bowl trip*
*~ courtesy of Michigan State University Archives & Historical Collections*

> *Educators' National Conference) at the national convention in Chicago. And all of it paid for. And that was an eye opener for all these people from all over the country.*[79] *Mr. Hodgson was head of the department and he came back just bubbling with enthusiasm. He . . . talked to the band at a rehearsal and said, "I wish I could tell you how the people mobbed me in Chicago after your performance to tell me what a wonderful thing they'd heard. They didn't even know where Michigan State was located, some of them." And so it's that pride, they took greater pride in the band, they appreciated the fact the band was up to the level it should be.*[80]

When the Concert Band was invited to perform for the Michigan School Band and Orchestra Association's Midwestern Conference on School Vocal and Instrumental Music ("The Midwest") at Ann Arbor's

Hill Auditorium 1958, it was offered a unique opportunity to carry the Michigan State-Michigan rivalry from the gridiron to the concert hall. The conference, held the second weekend in January, naturally had always been the showplace for the University of Michigan Band. But there was a problem in accepting the engagement since the time between the end of marching season when the Concert Band normally began to function and the January performance was slim—and with a long holiday break between. But with Stover's assistance with the Marching Band, Leonard felt free to suggest an unprecedented fall rehearsal schedule for the Concert Band which began the first week of school and included a two-hour practice every Tuesday evening. The result was that the audience of about 3,000, including most of Michigan's school band directors, was astounded at the beautiful tone, sensitive playing, and brilliant technique of Michigan State's band.[81*]

> **Leonard Falcone:** *(Revelli was) a public relations man, 100%, as well as a good musician. . . and with his tremendous facilities and resources, which we don't have at (State), he was able to develop a national image. Our band had been held down because it was not known. But in Ann Arbor there were people from all over. . . a tremendous exposure. I'd meet people later in my travels, and they'd say, "I was there! My, what a performance!" From that point, on, I personally became known throughout the country, and that led to other engagements.*

> **Myron Welch, clarinet, bassoon, MSU band 1962-1966:** *Many people told me how it just shocked everybody. In their words, (State) outdid the University of Michigan band.*

> **Leonard Falcone:** *Yes, they told me that, too.*[82]

It was also in 1956 that the annual meeting of the College Band Directors National Association's North Central Division was held at Michigan State and Leonard, chairman of the North Central Division, served as host. There, from his "bully pulpit," he decried what he saw as a lack of new and exciting works for band in a speech to the membership.[83*]

**Leonard Falcone:** *What American bands need is original band music. Bands . . . suffer from a lack of new music and are forced to keep on playing over and over the same familiar pieces.*[84]

If a lack of original band works were the problem, then James Niblock, Leonard discovered, was at least in part the answer. At the 1956 winter concert, held during the two day CBDNA conference, the band premiered his "Soliloquy and Dance" in addition to three other original band numbers by other composers.

Another way Falcone found to bring some new excitement in his work and keep from playing the same familiar tunes over and over came in 1957, when 60 members of the Concert Band made their debut as a chamber band during the winter concert. The select group allowed him to work with a new sonority that was both challenging and exciting; it learned more rapidly than the full band and was able to perform a new catalog of band literature such as Haydn's "Concerto for Trumpet," Morrissey's flute solo "Hoopla," Paganini' s "Perpetual Motion," and the delicate "Dance of the Hours" ballet music from Ponchielli's opera "La Gioconda."[85]

The Concert Band had been making several one night tours under the auspices of Cap and Gown Series (since 1954), Michigan State's educational and entertainment service. But because the 1958 Concert Band had had more time than ever to prepare, Falcone planned a four-day tour during spring vacation which included the Michigan cities of Portage, Mt. Pleasant, Cadillac, Petoskey, Traverse City, Big Rapids, and Grand Rapids—a PR move that not only increased the band's exposure, but also allowed prospective music students to hear it and consider MSU. After their spring tour of the Upper Peninsula the following year, 1959, Dr. William Sur, chairman of MSU's music education department, invited the Concert Band to play at the North Central Division of the Music Educators' National Conference on May 8 in Chicago. It was all paid for by Oldsmobile, the only time they paid for a Concert Band trip.[86]

**Leonard Falcone:** *From a serious musical point of view, (it was) one of the most important engagements the band (had) ever been asked to fill.*[87]

They were a hit. After ending with a performance of H. Owen Reed's "*La Fiesta Mexicana*," they received an enthusiastic standing ovation, rare in those days, particularly from an audience that knew great (or mediocre or terrible) music when it heard it.

Many years later, in March of 1984, Leonard could still recite all the music played for that concert and, in many cases, the names of the students who played it.[88]

CHAPTER 13

# AUTUMN YEARS: 1960–1967

*"Say it with Music"*

**~ Irving Berlin, Music Box Revue song title**

---

Where are the songs of Spring?
Ay, where are they?
Think not of them, thou hast thy music too,
While barred clouds bloom the soft-dying day,
And touch the stubble plains with rosy hue;
Then in a wailful choir the small gnats mourn
Among the river sallows, borne aloft
Or sinking as the light wind lives or dies;
And full-grown lambs loud bleat from hilly bourn;
Hedge-crickets sing; and now with treble soft
The red-breast whistles from a garden-croft;
And gathering swallows twitter in the skies.

~ John Keats
from "To Autumn"

THE CHANGING FACE OF THE MSU CAMPUS lost another landmark in 1960, when the 22 year old band shell, which had been the scene of hundreds of spring concerts and events including commencements, pep rallies, "Lantern Night" and "May Morning Sing" festivities, was razed to make room for a dormitory. It occurred not exactly in the dead of night, but close enough to it, and it was an event that seems to have nearly broken Leonard's heart.

> **Leonard Falcone:** *Nothing was said about the removal of the shell. It was just done. It was knocked down, and Bessy Hall and a parking ramp put up. Not even a consultation, not even a word to me. Since then, there's no place for the band to play, really. A beautiful campus, and there's no place for the band to play.*
>
> *Of course I went to see the president, and he said "Oh, Leonard, don't worry, we have plans, you know, for another shell." He asked someone to look up blueprints for the new shell, but no one could find them. It was to be built a bit further up toward the east on the river. The president said they were waiting for someone to donate the funds, and I suggested they approach Oldsmobile and they could call it the "Olds Band Shell" as a lasting tribute to Mr. Olds. I asked if it would be proper for me to*

*Left: On the field, 1963*
*~ courtesy of the Falcone family*

*Above: Teaching the next generation*
*~ courtesy of Michigan State University Archives & Historical Collections*

> *call the Olds people with the idea. He said "No," and sent me on to (Vice President) Mr. Breslin, who did these sorts of things, and he thought it was a wonderful idea. He told me that these things take time, and "If for six months you don't hear anything, don't worry." Well, it's been over 10 years. Whether he mentioned it to Oldsmobile or not, I don't know, but nothing happened.*
>
> *At the time, we were the only school that had a band shell. No one else had one.*
>
> *Nowadays, students would raise the devil if they had any pride in the shell and realized the history.*[1]

> **Tom Gillette:** *Leonard NEVER got over the razing of the band shell for Ernst Bessey Hall, and spoke rather bitterly about it. He'd say, "They said they would build a new one very soon. . . but of course they never did!"*[2]

It was the end of an era ("balmy . . . spring evenings, out under the trees with music filtering in from afar or more resoundingly near. Young life at its best, and older life look(ing) on approvingly, with applause for present youth and maybe some fond regrets for other days"),[3] an era which for Leonard had undoubtedly marked access to some of the most poignant memories of his childhood. Its razing was not only a reminder to him of the distance he had traveled from home, but a contributor to the decline in the band's spring concert attendance: it went from thousands, to hundreds.

When Bill Moffit was appointed Assistant Director of Bands in September, 1960, he brought a fresh new marching approach to Michigan State. He called it "Patterns in Motion," and it featured not just fancy footwork and his own special arrangements, but more importantly, an almost stereophonic effect to the music as constantly evolving kaleidoscopic patterns that could be appreciated from nearly every seat in the stadium were formed. The innovation re-established Michigan State as a leader in marching band techniques, which at the time were saturated with formations, gimmicks, and picture shows. The 130-man marching band, largest in State's history, kicked off their new signature style at the MSU–Michigan football game (MSU 24, Michigan 17: Go Green!) and started a marching trend that swept the nation and brought the band not just national, but international fame. Moffit and Falcone referred to it, in a letter to the band, as a style that would make the Michigan State Band "the band of tomorrow—today."[4]

> **Leonard Falcone:** *Moffit did excellent work with the marching band here and so he was a big help to me. I appreciated what he did for the band and I admired his ability. He did a lot to popularize the band. Prestige. Exposure.*[5]

> **Walter Hodgson:** *Moffitt—he had considerable expertise with marching band. He whipped (it) into shape, and they liked him.*[6]

"Patterns in Motion" was a revolutionary art form, its influences still felt today in many contemporary marching band styles. It became so popular that Moffit published six books on the technique as well as taught it at band clinics across America. He is also credited with inventing the "spinning of the block-S," which the Spartan Band still uses to open its pregame show.

When in 1960 State's head basketball coach, Forddy Anderson, suggested band music would promote spirit for Spartan basketball, it was Moffit who organized the 50 piece brass and percussion "Spartan Brass Band" that included both men and women. When he also alternated teaching "Techniques of Band Formations" and "Band Arranging" with Falcone during the summers and assistants took over all class instrumental instruction, Leonard's class load became more reasonable than ever before: along with his duties as Director of Bands, he now taught only the applied baritone and tuba students. Perhaps that is why he was able to find the time to collaborate with the First Division Band Course Co. in 1962, with the publication of *The Leonard V. Falcone Baritone Solo Series* and *The Leonard V. Falcone Trombone Solo Series,* and to take a trip with his family to Switzerland, France, England, and Italy during the summer of 1963— the third trip "home" for him, but the first for his family, most of whom his relatives had never met. It was a memorable visit, and one that served to again remind Beryl,

Mary, and Cece that though a proud American, at heart he was as Italian as gelato or the Bernini colonnade.

> **Cece Falcone:** *I remember mom driving and dad getting out somewhere to ask directions. When he got back to the car, he proceeded to give them to her. . . but in Italian!*[7]

> **Beryl Falcone:** *He loved Italian food. We were in Naples and Leonard wanted calamari. He was so excited because he could get it right from the sea! I thought it looked messy and I wouldn't taste it. I didn't want any part of it.*[8]

Daylight lengthened and shortened as the seasons clicked through campus, until suddenly it was January, 1964, and the Concert Band was once again given the honor of performing for the Ann Arbor Midwestern Conference. Musically, all went well. But when six clarinetists stood to play Paganini' s violin extravaganza "Perpetual Motion," a low laughter spread throughout the audience as it took in clarinetist G. James Gholson's legs, cuff bracelets of hairy skin highlighted between his socks and trousers. The trousers, hemmed six inches from the floor to highlight the Marching Band's white spats during fancy footwork, were the cause of President Hannah's being flooded with descriptive letters of the incident from James' friends and embarrassed alumni. The result was that when Falcone approached the President for new uniforms, he got them— and without delay. For the first time, the women in the Concert Band, who had previously worn simple black dresses, had a uniform similar to the men's. Theirs was a forest green A-line skirt and short bolero over a white blouse, while the men wore the same color in a tuxedo-style coat and pants with a dark tuxedo stripe down the trousers, and "Michigan State" written in white across the jacket cuff. The marching Spartans added a white leatherette overlay with a large block "S" on the front, a MSU monogram across the back, white spats, white gloves, and caps of white plastic with two toned green and white plumes.[9]

In an interesting innovation for the 1964 Marching Band, one that worked out quite a bit better than the helicopter idea a decade earlier, Bill Moffit developed a short wave hookup between the press box and 3 men on the field: the drum major, Sam English, and two of the band's bass drummers. English's receiver, a sound device, was placed in his hat, while the drummers had flashing devices mounted on their instruments. The setup was intended to rectify a problem Falcone had encountered across his years as band director.

> **Leonard Falcone:** *A drum major is . . . not a sensitive musician . . . Occasionally, he doesn't set the right tempo.*[10]

With Moffit in the press box controlling the tempo by tapping a 50-cent piece on the short wave transmitter as well as giving verbal instructions to the drum major between numbers, the problem dissolved. One more took its place, however. The weight of the receiver in English's hat often caused it to go lopsided.

Though Marching Band always ended after the football season, in 1964, when it had the opportunity to represent the State of Michi-

*MSU drum line*
*~ courtesy of Michigan State University Archives & Historical Collections*

*1964–1965 Concert Band*
*~ courtesy of Michigan State University Archives & Historical Collections*

gan during Michigan Week Activities at the New York World's Fair, it was recalled for the May celebration. Oldsmobile once again paid for expenses, this time transporting the band for the first time by air. The band first played at the Waldorf at an alumni breakfast being held there, and then appeared at the fairgrounds, where it marched the mile from the main gate to the United States Pavilion, then on to the Belgian Rathskeller, where it left behind Michigan's Gov. Romney and New York's Gov. Nelson Rockefeller. In gratitude for Oldsmobile's support, it gave a special concert at the General Motors Pavilion on the fairgrounds to a crowd which included most of the 1,200 loyal Michiganders who had stormed the exposition in support of "Michigan Day." Later, in a four encore concert from the lower plaza of Rockefeller Plaza, the band "shook the walls of the concrete canyon" as hundreds of New Yorkers stopped to listen and see the show on their way home from work.[11]

The 1964 marching season was notable for a number of reasons, most good. Very good. But the riot at Notre Dame (State 7, ND 34) stands as an exception. There, the band took as much of a beating as the football team as one bandsman was knocked unconscious, many others suffered minor injuries, and serious damage was done to instruments.

> **Merritt Lutz, drum line, MSU 1962-1967:** *We were marching in the stadium, and as we came through the tunnel the dormitories were on the left. We had these hats with chin straps and a plume bolted on top, and as I glanced to the back of the band I saw a little clarinet player—we had clarinets back then—and a Notre Dame guy and a girl who had come up behind him. He didn't know what was happening. They were trying to reach up and steal the plume, but that would have hurt the kid, who was about 5'2", and it would have ripped the hat. Anyway, when I saw it, I said to the guy next to me, "Bill, I'm going back there —you keep playing," and he said, "Yeah, okay." So I go back and I'm gonna hit the Notre Dame guy over the head with my drumstick and when I run up to him I can see he is frightened. I thought, "Good!" and I took a swing to hit him over the head—but I missed and hit his knuckles, and he cried "eh!" and began hopping around. Mission accomplished. When I turned to go back to the band, I saw that the whole drum section had followed me out. Once I broke rank, they did too—and they were all fighting because the dorms had begun to unload and the Notre Dame students were running out to join the brawl. So when the drums quit playing, the band quit marching, and all of a sudden everyone was fighting like crazy. I had a friend of mine wrap his trumpet around someone's head, another guy hit somebody with his baritone, and some of the drummers were beating guys with their drum sticks.*[12]

Bill Wiley (cornet, MSU 1964–1968), who had come back from the melee unscathed and with his cornet bent nearly in half, spoke of the Notre Dame riot with some pride for the rest of his life. He had held his own, and maybe then some, and had an icon to prove it.

> **Fritz Stansell:** *I remember Leonard telling me, and I believe this is a direct quotation, "In all my years at MSU I had rarely let the band out of my sight. I was dumbfounded by what I saw."*[13]

> **Merritt Lutz:** *Falcone was in the men's room when it happened. He had gone to the bathroom. I was the band's drum line leader and*

*he ran up to me and said, "What's happening?" and I said, "Looks like they are fighting to me." And he said, "I can see they are fighting, goddammit! Stop them!" So I started playing the Series*[14]* *and the drummers picked up their drums and gathered around me. Eventually the band came back and lined up with their hats broken and parts of their uniforms ripped off and we all marched back to the buses looking like a bunch of homeless people or something. Leonard, too. Somebody stole his hat. Took it right off his head.*

*When we went back on Monday and met in the band room, Leonard asked, "Does anyone know what happened?" And I looked around at the drummers thinking, "If you guys tell on me, I'm dead." And someone said, "They just came out of the dorms and attacked us!"*

*Later, when he talked with me about it privately, he said, "Goddammit, and they took my hat, too!"*[15]

The 175-piece Marching Band, the largest in MSU's history, returned to Notre Dame to play at the annual game the following year (State 12, ND 3), after football coach Ara Parseghian and Fr. Theodore M. Hesburgh, Notre Dame's president, sternly warned the students to be on their best behavior.

**Leonard Falcone:** *They (ND) expressed many regrets. They paid for damage to the instruments and there (were) several entreaties for us to return. We (felt) we should go back there to show (there were) no hard feelings.*[16]

**Merritt Lutz:** *I thought, "Those jerks! Those jerks!" The whole country was down on them. The next year we had to go back, and then the year later, too. And when we went back there they treated us like royalty.*[17]

On a more personal level, 1964 was the year Leonard made the first in three volumes of recordings for baritone which, to this day, remain staples in the recommended literature for the euphonium. ("Leonard Falcone and His Baritone," "Leonard Falcone—Baritone Volume II," and "Leonard Falcone—Baritone Horn") in Golden Crest Records' Virtuoso Recital Series in 1964, 1966, and 1969 with Joseph Evans, MSU's piano accompanist. *The Instrumentalist* magazine, in a critical review, claimed that Leonard demonstrated his "sound musicianship" and "competent performance and feeling for . . . various styles."[18]

The "various styles," reminiscent to students who studied with him of his programming suggestions for their recitals, are primarily traditional pieces from the Romantic, Baroque, and Classical periods, with little that is contemporary. The recordings survive today in CD and mp3 formats[19*] as part of Falcone's enduring musical legacy, and though the selections themselves may be unsurprising, what continues to thrill and astonish the listener are the infinite, deeply musical gradations of Falcone's lustrous tone and velvety touch, each phrase a discovery and an adventure of the imagination. Four years after the final volume was produced, Leonard's competitive rival, a man not known for his effusive compliments, had this to say about Leonard as a musician:

*Leonard with his recordings*
*~ courtesy of the Falcone family*

**William D. Revelli, Director of Bands, University of Michigan:** *As a euphonium soloist, he simply is the greatest of our time, possessing a beautiful, vibrant, rich tone, impeccable technique, control, and sterling musicianship; a truly great artist.*[20]

Many years later, a nostalgic Revelli again spoke kindly about Leonard.

**Bob Piatt, Sousaphone, MSU Marching Band, 1958-1960:** *I have been a member of the Ann Arbor Concert Band for nearly 30 years, and during one of those years Dr. Revelli was our director. He was over 90 years old at the time. When I asked him what he recalled of Leonard Falcone, his responses reflected his utmost respect for him as a musician and friend. He was pleased to have the opportunity to talk about him.*[21]

In January, 1965, the Spartan Marching Band, again sponsored by Oldsmobile, was recalled to march in President Lyndon B. Johnson's Inaugural Parade, making Johnson the fourth President to hear the Michigan State Band under Falcone's direction and the fifth to hear the band. Though Inaugural Parade rules limited bands to 100, an exception was made for Michigan State and all 155 members marched. Described by the television announcer as "The finest band in the Midwest, a place known for its fine bands," it swung into the "MSU Fight Song" as it moved within earshot of the president.[22] But not without some serious drama in the drum section first.

**Merritt Lutz:** *We were invited to the 1965 inaugural parade and we took trains out to D.C. The band was very large, though not as large as today, and the streets in Washington are very narrow. As we were coming up to the White House there was a place where the band was on three different streets at the same time. It was hard to see and to know what was going on. The drummers were behind the tubas and you can't see anything behind those guys. You can't hear anything, either, and the crowd was going crazy. So the tubas turned to me and said, "The drum major wants the roll off." You have to remember the drums don't*

> *play the roll off until the section leader, which was me, blows the whistle. But I can't see the drum major and I can't hear anything, and the tuba guys kept saying, "He wants a roll off!" So I blow the whistle that signals one, and as we're playing it I see a sign that says,* "BANDS DO NOT PLAY OR YOU WILL BE REMOVED FROM THE COURSE," *and at the same time I see Falcone with fire in his eyes coming at me and screaming to the band, "Don't play! Don't play!" because there were other bands around the corner already playing for the President. Leonard is running through the drum line grabbing drum sticks and holding people back and screaming, "Son of a bitch!" We went right back to playing the Series, and once we did that we were fine: we came down Pennsylvania Avenue and played the roll off again, this time at the right moment, and performed for the President.*
>
> *Leonard called me in on Monday and asked, "Why did you do that?" And when I told him, he said, "Don't ever listen to tubas or sassaphones. Never!"*[23]

"Sassaphones?". . .er, saxophones? What do they have to do with the price of peas? The answer, as it turns out, is relatively simple: "jazz music" was an oxymoron as far as Leonard Falcone was concerned, and the "sassaphone" was its symbol. He flat out didn't like them.

> **Fritz Stansell:** *At MSC in the '50s, it was not allowed to major on saxophone. If you were a saxophonist, you were required to study clarinet, and if you wanted to have a jazz band, you had to play or rehearse at the Union or in a dormitory. It was so ridiculous at MSC that the music school hired a man, Mr. Gorton, whose job description included patrolling the music practice building to ensure none of us were playing jazz or popular music. This is absolutely true! Of course, part of his job probably also included seeing that the place didn't become some sort of den of iniquity.*
>
> *Because the saxophonists in the band were always non-music majors, they were generally not well educated in the fundamen-*

> *tals of classical music. Nevertheless, some of these people were highly talented, and they were very capable jazz performers. Many gigged around campus in big bands and combos at dances, clubs and fraternity parties. Because Mr. Falcone didn't like jazz and inevitably some jazz articulations or concepts would creep into their performance of concert band music . . . the saxophone section was always a target for him.*
>
> *In addition to his continual lecturing to the saxes about style, articulation and tone quality, and every other aspect of performance in the concert band, every time he spoke to them, he mispronounced the word "saxophone. It always came out "sassaphone." I have countless recollections of band members imitating him by gesticulating with one hand and talking through clenched teeth, saying: "Sassaphones, I don't understand how you can play like that and have such innocent looks on your faces!"*[24]

Not surprisingly, Merritt Lutz wasn't the only one Leonard directly told to be wary of the wailing, barking instrument . . . *and* of its players.

> **Kent Krive:** *One year I conducted the Northport High School band during a district festival and Dr. Falcone was among the adjudicators. At the end of the day he singled me out, his serious demeanor indicating that he had information of profound importance to convey. After making sure he had my full attention, he said, gravely, "You know, Kent, there is something very important for you to keep in mind as you continue your teaching career: always be careful of those damned SASSAPHONES!"*[25]

Karma, it seems, can be a bear. In an irony of the first magnitude, the premiere "Leonard Falcone Festival" held in Roseto Valfortore, Italy, September 26-27, 2009, in honor of its favorite son, consisted in large part of parades and concerts performed entirely by saxophones. Master classes on the instrument were also conducted, in addition to conferences on Falcone's life and works.

During the 1965 football season, Michigan State's team turned in a perfect record of wins, was sent to the Rose Bowl, and there, was heavily favored to defeat UCLA. It had been a crazy season of surprise wins and losses, one which continued as the Bruins took on Duffy Daugherty's #1-ranked Spartans. When it was over, more than 100,000 exhausted spectators and millions more on television had witnessed the biggest bowl upset of a weekend of unforgettable upsets. The final score: State 12, UCLA 14.

At 3 a.m. the morning of the game, the band had been jolted from their slumber when a fire alarm had inexplicably gone off (in Sproul Hall on the UCLA campus, where the band was being housed. . .hmm-mmm). For the superstitious who believed it to be a mysterious occurrence, it was, perhaps, an omen that the day would not go entirely well for the Spartans. But in spite of the team's fortunes, the band came on strong, and went on to be "the star in the parade and the game."[26]

Oldsmobile did not pay for this, the band's third jaunt to California (though they were allowed to pay for a side trip to San Francisco) because of a 1961 Big Ten decision that commercial firms could no longer sponsor bands to the Rose Bowl. The stated reason was that some bands could not find a sponsor while others were becoming overly commercialized. Expenses were therefore to be paid for from a $50,000 account set up by the Big Ten Inter-Collegiate Conference, an amount much less than what Olds had paid for the band's 1956 trip. And so, because it was less expensive, MSU's "Green Machine" flew (the first flight for many of the bandsmen) instead of taking the train to California, a decision which, on the plus side, made it a shorter and less tiring journey, but on the minus, caused it to miss the opportunity to perform for tens of thousands of fans and appreciative alumni along the way. But to those lucky enough to attend the 77th Tournament of Roses parade[27]* and hear the sound of MSU's drums cutting through the air as the band approached, it hardly mattered how they got there. It was a moment of pride and inspiration.

**Fred W. Stabley, author:** *To Spartan loyalists it is soul stirring to hear the band's distinctively rich, full-bodied sound growing*

> *louder and louder in the distance and then see the green flood engulf Orange Grove Avenue past the main reviewing stands. The colorful parade provided a stimulating prelude to the main event—the big game in the nearby* Arroyo Seco *("arid gorge").*[28]

Even without stops on its way to and from California (except for re-fueling), the band was far from without activities and performance opportunities during its seven-day stay on the West Coast. After leaving Lansing via a prop plane on a cold December 28th morning, it arrived in LA and, though the first rehearsal was cancelled because of rain, was able to make two special appearances on the 30th: one at "Michigan State Day" at Disneyland, where the band paraded down Main St. and then spent the rest of the afternoon enjoying the rides, and the other a concert that evening at Pershing Square. At the Rose Bowl game itself, seen by millions, it entertained the live and television crowds with a kick step blast onto the field, spatted feet moving like 352 perfectly synchronized pistons. "The Michigan State Fight Song's" swaggering dare to the opposition was followed by a "Tijuana Brass" style version of "A Taste of Honey," complete with Rockette precision footwork. As the pregame ended, Leonard, the "Dean of the Big Ten Band Directors," conducted the combined bands of Michigan State and UCLA in the "Star Spangled Banner." At halftime, jazzed up versions of "Goody-Goody" "Tea for Two," and "Slaughter on 10th Ave." featured the band's signature "Patterns in Motion." Later, after the game, the band flew to San Francisco for a special concert in Union Square, and then took a tour of the San Francisco area, compliments of Oldsmobile.

The following year, 1966–1967, was an important one for Leonard and the MSU band. The spring tour of the Concert Band took the ensemble to, among other places, Roseto, Pennsylvania, a city inhabited by many Italians from Leonard's hometown, Roseto, Italy. There, because of a promise Leonard had made to his friend Nicholas Ronco, the band played a fundraising concert which helped the Bangor Area High School Band earn money for new uniforms. Leonard's wife, Beryl, rarely remained for the entirety of a concert. But for this one, she did.

**Beryl Falcone:** *I knew he (Leonard) would give it something special.*[29]

The audience was the largest and most receptive of the tour, and the band, in appreciation of the music lovers' refusing to leave the auditorium and clamoring for "More! More!" extended the program by four selections, including, at the end, the "Michigan State Fight Song." In both Italian and English, Leonard thanked the audience for their touching reception and generous gifts, which included a bouquet of red roses for Beryl, Mary, and Cecilia, a book on the life of Donatelli with mention of Leonard himself, and souvenir presentations to Bill Moffit and the band.

**Merritt Lutz:** *It was a very warm atmosphere with a lot of hugging, and the reception that the band got was amazing. It was standing ovations and all the rest of it. And I remember as we were walking around—it was a little town—that there was a street sign in one of the areas where the people lived that said "Falcone Avenue," and we walked by and everybody thought it was kind of funny and interesting. So when Leonard left, some of the guys went back and shimmied up the pole and stole it and presented it to Leonard once we got back to East Lansing. I was not one of the guys who went up the pole, but he was appalled that that sign had been stolen. Yet you could also tell he was quite pleased by it. He took it, and he had a smile on his face and he didn't know whether to say "Thank you," or what. But I'm sure he took it home and that it became a treasured possession of his.*

*I was not involved in the private things they did for him in Roseto, but I can tell you that he was a celebrity there—a tremendous celebrity in the town. It is an isolated place in the hills of Pennsylvania, and there are a lot of proud Italian people there.*[30]

**Dick Lodge, percussion, MSU 1965–1969:** *My mother, who then lived in Michigan, traveled with a friend to Roseto unbeknownst to me to see me play the concert there. Well, Leonard was the one who actually told me my mother was in the audience, and*

> *he escorted me to her seat to say "hello." This act was well beyond the call of duty, and it made me feel like I was more than just a member of the band, but an appreciated, close friend of Leonard's. He immediately became much more inspiring to me after that gesture. My mother, who is currently 92 years old, still remembers him as being very gracious.*[31]

Leonard, now in the autumn of his life, began his 39th year the following fall with an announcement to his bands: he would be retiring at the end of the 1966–67 school year. Earlier that spring, he had informed the university of his plans and asked that he be allowed to make the announcement personally to his students. Though mandatory retirement would not occur until he turned 70, he wanted to leave the university while he was still in good health and at the top of his game. He had seen the campus grow from an enrollment of approximately 2,500 students in 1927 to over 40,000 in 1967. His single 65-piece Military Band had developed into four units: the 175-piece Marching Band, the 115-piece Concert Band, the 100-piece Activity Band, and the Spartan Brass. He had raised his Concert and Marching Bands to positions of national prominence through the sheer force of his personality, his musicianship, and his unrelenting demand for perfection, made many guest appearances as a baritone soloist, cut commercial baritone LP records, popularized the once obscure instrument, served in professional societies, acted as host and chairman for numerous solo and ensemble and band and orchestra festivals at State, authored ten articles for professional journals and published trombone and baritone music books for students, brought renowned musicians to campus, conducted numerous clinics, transcribed and arranged music for band, acted as an adjudicator and guest conductor at several universities and high schools and at Interlochen, appeared with his bands at football games, concerts, and on television innumerable times, as well as performed for four presidents (Herbert Hoover, Franklin Roosevelt, Harry Truman, Lyndon Johnson), at three Rose Bowl games, the New York World's Fair, and in Rockefeller Center. He had educated and mentored thousands of musicians and made a name not only for himself, but for the university he served. In his letter to Dr. Niblock of April 17, 1966, he said simply, "On April 5,

1967, I will have reached the age of 68, and by July 1, 1967, I will have served the university for forty years. In consideration of these factors, this seems to be the proper time to retire."[32]

When a week later Dr. Niblock notified Dean Paul Varg of the College of Arts and Letters that Leonard wished to make the announcement of his retirement himself, he also requested that Falcone's successor be named at that time to avoid receiving a flood of applicants, and asked that Leonard be awarded a one-year consultantship leave at full salary. Both requests were granted, and when the great maestro broke the news to his stunned students, the university made it publicly official and simultaneously named Dr. Harry Begian, Director of Bands at Wayne State University, as the new Director of Bands at Michigan State.[33]

Begian was no stranger to State, nor to Leonard Falcone. In a moment reminiscent of the teenage Boy's Nation delegate Bill Clinton meeting his predecessor President John F. Kennedy in the Rose Garden, they, too, had had a fateful, prescient encounter years before.

> **Dr. Harry Begian:** *I was a thirteen year old in junior high school when I first heard Mr. Falcone when he appeared as soloist on the euphonium—the baritone, as he called it. I was visiting my uncle's home on the weekend, and my cousin asked if I'd like to hear his high school band play a concert that afternoon at Highland Park High. He said, "You'll hear the world's greatest baritone player if you do," and I said, "Who is that?" "Leonard Falcone," he said. "Haven't you ever heard of Leonard Falcone?" And I said, "No, I have not." So we went to the concert, and it was the first time in my life I heard an artist play on the baritone, and it was the most wonderful playing I'd ever heard on the baritone, or on any instrument for that matter. And the important thing I got from that at an early age was what people meant when they say "expressive playing." It was what I heard when I heard Mr. Falcone play for the first time. I remember how clean it was, and how expressive. I never forgot that, and I never forgot what he played.*
>
> *Years later at Michigan State I was talking with Mr. Falcone about when I first heard him perform, and he said, "You did? Do you remember what I played?" and I told him, and he said,*

*"That's amazing!" It was one of his favorite words: "Amazing!" I said, "I'll never forget it! It was the 'Fantasia di Concerto' by Boccalari, and 'O Solo Mio' was the encore."*

*He played 'O Solo Mio' unaccompanied, and I looked around and you know, all the little old Italian ladies were close by and when he played it I saw a couple of them pull out handkerchiefs.*[34]

That fall, the halftime show of the final 1966 home football game was dedicated to Leonard Falcone, the "Dean of Big Ten Band Directors."[35]* It was a tribute that nearly didn't occur.

**Merritt Lutz:** *The last game of the season it snowed like crazy from Tuesday to Thursday, and so Biggie Munn, the athletic director, said "The field is so bad I can't let the band practice on it." This was for Leonard's farewell show! And Leonard says to the band, "Looks like we can't play halftime on Saturday because we can't practice. Landon Field is all snow." So on their own, a group of MSU people went over to see Biggy and said, "You can't do this—you just can't do this!" And Biggy gave in and said, "Okay." But then it was all up to Leonard. "It was nice of you," Leonard said, "but we can't go on—we can't practice on that field. There's too much snow." Some time on Thursday it finally stopped snowing, and we all went out there—the whole band with girlfriends and roommates and shoveled the entire field—blisters!—so the band could practice. And so we played Leonard's last game that Saturday. I can get teary about it today. It was a tear jerker. It was really something.*[36]

76,000 fans cheered for over five minutes,[37] and as the band played "The Sound of Music," the announcer, speaking directly to the crowd, said:

*Leonard Falcone is recognized throughout the world as a baritone horn virtuoso. National authorities have proclaimed his bands to be in the first rank among universities. He is in constant*

> *demand as a soloist, guest conductor, adjudicator, and clinician. As a teacher, students from across the nation come to this campus for the privilege of studying under his guidance. Fellow musicians respect his musical standards, personal integrity, humanistic values, and maturity of judgment. He stands before you today at the head of his profession, as a giant among men.*

And then the announcer addressed Leonard himself.

> *Leonard Falcone, you have given much to Michigan State University. In return, we recognize your achievements, your contributions to the profession and your great personal influence on your students and in the history and development of Michigan State University. . . . Through these years, past and present, to all who have known you, to all who have seen your bands, you are to them the sound of music at Michigan State University.*

Standing in the spotlight of praise and attention was what a humble person like Falcone might think being in hell was like, only there he wouldn't have to act like he was enjoying it.[38*] Nevertheless, those who knew him well could see that the tribute had deeply touched and moved him. How could it not?

It was sometime around this period of Leonard's final year at MSU that he had an encounter with a group of long haired radical students who came to his office with a demand. Campus unrest was gearing up across the country. "Sex, drugs, rock and roll!" and "Power to the people!" were the rallying cries of a student population fed up with national politics, the Viet Nam war, and the slow progress of civil rights. The Kennedys, King, Carmichael, SDS, the Beatles, Bob Dylan, Malcolm X, were names on the lips of college students everywhere. This was the situation on campuses across the country in the mid to late 1960s. And this was the situation with Leonard Falcone: straight arrow, family man, WWII veteran, loyal American. One can imagine how, through clenched teeth and a mouth the shape of a mail slot, he told the students gathered in his office "No," he would not suspend the playing of the "Star Spangled Banner" at football games, that the Michigan State Marching Band was not going to do any such thing. Perhaps he added, as his right hand lightly slapped his left to punctuate salient points, that he was a naturalized citizen, a man who loved his country. And possibly, his expressive blue eyes betraying his curiosity, his hands made the "magic circles"[39]* so familiar to those who knew him. It would have been the (much imitated) Falcone way to deliver the message. At any rate, case closed. The students left his office peacefully, and the "Star Spangled Banner" remained an integral part of the pre-game program.

That winter, by invitation of the Commencement Committee, Leonard appeared as euphonium soloist at the 1967 winter term commencement, the last indoor commencement ceremony to be held during his 40-year tenure.

Though the talent in the band in the mid-sixties was better than ever and it would have been relatively easy for Leonard to keep the band at the same level of performance as previous years, he was never satisfied with *status quo*. The better the group played, the higher he set his standards and the more he expected. Nothing new there. And his expectations were no different with his applied students.

> **Earle Louder:** *In my lessons with him, the more I did, the more he gave me to do, the more he gave me to do, the more I did. That comes from the respect I had for him as a performer and teacher.*[40]

Always looking for something new, new music, new places to play, new effects, new sound combinations, and even new ensembles, he pushed himself and others to learn and grow.[41] No surprise, then, that in 1967, his last concert season, the Concert Band reached its second pinnacle of perfection at a concert at Hill Auditorium on the University of Michigan campus, this time for the Fourteenth National Conference of the College Band Directors' National Association on February 9, 1967. Appearing there were the University of Michigan, Ohio State University, University of Minnesota, University of Montana, and Ithaca College Bands. Of them all, Michigan State's band received the highest critical acclaim from the nation's top band conductors, composers, and musicians. After 40 years at Michigan State, Falcone had only been completely satisfied with his band's performance two times: the performance at the Midwestern Conference, Hill Auditorium, January 10, 1958, and this one.[42]

> **Leonard Falcone:** *I must admit that on these two occasions the band played perfectly. I could not correct a thing.*[43]

> **Tom Gillette:** *One fond memory from 1978 or so, heading to Ann Arbor to listen to various groups at their annual "Midwest Conference": the University of Michigan Symphony Band ended their concert with a stunning performance of the Finale to Tchaikovsky's Fourth Symphony. It was impeccable—probably the first time I could put aside the rivalry, nod my head and applaud loudly. On the way out of the balcony several of us encountered Dr. Falcone in the stairwell. He asked our impressions of the performance, and we mustered up what we could, enthusiastically. "Have you heard my recording of my band playing this?" he asked. No . . . we hadn't. "Meet me in my office tomorrow morning at 8:00."*
>
> *You don't turn down an opportunity like that, so several of us made it there. He was beaming as he put the record on the old record player. And Michigan State's performance WAS better . . . very nice, and also recorded at Hill Auditorium.*
>
> *There was just enough competition in the Old Man to make him very proud of his accomplishments, and he smiled broadly as we congratulated him on it. It was a special moment, and I was thrilled to buy a copy of that 1967 recording on eBay a year or two ago.*[44]*

On May 21, 1967, Phi Mu Alpha Sinfonia and the Michigan School Band and Orchestra Association held a Testimonial Dinner for Leonard at the Lansing Civic Center. Nearly 400 students, faculty, alumni, and friends came to pay tribute to the man they loved and admired for, among other things, raising MSU's marching and concert bands to positions of national prominence. Of the gifts presented, there was a portrait, which was to hang in the campus' new "Leonard Falcone Music Practice Building," a new composition by Norman Dello Joio, "Variations on a Theme by Haydn," which was commissioned on his behalf by the Michigan School Band and Orchestra Association, and the establishment of a scholarship fund in his name which was to become part of his legacy to future musicians at Michigan State University. Speaker for the evening was Col. William F. Santelmann, retired, Honorary Director of the United States Marine Band,[45] and the guest soloist was former student Earle Louder, then with United States Navy Band, a man whose musicianship Leonard highly respected.

> **Leonard Falcone:** *I admire other performers very much. For instance one of my own students. Earle Louder. He plays beautifully. Tone, technique. I can tell you (he is) the most successful . . . the one who has pursued the profession, and the top student I've had.*[46]

> **Earle Louder:** *There's one distinct honor I've had in my life that I hold with great pride: I was asked to come to Lansing in 1967, Leonard's 40th anniversary banquet in downtown Lansing. They invited me to come as a soloist in honor of his anniversary. I was on tour with the Navy Band, but I flew from Youngstown to Lansing and played two solos at the banquet for him. I was so honored to be a part of that celebration. That is a highlight in my life that I never will forget doing it.*[47]

On Sunday afternoon, May 21st, 1967, Leonard Falcone conducted his final concert as Director of Bands at MSU at Kresge Terrace to an overflow audience. It was a nostalgic affair with a variety of music, and when the band reached the end of the program with Sousa's rousing "Stars and Stripes Forever," US Marine Corps Col.William F. Santelmann made a surprise appearance, which led to the playing of "The Marine's Hymn" and some lively toe-tapping on the part of the audience.[48]

And then it was over.

*Leonard with his baritone*
*~ courtesy of Michigan State University Archives & Historical Collections*

## CHAPTER 14

# WINTER YEARS: 1967–1985

***"There is nothing in my life that I regret. It's all been valuable."*[1]**
**~ Leonard Falcone**

---

*"If you're on time, you're late," he was fond of saying, and accordingly he and his wife had arrived early that morning for their first visit to the arts camp. Though anxious to see his old friend, a former student who had founded the place, he took several minutes to look around. Pausing on a hill, he saw a lake ruffling in the breeze some distance below, where the last of an early morning mist blanketing the shoreline was gradually burning off under megawatt sunshine. A sigh and rustle of leaves, and then the plaintive tones of a lone baritone floating on a puff of air. A lively group of neatly uniformed teenagers emerges from a forest trail, heading for breakfast at the nearby dining hall. "I'm going to like it here," he mused, satisfied. And heading toward his friend's house through a serene forest of large white and red pine, oak, and maple trees, he turned to his wife and said so.*

In 1968, Leonard's first retirement year, Lisa Fulton was born, an event that made him a grandfather.

> **Lisa Fulton:** *I think of him as my dad. I was brought home from the hospital to my grandparents' house, and they were who raised me. When I was very young, from around ages 8 to 11, we would play badminton together in the front yard. That was one of my very favorite things to do with him. Later, when I was a teenager, he would shoot baskets with me. He was in his late 70s at that time. When I came home from school and he'd be there playing his records, sometimes opera, sometimes the NBC Symphony Orchestra. He would want me to sit with him and listen, and he would explain things and try to make me interested. Sometimes I'd try to have a really personal conversation with him, like maybe about a boy I was attracted to, and he just wasn't interested. But he always entertained my friends when they came over. He wasn't stand offish at all.*

Like others in her family, Lisa became an accomplished musician, too.

> *It was never a thought whether I'd play an instrument or not. I started piano when I was 6, and beginning about then my grandfather would bring home his euphonium at Christmas time and we would play carols together. I accompanied him on piano, and often, when I messed up a chord, I'd tell him he was the one who made the mistake. And I was serious. I didn't think of him as a fantastic musician, I thought of him as a father and a teacher. We did that for many, many years, and he always seemed to enjoy it.*
>
> *I started cornet at age 7 or 8, and in 5th grade, he arranged for me to play a recital for my classmates. We practiced, and I played 3 or 4 songs for them. All through middle school and high school, grandfather was my trumpet teacher.*[2]

Leonard, though retired, was not without plans for the future. In addition to helping raise his granddaughter, among other things they included teaching baritone and tuba part time at Michigan State in the early 1970s, a continuance of guest conducting and adjudication, a participation in band clinics, and a 17-year involvement (1967–1984) with the Blue Lake Fine Arts Camp in Whitehall, Michigan.

At State, Leonard held lessons in his office in 319 MPB, a pleasant room and favorite spot for his studio classes. There, each student played for the very same group they were in competition with for band chairs as Leonard made open, blunt comments on each one's progress—or lack of it (*"Now John has been having trouble with his range . . . his tone is not well-developed . . perhaps his embouchure is causing the problem . . . and his technique needs much work. O.K., John . . . we're all ready to hear you play now"*). These were unforgettable sessions with his "boys" (and rarely, a girl) who, like those before them, were in awe of his prodigious talent, not to mention his ability to astutely analyze and diagnose performance problems all while seemingly concentrating on something else.

> **Tom Gillette:** *Sitting or standing outside 319 MPB, I'd listen to "the Old Man" warm up. It might be 10 below out, snowy, whatever...and I might have rolled out of bed at 7:45 for an 8:00 lesson, but he'd have been there long before me, and I would hear him rip through scales, arpeggios, excerpts of whatever popped into his head . . . it was truly fascinating. The playing would stop, promptly at 8, the door would open, and that big smile would cross his face as he'd ask how I'd been over the week, or make some comment on the weather . . . whatever. The lesson was about to begin.*
>
> *If you had one of those early morning lessons, there was most likely a fresh STATE NEWS on the desk, laid out very carefully, deliberately. "Why don't you begin with* <u>this</u> *exercise?" He'd point to one, and sit down at his desk chair, looking at the paper. I'd plow into an Arban's or Rochut or Tyrrell exercise, and out of the corner of my eye, or with one ear, I'd see him look puzzled . . . or perhaps hear him turn a page. Maybe mumble . . . "hmmm" . . . another page turns . . . nodding . . . shakes his head. "Well, the pressure is off me," I'd think. "He's absorbed completely in the events of the day! Besides, I'm playing this rather well!" And I'd dive into the last section with real confidence. I'm done.*
>
> *It seems like an eternity, and he begins to comment on something he read in the paper . . . "Did you know that*

*President Carter is meeting with Anwar Sadat today?" or "I understand gasoline prices might hit fifty cents a gallon." He'd make a few observations about it . . . we'd converse briefly . . . then he'd stand up with the pencil. "All right . . . now there are a few things we should look at here . . . " The horn would come off the wastebasket, and he'd begin to demonstrate. He'd mark up my page, and by the time we were finished, I realized that he'd made more marks on the page than there were notes! But every one of them was right...zeroing in on a particular problem or concept that could have been presented better. He didn't miss a trick! Ever. Not that he was unfocused—not at all—because most of the lesson was spent with him standing alongside, playing, pointing, gesturing, nodding, shaking his head (the WORST!) and encouraging. And he REQUIRED good eye contact, and if you didn't give it, he'd put himself closer to you and always the smile, the nod, and the eyes. Very kind eyes, but curious and just on the edge of dancing. Then came the end of the lesson...after which the only POSSIBLE choice was to somehow stagger back to one's room and take a nap for an hour or two, or just stare at the ceiling and wonder how someone could work you over so intensely in one short hour. I'd give ANYTHING for one more of those hours!*[3]

On football Saturdays, Leonard would often be at the game in his role as Director Emeritus, where he would conduct "MSU Shadows," or the "National Anthem." Even there, where he was only minimally in charge of the half time performance, his students strove to impress him.

**Tom Gillette:** *I remember his being at a game vividly, a time when the band was in a concert formation which put my squad a few feet from the sideline right near the podium on the 50. Dr. Falcone was standing by to conduct "MSU Shadows," and we were playing the then-current Captain and Tennille hit "You Better Shop Around." Our part had some off the beat "pops" to accentuate the melody, and I cranked in as loud as I could in the* *wrong spot—a beautiful sound, a deadly force loud, but clearly in the wrong place . . . and right in the Old Man's face. To make it worse, when the spot repeated itself I stressed out about it so much I did it again, only louder. A few days later, at my lesson, he said, "I enjoyed the band's performance on Saturday, but I don't think I liked that song about going to the grocery store." I didn't like it much, either.* [4]

Most directors in his shoes would simply have shown up at the gridiron on game day, climbed the ladder, and conducted on autopilot. But not Leonard. He loved his craft, took his role as seriously as if the band were performing on stage at Carnegie Hall (which he once said he never got to do, but wished he could have).[5]

**Bob Piatt:** *The last time I was under Leonard's direction was, I believe, the last Alumni Band Football Reunion he attended. I was playing a sousaphone at the time and was standing directly under his portable platform. We were practicing our performance for the game, playing the "Alma Mater" on the practice field, and he started the band several times until he was satisfied that finally we were all together. He (was feeble) and needed assistance to get up the ladder, and there were hands to help him should he falter. I will never forget the moment.*[6]

In spite of advancing physical problems, he stayed active, and in addition to teaching and mentoring students majoring in brass instruments at Michigan State, adjudicated competitions and sometimes even appeared as a guest conductor.

**Joe Dobos:** *As a young band director I had Leonard as a judge quite often at band festivals and my students would have him in the low brass room. The first time I ever saw him, my first year of teaching, I had a student play baritone, and someone, perhaps his granddaughter, was doing the writing for him, and he would whisper to her. I thought, "Why is he judging? He is very frail, and he can't even write anymore." Then we'd get the sheet* *back, and he wouldn't have missed a thing. He'd have heard every detail, and the paper would be covered with comments that were full. He might say, "I disagree with this interpretation," but then, "Here are things that would make it better." Even when he criticized, he suggested how to fix the problem. Here he was, the great Leonard Falcone, in his 70s and not a crotchety old man.*

*This is unheard of now days. Usually, it's the judge's way, or the highway. I'm now a judge and I try to be sure that if I disagree with something, I am open minded about it, like Leonard, and try to be helpful.*[7]

**Ken Glickman:** *My first recollection of Leonard Falcone dates back to about 1970 when I was a music student at Indiana University. It's a fond memory of a man I could later say was my friend. Our band was playing at the American Bandmaster's Association convention in Elkhart with famous band directors from all over the country conducting us . . . This outwardly gentle man, we soon found out, had musical convictions as strong as steel. (Unlike others) he was not consumed by his own ego or with proving his authority to us. He was only concerned with performing beautiful music WITH us.*[8]

Summers were spent at Blue Lake, where memories of his presence run deep. Perhaps most unforgettable were the times he conducted the Festival Orchestra, a group comprised of Blue Lake's faculty and staff, which still functions today and has existed since the very first season in 1966. Sometimes, his way of putting his stamp on that professional group would take those who didn't know him aback. At least in the beginning.

**Tom Stansell, clarinet:** *It was our first rehearsal with Dr. Falcone, and he had chosen to perform the L'Arlésienne Suite No. 1 by Bizet. Many of the Blue Lake faculty and staff were meeting him for the first time. The principal flute had a long, lightly orchestrated, and very exposed solo to play, and she sight read it beautifully—except at the very end of the passage, when she made a blooper.*

*Dr. Falcone stopped the orchestra and began to talk about the importance of accuracy and being prepared for rehearsals and solo passages. As he went on, he explained to everyone that he had played baritone all his life and that while performing in rehearsals or concerts he didn't make mistakes. "I don't understand how musicians can make mistakes," he said. And he meant it.*

*People were stunned. The flutist took the lecture, but at this point, she had steam coming out of her ears. The orchestra was as quiet as a morgue, and the anxiety was palpable.*

*It took a couple rehearsals for everyone to realize he meant no malice, and that his comment that he never made mistakes wasn't arrogance on his part—it was simply true. He had a thirst for musical perfection and knew how to achieve it, and the result was that eventually we played at the very top of our potential and grew to love him.*[9]

And as with much that Leonard said, his comments to the orchestra that day were to have a comic upshot as the group repeated them, complete, of course, with the requisite gestures and accent. Not surprisingly, the orchestra received outstanding reviews for its concert.

In another shake-up measuring a near 4.0 on the Wagner scale, one that delighted those coming from band backgrounds but was a jolt to those orchestral musicians who consider themselves superior to bandsmen (and their numbers are legion), Leonard, during a Festival Orchestra rehearsal of Verdi's overture to the opera "La Forza Del Destino," remarked, "You know, I like this better for barr-tones." Accustomed to conducting a fine band arrangement of this piece with eight or so tubas, a myriad of low woodwinds, and perhaps eight baritones doubling the cello lines, the orchestra, with its six cellos and four basses, just couldn't produce the full, resonant sound he'd hoped for—particularly in an outdoor shell. It was an unintended put-down to the strings, one that few band conductors could have gotten away with. Leonard did.[10]

That Leonard preferred baritones over other instruments was no news flash to the bandsmen who knew him. It was the stuff of many a story.

**Kenneth G. Bloomquist:** *One thing Leonard would do was look back at the baritone section and say "More barr-tone!" The section always had a bet between them to guess how long it would take before he said it.*[11]

**Bob Walters, trumpet, MSU 1968-1971:** *We were to perform "Bugler's Holiday" at Blue Lake at the Wednesday night "Concert in the Park." Having only two trumpets willing to tackle it, a baritone player volunteered to help out and play the third trumpet part with us. After the concert, Dr. Falcone came up and enthusiastically said he enjoyed our rendition—that, in fact, he'd never heard it done better! I suspected that had it been entitled "Euphonium Holiday" and played with three baritones, he would have liked it best of all.*[12]

**Tom Gillette:** *There's a story that's become legend, but many are on hand to state it as fact, that Leonard was given an opportunity to conduct the Detroit Symphony Orchestra, and during the course of the rehearsal, he asked the cello section to "try to play more like barr-tones" (as he would have pronounced it). The story is consistent with what I know about the man from personal experience, and must have raised a few eyebrows!*[13]

Others at Blue Lake recall his directing high school groups, conducting and touring with them internationally. The first tour, in 1971, was a nearly month long jaunt through Holland, Belgium, Austria, Switzerland, Germany, San Marino, and Italy, arranged by the camp's International Exchange Program. It was an exciting time for Leonard, and at one point it brought to mind an old friend—and competitor.

**Fritz Stansell:** *When we were discussing how unusual it would be to take a band on a European tour and how impressed everyone would be that he was taking on such a project, he mused, "Well, what do you suppose Revelli will do now? Take a band to the moon?"*[14]

As for the students themselves, they found his brilliant conducting, hard work, and gentle spirit inspiring. Even the music Leonard had selected for them to play on the tour captured their imaginations.

> **Jane Church, alto saxophone, MSU 1971–1977:** *As the date drew near, we moved rehearsals (from Michigan State) to the camp. Although practicing took the major part of the day, I was so completely engrossed in the college level music we played that I was oblivious to the heat, humidity, or length of each session. Apparently Dr. Falcone was, too. Rehearsals were so intense that he would have to change after each one because his shirt, which was always a white long sleeved dress shirt, would be soaked with sweat. He was 72 at the time, but I never once thought of him as a "senior citizen" because of his high energy.*[15]

Fellow musicians lucky enough to have a front row seat in seeing how he accomplished miracles with high school groups soon became his fans—even those who were, at first, reluctant to be so.

*Leonard at Blue Lake*
*~ courtesy of the Blue Lake Fine Arts Camp*

*Leonard rehearsing in the Falcone Pavilion at Blue Lake*
*~ courtesy of the Blue Lake Fine Arts Camp*

**Avis Heger, Director, Harp Program, Blue Lake:** *When my husband and I went to Blue Lake, everyone absolutely worshipped Leonard. As outsiders, we were only semi-impressed. Our connections had been with the University of Michigan and . . . so hearing all the Falcone praise was sort of a turn off.*

*By chance, in the early years he would rehearse his band within my hearing range. I would hear the progress. In three days the band would have the Falcone sound—especially the lyrical phrasing. I had only dealt with orchestras and have an ear for the strings, and yet I was hearing a string sound from a band man. He fascinated me, and I began to make a point of listening to him "turn notes into music."*

*After I knew him personally, I would tell him I was a convert to the "Falcone Worship Team." He was always amused by my being a convert!*

*On hot days, he and I would free up Beryl and have a McDonald's date in a cool spot and I would ask him about his teaching. His greatest comments? "Listen, listen, listen!" and "Tone, tone, tone!"*[16]

Other memories of Leonard at Blue Lake have their roots in having once studied under him at MSU. Former students found that the urge to please him did not fade with time, even though they, themselves, were accomplished professionals, and vague recollections of low brass classes where his sincere desire to help mixed with his innocent yet brutally stark honesty sometimes rose to a startlingly clear and present reality.

**Marty Erickson, tuba, MSU Band 1965–1967:** *I had been in the Navy Band for a few years and had been asked to perform a solo, some concerts, and present a master class at the Blue Lake Fine Arts Camp. My duties for the residency included playing with the Blue Lake jazz faculty in a solo jazz tuba performance in the afternoon for camp students. I finished the performance with encores and "screech tuba" in the spirit of the show, and immediately after was whisked away in a golf cart to the other side of the campus, where dozens of brass* *players awaited me for a low brass master class. I was comfortable with this, because I had time to relax and "warm down." Blue Lake's Festival Band director, Donald Flickinger, an old friend and school colleague, was to be there to announce me to the students, but when I arrived, there was a surprise. Sitting next to Don was my old teacher, Mr. Falcone, who asked if HE could do the introduction. I started getting more nervous by the moment, knowing how he felt about the jazz playing (he did not like his students playing in jazz bands because of the way it might affect their embouchure), knowing I had just played loud and long and was tired, knowing how meticulous a performer he was, knowing what perfection he expected as a teacher . . . As these thoughts ran through my mind, I heard him say: "Now students, when you hear Martin play, you will hear very clean playing and articulation. When he was with me, he had a very "airy" sound at first, and his attacks weren't so clean, but sounded little "peeahh" attacks, or air, before the sound." Horrified, I sat and listened to the growing list of my former playing issues!*[17]

*Leonard receives his Doctorate, March, 1978*
*~ courtesy of Michigan State University Archives & Historical Collections*

*Leonard posing in front of his NBA Hall of Fame portrait, February, 1984, with Ken Bloomquist*
*~ courtesy of the Falcone family*

Leonard nearly always refused compensation from BLFAC, preferring instead to donate his talents. In 1976, the Camp dedicated its new band pavilion in his honor, and in 1986, the year after this death, the Falcone Festival, which includes four divisions of internationally recognized and highly competitive solo competitions for euphonium and tuba, was founded there in his memory by his wife, Beryl, and several of his former students.[18*]

Sometimes, Karma can be first-rate.

In 1984, a year before his death, the walls of 319 MPB (Music Practice Building), Leonard's office, were covered with pictures of him as a young, handsome man, standing in front of his band on podiums throughout the country, with publicity photos of him as a baritone soloist, author, and teacher, and with various awards and lifetime memberships, several of which had been showered upon him since his retirement. There were honorary memberships in the Phi Mu Alphia Sinfonia Music Fraternity, the MSU Alumni Association, and the Kappa Kappa Psi Honorary Band Fraternity, which had also awarded him its distinguished medal for Outstanding Contribution in Music as a Performing Artist and Conductor at an MSU banquet honoring his 50 years of service, and awards and memberships from, among others, Excalibur, the Blue Lake Fine Arts Camp, the American Bandmaster's Association, the American School Band Director's Association,[19*] the College Band Director's National Association and the Michigan School Band and Orchestra Association. And among all these were two others, two that were possibly Leonard's most cherished, marking the pinnacle of his career. One, bestowed on him in 1978, was an honorary PhD from Michigan State honoring his 50-year contribution to the great university. Though Honorary Degrees are usually reserved for prominent people not affiliated with the university, a diligent group of Falcone supporters led by A. Thad Hegerberg, MSU Band President 1963–1964, made the argument that Falcone's untiring work in music education outside of his being Professor Emeritus at State should allow him consideration. They won their point, and in March, 1978, Leonard was awarded the degree "Doctor of Fine Arts." Though he never used his title and preferred to be called "Mr. Falcone," it was a highlight in his life, and he said so in an interview.

> **Leonard Falcone:** *As a little immigrant boy, shall we say, I have come to the top by being granted this doctorate.*[20]

The other came six years later in Troy, Alabama, when on Saturday, Feb 4, 1984, at the age of 84, Leonard was inducted in the NBA's Hall of Fame of Distinguished Band Conductors, the National Bandmaster's Association's highest honor. Accompanied by Dr. Kenneth Bloomquist and nominated by a grateful alumni, he joined the ranks of such American musical giants as John Phillip Sousa, Karl King, Edwin Franko Goldman, and Henry Fillmore, and preceded such other titans as Frederick Fennell, Col. Arnold Gabriel, Harry Begian, and Kenneth Bloomquist, the last two, his successors at MSU.

**Kenneth Bloomquist:** *Leonard was very weak and unable to get around easily, but he attended all the events including a morning induction ceremony where his portrait was unveiled and a concert in the evening where he was introduced to the full house crowd.*[21]

It, and his honorary doctorate, were surely the most important tributes of his lifetime. Dr. Bloomquist made the presentation, and concluded it with a statement.

**Kenneth Bloomquist:** *I think the Hall of Fame grows in stature with every year of its existence. This year, it grew a lot.*[22]

With his characteristic humility, Leonard, in his acceptance speech, shared with the audience his reaction to hearing that he would be inducted into the Hall of Fame.

**Leonard Falcone:** *I was floored. I could not believe it. I still can't. I hope some day I'll get over this embarrassment.*[23]

That he would be forever be associated with such prominent bandsmen incredibly, because of his unassuming nature, had surprised him. Nevertheless, the honor left an indelible mark of pride on his unpretentious spirit.

Of the many tributes given Leonard across the years, most never made it into frames on his wall. One of these occurred in 1977, when an acknowledgement not intended for him at all basked him in the reflected light of glory nevertheless. It paid a very public tribute to his brother Nick's significant contribution to the University of Michigan Band, and Leonard was on hand, in front of more than 100,000 spectators, to bear witness. What no one there who knew them could possibly fail to recognize was that their stories as bandmasters were inextricably tied: to honor one was to think of the other.

**Joseph Dobos:** *Nicholas Falcone's "M Men March," in a sense, began a series of events that led to the appointment of Nicho-*

*las Falcone as Director of the University of Michigan Bands and soon after the same for Leonard Falcone at Michigan Agricultural College. Looking at the music Nicholas performed, he must have had quite a band. This march is DIFFICULT! This is proof that there WERE bands at Michigan before Revelli! Many years later, Nicholas was honored at half time on the 50th anniversary of his appointment as Director of Bands. The combined Michigan Marching Band and Alumni Band performed "M Men March" in the Michigan Stadium where it had been played many times (as Nick conducted) in the late 1920s. Standing on the 50-yard line were the Falcone brothers—proud, erect, and all smiles.*[24]

It was the last time the two men made a public appearance together. Nicholas Falcone died at his long time home, 418 Thompson Street, Ann Arbor, on February 11, 1981. He was 88.

Just months prior to Nick's loss, in early summer of 1980, an incident occurred that nearly caused Leonard to precede him in death.

**Lisa Fulton:** *He had a fall in a shower at Blue Lake and got a hematoma. My grandmother (Beryl) took him in the car to the hospital, and that's when they discovered the blood clot in his brain. They did surgery, and they didn't think he'd make it. They called the priest to do the last rites. . . and then he recovered!*[25]

He awoke to see the concerned faces of a priest and his family hovering over him. After six weeks in the hospital, he went home, a testament to his spirit and will to live. Yet it seemed to be a turning point, and as he became more frail in his final years, it was getting harder for him, or anyone around him, to deny what was happening. His life was becoming a ceaseless round of reporting symptoms and visiting doctors. Walking became a slow and tedious task, and often, he needed help. And something else was wrong, he could sense it. But what?

**Lisa Fulton:** *The entire fall of 1984, he complained he wasn't feeling well. He'd go to the doctors, and they couldn't find any-*

*thing wrong. Finally, in January of 1985, he himself called an ambulance and had himself transported to the hospital. They ran a battery of tests while he was there and they still couldn't find anything wrong with him, but they put him in the care facility at Dimondale, on the care side first, not the nursing side. They ran more tests, and that's when they found early dementia. Alzheimer's. Nobody quite knew what that was back then. But he always recognized it. He knew.*[26]

During this difficult period at the end of his life, on September 30, 1984, his last autumn, he received one of his final public displays of love and respect when old friend Bill Moffit, now Director of Bands at Purdue University, surprised him at his home with 400 very loud (but orderly) drop-by guests. He marched the Purdue Marching Band from East Lansing High School down the previously quiet Burcham and Charles Streets to Leonard and Beryl's front yard, where it proceeded to play the "Michigan State Fight Song."

**Cece Falcone:** *The neighbors, quite used to strange things going on in front of the Falcone house, came pouring out of their houses to see what the hell was going on there now!*[27]

Beaming, Leonard appeared wearing his green game day Michigan State suit and Spartan tie. "Oh my God. This is tremendous!" he said. "We wanted to do something really special," responded Moffit. "Hold on, it's just beginning!"

The band proceeded to perform six numbers, one a can-can featuring a block long kickline, another, the final one, Purdue's fight song (complete with eye rolling from the crowd). "This is for one of the most important persons in my life," Moffit said as he presented Leonard and Beryl with Purdue t-shirts (which they immediately put on) and a medal honoring the aged maestro.[28]

**Ed Zabrusky, MSU spokesman:** *It was a real honor and a surprise for him.*[29]

**Cece Falcone:** *I will never forget the September Saturday in 1984 when Purdue played at MSU and Bill marched the band (big drum and all) down the street to play a concert in front of our house. Thanks, Bill, for some great memories!*[30]

**Bill Moffit:** *I wanted to come back and do something spectacular for a wonderful man, (to show) love for a super person.*[31]

Amazingly, sometime that fall Leonard also conducted a band in what was surely his final public appearance on a podium.

**Kenneth G. Bloomquist:** *We had him conduct whenever possible, once in the fall of 1984 just a few months before he died. We got two persons, one on each side, to help him on the podium. He got up there and he grabbed the music stand with his left hand and conducted with his right. The longer he conducted, the wilder he got – and by the time he ended he was conducting with both hands and holding on to nothing. Then, he put his hand on the music stand and gradually lay his baton down. I had a rack around the podium, and he turned very slowly and nodded to the audience. As he was conducting he had no problems. I think it was his last time conducting in front of an audience, ever.*[32]

Soon after, he was in the Dimondale care facility, and thereafter its nursing home, and though not his old self, was remarkably active, making plans to take the Michigan State University Alumni Band to Europe.[33]*

**Earle Louder:** *The last contact I had with him was just before he died. I was in Detroit playing the Detroit Concert Band that March, and Byron Autry, who taught trumpet, said that Mr. Falcone was in Okemos in a home. "If you want you could call, but he might not recognize you," he told me.*

*Of course I called, and when he came to the phone, I said, "Mr. Falcone?" and he said, "Earl!" There was no hesitation. We spoke for about 30 minutes, the most wonderful conversation.*

*He was going to take the band overseas and he had some of his better players. He was very much looking forward to taking the band to his childhood village. After 30 minutes, he said, "I'm tired and I should go to bed," and we said goodbye. And that was the last time we spoke. He died shortly after that.*

*It wasn't just music that was important to him. It was people. He knew who I was.*[34]

CHAPTER 15

# SUNSET: MAY 2, 1985

***"Good-night, sweet prince; And flights of angels sing thee to thy rest."***

**~ William Shakespeare**
***Hamlet***

---

*The old man lies still in his bed looking sweet and feeble on his blanched linen pillow. His breath heavy, he hears a faint voice drift into his dying consciousness like a melody. It whispers his name. His eyes remain closed, his breathing quickens. A beautiful, beautiful, aria wails tenderly from somewhere in the distance, calling mermaid-like to him, and he follows the sound. And then, as if there were a string somewhere under his left ribs that led straight to the heart of the little village of his birth, as though the cerulean sea, and hundreds of miles of land could not separate them, he drifts closer to its wellspring and bathes in its pure and lustrous silvery tones, until finally he hears his name again, this time loudly and called with some urgency from beyond. And now as he draws near to the source, he readies to answer the call, to be transported to a time and place that is not this time and place, and his breath turns to a shallow panting. He is near death.*

**Beryl Falcone:** *In the end, on his last night, he didn't want dinner. All he wanted was ice cream, and I finally managed to find some for him. He didn't want to get out of bed and eat, but the nurses didn't seem too concerned about it. Finally, I went home at about 7 or 8, and he just went to sleep. And they called me at about 10:30 to tell me he had passed away. He just kind of went to sleep. Lisa and I went there, and I went in (to his room) to tell him goodbye. He just kind of went to sleep.*[1]

**Lisa Fulton:** *We were in shock because we didn't realize it was going to happen that fast. I couldn't get myself to go in and see him when he died. I was just 16. I've regretted that my whole life.*[2]

LEONARDO VINCENZO FALCONE, "The Dean of the Big Ten Band Directors," departed this life on a Thursday evening, May 2nd, 1985, at the St. Lawrence Dimondale Center in Dimondale, Michigan.

Surely, it was comforting to the family to know that so many of his students and friends cared so deeply. Just the Monday before, an alumni group had come to the nursing home to sing to him, and on the afternoon preceding his death, he had a visit from old friends.

**Mary Platt, trumpet, MSU 1975-1982:** *We sang in four part harmony and this smile came over his face and he applauded and a nurse said, "You made him very happy."*[3]

**Kenneth G. Bloomquist:** *I saw him the day before he passed away when Dale Bartlett and I went to see him in the nursing home. It was memorable. We brought a tape recorder with big knobs on it— not difficult to run, because he didn't have the stamina to do anything— with his records on tape. So we bought this so he could listen to it. He was very, very quiet, very tired – he had no energy at all. When he would talk I had to get my ear an inch or two to his mouth to hear him, and he whispered, " Ken, why is this happening to me?"*[4]

During the evening of the day before he died, 30 members of the MSU Marching Band serenaded him in his wheelchair with MSU's "Fight Song" and Alma Mater, "MSU Shadows."

> **Mike Melnik, trombone, MSU 1981-1987:** *Here's a guy who's as close to God as you can get in a college marching band, who has had thousands of students play under him, and we were the last. Just being able to get a band that size together in the middle of midterms shows how much we cared for him.*[5]

"MSU Shadows," the last music Leonard Falcone heard performed in his life, was also to be the last tune played at his funeral.[6*]

Comforting, too, was the near certainty that in the weeks preceding his death, even though his ability to recall and communicate was greatly diminished, music was surely his constant companion, filling his mind with lilting strains that raced through the air and memories of his baton taking flight.

> **Cece Falcone:** *I never wear a radio at work or walking or at any solitary time, because something is always playing up there. It could be a church hymn or a commercial ditty or an old 60's song that was playing in the car. It will play continuously until replaced. Cheap entertainment- no iPod needed.*
>
> *If my head is anything like my dad's, and I'm pretty sure it is, then he had something playing in it all the time. In the months before his death, he may not have remembered what a piece was titled, who wrote it, or been able to discuss it on any level, but I doubt his memory of music itself ever faded. It probably comprised most of what little recollection he had left near the end, and it may have been ALL he had of his old self in the final days of his life. I can't know that for sure and it's too late to ask, but I truly think that this is so.*[7]

Days later, hundreds of former and current MSU band members from across the nation attended his funeral mass at the St.Thomas Acquinas Church in East Lansing, with several of them participating in the service. One former student, Roger Behrend,[8*] who at the time was with the US Navy Band in Washington, D.C., was given the honor of being asked by MSU School of Music Director Kenneth Bloomquist to play his euphonium. Most fittingly, he chose "Ave Maria."

**Roger Behrend:** *(It) was the ultimate tribute and honor I could pay to the man.*[9]

Those who knew Leonard well not only stressed his humility, integrity, and insistence on excellence, all of which became a model for hundreds of thousands of music students across the nation, but also his contribution to Michigan State University and the American Band Movement.[10]*

**William Austin, MSC 1933-1937:** *He (was) loved by thousands who played under his inspired baton. Actually, he (was) loved by the entire music world.*[11]

**Burton Bronson:** *He was demanding in the sense that he wanted you to achieve your greatest potential. He made all the difference in my life.*[12]

**Robert Sack:** *He was one of a kind. Such a fine musician and person. So talented. He was never unfair. He was strong. He did not allow people to mess around. We were lucky to have Leonard Falcone. He was not only a great educator, musician, and band director, but he was also a person that everyone really admired.*[13]

**Keith Stein:** *One of the finest men I've ever known. Totally honest. Totally above board. Never had a rotten word for anybody, or, if he had one, he didn't speak it. One of the great guys. And he always was exemplary in that he didn't say, "Do as I say." It was, "Do as I* do.*" He practiced. I could hear him. (My office) was below his. And he played concerts—he didn't just conduct . . . He stayed active. How many guys do that? He stayed active all his life. And he was a great disciplinarian, which I think is tremendously important. And he disciplined himself equally. So he was exemplary in every way. A tremendous man.*[14]

**Henry Nelson, MSC Band 1940-1943, 1946-1947, flute, sousaphone, string bass, saxophone:** *Leonard Falcone was one of the most moral and honorable men I ever knew. I had to become an adult to realize all of this. I learned then of his help to his students financially, vocationally, and in so many other ways.*[15]

**Kenneth Bloomquist:** *Falcone was revered in the profession of band conducting as being one of its giants, not only as a conductor, but as an arranger. His reputation nationally was unequalled as a euphonium soloist.*[16]

**James Niblock, Chairman MSU Music Department, retired:** *I have been proud to be a part of a university whose conductor of bands was so progressive in bringing his students into the music world of wind ensembles, wind orchestras, and various wind and chamber organizations. His incomparable musicianship elevated BANDS to higher levels.*[17]

**Harry Begian:** *His most important contribution was in developing one of the finest college bands in the country. He was an excellent musician and he produced students that always played at a very high level, with outstanding qualities both musically and on the marching band field. That's my sincere feeling, and the feeling of most of the people I associate with.*[18]

**Fritz Stansell:** *One of Leonard's many legacies is that he had a hand not just in the evolution of college bands, but high school bands as well. He and Revelli and other university directors from that era helped the fledging MSBOA get started because they could see its ultimate impact. They were mindful of the fact they had to help the high school bands be successful in order to produce good college bands, and then their college bands produced music students that went back into the high schools to teach. I spent 2 years with the Muskegon High School orchestra, and what became apparent was there was no one in the state that took an interest in high school strings the way that Leonard Falcone took an interest in helping school band programs.*[19]*

**Dale Bartlett, retired Assistant Chairman, MSU School of Music:** *He brought to the university a national prestige. He was one of the kings in the band field. John Phillip Sousa is a king, and so is Leonard Falcone.*[20]

As for his youngest daughter, she found it impossible to imagine her father, though gone, without his music.

**Cece Falcone:** *I believe that dad willed himself to die. I really do. At the end, when he could no longer do the things he loved to do in this world, he longed for the next. I think he's in a spiritual realm right now with his music, and someday I'll be able to play for him again.*[21]

As a final gift to Michigan State University, Leonard Vincent Falcone, who had already given so much to the school and its students, in a gesture of unbelievable generosity literally gave himself, and willed his body to Michigan State's Department of Anatomy.

*Last known picture of Leonard Falcone*
*~ courtesy of the Falcone family*

CHAPTER 16

# CODA

***A teacher affects eternity; he can never tell where his influence stops.***
**~ Henry Adams**

---

In 1927, Leonard Falcone found a marching band which was known and respected locally and regionally, and a concert band that was practically unknown anywhere. Probably his biggest contribution to MSU was that during his lifetime, he raised both groups to national prominence and made the music department a powerful force at the university.

Underpinning his every action and decision was his philosophy of the role of the college band, that it is not only an end in itself as a musical medium but that it is an important means of training music education majors who would themselves train future generations of musicians long after he was gone. His influence as a musician and a human being on his students and peers runs deep, and it reverberates in their lives even today.

> **Henry Nelson:** *He was so instrumental in shaping the lives of so many of us—responsibility, dependability, punctually, morality, and I could go on. I haven't even mentioned his musical influence.*[1]

> **Myron Welch:** *Leonard Falcone made an enormous impact on the music world, and how he did it is both complex and simple.*

*The sheer force of his dedication and his enormous talent play a large role, but perhaps most important of all, the lesson of his life is that he was a hero as a human being.*[2]

**Tom Gillette:** *Leonard Falcone was one of only a very few profoundly GOOD influences on my life, from a musical standpoint, from a "global" how to look at music's place in the world, to just plain being a gentleman . . . having a clean shirt on, a crease in the "T-rousers" and so forth. He poured all of the good things that were him into us, and some of them took root and grew.*[3]

**Kent Krive:** *His character, musicianship, warmth, and humility have left an indelible impression on me, setting a standard higher than I can reach, but one which inspires continuous reaching.*[4]

**Merritt Lutz:** *I believe Leonard is one of the very few special people that affected my life. He was such a great man, such a moral guy. He always took the high road; he always did the right thing. The man himself, how he was, you know, even aside from the music, you learn from a guy like that.*[5]

**Fritz Stansell:** *He was a musical icon. Though he never discussed with me anything like the meaning of life, religion, politics, or philosophy, by example, he always set the highest standard for honesty and personal integrity in all he did. I feel very lucky to have had his friendship.*[6]

**Pat Facktor, MSU 1958-1962:** *In the spring of 1958, I was a 17 year old high school senior playing in the State Solo and Ensemble Festival, held that year at Michigan State. As my father and I were walking out of the music building, a gentleman passed us in the hall, nodded a greeting, and suddenly said, "Loomis! Grand Rapids! Trumpet"! My dad had attended Michigan State College for just one year, Mr. Falcone's first year, 1927-28, and Mr. Falcone had remembered him from 30 years past! He asked what we were doing in the music building, and when we ex-*

*plained that I had just played in the solo and ensemble festival, he asked if I would like to go to Michigan State. I declined, stating that I had been accepted at Central Michigan College, and even already had my roommate. But he persisted, and so I played for him, and he offered me a scholarship to attend Michigan State. And I accepted.*

*I can only say that that 5-minute encounter with Leonard Falcone changed my life completely. Whenever anyone asks me if I can define a changing moment in my life, this is the story I tell them. If we had not run into Mr. Falcone, I would NOT have gone to MSU. I would not have met my husband and, as my granddaughter once correctly stated, "Grandma, I wouldn't have been born!"*[7]

**Robert Sack:** *He was an influence to all of MSU. He was the premiere baritone player in the United States during his lifetime, and was highly regarded as such, he was at State for so long and was respected highly and honored by all the conductors in the Big Ten, and he developed a very high standard of music and professionalism to a generation of students which impacted a lot of their lives for the good.*[8]

**Dan Pearson, Band Manager, 1957-1961, business major:** *I learned so much from him. I told some of my business professors that I learned as much from Professor Falcone and the band about managing people, getting along with people, as I did in some of those business courses. He was a strict disciplinarian, no monkey business, and he treated everyone the same. I learned discipline from this man.*[9]

**Kenneth Bloomquist:** *Leonard was like a father to me. He was one of the warmest and most musical human beings I have ever known. I will never forget him, and the world shouldn't, either.*[10]

Though perhaps Leonard's greatest achievement was his influence upon the lives of the thousands of students who came under his direction, many of whom went on to found a music camp or attain prominent positions as college, high school, or community band directors, concert stage musicians, or service band members, the beauty of Leonard Falcone's life is that his influence doesn't end with his students or with MSU. As a figure in the American College Band Movement, even now, long after his death, he stands at the pinnacle alongside only four or five others. His musical spirit extends into the lives of hundreds of thousands of today's young people, who have had it infused in them by those he taught.

**Earle Louder:** *I definitely inherited his instructional philosophies and teaching style. You can't help but absorb the things you see and are involved in as a performer in the band with him in front of you as the conductor – or being in his office and having him sit next to you, one on one. He taught, for lack of another phrase, through the "back door." I do this, too. Say you have a problem in articulation. Mr. Falcone would never say, "Here's and exercise you can do to address that problem."* No. *He used the music we were working on to address it so in your mind, then, you would not be saying to yourself, "I have a big problem with articulation." He'd get your mind off the difficulty you were having, but through the music it was addressed automatically. It was back door teaching, and I've inherited that from him. I use that when I teach.*[11]

**Tom Gillette:** *Sometimes it comes to mind when I'm in my basement with a fairly talented 8th grader on trombone. I find myself being "L.F." First I shake my head, look gravely at the floor, and wonder just how in the hell I am going to fix this mess. I ask the kid if he practiced, and he politely explains about homework, wrestling, etc.*

*Then I pick something to work on. Last week I picked on a legato tonguing issue, demonstrating Leonard's "thu-thu-thu-" tongue, which is bizarre, but it works in some cases . . . and suddenly this little figure came out from this kid. I don't know how he did it, but I laughed inside and said, "Thanks, Leonard."*[12]

A strikingly similar comment comes from a man who found himself teaching a master class with (surprise!) Maestro Falcone sitting right next to him.

> **Marty Erickson:** *When I teach, I often recollect "My Master's Voice" instructing me and I simply pass on the lesson. This time, the voice wasn't just in my mind, because sitting close to me for the presentation was Mr. Falcone saying under his breath, "Don't forget to tell them about . . ." "Remember that . . .", etc. I had my own world class "prompter" the whole clinic. Everyone loved seeing this interaction, my nervousness, and the shared respect. Things went very well, and it probably wasn't until THAT moment, that I "came of age" as a professional.*[13]

And then there is the realization, one made by many former students, that what was learned from Leonard is now so second nature that it is hardly identifiable as something separate from the everyday way of doing things.

> **Ted Thompson:** *(Leonard's) influence on me personally was considerable, but I find it somewhat difficult to pinpoint or put into words. I believe I just grew with him without being aware of the things I was absorbing. I suspect that I emulate his techniques, his conducting style for instance, without really being aware of it.*[14]

Leonard Falcone's deep devotion to his music, his students, Michigan State University, and his family formed the central meaning of his life, providing it with great dignity and purpose. The memory of his enormous talent and humanity, his exactitude, dedication, integrity, and even his innocence and unique mannerisms, has been raised to mythic proportions amongst those who knew him, most particularly his students, friends, and family, who all gladly share their remembrances of this extraordinary man.

# Memories

**"Put your talent into your work, but your genius into your life."**
**—Oscar Wilde**

**Dr. Harry Begian:** *I was on staff for 10 years in the 1960s at Michigan State during the summers when they had high schoolers on campus for the Youth Program. One day, Mr. Falcone said, "I'd like you and your wife to come over for dinner tonight" at his home with him and Mrs. Falcone, and a music publisher, a Mr. Malecki, who was there to talk with him about a music order for the Michigan State Band in the fall. And I said "Sure!" Everybody had heard about Mr. Falcone and his Italian spaghetti dinners. That evening, we were sitting at the dinner table enjoying the meal, when all of a sudden there was a clamor outside. The front door was open, and we heard a kind of loud chattering. About the same time, Leonard's girls came to the table, and one of them said, "They're back!" and Mr. Falcone, sharply rising from his chair, barked, "Those damn nuisances!" Without another word he went to a nearby closet and pulled out a shotgun!*

*"Excuse me," he said, as he politely stopped at the table and pumped the gun. Amazed, we watched as he went outside, took aim at the trees, and began shooting. "Damn birds!" he said as he came back in. Then he put his gun away, and sat back down at the table as though nothing out of the ordinary had taken place. Apparently, starlings had congregated in the trees, and with this shotgun, he scared them away. It was a funny experience.*[15]

**Cece Falcone:** *I remember the summer of the starlings. There were bazillions of them in the trees that lined the street. Someone had loaned my dad a shotgun which he and other neighbors would shoot off to try to disperse them. I was amazed at my dad for using a weapon and used to show the hidden gun to my friends. Boy, today he (and the others) would have been hauled off to jail* *for shooting firearms within the city limits and for having unsecured weapons. I'll take the old days, thank you.*[16]

**Lisa Fulton:** *My grandfather enjoyed making his famous spaghetti dinners. They were literally always the same in terms of preparation. My job was to set the table and carefully pour water in the water glasses, and also to bring in the different entrees. The meat was always served separately, something like round roast or something. You had meat with a very plain sauce and of course pasta with a sauce flavored by the roast, bread, salad, and finally a dessert. Sliced carrots, sweet pickles, black olives for hors d'oeuvres. For those meals, he always did the cooking, and he would always serve. He was very proud of it. He liked having a house full of people and entertaining.*[17]*

*Pasta time*
*~ courtesy of the Falcone family*

**Beryl Falcone:** *We always invited visiting conductors over for spaghetti at the house and they often brought their wives. I don't think we ever had the Revellis—they always had to go back to Ann Arbor immediately with the band.*[18]

**Walter Hodgson:** *We'd have wine, and then a big spaghetti dinner. His brother would come over. After the spaghetti they'd come in with a big platter of fried chicken or something. And then we'd have an Italian dessert on top of that. We'd stagger out, stupified.*[19]

**Earle Louder:** *Louise and I raised a couple of kids while I was an undergrad at MSU, and I painted cars, houses, and played in dance bands to make ends meet. Something the Falcones did—they would have Louise and I and our little son, Joe, over to the house for spaghetti. Leonard would kick Beryl out of the kitchen and he would put on a chef's hat. It would take him all day, and it was served in traditional Italian courses. It took a long time to eat it. He took such pride when he did this. It was wonderful. It made us feel like we were part of the family. When we asked him, "How do you eat spaghetti in Italy? Do you twirl it in the spoon?" he took some on his fork, put it in his mouth, bit it, and let the rest fall into the plate. This is how you eat spaghetti.*[20]

**Beryl Falcone:** *Leonard made his own pasta from scratch, and he did the cooking and serving of it. But the rest of it I did so things were ready when guests came to the house. When we first got married I was an amateur cook at that point and I would experiment with things, and he'd say, "I like this," or "I don't think we ever need to eat this again." I knew where I stood, anyway. But he was always a great cook. He cooked lots of Italian dishes, and would cook for the family every Friday.*[21]

**Cece Falcone:** *Dad never forced weird Italian foods on us, but I know he liked squid and he used to make this awful stinky mess with chestnuts.*[22]

**Lisa Fulton:** *The second time I went on a European tour with Blue Lake International we got there 12 hours late and our host family prepared a meal that we ate at midnight. They had a salad with weird little things on it. I was pleading with my eyes to my grandfather and he started taking them off my salad and happily eating them himself. They turned out to be anchovies.*[23]

**Tom Gillette:** *I had the opportunity for a couple years to spend many Saturdays doing housework at the Falcones. Once when I was there he made pizza. He demonstrated how Americans did it wrong with the cheese on top, then the meat, and explained how soldiers during WWI did it wrong. I tasted the pizza and it was certainly different. Ten years later, when I moved to Chicago, I understood that he had been making Chicago style pizza. He seemed to know his way around a kitchen all right.*[24]

**John T. McDaniel, baritone, MSU 1972–1976; MSU Technology Coordinator:** *I worked for a number of years from the late 1970s to mid-1980s recording the Spartan Marching Band performances in Spartan Stadium. This was when the Photo Deck of the press box was at the bottom, and was open air. At many games, Leonard would come and sit with us to watch the game, especially the colder games late in the season. At one such game, late in the 1982 or 1983 season, Leonard, fresh from a hospital stay after surgery, joined us. He was looking hale and hearty, and was wearing his heavy black wool overcoat, hat, and those buckle galoshes of his. As the game concluded, he asked if I could provide a ride home, as Beryl and granddaughter Lisa were at Blue Lake for an International Band rehearsal weekend. Certainly I could provide a ride. Well, he said, he had to stop by the store for some medicine on the way. That would be fine.*

*As we left the deserted stadium I asked for directions. We headed west on Michigan Avenue past Frandor, and I was surprised to think there was a pharmacy in this direction, or at least one open this late on a Saturday afternoon. Well, the store turned out to be Coscarelli's Market, and the "medicine" con-*

*sisted of ingredients for a sauce, pasta, a wedge of cheese, and some bread. As soon as we entered the store (we were the only customers there) everyone greeted Leonard as if he were royalty and seemed to know exactly what he wanted. He explained that before his surgery, food had lost its flavor and he'd lost interest in eating. Now, he was looking forward to going home with the women gone and cooking up a big meal! Part of his purchase included two packages of Stella D'Oro Vanilla Egg Biscuits. When we arrived at his home on Charles Street, he handed me a package of the cookies. "I want you to have these. They are very good with coffee in the morning." He was right, they are very good with coffee in the morning, and each April, I try to find a package of the "Leonard Falcone Egg Biscuits"at the grocery to celebrate his birthday.*[25]

**Cece Falcone:** *When we cleaned out dad's office after he died, we found Stella D'Oro cookies stashed everywhere. His office was the only place they would be "safe" from the rest of us!*[26]

**Lisa Fulton:** *My grandparents used to have band boys help out around the house on the weekends. My bedroom was painted by baritone students annually. I loved it. It didn't need it, but it was great fun picking out a new color every year.*[27]

**Beryl Falcone:** *Leonard's students did work around the house. It was a good thing, too. When we first moved in, the whole place needed paint. I did the painting, and one hot summer day I was painting the linen closet upstairs when he said, "Let me help you," and took the paintbrush from me. I went and did something else, and when I came back . . . so you know how an artist paints? Well, he was painting like an artist would at an easel. One little brush stroke here—and then one little stroke there—and then a little leaf and then a fine blade of grass. I stood there, and I looked at it and I thought, "Ok, well, that's the end of that." He just did not know how to do it. It finally came all together—and the paint did not leave any marks. Nevertheless, around the house he was not* *real handy. He didn't even know how to use a screwdriver—he just didn't know.*[28]

**Henry Nelson:** *No, he was not handy. Stan Finn, formerly a clarinet instructor at MSU, told me that he and Leonard were on their way to a judging event with Leonard driving (yikes!) when a tire blew. As Stan heard the ominous "flubbity-flubbity," he said to himself, "One of us will have to change that tire, and it won't be Leonard Falcone." Moments later, as Stan was changing the tire, Leonard came up behind him and said, "Let me help you, Stanley," and handed him a pair of pliers.*[29]

**Tom Gillette:** *Beryl kept me and a couple other guys busy with some cleaning and yard work projects along the way. She ran her household (where we cleaners were concerned) with the precision of a drill sergeant, and explained processes very clearly...ever the teacher! Lisa was a pleasant little girl of around 8 when I was there, very polite and fun. Her grandfather doted on her almost to spoiling.*[30]

**Lisa Fulton:** *I had him wrapped around my little finger. I don't remember him ever really disciplining me. It was always my grandmother. He was not the kind of person to be confrontational.*[31]

**Tom Gillette:** *They were generous in providing work, and paid quite fairly. When it would snow or something unusual, there might be an early call to shovel out the drive, sometimes followed by hot chocolate and a Stella D'Oro ("The name means "Gold Star," Leonard would explain). It wasn't exactly "make-work" but we were there about every weekend and when needed.*[32]

**Earle Louder:** *I painted the Falcone's basement walls, they were cinder block, 4 or 5 times when I was a student. Because he would recognize that Louise and I had some financial problems, he would have me come over and let me earn money. That was the perceptive side of him—he was perceptive of needs, and did not want to make me feel like I was getting a handout.*[33]

**Marty Erickson:** *Mr. Falcone seemed to be able to sense when his students were in "distress" financially and would invite us over to his house to perform some odd jobs for a little money. On one of these occasions, I appeared at the Falcone home on a late Saturday morning to await whatever work was to be done. Mr. Falcone greeted me warmly, and, as it was fall, assigned me the task of raking the leaves in the yard; he said I'd find the rakes and leaf bags in the back. Glad to have something to do, I walked out to get my rake, but noticed that the yard was absolutely pristine in its "unleafiness." I picked a single leaf off the ground and offered it to Mr. Falcone as evidence. He said: "Hmmmm . . . oh, that's right, I had a student do this already. O.K. then . . . ummm . . . oh yes—I would like you to clean the windows!" So, with rag and window cleaner in hand, I trudged upstairs where I expected to find filthy windows awaiting my attention. But again, someone had beaten me to the job. You could eat off these windows! Disappointed, I reported to Mr. Falcone that the windows were already, quite literally, squeaky clean. Once again, he remembered that this task had been done during a visit from a different student. So . . . after puttering around picking up a piece of paper, moving a chair a couple feet in a different direction, etc., he simply said: "Well, let's listen to some music!" I sat on the sofa and we listened to recordings of the bands and some Italian songs for more than an hour or two, and then he (or perhaps Beryl) fixed some spaghetti for a late lunch. We talked about my family, the music, my plans for the future, and more. Finally, it was time to leave, and as I prepared to go, Mr. Falcone said: "Oh, wait! I forgot to pay you!" I said, "Thank you, but I didn't really do anything." "Oh, of course you did!" he replied. "You were here for over 3 hours and we agreed on $3 an hour, so here is your money." I hadn't remembered an "agreed upon" fee for my "services" and $3 an hour was a LOT in 1966.*

*Years later, those of us who helped around the house realized that our visits had less to do with managing household chores than with mentoring, caring, teaching, setting an example, sharing quality time, and so much more. Just telling this story makes my tears swell and my heart ache for this incredible, gentle man.*[34]

**Kent Krive:** *Dr. Falcone seemed to have an insatiable desire to counsel his band members. . . his beloved band members. I say "beloved" because the kind of abiding concern implied by the attention he paid us could only have arisen out of love.*[35]

**Cece Falcone:** *He truly liked to help. Of course, it might also be considered "butting in" from a kid's perspective. For example, when I was in high school, I played in a woodwind quintet. Not to be boastful, but we were great (with our parents in the music department, how could we be otherwise?). Every evening we would go to Howie Niblock's house (James Niblock's son), set up our stands, tune, and then play euchre the rest of the night. Nobody ever bothered us (and we always got straight 1's at festivals!). Well, once we went to my house. We set up our stands, tuned, and then dad appeared, and had us actually rehearse! The nerve! No euchre that night! We never rehearsed at my house again, and any time I was practicing and his car pulled in the drive, that horn went back in the case, pronto. He was never critical—he just thought we were all as dedicated as he was and wanted us to succeed—when maybe we would rather have been playing cards!*[36]

**Mike "Screech" Dineen, trumpet, MSU 1981-1984:** *We played for Dr. Falcone at his home on Halloween of 1982, the first time I met him face to face. He was 83 then. When we arrived at his house, he came out onto the front porch to meet us and we played the "Fight Song" and the theme from "Flashdance." When it came time for us to play and sing the "MSU Shadows," everyone sort of looked at each other for someone to conduct—we were all terrified at the thought of doing it in front of Dr. Falcone. I volunteered finally, made my way to the top step of the porch, gave him a nervous "Hello," and turned to face the musicians. "Chord, sing, play," I said, and with my trumpet cradled in the crook of my left arm, I raised my right to conduct. We played the chord and were about to begin singing when Dr. Falcone suddenly said in his famous accent, "What chord is that?" Assuming the question was for me, I replied, "A-*

*flat." "That's right!" he grinned. You must be a music major!" We finished singing and playing the "Shadows," exchanged goodbyes, and though we moved on, for me, the moment is frozen in time. The thrill of hearing those words, "You-must-be-a-music-major," from a living legend on that October night defies overstatement.*[37]

**Cece Falcone:** *The band habitually serenaded. Every year at Halloween a group would march down the street after dark and play in front of the house. Then at Christmas a group would come and sing carols out front. Dad always had apples for them at Halloween (even though it was a "surprise") and hot chocolate at Christmas. Good memories.*[38]

***"Man is distinguished from all other creatures by the faculty of laughter."***

**~ Joseph Addison**

**Fritz Stansell:** *I've been trying to figure out the answer to the important question of why Leonard Falcone has become, in the memories of so many of his students and others, almost a mythic character, and why so many seemingly mundane incidents that he was involved in became so humorous. Perhaps it was because he was extraordinarily gifted musically and so straight forward in all his dealings with people. Certainly, because English was a second language, he missed much double entendre. Also, his Italian accent played a part. Almost every band member, when quoting him, to this day tries to imitate his speech mannerisms and hand gestures. His honesty, innocence, and naiveté made him a perfect "straight man" in setting up humorous situations.*[39]

**Cece Falcone:** *My dad wasn't a comedian and I only heard him tell one joke, ever (and it was off-color!). I think it was just his honesty and innocence that lent for amusing comments, actions, and encounters.*[40]

**Beryl Falcone:** *He had a good sense of humor, but he didn't always get a joke. I think former students pulled jokes on him and he never did get the point.*[41]

**Tom Gillette:** *There were little head games his private students would play. These were harmless things, and the tradition had continued for years. For example, back in the days when his office was next to the band room, someone would point out the window and tell Dr. Falcone how nice the bushes looked. Word would be passed to the next student to do the same . . . and so it would continue, and upon hearing this, a big smile, and a nod, and an eager, "Yes, they DO look especially nice, don't they?" This would culminate in seeing the Old Man outside at the end of the day, taking in this beautiful scene. No harm no foul. In later years it might be something as simple as "Tell him you like his tie!" and it would continue through the day, or "Your windows look cleaner than ever!" I don't know why we did it . . . probably because he seemed so genuinely PLEASED with these things, and it was just cute!*[42]

**Lisa Fulton:** *He was so pure in so many ways. His mind didn't fathom how someone could choose to do something they weren't supposed to do. His mind just didn't go there. Part of it was his culture, the family he came from, the fact the world was changing so quickly. I could get away with things he was oblivious to, though I seldom took advantage of it. But one time I drove the car before I was 16. I was 15 and I only had my learner's permit, and I said, "I'm leaving now and I'm taking the car," and he said "okay!"*[43]

**Beryl Falcone:** *In a lot of ways he was very innocent and I heard a lot of people say that about him.*[44]

**Fritz Stansell:** *During a rehearsal of the Concert Band (in about 1951), Leonard was rehearsing with his usual intensity . . . demanding absolute precision in technique while, at the same time,* *asking for sensitivity and expression. I don't remember the piece, but it may very well have been the overture to "La Forza Del Destino" by Verdi. In any case, the music was pulsating in rhythm, and technically demanding. As with many such 19th century orchestral transcriptions for band, the use of a sudden silence with tension is a device used by many composers. In other words, during a rest for the entire ensemble, one can still feel the press of the meter as you wait for the re-entry of the group. These quiet spots are the very likely places for someone to make a mistake . . . or play on a rest. As the music progressed inexorably to a climactic grand pause, the musical tension built. When we arrived at the totally quiet moment, the sound of someone releasing gas was unmistakable to at least the back rows of the band. Instantly, sniggering broke out, partly because there was a good attack and the tone was full (not to dwell on it, but the release was excellent . . . and it was in rhythm!). A few of us seated near the soloist were unable to resume playing when Leonard continued conducting the score. In growing frustration, he stopped the band and started over. By this point, more and more members were trying desperately to hold back laughter. After another failed effort to get the band playing again, he stopped, and while beginning to smile himself because he could tell that everyone was greatly amused . . . he then asked, "Did I do something?" . . . and then the entire band exploded with uncontrolled guffaws. As you may imagine, it was quite some time before the band could resume playing. This is an absolutely true story. I was there (but not responsible)!*[45]

**Anonymous, one of the mid-'70s bawdy "boys:"** *He had an innocence. We had a thing with him, using the phrase, uh . . . "Mangia Mia" or something . . . a bunch of us in Marching Band using pigeon Italian to describe . . . um . . . uh . . . "Eat me." It has the same number of letters as in "S-T-A-T-E" and worked well with some cheers of the day. Here we were on the sidelines at a football game yelling "Mangia Mia!" . . . and suddenly there is Leonard right beside us! He pulls* *us aside and explains that our grammar is wrong— that we need to add a word . . . "What you boys said was 'Eat ME' . . . and what you meant to say was (some Italian like 'Mangia Tu Mia') . . . which means 'Eat WITH me' . . . Or maybe you meant (more Italian), which means 'Eat AFTER me.' It went on and on, and he kept saying "You were saying 'EAT ME,' which doesn't make any sense at all, does it?" And we somehow managed to keep straight faces!* [46]

**Merritt Lutz:** *He often didn't get it. He was so literal. I remember in 1964 or 1965 when we played a Henry Mancini tune related to the Pink Panther, and Leonard would say, "Let's play that song about the cat."*[47]

**Tom Gillette:** *Just strange ways of describing things that gave you a look into his life...one piece, for example, "Concerto" by G. Mangnan, had a section near the end that had these quick, successive 16th notes outlining ascending chord members 'Da-da-da-da- DAAA-AAAAH, Da-da-da-da- DAAA-AHH." Somehow it sounded familiar. "This part reminds me of that bird...that bird on the television," he said. I'm lost in thought trying to put this together, and then he played it...and I had this vision of Leonard Falcone, sitting in his living room, for some reason watching Woody Woodpecker. He obviously had, or he wouldn't have the reference. Whether or not it was a favorite, I don't know— although I PERSONALLY think Woody's "Barber of Seville" is far superior to the portrayal by Bugs Bunny and Elmer Fudd.*[48]

**Earle Louder:** *Even from the podium he had some real fun with us at times. I remember one time we were rehearsing a piece called "Divertimento for Band" by Vincent Persichetti, 3 short little movements. This was in 1950, and in that day, this music was out in left field. You'd play like two fragments of a melody, and then jump to another melody. He was conducting along, and all of a sudden he gave a cut off very quietly, and he laid his baton on the stand and slowly crossed his arms. He got this quirky look* *on his face and with a gleam in his eye he said, "You know, this music is like alphabet soup—all the letters are there—but they don't spell anything."*[49]

**Fritz Stansell:** *He had a sense of humor, but I never heard him poke fun at himself.*[50]

**Cece Falcone:** *Long before cd's existed, way back in the '60s somewhere, dad adjudicated this band somewhere and they were so awful he asked for a copy of the tape. They had played the* 1812 Overture, *and the conductor was yelling "BOOM!" where the cannon shots were to be heard. Dad did get his kicks out of it. One other time I remember him laughing until he cried was up at Blue Lake when Bill Cosby was doing a show. Dad was in a lawn chair on the unsteady ground near the shell. He was laughing so hard, I thought he was going to tip over! I got a bigger kick watching him laugh than watching Bill Cosby.*[51]

**Carl Bjerregaard:** *In the last days of Bill Stewart's tenure at Muskegon High School, Leonard was asked to be baritone soloist with the band. They were having their final rehearsal before the concert that night when suddenly the outside door opened with a blast of cold wintry air. Covered with snow, he came in, took off his coat and galoshes, and placed his horn case on top of a nearby old fashioned steam radiator. Bill finished rehearsing one of the more involved pieces for the concert, introduced him to the band, then asked if he would like to warm up. Leonard walked to the radiator, opened his case, and picked up his baritone. Feeling the bell, he said, "Feels warm to me!" and stepped to the front of the band, ready to play.*[52]

**Harland Nye:** *I never heard him "warm up." He just picked up his baritone and played.*[53]

**Dr. Jon P. Nichols, MSU 1973 and 1979:** *At the Midwest Clinic in Chicago in 1977, Bill Berz (MSU '73, '78, '82) and I sat with*

*Mr. Falcone in the balcony of the Chicago Hilton during a concert. Afterward, he asked if he could buy us some "refreshment," and we accepted ("how could we not?) and proceeded with him to the old horseshoe ice cream counter at the hotel. We were all enjoying the treat when all of a sudden a straw wrapper came flying over the counter right into Mr. Falcone's ice cream. His blue eyes went black and he became indignant—until he looked over, and saw that it had been blown at him by Raymond Dvorak, retired Director of Bands at the University of Wisconsin. Mr. Falcone broke out into a smile. "Well, Raymond," he teased, "I see you still have good lung capacity from your years directing the Glee Club at the University of Illinois. That was back in 1926, wasn't it?"*[54]

***"To be nobody but yourself in a world which is doing its best, night and day, to make you everybody else, means to fight the hardest battle which any human being can fight; and never stop fighting."***

**—e.e. cummings**

**Dr. Harry Begian:** *I think of him as a very gentle man, a calm person who spoke very well and who was able to get the results he wanted. At times he'd say, "I don't express myself very well," and I'd say, "You express yourself beautifully." Because he was very thorough in everything he did, I think his speech was something he was always sensitive about. I understood this concern, as Armenian is my first language—I didn't learn the English language until I started school. My parents were from the old country. Mr. Falcone coming from Italy spoke very, very well, and expressed himself clearly so that people knew what he was saying.*[55]

**Lisa Fulton:** *I asked him one time why he didn't speak more Italian, and he said, "I'm an American. I speak English." That's all he said to me. For years and years and years, the local Italian chapter here would invite him to dinners on Columbus Day, and* *he would never go. He was very proud of his Italian heritage, but I think he wanted very much to be an American and to be accepted as one.* [56]

**Beryl Falcone:** *He had a slight accent. He would get certain words . . . I can't think . . . there are students stories that bring that out.*[57]

**John Underwood:** *We, as I'm sure all the bands over the years, were often reminded by Dr. Falcone that members need "individual prat-is."*[58]

**Fritz Stansell:** *His speech mannerisms were constantly imitated by nearly all of his students (always behind his back and, of course, respectfully). The typical impersonator would speak through clenched teeth while gesticulating with the right hand. I don't think Leonard could have talked without using his hands in countless expressive, interesting and arcane gestures. It was fun to watch him as he spoke. "I can't understand how you can play when there is no note!"or "I can't understand how you can play like that and then sit there with those innocent looks on your faces!"or "I can't understand how my own students could do such a thing!" were typical quotations.*[59]

**Earle Louder:** *He had that little shake of his hand. He would have his hand out and accentuate words with motion. He'd lift his hand up and rock it back and forth with the rhythm of the words he was saying. Not a hard motion—a rhythmic motion. It could be either hand, depending. It was something he did automatically. An automatic reaction. A sort of motion.*[60]

**Lisa Fulton:** *Sometimes it was just the way he said things that was different. He used to call the "7-11" the "7-Up." I never sensed his having any kind of accent when he was alive, but since he's passed away I've heard tapes of his voice and I've been surprised to hear a little bit of an accent there.*[61]

**Fritz Stansell:** *He had favorite words. The way Leonard always summarized apparent procrastination, apathy, lethargy, was to say he/she has a "lackadaisical" attitude. I swear that he loved to use this word. I heard him say it many times. Example: "The sassaphone section has a lackadaisical attitude." Perhaps he liked it because it has that musical, mellifluous and rhythmic sound of Italian. Of course, working with young musicians I suspect he felt he was always surrounded by lackadaisicalness.*[62]

**Merritt Lutz:** *He didn't want people bad-mouthing or trash talking anybody. He was professional. He always said, "That is not professional." "Professional" is showing up on time, "professional" is saying nice things, etc. Leonard would never say anything bad about Michigan or Revelli—and when someone else did, he'd say "We need to be professional." That was one of his favorite words. It was a code of behavior—always positive, always clear, always honest.* [63]

**Joe Dobos:** *I listened to a couple of tapes of my interview with Leonard, which was the only time I really had a conversation with him. He had a gentle, flowing tenor voice. Very melodious. An excellent vocabulary. He had a lot of expression. "Amazing!" or "Marvelous!" he would say.*[64]

**Tom Gillette:** *It wasn't just his speech that was unique to him. In 1970s, it was the "Ted Baxter" era, Jimmy Carter was in the White House, and other music professors were sporting turtlenecks, plaid pants, leisure suits—some even wore the "Full Cleveland" (Google it . . . it's a stitch!). But Dr. Falcone usually wore gray trousers, pressed, blue blazer, or a brown suit, a white shirt, conservative tie, shined Oxford shoes. Often there were rubbers or galoshes in the corner.*[65]

**Beryl Falcone:** *He was particular about his grooming and he wanted his students well dressed. We went to a program in an* *auditorium once and a man came in a plaid shirt; it was winter, and I remember Leonard saying something to me about how incorrect it was for someone to come to an evening performance like that.*[66]

**Tom Gillette:** *Blue jeans were in vogue in the '70s, and one wore them EVERYWHERE at MSU...except for in Dr. Falcone's office. Another euphonium student once did, and was immediately asked, "Did you come from another job? I see you're wearing dungarees." And throughout that day, and that week, LF's concern about this matter came up to other students . . ."Do you know if ___ is working at another job early in the morning? He came to his lesson wearing dungarees." It was a tacit reminder.*[67]

**Beryl Falcone:** *When he bought a new suit, he would fuss over how it was made. One summer shortly after we moved into our house I decided to make draperies. I'm really not a seamstress, and I was struggling away with it and finally one day he said, "Put it all down, I'll finish it." And he did. He took over the sewing machine and he made them. They looked good, and they hung on our windows for a few years.*[68]

**Joe Dobos:** *When we were interviewing him (January, 1984), he took his coat off and showed us the stitching and how lousy it was. He said he could have done it much better.*[69]

***"Hide not your talents. They for use were made. What's a sundial in the shade?"***

**~ Benjamin Franklin**

**Carl Bjerregaard:** *He was respected by everyone, even students meeting him for the first time. While I was band director at Muskegon High School, Falcone guest conducted the "Finale" to Tchaikovsky's* Fourth Symphony. *I had been rehearsing in a fast* *four, slightly slower than the traditional tempo, and he started conducting in two, almost twice as fast. He stopped and asked, "Can't you see my beat? It's very clear. Two beats per measure." Wide-eyed panic set in. Backs straightened, students moved to the fronts of their chairs, and each did his or her best to keep up with the faster tempo. Every horn went home after school and that night, before the concert, the practice rooms were ablaze with activity. Students understood the challenge, and had great respect for the man and his musicianship. In just one rehearsal, he had built an amazing rapport. The performance was a great success, and afterwards, Leonard Falcone was a happy man. Needless to say, many of those students later attended MSU.*[70]

**Carol Burt Porter, saxophone, MSU 1957–1961:** *He had such a natural way of getting us to do our best, and demanded such respect that there was never a thought of not paying attention. And whenever another conductor would take the podium . . . wow! We'd struggle to follow him, and realize again just how good Dr. Falcone was!*[71]

**Kent Krive:** *One day, Dr. Falcone was tuning the band, one by one, using the venerable Strobo-tuner. When he reached the trombones, the principal player, Don Thornberg, couldn't seem to hit the proper pitch. On each try he was either above or below it. In mild frustration, Dr. Falcone marched to Don's side, demanded his trombone, and announced "This is how it should be done." Then, looking elsewhere than the tuner, he put the trombone to his lips and gave an assertive blast of air. It was a tuning Bb, all right. He did it three times, and each time, the Strobo-tuner's visual pattern came to such an abrupt stop (indicating perfect agreement), that the wave of snickers was barely audible. Just another instance of Dr. Falcone's impeccable ear.*[72]

**Earle Louder:** *I heard him play when I was in high school, and it knocked my socks off. I knew right then I wanted to study with him.*[73]

**Beryl Falcone:** *He had perfect pitch. We were in Paris, and a police car went by and I remember asking him, "What pitch is that?" And he would whistle it and tell me.*[74]

**Ron Salow, cornet, clarinet, MSC Band, 1946–1951:** *During a Wednesday night rehearsal in 1950, we were playing Nicholas Falcone' s marvelous arrangement of the* Carman Suite. *There was a section with a short piccolo duet, but as only one piccolo had shown up for rehearsal, I naturally didn't expect to hear two parts playing. Yet when we got to the duet, there they were. . . two piccolos, as clear as a bell! I shot a glance over to the first row where Roger W. was playing the first part, and saw that sure enough, next to him was an empty chair. Guess what? Leonard was whistling the second piccolo part to perfection. Just another talent of that fantastic man.*[75]

**Leonard Franke:** *We were rehearsing in what at the time was the new music building—they were just finishing the work on it—and during the rehearsal somebody with a sweeper was going down the hall, and it was kind of loud. Mr. Falcone stopped the band and said, "Will somebody go out there and tell them to stop that noise? It's in the key of F and we're playing in E-flat!" He asked a flute player to play in both keys, and sure enough, he was right.*[76]

**Kenneth G. Bloomquist:** *After he retired, every time we got him to conduct the Marching Band for sure he would always conduct the "Alma Mater" and the "MSU Fight Song." He had wonderful sense of pitch. He would raise his hands and hum the starting note to the band.*[77]

**Harland Nye, tuba, MSC 1949-1953:** *One time in a lesson I was working on high notes and felt I had reached my limit. I said so, and thinking that the mouthpiece was the problem, suggested that a smaller one might make those notes easier. Mr. Falcone took my horn, my mouthpiece, and easily played not only the* *note I was having trouble with, but an arpeggio an octave higher. "It seems to play," he said simply, handing the instrument back to me.*[78]

**Carl Bjerregaard:** *During a 1959 summer session rehearsal in the MSU band room when I was a student there, Dr. Falcone was rehearsing Rossini's* Semiramide Overture. *In the famous horn quartet section, the first French horn player was struggling, playing some wrong notes and having intonation problems. He stopped the band, said a few words to a young lady to correct the problem, and started that section again with no improvement. He stopped again and patiently proceeded to relate the corrections to the "young lady" more emphatically. Again, the same problems occurred. "Young Lady," he repeated, and gave her a short lesson and lecture with obvious irritation. Again, little improvement. In frustration, he left the podium and headed toward the French horn section as band members quickly moved stands and chairs, creating a clear passage. He borrowed her horn, and with the bell in the air and without using the valves, played the part perfectly. Of course, it sounded more like a baritone than a French horn, but "Young Lady" got the message and the rehearsal continued.*[79]

**Dr. Harry Begian:** *He was the most thorough musician I've ever seen. Wonderful as a conductor, a performer. I never saw him make a mistake. Mr. Falcone make a mistake? Unheard of! It was a gift. He had an intensity that he applied to whatever he was doing. It was something he had.*[80]

**Harland Nye:** *In four years, I never heard him play other than perfectly. Never a bad note or sound.*[81]

**Tom Gillette:** *Make a mistake? In performance? No...never. That's part of his legend. During practice as I listened outside his door? Yes . . . he might chip a note, but he would go back and BLAST the correct one. This was consistently a LF means of beating mis-*

*takes for his students. "Play that note very LOUD," he would say, and you would. He was MILES ahead of* Zen and the Art of Motorcycle Maintenance, *which I read at that time and tried to explain to him—the concept of implanting a "right" idea into your mind* and *body so that the two work together. But he simply said, "I don't know what this has to do with motorcycles. Let's get back to the music." He was EXTREMELY accurate. His recordings were generally made in one take.*[82]

***"Always be a first-rate version of yourself, instead of a second-rate version of somebody else"***

**~ Judy Garland**

**Robert F. Meyers Sr., MSU Concert & Marching Band 1957-1959:** *Mr. Falcone was a perfectionist and this trait demanded 100% effort of those lucky enough to be associated with him.*[83]

**Cece Falcone:** *I heard this second hand from who knows whom so I don't know if it's true or not, but it was that he quit performing because he was afraid that he would make a mistake. Dumbfounding to start with. I would never have played note one if I had set that high a standard for myself. It shows the perfectionist that lived within.*[84]

**Kenneth G. Bloomquist:** *I asked Leonard if he would perform Verdi's* Manzoni Requiem, *orchestrated with a euphonium and trumpet replacing the male vocal solos, with the Symphony Band in the early 1970s (he would have been in his mid 70s then). Though he told me he didn't perform any more, I didn't give up. "I can't do it," he said, and I said, "You've never played for me as a soloist when I am conducting." Finally, he said, "I will do it, but I want to sit in the back next to one of my students in case I need help"—which he, of course, didn't. He played it beautifully and he never faltered. I'll never forget it.*[85]

**Dan Pearson:** *He was meticulous about a lot of things. The managers and I would have music set up for rehearsals—the racks set up—we'd have the chairs set up and everything ready to go at a certain time, and I mean it. He wanted those chairs on those squares on the floor of the old music building. Every chair had to be at the right square. He'd come in and he'd conduct. He would get up on podium, and it was all business.*[86]

**Joe Dobos:** *When Leonard was a student at Ann Arbor's School of Music, Gustav Holst conducted May Festival one year, and he visited Nick's theory class to give a lecture. Later, they went to the concert that Holst wrote for orchestra and choir and during the concert something wrong happened so he stopped the whole thing, and made a correction. The audience applauded and then they went on. Leonard's comment was "Those Englishmen, they can't stand one little mistake."*[87]

**Fritz Stansell:** *Part of Leonard's perfectionism was his punctuality, which was legendary. Band rehearsals began at precisely 5:00 p.m.*[88]

**Beryl Falcone:** *One of his favorite phrases was "If you are on time, you are late." He expected you to be in your seat and be ready to play at the beginning of rehearsals.*[89]

**Earle Louder:** *One time I was sick with the flu. I was never late to a rehearsal, never except this one time. As I walked up to the door, I heard the band playing and I thought "Oh, no!" His treatment of someone who came late to rehearsals was unique. If you came in late and he was conducting, he would very gently stop, cross his arms, and his eyes would follow you until you got to your seat. The band would be stone silent and you'd feel 2 inches from the floor by the time you were seated. Then he'd pick up the baton and would go on with the rehearsal. He could have flown off the handle, and yelled like I've heard other band directors do in the same situation, but he didn't. That to me was a show of kindness—as well as a show of learn.*[90]

**Robert F. Meyers Sr.:** *Years before my first appearance as a member of the MSU Marching Band I stood curbside as the band marched to Spartan Stadium. As the proud Green and White Corps passed I vowed, "Someday I will march in that band!" Years later my time came. Though I went to the music building a full hour early to prepare, I ended up on the practice field 2 minutes after the "fall in," and after the band was already in formation. Mr. Falcone (from his raised platform) and everyone else stared at me in my running approach as I fell into rank. "Nice of you to join us," he said in his most sarcastic tone. Since that experience I live by his maxim, "If you're on time—you're late!"*[91]

**Earle Louder:** *It didn't matter what status you had with him in the studio. If you stepped out of line, you were quickly brought back into line.*[92]

**Denny Morrill, cornet, MSU 1960-1964:** *Fall, 1963, we were becoming slack in the attitude department about Wednesday night concert band rehearsals because of all the hot, grueling marching we'd been enduring during the day. Dr. Falcone, increasingly irritated by our lack of discipline, finally reached his breaking point one Wednesday and grimly mounted the podium to give us a piece of his mind. "First of all," he accused, "some of you are sliding into your chairs a minute before rehearsal begins. You cannot properly warm up, tune, and get your music and mind organized without adequate time to prepare. If you aren't at least 15 minutes early, you are late! Second, some of you are becoming careless in your dress. You are not to wear Bermuda shorts, sandals, or sloppy t-shirts in rehearsals. It is unbecoming."*

*We all slunk down in our chairs as he ended the lecture, gently opened his score, and raised his baton. At that moment, to our horror and entertainment contra-bass clarinet player Jim Leet, a reed dangling like a cigarette from his lip and swinging his instrument case with his music stored under his armpit, sauntered in through the door behind Mr. Falcone, a full five minutes late. His clothing selection for the day? Bermuda shorts and a t-shirt.*

*There was a collective gasp that all but sucked the air out of the room as we awaited Jim's execution. And then, a miracle: Mr. Falcone merely shot him a glance, paused, and gave the down beat. Later, we heard that Jim had received permission to arrive late—but why Mr. Falcone decided to allow him to live another day after wearing shorts and a t-shirt to band rehearsal we'll never know. Had he decided he'd already said all there was to say on the matter?*[93]

**Charles Aurand, MSC 1950–1954:** *As a new freshman at Michigan State College in 1950, I recall going through my first class registration in the "bull-pen" at the Auditorium. Students at that time picked up class cards for each of the courses they planned to take for the term. Being totally inexperienced at this new process, it took me longer to complete than one might normally expect. The result was my arrival at the 5:00 p.m. marching band*

*Leonard at his desk*
*~courtesy of Michigan State University Archives & Historical Collections*

*rehearsal at 5:05—five minutes late. The band was on the field next to the Music Building and Mr. Falcone, on an elevated observation platform mid-point of the field, saw me running to my position on the field. "Aurand, see me in my office following rehearsal!" he barked. Later, I found our Director seated behind his desk. His instructions were brief and unemotional, but firm:"Charles, don't ever let this happen again." And I didn't. The lesson that I learned, don't be late to an appointment, arrive early and be fully prepared, is one I've never forgotten. Mr. Falcone taught me not just musicianship, he taught me responsibility.*[94]

**Fred Elmore, tuba, MSU 1966-1970:** *I was a freshman in the fall of 1966, Dr. Falcone's last year as director of the Marching Band. I was the alternate, i.e., the last one in the door and admittedly the least talented of the tubas. I recall Dr. Falcone's very strict definition of "on time:" practice starts at 5 PM, meaning you are in your seat/position with a pencil ready and your instrument tuned. One time that fall we had had a practice in the field house—I do not recall why, but we did—and though I was on time and in position, one of the tubas was not. Dr. Falcone walked down our row, noticed the empty tuba position, saw me standing between the rows, and said, "What are doing out there?"*

*"I am the alternate, sir," I said.*

*"Not anymore!" he boomed.*

*The tardy tuba showed up shortly afterward and confronted me. "You are in my spot," he said.*

*"Leonard Falcone put him there. Nobody moves him!" piped an upperclassman.*

*A good lesson learned: I never missed marching in a game for four years.*[95]

**Fritz Stansell:** *Leonard rolled his car once on the way to Blue Lake. He was on the expressway and exited without slowing down—and rolled the car. He wasn't harmed, and here's the thing: he arrived on time for his rehearsal, punctual as always.*[96]

**Kenneth G. Bloomquist:** *When he got home, he couldn't find his keys for the university, and he thought he'd lost them when the car rolled. He went back the next day to the accident site and found them.*[97]

**Beryl Falcone:** *Sometimes he was a speeder. And he had a bad habit of driving and talking to someone in the back seat. He looked at the people in the car instead of the road.*[98]

**Earle Louder:** *I rode with him to Ann Arbor once for one of the workshop conferences he used to have and it was one of those times you find yourself holding the door handle.*[99]

**Harry Begian:** *I remember driving with him one time, and it was pretty fast . . . He was not completely on the road.*[100]

**Henry Nelson:** *I was judging a festival with Leonard, and was driving. We stayed the night before in a motel in Ionia. When I picked Leonard up the next morning, he told me that he had been sick all night and couldn't possibly judge that day. We discussed what to do as we drove to the nearby festival, where it was decided that Leonard would return to East Lansing driving my car, a shift Mustang. It was then that Leonard announced that he couldn't drive a stick shift (even in good health), so we all trooped out to the school parking lot where he practiced driving around and shifting. There was some concern amongst the group about the wisdom of my loaning Leonard my car, but after we somewhat dubiously ascertained that he could drive it, he took off.*

*All through the day I wondered and worried about the outcome. Finally, at the end of the day, Joe Scott, who was also judging, drove me to East Lansing. There sat my car in front of the Falcone home on Charles Street . . . with the keys in the ignition! I got in, drove home, and never said a word.*[101]

**Cece Falcone:** *When he was in the service, he directed some post band and also was a driver (Oh my God!!!) for some officer.*[102]

**Henry Nelson:** *He went to Fort Custer in Battle Creek where one of his early duties was that of chauffeur. He was assigned to an officer who was a follower and admirer of his as a performer and director, and who was chagrined and embarrassed to have a person of Leonard's stature and reputation as his chauffeur. Leonard was later in the Fort Custer band, where he played* fourth *chair baritone because he was militarily outranked by the players in front of him. Leave it to the army! He was finally given leadership of a band at a glider base in Arkansas. He told me, "Henry, they sent me 16 men, and only 9 of them could read music!"*[103]

**Earle Louder:** *The word "fear" comes up sometimes in discussions about Leonard. But a better word for that "fear" of him is "awe." Respect. You feared him in that you didn't want to do anything wrong—you wanted to do everything right for him. Not that you would be punished for it. But you had desire to do right for him. He would bend over backwards to bring home a concept, and make it understood. For instance if I were playing an excerpt and not quite getting right musical expression, he would take his horn and say, "Try it this way." He would never say, "No! That's not right!" He was very respectful. Very humble. He had a positive approach to teaching.*[104]

**Carol Burt Porter and Robert Sack, saxophones:** *One time at a practice we were playing a technically difficult piece when there was a rest, and someone played a note. Suddenly, off the podium flies Dr. Falcone, and down through the band he plows, music stands and chairs parting like the Red Sea. We '"sassaphones" were too frozen to move. He reached our music stand, and pounding on it with his baton, roared, "Now why did you play that note there? How did you know what note to play? There's nothing written!" And he was serious. The rest of us settled our stomachs and tried to continue. It took a while, but now I (WE?) laugh about it, and have had so much fun telling it.*[105]

**Fritz Stansell:** *Leonard never could understand how any of us could do such a thing as to play on a rest.*[106]

**Kent Krive:** *He was a natural musician. Implicit in the term "natural" is the notion that mundane operations involved in the making of music, such as counting, tuning, even expression, seemed to be inborn, not requiring conscious effort. Roger Topliff, one of the most outstanding clarinetists to ever grace the principal chair of the MSC Concert Band clarinet section, enjoyed a warm friendship with Dr. Falcone. In the course of one conversation which must have occurred during the early 50's, Dr. Falcone mused to Roger, "You know, Roger, I've always wondered why band members would play in the wrong places in the music. How could they play when there are no notes to play? Or how could they play notes other than the ones written? I've finally figured it out: THEY DON'T COUNT!"*[107]

**Ted Heger:** *We were sitting together (at Blue Lake Fine Arts Camp) at a final Sunday concert and a middle school band was performing "American's We" at a comfy tempo. Mr. Falcone said, "I can't understand why young people's tongues are so slow!"*[108]

**Dan Pearson:** *I want to say what a humble gentleman he was, how I would often visit him in Music Building 116. He might be playing his baritone horn, but he'd want to see me. He would put his horn in the garbage can and we would talk, we would make plans. Specifically, he had me come down in the fall to go over things. I would go over to his house at 519 Charles. I happened to live with an elderly lady on Charles, and I'd walk over to 519 and Mrs. Falcone would give us tea and we would talk about the upcoming band season. It may not sound like a big deal, but to a farm boy from West Michigan, I was quite awed by this man. I realized, even at that age, that I was seeing him in a different way, or in a different light, or at a different time, than many of the music majors.*[109]

**Joseph Dobos:** *Listening to my interview with Leonard about his brother, almost constantly, he takes great pains to not praise himself. "This is about Nick, not me." When speaking of himself, his accomplishments, his musical gifts, he would say, "I'm embarrassed to talk about it." "I shouldn't bring this up, but I got this honor. . .but I was just doing my job." I would never get that from Revelli.*[110]

**Tom Gillette:** *He had such integrity. On one occasion, when the university was about to hire a new trombone teacher, one of the euphonium students got a small piece of information . . . that the name of the front-runner started with an "O." This got a lot of speculation going—Alan Ostrander, a friend of Dr. Falcone's who had played with the Boston Symphony and was about to retire, came to mind. He was a heavy hitter . . . and we were excited about that possibility. Dr. Falcone overheard some of this, and spoke with each one of us about what we knew, what we thought, and what we had heard. Then he put the rumor to rest, not by calling Alan Ostrander and confirming or denying it, but instead, (at least with me) explaining clearly first that "Mr. Ostrander is my friend," and then squashing it, not because it was true or not, but based on the absence of good information. In that sense, I realized that he was teaching me something about the nature of rumors (I remember his telling me that), and how sometimes rumors could be damaging. "Let's wait and see how this turns out," he finished. A couple of weeks later, we met Curtis Olson, the new trombone teacher, who was/is a wonderful addition to the MSU faculty. We learned that only part of the rumor was true, and that once again the Old Man was right.* [111]

**Joe Dobos:** *I graduated from U of M in fall of '71 and we played at MSU. As the Marching Band came off the field, there was Leonard saying "Sharp! Sharp! Very sharp!" Typical of him to go to the visiting band and congratulate its conductor.*[112]

**Leonard Franke:** *He was a great conductor and a great guy. He was honest. He was always straight with us, even if we were making mistakes or whatever.*[113]

**Daniel Hornstein, euphonium, MSU band 1965-1968:** *Mr. Falcone had insisted at my scholarship audition that I needed to change my embouchure—I was ducking my head and "smiling," which limited my range. And so I spent a summer in misery, having to go back to the Belwin Band Booster Book I, which I had used in 5th grade, and watching myself play in a pocket mirror so I wouldn't slip back into the ways of the wicked. The process was not by any means complete when I showed up that fall, and my first lessons with Mr. Falcone were somewhat rocky. But finally, about November, I felt things were falling into place and I thought I had delivered a pretty good lesson. But as I was walking out of his office, he patted me on the back. "Never mind, Don," (his Italian accent could never quite manage "Dan") he said, "It should go better next week." I teared up, and headed back to the practice room.*[114]

**Harland Nye:** *I learned early on that he was not a person to give individual compliments. In my lessons, when I was working on a study or etude, the closest he would come to sounding pleased would be to say, "Well, we'll let that go for now." I played the Williams' "Second Concerto for Tuba" for a student recital, and following the performance, he spoke to me about it, saying (in all sincerity) "Harland, that was almost musical!" Was that a compliment?*[115]

**Dan Pearson:** *I came to MSU fall of '57 with no intention of being in band. My roommate was a senior, a music major. He talked me into playing a walk-on. So I got out the alto sax I'd played in high school, and went to audition for Mr. Falcone. He asked me to play "Barnum and Bailey's Favorite." I tried. He cleared his throat. He said, "In band we have a position for Band Manager." I took it.*[116]

**Robert F. Myers:** *Under his tough shell was an ever-present compassion. Never would he utter an insult, and as a true teacher, he strove to find a path for a student to follow to his or her fullest potential. As a high school student, I was a large "bug" in a very small puddle. I had played the accordion for 12 years and been an adequate euphonium player in my 25 piece high school band. Then I presumed to enter MSU to study euphonium as a Music Ed. Major. After a few lessons, Mr. Falcone very respectfully suggested I change majors.*

*"But music is my life!" I responded, to which he replied, 'Then you have this term to prove it."*

*Four years later, as our last lesson came to an end, he said," you've worked very hard and come a long way. Don't stop now."*[117]

**Fritz Stansell:** *Leonard didn't make the rules, but by his very nature he had to conform. He was frankly, in the best sense, a conservative. . . a status quo guy. He was never an innovator. Neither was J.S. Bach, but they both were masters of the environment in which they found themselves.*[118]

**Lisa Fulton:** *He was conservative in many ways, and I always sort of knew we were a conservative family politically, though we never talked politics, ever. When the first female ran for vice president, Geraldine Ferraro, I wore a huge button on my jean jacket and I heard her speak at Michigan State. She's a woman, she's Italian, and that was good enough for me! I came home with that huge button on my jacket and he looked at it and shook his head as though to say, "What are you* doing*?!" The problem, I think, was not that there was a woman on the ticket, but that Mondale-Ferraro were Democrats.*[119]

**Cece Falcone:** *When I wanted to get a car, he didn't say "No," he said "Get a job." I think he had to earn everything he had and taught the same lesson to me. FYI, he never bought anything on credit, even the house. That's the way he was and my* *mom could never convince him otherwise. He thus had no credit rating at all!*[120]

**Tom Gillette:** *Politics? World View? This is a side I don't know...I don't suppose we ever talked about that. . . .But he was conservative in his concert programming, his speech, even what he drove. I remember a couple of cars. . .one a small Oldsmobile, silver, replaced by an Olds Omega, maroon—not sporty, not big, not small. . . velour upholstery with a whisk broom near the driver to keep it clean.*[121]

**Beryl Falcone:** *When we were married, he had a Plymouth. Later, we drove Oldsmobiles. They would give us a deal.*[122]

**Tom Gillette:** *And as I said, he was also traditional in his conversation, always careful, in speaking of former students, to call them "Mr." or "Dr." to me.*[123]

**Dr. Harry Begian:** *They are titles of esteem. I never called him anything but "Mr. Falcone" because I felt so much respect for him as a wonderful man besides being a wonderful musician. Out of respect, I could never call him by his first name.*[124]

***"Rivalry adds so much to the charms of one's conquests."***

**~ Louisa May Alcott**

**Anonymous:** *He was a good disciplinarian. In the folklore of the brilliantly talented pioneering college band directors of Mr. Falcone's generation, such as Leonard Falcone himself, Glenn Cliffe Bainum (Northwestern), Ray Dvorak (Wisconsin), A. Austin Harding (University of Illinois), William Revelli (University of Michigan), and Clarence Sawhill (UCLA), there are several legends of tyrants who degraded their bands and belittled individual players for minor errors—this, supposedly in the service of dis-*

*ciplining them in a way which was supposed to lead somehow to producing great music. Yes, they received excellent and sometimes even spectacular results—but with hurt feelings and broken spirits in their rear view mirrors. Mr. Falcone had respect for his players, so when he disciplined them, it was never malicious. He valued his players as musicians and human beings, and because he did, he received not only their respect, but their great love as well. I believe that his respect for others is the greatest lesson of his career, and of his life.*[125]

***Harry Begian:*** *Never, never, never, did he say an abrasive word when talking with his students or his colleagues. That's the kind of guy he was.*[126]

**Dan Pearson:** *There was a trumpet player in the band, a terrific player, who had an attitude and an ego. Falcone had a way of whipping him into shape, just by looking at him and being Falcone. He had a way of doing it without putting anyone down. Stern, but I don't remember him ranting or raving or shouting. Falcone's way of disciplining was not like Revelli's. We used to hear about Revelli at Michigan doing that, but not Falcone.*[127]

**Dave Wisner:** *I never talked to a UM band member who actually liked Revelli, and I never talked to a State band member who didn't like Falcone. Not that Revelli wasn't good. He was. But we always laughed because it seemed like U of M's band was billed as*

**WILLIAM D. REVELLI**

AND THE *UNIVERSITY OF MICHIGAN BAND*[128]

**Leonard Falcone:** *(Revelli) is a very strong minded person. Right or wrong. He takes a stand and that's it. And it could be completely wrong, but he'll stick to it until he makes everybody think it's right. It could be that six months later, he'd make a complete change the other way and then insist that that way is right. It's* *in his personality, his mentality. He's determined to espouse a definite line and stick it out, and if you don't agree with him, well, that's too bad. If I had to share a position with him such as co-director of an organization, I'd refuse. I don't believe in being so dogmatic. That's for him. . . . I will not try to impose my feelings on others forcibly. I think other people have a right to an opinion.*

*He's extremely articulate, a very fine public speaker who can project his ideas and principles very strongly. He has not only confidence in himself, but the strength of character to maintain his point. Couple that with the fact that he has the means to do it, such as his position at the university with all his resources and his first class students, and well, he can do those things. I didn't resent Revelli. I realized why the eminence was there.*[129]

**Beryl Falcone:** *The men argued once in a while about certain things. I remember a game when Leonard was very upset because Revelli took too much time at halftime. The game would have happened here. Whoever the visiting director was, they would divide up the time. Leonard always claimed that the Michigan band took more time than they were allotted, and it took time away from the State band. Halftime would be over and State hardly had any time on the field. He'd talk to Revelli about it. That's where the arguments came in. Mary Revelli and I were always very cordial with one another.*[130]

**Earle Louder:** *I witnessed an argument between Bill Revelli and Leonard once. They were at a game, and after the game the Revellis and the Falcones were in a line and Louise, my wife, and I were there. Mrs. Falcone was first in line, then Dr. Revelli, Mr. Falcone, Mrs. Revelli, then my wife and me. They got into it, and Mrs. Revelli and Mrs. Falcone stepped in between them to keep them apart.*[131]

**Gretchen Stansell, French horn, MSC Band 1952–1954:** *In 1953, I was sitting at the 50 yard line of some football game, and it was* *after the half time shows. Leonard and William Revelli walked by using their hands very expressively, the way you sometimes see Italians doing, and both were going at it in angry, loud voices. I don't know what it was about, but if I had to guess, I would say it had something to do with time spent on the field during halftime.*[132]

**Fritz Stansell:** *Naturally, as visitors, Michigan would have gone on the field first, and if they took too much time, the MSC band would have to have curtailed their program in order to prevent a delay of the second half. This might have caused a penalty for MSC because of the band. I'm certain that for years, Leonard had been very careful not to let his band go overtime in Ann Arbor. It's easy to understand his anger when Revelli was careless or deliberately went long in East Lansing.*[133]

**Anonymous:** *The background of their rivalry is enormous. Nick, Leonard's brother, never got much credit for the success of the UM band from Revelli, and this had to have bothered Leonard, though I doubt he ever spoke of it.*[134]

**Joe Dobos:** *When I interviewed Leonard in 1985, we listened to a recording of some clarinets—and he stopped the recording and said, "Ya know, Bill (Revelli) did not have the only good band in the state!" Leonard had the highest respect for all band directors—but he was soft spoken, never pushed his way into something. Revelli was like a bull-moose—a born salesman . . . (He was) a hurricane, a tornado, and Leonard was like a gentle breeze. I still have Revelli nightmares sometimes. He could make you sweat. He was rough—but underneath it all we knew he loved us a lot—and that counted for something.*[135]

**Leonard Falcone:** *You can't help but sense the competition, particularly on the football field . . . But let's put it this way: I never felt antagonism toward Revelli. It was a very strong, friendly rivalry.*[136]

***"If you enjoy what you do, you'll never work a day in your life."***
**~ Confucius**

**Tom Gillette:** *Dr. Falcone's office was on the first floor, next to the bandroom back in the day. . .116 MB which was/is always the Director of Bands office. It was about when he retired in 1967 that the Music Practice Building, the god-awful ugly thing next door, was built and he had an office on the 3rd floor, having given up 116 to Harry Begian in 1967 and later to Ken Bloomquist, Stan DeRusha, and others who came later.*

*Now, ascending into the 1970s and early '80s, we walk from the basement of the old music building through the tunnel and up the stairs and/or elevator, and towards 319MPB, the post-"retirement" office of Leonard Falcone. The door is open. To the left is his gray record player and a good stack of records . . . some Toscanini, some Enrico Caruso, some band records, one with familiar handwriting on it in black marker saying "Bad note . . . do not listen." To the right, in the corner, is a utilitarian steel desk. On that desk sits a dial telephone, which is always answered "Lllllllllllllleonardfalconespeaking" in a crescendo/accelerando fashion. Next to the phone is the famous little typewriter where Dr. Falcone bangs out little notes to his students, two fingers, with amazing speed and interesting commentary as he mentally and verbally corrects himself. A* State News *is on the desk, open. Ahead of the desk is a work table with a score or arrangement in progress. Next to the record player sits a box, and atop the box is the prototype for the "Falcone Model" made by the Holton Company, which is essentially a copy of his old Conn instrument. And next to the desk is a square wastebasket. Into this wastebasket, little paper finds its way, but the wastebasket is the perfect spot for his gold-plated 1928 Conn baritone to perch. It is always there, right next to where the Old Man stands in lessons, within easy reach, and the wastebasket fits it perfectly. Occasionally a dirty Kleenex might be stuck to the tubing when he picks it up, but the waste basket works well for him.*[137]

**Kenneth G. Bloomquist:** *When I became Director of the School of Music 1978, Leonard would arrive at the Music Building rather early every morning. It was very common for him to knock on my office door before 8:00 a.m. just to sit and talk. Since I was an administrator rather than a band director at that time, I loved those conversations about "the good old days." One morning in the early 1980s he knocked on my door and cried, "My barrtone's been stolen!" Shocked, after a brief conversation with him I called the police who were at my door in a matter of minutes. They reported the theft and proceeded to contact their sources, which included pawn shops all over the area. Announcements on radio stations and in the newspapers let the world know that "A famous euphonium player and teacher" had had his valuable instrument stolen.*

*On the third day after the theft, a petite lady who was a new custodian came to my office and, after some effort on my part to engage her in conversation, said, "I heard that a famous man's instrument was stolen." I confirmed this. "I have it," she said finally. "It was in the garbage can, and I thought it was trash. My little grandson really likes playing with it— should I bring it back?"*[138]

**Tom Gillette:** *One day, Dr. Falcone was fit to be tied. He had had his horn in the shop for some work after it turned up missing, and it just felt WRONG. He was frantically moving the valve buttons from one place to another, and grumbling that it just didn't feel right. He'd play for a bit, and stop and mumble, and switch 2 with 4, play some more, switch 4 with 1, and so on. This went on for a week or more. "There was a new caretaker in the building, and she thought my instrument was garbage," he told me. Apparently she took it home. It took some time to find it, and I took it to Marshall Music to have it cleaned. She meant no harm . . . she just didn't know."*[139]

**Kenneth Bloomquist:** *Leonard, at the end of the day, would always put his "barr-tone" in the wastepaper basket in the corner* *of his studio rather than in its case—everyone in the School of Music knew this and thought nothing of it. Moments after my conversation with the custodian, she literally ran out of my office. The instrument was dropped off at my secretary's desk about an hour later.* [140]

**Keith Stein:** *He (was) a great man, with his two finger typing. Amazing. Very much dedicated to the band. Mr. Richards just implored, then finally made him have a secretary. "You must have a secretary, you can't just peck away like this constantly. It takes too much of your time." But he dismissed her after 2 weeks. I think he thought he could do it better himself.*[141]

**Tom Gillette:** *It's easy to forget today what communications were like just half a lifetime ago. For Leonard Falcone, one very real link to the outside world was the small, old portable typewriter that sat squarely in the middle of his studio desk. Sometimes the door was open before my lesson time and I would hear the "duet" . . . first the non-rhythmic tapping of the keys, as a sort of ostinato, punctuated and accompanied by vocalizations; either actual words: "No . . . that's not what I wrote . . . " or "Uhhhh . . . hmmmmmmmm . . . oh . . . um . . . oh-oh." Then the scratching of the eraser, or, more likely, the sound of many over strikes, the backspace and the proper key used much in the fashion of rocking a car out of a snow drift. "Come on in," he would smile, "I'm just finishing this letter." I'd put my books on the stand, take a seat on the piano bench and watch. He typed with two very fast and not always so accurate index fingers, his eyes searching for the next letter almost like a curious kitten watches a moth. And always the commentary and vocalizations. Dr. Falcone's typewriter affected euphonium and tuba students in a tangible way. Walking into the Music Building on a given day, one might glance at the bulletin board just inside the door. There might be a collection of little notes, neatly folded and tacked up. One of these notes might have my name on it. There, typed, overstrikes and all, on a small sheet of note paper: "Please pick up* *the following books and solos available at Marshall Music and bring them with you to your lesson at 10:00 on Tuesday morning." And then the list . . . a LONG list, always, and expensive. You prayed it didn't include French music from Alphonse LeDuc because it was terribly costly. But sure enough, at the end, "36 Etudes Transcendentals/Charlier."*

*Here was the problem—(1) How to pay for this stuff. It was the middle of the term and the checkbook was overdrawn. (2) No car . . . hiking out to Marshall Music was a cold walk (3) Time—it was 4:00 on Monday, and you needed this stuff by the next morning. Sometimes one tried the music library, or one would borrow a book. You only did this once. "Why, this is from the library. We can't write on it, so it does us no good." Or . . . "This isn't your book, is it? If you use his book, what will HE use?" It never worked to try to put one over on the guy. So when the typewriter struck, you had to call home, beg money, take a cold walk, and bring this stuff to the lesson in the morning where you'd hear, "Very good! Except for this ONE solo. I'm not sure I like this edition . . . why did you get it?"*[142]

**Earle Louder:** *Oh, yes. The bulletin board. One Monday morning when I was a junior I came down the hall, and on a little typed note posted on the board was a list of who would be playing in the Thursday recital and I saw my name there alongside the "Concerto for Trombone" by Rimsky-Korsakov. I went to Leonard right away, and said, "You didn't tell me I would be playing," and he said, "Don't worry. Something is wrong, your name is on there wrong" . . .and then, "Wait a moment! We're working on the Rimsky-Korsakov, aren't we?" And I said "yes." "Okay, then let's do it!" he said. I said I wasn't sure I* could *do it. "I have confidence you can," he said.*

*On Tuesday and Wednesday I was in that practice room making sure I had it all memorized, and then I met with my accompanist. This was not about me – but in his saying, "I have confidence in you." I was shaking in my boots.*

*And I did it! Later, Louise (wife) said she couldn't believe it.*[143]

***"If you obey all the rules, you miss all the fun."***

**~ Katherine Hepburn**

**Earle Louder:** *Mr. Falcone was businesslike and ready to work when he was on the podium, but there was a side of him off the podium that was not all business. In 1956 when we went to the Rose Bowl, my brother in law loaned me his camera for me to take pictures along the way. I tied it in my baritone horn so I could reach back and take a picture while I was playing. I took some pictures at Pershing Square in LA, and I had some pics of Mr. Falcone because I was in front of the band. Years later we were looking at pictures and he saw these particular ones and said, "How did you get these?" We were not supposed to have cameras. He got a kick out of it.*[144]

**Henry Nelson:** *I no doubt enjoy the dubious honor of being the first at State to get the entire band inebriated. On a beautiful fall day in 1946 when MSC upset Penn State (19 to 16), the band marched back to the train station in heavy band overcoats and immediately discarded them on the train. We were hot and sweaty, happy for the victory, and thirsty. I noted a veteran's club near the station, and suggested to some of the older veterans—we were 24 or 25 at the time—that we might be able to procure a drink there. A bunch of us wandered over and rang the bell. When a steward came and suspiciously looked us over, we assured him that though we were not club members, we were all veterans—and on top of that, that we were still members of the ROTC, as stated right there on the sleeves of our MSC band uniforms! He thought about it a moment, and probably thinking of dollar signs, finally admitted us.*

*After enjoying a few brews, we drifted back to the train only to find out that there had been a delay before departure. Of course, we all returned to the club, only this time, practically the whole band joined us. We enjoyed our refreshments for some time, and then, upon hearing that the train was ready for departure, we all dragged back, smelling like a brewery.*

*Immediately before leaving, Leonard walked the aisles of the coaches checking up on us. He had to be aware of our aromatic condition, but he never looked right or left, and he never said a word. I always felt that he was so pleased to have so many of his "boys" back from the war that he overlooked our indiscretion.*

*Years later, when I told this story to Beryl and mentioned that he must have known what was going on, she said, "I'm sure he did."*[145]

**Beryl Falcone:** *The year we went to Ohio State for a football game, on the train, thanks to Oldsmobile, it poured down rain – it was a miserable day. The coach of OSU, Woody Hayes, would not allow the bands to take the field because of the soaking the field was getting. Wilma (Moffit) and I and the kids sat through the half time and then we went back to the train, which was on a siding very near the stadium. Now Leonard was not much of a drinker at all, but on that rainy day in Columbus, Wilma had brought some thermos jugs filled with mixed drinks. When the men got back on the train they were soaking wet (we hung uniforms all over that train trying to dry everything out), and Leonard was terribly thirsty. And so he asked, "What do you have to drink?" Meaning water. And Wilma said, "Oh, I've got something good right here in the thermos!" and he drank down a pretty tall glass of it. I don't think he ever really knew what he was drinking.*[146]

**Gretchen Stansell:** *The 1978 Blue Lake International Band was performing in a beer tent during the town's annual "VolkFest" in Hainburg, Germany, near Frankfurt and the Bavarian border. Leonard was conducting Wagner—"Liebestod" (Love Death) from Tristan and Isolde—and Fritz's German cousin, Gunhilde, a very dignified lady, was in attendance. I remember her putting her head in her hands and shaking her head and saying, "I cannot believe that I am listening to Wagner in a beer tent!" Anyway, someone in the audience brought a big Bavarian size mug of beer to Leonard, and between numbers, he would take a swig* *to the great enjoyment of everyone there. The kids in the band all took it in stride, and enjoyed seeing Mr. Falcone in a more relaxed (than normal) situation. Beryl and Lisa and Heidi were there, too, as well as Father Marek, who spent some time in the wine tent next door teaching the girls in the band how to waltz! What a night!*[147] *

**Dan Pearson:** *We used to take the train in the late '50s—the band was 160 men, plus extras—to Columbus, Champaign, Urbana, Lafayette, and other places. We'd take a bus to Notre Dame and Ann Arbor. Wonderful band trips. Instruments were kept in the baggage car, and I had the key. I would let the guys in there at night. Once we were in the stockyards in Chicago, and the guys were in there jamming. We are so thankful Leonard never found out about the jam sessions. He would not have approved. Supposed to be in our berths. We had some great train trips, all right.*[148]

**Jack Bates:** *One May or early June of 1936 or '37, the band was all bused up to Traverse City to parade in the Cherry Festival. We rode up in the early morning and returned to East Lansing that night. Our supper was furnished by the women of some church en route back. I didn't know what was going on during the meal, but apparently some band members helped themselves to sugar bowls. A few days later Mr. Falcone addressed us, telling us that the theft of the sugar bowls was most improper and that we were to pay for them from money in our band fund. He was not one to hand out a "boys will be boys" award when there was misbehavior. We were expected to 'toe' the mark with no fooling around.*[149]

**Dave Wisner:** *I was band president in 1958–'59 and spent a few moments in Mr. Falcone's office before almost every rehearsal. I remember one instance where we were in mild disagreement over smoking in uniform. I lobbied to get my point across, and was meeting with little success. He had a couple of historical stories to tell me about smoking on campus. Finally, in a last ditch effort,*

*I said, "How about if we have the band vote on it?" He looked up at me from his desk and in his kindest and much imitated accent said, "Dave, a band is not a democracy. It's a dictatorship. There can only be one person in charge, and in this case, that person is me." I left his office that day having learned yet another valuable lesson from him.*[150]

**Kenneth Bloomquist:** *His way was the right way and the only way, but he got what he wanted in a very gentle and kindly manner.*[151]

***To live is not to live for one's self alone; let us help one another.***

**~ Menander**

**Walter Hodgson:***(Leonard) got to know the boys real well. He kept track of them. He answered the letters they wrote him, and he didn't dictate them. He wrote them out.*[152]

**Merritt Lutz:** *I moved to Washington D.C. in early '70s. Lived at 4th and G SW. Anyway it was a Saturday and I was there by myself. I get a phone call. "Is this Merritt Lutz? This is Leonard Falcone." I thought it was a joke. He said, "Can't you tell my voice?" I said, "Where are you?" and he said, "I'm in Washington. I'm here to adjudicate some bands. I wonder if you want to have some lunch. I'd love to see you." Of course I said "Yes," I would. So I met him. I was so flattered that he had somehow found where I lived and called me. It was '74 or '75, and the last time I ever saw him. Here is a guy who had been out of MSU since '67, but it was like, "I think of you, and I still love you."*[153]

**Earle Louder:** *Quite a few of us stay in touch, even after all these years. Fritz and Gretchen Stansell and Dick Goldsworthy. From year to year I run across people I had an association with. I play with Burt Bronson the tubist in Detroit. John Lypratt played* *baritone and I do Blue Lake and Falcone Competition every year, and we all communicate.*[154]

**Dan Pearson:** *I often tell people band was my fraternity. I couldn't afford fraternity, so I had 2 years in a dorm, then 2 years off campus at $7 per week at Mrs. Ralph's house a block from Professor Falcone's. I don't regret any time I spent in that band. Not a minute.*[155]

**Dick Lodge:** *My experiences at MSU, and especially the MSU bands, are many of the most fulfilling memories I have in my life.*[156]

**Earle Louder:** *His philosophy, though he never stated it, was, "You don't play euphonium, and I don't teach euphonium. You express yourself through the horn you have in your hand." He didn't teach music, he taught people.*[157]

CHAPTER 17

# THOUGHTS: SPRING, 2011

***"Music gives a soul to the universe, wings to the mind, flight to the imagination, and life to everything."***

**~ Plato**

---

I FIRST MET LEONARD FALCONE in the spring of 1964, though I had seen him from afar many times before that when our little high school band from North Muskegon, Michigan, came every fall to play for MSU's annual Band Day. Mr. Falcone would show up for morning rehearsal on a practice field, and then again on the gridiron during halftime to conduct the 25 or so high school bands that converged there from all around the state. I was in awe of him, his reputation as a virtuoso musician and "Dean of the Big Ten Band Directors" having filtered to even my small little village situated on Muskegon and Bear Lakes, near Lake Michigan. He would mount tall, mobile steps, tower over us as though on Mt. Olympus, and when the time came to play, beat in huge, grand gestures that pretty much kept the drum majors and bass drum players from each band in tempo. We would play a march or two, and then the "Star Spangled Banner," which was always a trip in terms of synchronizing 25 or more simultaneous cymbal crashes.

But in early spring of '64, I found myself walking the Green Mile, the long, lonely walk down the corridor of MSU's music department and into Room 116, his office at the end of the hall to the right of the band room, to audition for a spot in MSU's Concert Band. I was in a total state of nerves—nothing new for me when it came to playing in front of someone, but much exacerbated by the knowledge that this man, a driven perfectionist known for his assiduous attention to the most minute detail, a big footprint conductor/teacher/composer/bandsman/musician who had earned his place in the pantheon of the greats, was there to judge me as worthy or unworthy of being in his band, and in the end determine whether or not I should declare music as my major and for all I knew at that point, perhaps even if I was going to get into MSU. I felt very small, a sacrificial maiden headed for the Minotaur.

I was sure he could hear my heart pounding as we introduced ourselves. Or perhaps, I thought, the sound was coming from beneath one of the cairns of books and music I saw on the tile floor, possibly placed there to obscure a trap door under which was thumping the still beating heart of the last student who had played a wrong note, or worse, played on a rest.

"What have you prepared to play for me today?" Mr. Falcone asked from behind his big desk. A slight man, about 5'8", and thin, he had a serious face that seemed to be chiseled from stone. But his voice and eyes were kind.

"The Von Weber Clarinet Concertino," I answered, sounding more confident than I felt.

"Oh, yes. . .very good," he said, his blue eyes soft and curious. "I'm also going to hear you do some sight-reading. It's on your stand, and let's begin with that. Take a moment and look it over." He gestured toward a couple music folders on his desk. " I hope you don't mind. . . but I have a few things I need to do." Rising from his chair, he turned around and quietly began making space in a file cabinet directly in front of me. I eyed him for a second, scanned the first sight-reading piece, and took a couple of deep breaths. Was his kindness part of a diabolical plan to win my confidence and then shatter it to bits, or was what I was dealing with here a genuinely thoughtful man, doing what he could to provide a tranquil environment to calm my nerves? By the time I was ready to play he was seated again, quietly looking at the open *State News* on his desk. I had my answer, the thumping stopped, and I began.

Later on I related this story to my high school band director, a former student of Dr. Falcone's. "You were lucky," he said.

"How so?" I asked.

"You got special treatment. He didn't usually do things like that."

"No?" I asked. "What did he usually do?"

"Well," he replied. "Stare, I guess. He usually stared at whomever was playing."

Yikes! I'd been lucky, all right. Dr. Falcone's expressive face could emanate a deep gentleness or call a student to attention faster than a "Ten-Hut!" from a drum major. Had he decided to watch me play, one frown or shake of the head surely would have shot my nerves through the roof.

Now that I know him better, I can't help but think that this sensitive and gentle man picked up on how frightened I was on that lovely spring day in 1964, and in a move that was somewhat atypical for him, decided to make himself as invisible as possible. Whatever his intention, he succeeded in creating an illusion for me that I was alone in a practice room doing a final run through, and not in front of a lion of the music world in an audition that might well decide my future. The result was that I made it through his sight reading selections without too much trouble, and through the Concertino, too. And I got in the band. That's me on page 199—second row clarinets, third chair.

Rita Comstock, clarinet
MSU 1964–1968
Go Green.

# APPENDICES

## A. In His Own Words: Leonard Falcone on Teaching Methods

*Teaching style? That's a big question. Let me say what I expect a student to be able do eventually. I would like for my students to have a very good tone to start with. I agree with the idea that tone is the most important thing. There was a time I didn't agree with that because it seemed to exclude everything else.*

*I try to develop a firm tone, a good quality of tone. A good tone is free, it's open, it's round, one might say. It has no restriction, no pinched lips or tight throat. And then I like to have them [students] have a good wide range, especially in the upper register so that they will not feel restricted or feel incapable of playing freely the high tones especially required in solo literature. And then I like them to play with a very firm tone, a strong tone, so that every note they play is firm—you can recognize it. When they play a passage you can hear every single note in that passage, not just the first and the last note. And then I like to have the instrument very flexible, very expressive. I would like to hear* the baritone played as closely to a cello as possible, a singing style, very sensitive, very delicate. But to do this, you have to first have developed a very firm tone, very definite.

Now, in the process of doing this, I ask my students to blow as loud as they can. My experience has been that the majority of low brass players, baritones, tubas, and trombones, that come from the public schools have a small, pinched tone. That's due to the idea that you start to play by buzzing your lips, an idea which I don't subscribe to completely. As a last resort to start some kind of a tone in the beginner, it's successful. If nothing else works, that will. But somewhere along the line, as you progress, that has to be changed because the buzz means closing the lips firmly and pushing the breath through in order to get it to vibrate And while that's a very fine method to begin with to start a tone in a beginner, in say six months or a year it has to change. So it has been my role to project this to students.

I find that beginners and even [the] advanced [players] play in a superficial way. It's so light that you are not positive what the notes are. And there's a constant pecking and scratching of a note and a weak tone here and there and that stems from the fact they can't locate where the tone is in the instrument. You can't see the note, you can only feel it. I think that playing with a very strong tone you have a better feeling of that particular tone by staying right with it. This is it! It's here! When I play this particular tone, or this pitch, the muscles of my stomach feel this way, the pressure of my mouthpiece is always such. It's a feeling. I have used the process of long tones to develop this tone quality, strength of tone, and range. Long tones can be 8 or 10 beats long. It's required to strike the tone accurately through the process of finding where the tone is, first, and then constantly attacking the tone until it's precise, clean, and then [with] a great extention—which means a lot of blowing and pressure on the mouthpiece, which develops the muscles of your lips. And then the control of the tone through the expansion and diminishing. It sounds complicated, but it's a method that works and is still working. It's a long process and it's fatiguing and it's tiring. And sometimes it's *discouraging. But unless there is a very definite physical handicap in the shape and construction of the mouth or teeth or lips, all my students have succeeded, and they all have a wide range—at least all those who apply themselves and continue with the study.*

*And so after that, when they have a good control, then of course we proceed with other studies, to develop the dexterity of the fingers and general technique—various types of tonguings, the embellishing of the tone through the use of the so-called vibrato, and the phrasing, breathing, where to take a breath, the business of the musical phrase, and the general concept of the expression and playing. This is the main thing I work on the first year. At very first, it may take a whole period of a lesson, 45 minutes, an hour, until they [students] understand what to do. This is quite complicated at first, and the students forget and they don't understand just what to do.*

*And then along with it, I teach some basic style, such as the rhythmic style of playing, the type that we use in marches, where you attack the tone sharply and then it's tapered off, the release, and then how to release it, and then the spacing between the tones. And I use the rhythm system for that.*

*Most of the music we play is based on 8th note rhythm. In other words, it's important to feel the end beat between the beats, the ends of the beats. Without the ends of the beats, we're in deep trouble. If we play a whole note, which means 4 beats, and we think of each beat as 2 eighth notes tied together, so that we have 8 eighth notes tied together for a whole note, and we play that note from the beginning to the 7th eighth note straight, and then from the 7th to the 8th, we release it—that's where the tapering off of the release takes place. And then if we have another whole note, then the spacing between the two is between two 8th notes. I'll sing it out for you [sings and counts to 8]. So that there's a space between 8th notes. And this release is very important because some students will play all the way through two full notes [sings 2 long notes with little separation], which is not a rhythmical type of playing. You see, spacing. Separate the tones. And when they cut off the tone [sings] there is a choking effect at the* *end. To avoid that choking effect, taper off [sings, separating and rounding off the notes]. With dotted half notes, we have six $8^{th}$ notes [sings]. We call this a "round." Round out the release of the tone. Half notes [sings]. See? We never (sings, choking off the tone) We do this sometimes for special effects, but normally, we don't. Quarter notes? Just two [sings]. There's a space. There are exercises specifically for that in the Arban book for cornet and low brass. I'll give an instance: if we play the University of Michigan, "The Victors," the trio, which is in cut time, by the way, half notes, but the half notes become quarter, we don't play [sings in a staccato style, then legato]. There should be a softening on the release. Our fight song here is in $^2/_4$ time, so that's quarter notes [sings]. This is the rhythmical type of way to play marches. There's a lift. If you sustain the notes like some high school bands do, [sings] there's no separation. But if you separate without the release, without the rounding, there's a choke. That's the basic. There's a lot of variations to it.*

*On the other side of the spectrum, you might say, we have the lyrical type of playing—that's entirely different, where we use the legato tongue then to connect the tone, very easily. We can pick out anything that's lyrical or any phrases where the tones are to be tongued, but very lightly, so that . . . as far as the ear can detect, there's no separating, no stopping, but just a pulsation [sings "I'll Be Loving You, Always" to demonstrate]. So that's entirely different. That's continuous. Like a chorale.*

*[Teach] the rhythmical first, absolutely, then the lyrical. The lyrical is sometimes difficult, but usually not. The process is the same thing. A continuous tone. No tongue. The breath is continuous. And then when that's settled . . . when the student learns how to do that with no sense of separating the tone, then he needs to learn to add the tongue, but very lightly. Learn how to control the air column first. Now some people use syllables "Du-du-du"or "La-la-la-la," and that's all right if it works. Personally, I don't think of syllables, I think of the music itself, the way I want to have it sound, and then the tongue will do what I want it to do.*

*Vibrato is a technique which is to be used sparingly in an appropriate type of music. Because of that, it has to be taught or acquired in such a way that it is used if you want to, or not used if you don't. Some people get in the habit of using it continuously, and they can't stop it. Speaking of brass only—not oboes or other instruments—but the brass, because of the difference in shape of the different instruments, there are different kinds [of vibratos]. For example, on the trombone, because of the slide, it's very simple to have a vibrato because of the slide. Now some trombone teachers object to that. Cornet players will use their hands. On the baritone and tuba, it's not possible to use the hand because they're (baritones and tubas) too big. Now I use what I call the jaw, a lip vibrato, really, but you don't use the lip because you can't move the lip, up and down in other words, you cannot without moving the jaw. Mine is actually what I call a pitch and a dynamic vibrato done by the movement of the lip and jaw, it's not a breath. It's not a breath vibrato. I teach the vibrato, again, by rhythm. We start with a sustained tone, and have the jaw go up and down rhythmically, let's say in quarter notes . . . and the pulsation is when the jaw drops down in a regular position–it's brought up, and then down—(sings) very quick, in quarter notes. Now when they (students) can do that, first on one note, you know, to get the feel of it. . . it takes a long time. . . . It's a matter of time. And then of course we try every note. And then when the student can play the quarter rhythm note quite well, then we speed it up and progress to eight notes per beat, then gradually progress to triple eighth notes and to sixteenths. The sixteenths will speed up the tempo to about 84 to 86 on the metronome, and that's about the fastest I think it should go. You can go too fast, you know.*

*And then it (vibrato) has to be applied. . . all in rhythm, in different rhythm patterns. Some in ¾ time, tripled eighth notes or tripled sixteenths, slow. Others in six notes per beat, say a slow 3/8 time. I find that one problem that everyone seems to have: in the concentration to use the jaw vibrato, they, the students, are not enveloped with a full tone. Unless the tone is strong and full, it weakens the tone and you'll have a weak wa-wa-wa-wa weak kind of tone. So that's the hardest thing to do—to combine them both, keep going, and then have this variation.*

*Eventually, we get away from the rhythm part of it (the lessons) altogether. . .oh, yes. Perhaps the player will use a faint vibrato, but the listener is not aware of it. You know, we have rhythm sometimes that changes in one way or another. The performer knows it, but the listener is not aware whether he's played 3 and 3 or 2-2-2. Oh yes, we get away from the vibrato [in lessons]. Eventually, the vibrato, the deviation away from the center of the pitch, we'll say, is quite definite. If it isn't definite, then it becomes diffused and we hear a little flickering here and nothing there and all of a sudden the tempo is this way—very fast—and then it settles, and then is fast again. That's not stable. There has to be stability there, but not at the point where it is obvious. Take Saint Saen's "The Swan" [demonstrates a very strong, obviously rhythmic and overdone vibrato] You can't have that. You see, that's a 6/8 time. Four pulsations to a beat, let's say. It's too obvious. The deviation is so slight that you just know that there's a warmth in the tone but you couldn't pound the pulsation, nor would you feel it too objectively, too definitely. And then the lip comes into it. At first, to start, the lip is wide in order to get the jaw to move. And then we get closer and closer.*

*There's another type of vibrato that varies from one style to another. The type of vibrato I'm talking about now—the pitch is raised rather than lowered, by closing the jaw and bringing the chin up. That raises the pitch as well as closes the tone somewhat. The type of vibrato that's used in a dance band is just the opposite. Rather than going up, the jaw goes down, so it brings the pitch down, and you have a sort of a flat type of tone. It's the pitch. If you hear two players play, and if one lowers the jaw too much and one doesn't, you can tell the difference. You'll say, "there's something wrong with this one here . . . what is it? It just doesn't sound right to me." And what it is, is that the tone goes down rather than up. When it goes up, we're not aware of it. It's sharp. It just seems to stay there. The one that goes up, you hear the vibrato but you don't hear the pitch change. But down, you do.*

*These are the things I've learned to diagnose in the process of teaching. Teaching—there's no end to it. You find new problems every day. It's wonderful, in a way. It doesn't mean you know anything about it either—some of your ideas, they don't work with everybody. You have to figure it out.*

*The vibrato I learned originally in Italy [playing lower brass instruments] was a flute vibrato. It was a breath and throat vibrato. Nobody taught me that, but I developed it in listening to other players. It's not that effective, especially in the upper tones, because in the upper tones, when you tighten your throat, that pinches the tone. Also, at times, the breath, the guttural sound, comes through the tone-eh-eh-eh-eh-eh-eh. Eventually, I abandoned that altogether, after I was here. It wasn't satisfactory. I didn't like it, so I changed it, though it's widely used by others on low brass instruments.*

*As far as the cornets are concerned, I think the movement of hand is less and less sufficient.*

*And of course there are different ideas about vibratos, how wide and how fast. Sometimes the intensity is greater in the higher tones than it is in the middle or lower, it's faster. I emulate the string instruments. You see, with the string instruments, there's that variation in pitch. They never get to the point where it's too low and it sounds flat. They stay right there. As a matter of fact, the finger never leaves the string.*

*I have a basic repertoire that I expect my students to cover. The Arban Method is to me is the most complete and exhaustive method book in existence; it has everything, everything you could ask for. All the fundamentals. It's not for young students, it's more for high school and university students because it progresses too rapidly for class work. If you're starting right from the beginning, then the books published by Rubank are good. After that, I would go to the Arban. The Arban is very complete and can serve the purpose until the student is a senior practically. There are difficult etudes included, and it has material that no other book seems to have, such as embellishments like* grupetto *and* mordente *and grace notes and trills, just how they're done. Of* *course I supplement it with other things, such as the book by H.W. Tyrrell—it has a series of etudes that are very nice [*40 Progressive Studies for Trombone*]. They are for trombone, but can be used for baritone, too. And then there are trombone books by Wiser and by Sidell that are good supplements. And then as the student progresses, then we have the Rochut etudes, which are purely lyrical style. It's known as the Marco Bordogni Vocalises. Mr. [Johannes] Rochut transcribed them for trombone and baritone, and tuba, for that matter.* Melodious Etudes for Trombone, *published by Carl Fischer. And then there are other, more complicated studies.*

*One of them . . . let me see . . . I believe in keeping notes on every lesson for every student . . . oh, yes—etudes by Edmond Vobaron are excellent. Still more advanced are the studies by Kopprasch. They are well known studies, and very complicated. There are a great variety of them. The last 10–15 years the French literature, essentially for trombone, is very good. The best students in baritone have been going to cornet literature, some studies by French composers that are very complicated. They are extremely musical. By Eugene Bozza and by Henri Tomasi. And the Herbert L. Clarke studies are excellent, particularly the second and third series [*Technical Studies, Characteristic Studies*]. Then we have the [Theo] Charlier studies for cornets, which I would say is about the top for advanced players. It requires advanced musicianship, even from a rhythm standpoint—very difficult rhythmically. The unusual intervals you play—I would say that half of them would be wrong notes the first time because you don't expect them. In brass playing, you have to be able to hear the pitch before you play, so it becomes very hard. I also use 2 or 3 transcriptions for trombone of the cello suites by Bach. I use Andre LaFosse. When you look at it, it looks simple. But when you play it. . . .*

*It's a very wide repertoire. There's no end to it. It's primarily due to some very fine French composers.*

*I play for my students continuously. The day will come when I can't play—teeth, you know—but when that day comes, I don't know what I'll do. I don't know that I could teach and not do that [demonstrate]. There's just so much you can do with words. Demonstrating it seems to be the quickest way, and perhaps the only way. I don't play all the time, just when it's necessary to set a concept. All my string teachers in Ann Arbor, they all played. In Italy, I heard the soloists play all the time. I don't sing for my students very often. I don't admire my voice—as a matter of fact, the sound seems flat when I hear myself on a tape. I don't sing.*

*I always play from memory, and I like my students to, too. I feel that if you really know the music . . . I never had any fear of lack of memorization. If you are convinced, if you know the music well enough, then you have no fear of suddenly forgetting. I think that part of it is perhaps due to the fact that I can hear the pitches, I can hear the tones. Some people call it perfect pitch, but I don't believe there's such a thing, myself. But it's close. You strike something on the piano, and I can tell you what it is. The music is right there, I see it, and I immediately relay to the fingering of that tone . . . I think you can play so much more effectively if you think of the music itself, the phrasing, the tone quality, the intensity, the expression, rather than look at the music itself. Whether that's possible to continue to do that is another question, because some of the music being written for brass instruments today is too complicated; it's so fragmentary, a note here, a note there, that [it] becomes extremely difficult to memorize. I think that's the reason why contemporary composers make such a strong plea to play and not memorize. Even if it's not necessary to play by memory, I think it's a good thing to develop because it has a carryover. If you have a good idea of what to expect, of how the music sounds, it helps.*[1]

### B. Granita di Limone

*3–4 lemons, enough to make 2/3 C juice*
*1 C sugar*
*4 C water*
*Dash salt*

Use a vegetable peeler to cut zest from ONE lemon only. Squeeze the lemon and reserve its juice. Using the metal blade of a food processor, process the zest and sugar until the zest is finely chopped. Place in a 3 qt. pan with the water and salt, and heat just until the sugar dissolves. Cool.

To the reserved lemon juice, add more juice from remaining fresh lemons to measure ⅔ cup. Stir the juice into the cooled sugar mixture and freeze in divided ice cube trays. Later, you may put the cubes in plastic bags and return to the freezer.

To serve, use the metal blade of the food processor to puree 5 lemon cubes at a time until you have made a smooth slush. Scoop into serving dishes or store, covered, in freezer until ready. Makes 4½ C, serving 4-6 people.

~ recipe courtesy of Donato Bracco

## C. Leonard Falcone's Graduation Recital

University School of Music
Students' Recital Series
School of Music Auditorium
Ann Arbor, Michigan

---

Graduation Recital
Leonard V. Falcone, Violinist
Assisted by
MEMBERS OF THE ENSEMBLE CLASS

---

Twenty-first concert — Complete Series 1529
Friday, May 28 1926 — 8:00 P.M.

---

PROGRAM

Sonata, D major................................................................*Handel*

Adagio-Allegro
Larghetto-Allegro
Mr. Falcone

Trio, D major, Op. 70, No. 1............................................*Beethoven*
(First Movement)

Mary Alice Case, Violin
Zona Eberly, Violoncello
Saime Mouhidden, Piano

Guitarre..................................................*Moszkowski-Langey*
Prelude, G minor, from the First Solo-Sonata.......*Bach*
Muzurka de Concert, D...............................*Musin*

Mr. Falcone
Accompaniments by Donna Esselstyn[2]

D. Theater Programs

Arcade Theater

Friday and Saturday, June 1st and 2nd, 1923
Overture . . . . Arcade Orchestra
Leonard Falcone conducting
Organist, Paul Tomkins

The Arcade Presents:
"Where There is a Will"
A Sunshine Comedy

Presenting the Great
Saturday Evening Post Story
"Backbone"

International News

Marches. . . . Selected

* * * * * * * *

Wuerth Theater:

Pique Dame . . . . Suppé
From Verdi's Opera "La forza del Destino"
Leonard Falcone conducting:

* * * * * * * *

Majestic Theater

"Spanish Holiday"
Interpreted by Leonard Falcone, violinist at the Majestic

Also

2 Reels of Laughs
Anne Cornwell with Jack Duffy
in
"Chicken Feathers"[3]

## E. "Van"

Hoag had this to say about the bouncer when, in 1927, the Majestic became devoted completely to movies and the deluxe Michigan theater was opened for stage shows: "We figured on bringing all the loyal (Majestic) employees over (to the Michigan) as a reward—orchestra, stage hands, cashiers, doormen, etc. My problem was what to do with Van, as we intended a considerably different policy of maintaining order. The result was that we dressed Van up in a tuxedo with shiny lapels, black bow tie, etc., and instructed him, under all circumstances, to say, and always with a smile, the words: "Please be a gentleman." Van's accent was funny, too.

After a few weeks in the new house, the students learned that Van was no longer fighting. So they devised a trick of coming up alongside, quietly, and pulling his tie out of being tied. Van's face would always get redder, and he would mutter, "Nex time I poke him vun!"

One night, a student rushed in while the stage show was on, pulled Van's tie, then rushed to an aisle seat about 5th row. As soon as he was seated, he reached into his pocket and tossed a penny on the stage. Van had just replaced his tie when he saw the incident. He rushed down the aisle, leaned over the student with those shiny lapels, and with a flushed face and a big smile, blurted in a thunderous tone heard over the entire house, "PLEASE BE A GENTLEMUN, YA SON-OF-A-BITCH!"

Probably no other audience has been so rocked with laughter for a longer period.[4]

## F. The Band/ Orchestral Connection

Many of Falcone's musical concepts regarding band performance resulted from his violin study and orchestral experience. Stressing the blend inherent with string instruments, he never allowed his bands to sound harsh, ponderous, or loud. Even his concern with tonguing style stemmed from his orchestral experiences: he insisted that rapid passages be played with a flexible style of tonguing, comparable to the detache or back and forth bowing of a stringed instrument, as opposed to the spiccato, or bouncing bow, analogous to rigid tonguing.[5] "I don't think a band should sound like an orchestra, but from a musical standpoint, we can come close," he once said.[6]

Speaking as an euphonium artist, he noted that he felt that his style of playing had been unconsciously influenced by his interest in string music. "Automatically, I try to imitate the cello in the orchestra, both in terms of techniques, tone quality, and expression. When I study a piece of music, if it is a lyrical type of composition, I think of the cello and try to inject the same expression the cellist would. For example, if I were to play "The Swan"(*Carnival of Animals* by Saint-Saens) on the euphonium, I would try to assimilate my performance to the way a cellist would play it because it was written for cello originally. That is why my style is somewhat different from the general concept of euphonium playing. I like a very expressive sound, a very expressive tone and at the same time, if it's a technical type of music, I would like to make it as brilliant and exciting as possible."[7]

## G. The "MSU Fight Song"

The "Michigan State Fight Song" was written by class of 1916 "yel-leader" F.I. Lankey, an Air Force Lieutenant who lost his life in a plane crash while on a War Bond tour in 1919.[8] Lankey wrote it in 1915, two years after Michigan State's first victory (12-7) over Michigan on October 18, 1913. Led by the MAC. ROTC Cadet Band, hordes of "Aggies," paraded through the streets of Ann Arbor after the game singing the U of M.'s "The Victors" because they had no fight song of their own. Lankey determined to give them one. An accomplished pianist and composer, he based the tune on "Stand Up, Stand Up for Jesus" and enlisted the help of Arthur L. Sayles, an engineering senior, to write the lyrics. When four years later the Varsity Club managed to come across a copy of the song in the hands of one of Lankey's many girlfriends, they had 770 copies of it printed and sold them for 50 cents apiece at a homecoming pep assembly as a fundraising effort. The song was a hit: in half an hour, all 770 copies had disappeared into the hands of eager students. J.S. Taylor, the new director of the Military Band, had the "Michigan State Fight Song" orchestrated for band in 1920, but ironically Lankey didn't live long enough to know.[9]

Basically, two arrangements of the "Michigan State Fight Song" are currently played: the "Falcone Fight," and the "Pregame Fight." Though the Michigan State University Marching Band refers to the "Falcone Fight," the fact of the matter is that Leonard Falcone wrote many arrangements of the "MSU Fight Song," as can be heard in the various recordings of it in the university's music library. The version of the "Falcone Fight" used today includes the opening verse of the song, the chorus, which is sung by the band with percussion and tuba accompaniment, the breakstrain, and a final instrumental repeat of the chorus. Yet another example of Falcone's lasting musical legacy at MSU, it takes just under 2 minutes to play, and is usually performed during parades or long breaks during athletic events.

A second styling of the "MSU Fight Song" played by the band, the "Pregame Fight," is primarily used for football pregame shows. It lasts about a half minute, is completely instrumental, and is comprised of part of the breakstrain and the chorus. After a touchdown, a particularly good play, or during a stop in the game, an even briefer version of the "Pregame Fight" is played, beginning at the line "See their team is weakening," and ending with "Victory for MSU!"

**Current "MSU Fight Song" Lyrics**

On the banks of the Red Cedar,
There's a school that's known to all
Its specialty is winning,
And those Spartans play good ball;
Spartan teams are never beaten,
All through the game they fight
Fight for the only colors:
Green and white.

Go right through for MSU,
Watch the points keep growing,
Spartan teams are bound to win,
They're fighting with a vim!
Rah! Rah! Rah!
See their team is weakening,
We're going to win this game,
Fight! Fight! Rah! Team! Fight!
Victory for MSU!

**Original "MAC Fight Song" Lyrics**

On the banks of the Red Cedar,
There's a school that's known to all;
Its specialty is farming,
But those farmers play football;
Aggie teams are never beaten,
All through the game they'll fight
Fight for the only colors:
Green and white.

Break on through that line of blue,
Watch the points keep growing,
Aggie teams are bound to win,
They're fighting with a vim!
Rah! Rah! Rah!
Michigan is weakening,
We're going to win this game,
Fight! Fight! Rah! Team! Fight!
Victory for MAC!

## H. Leonard Falcone's Published Articles

"How to Choose a Solo for the Baritone." *Educational Music Journal*. 1932.

"Chin Up When You Play the National Anthem." *The School Musician*. 1937.

"An Appeal for Solos for the Baritone Horn." *Music Educators Journal*. Dec. 1939.

"If I Were Choosing a Solo for the Baritone." *The School Musician*. Dec. 1939.

"The Euphonium—Cello of the Band." *The Instrumentalist*. Nov. –Dec. 1951.

"How to Produce a Beautiful Tone on the Baritone." *The School Musician*. 1952.

"The Best in Band Music." *The Instrumentalist*. Apr., 1958.

"Marching Trends in the Mid-West." *The Instrumentalist*. June. 1963.

"Let's Not Forget the Outstanding Band Literature of Yesterday," *The Instrumentalist*. June. 1967.

"My Forty Years at Michigan State University," *The School Musician*. Dec. 1967.[10]

**I. Dave Wisner:** A song I recall that we used to sing on the bus went like this:

*I want a band, just like the band that ole Falcone has!*
*It is the band, and the only band that makes Revelli mad!*
*A good old fashioned band with lot of pep,*
*One that never marches out of step.*
*Oh, I want a band, just like the band that ole Falcone has!*

*Oh, what a band, let's give them a hand,*
*For showing how it's done!*
*240 per, and the kick step,*
*Sure puts them in the sun!*
*Hear them coming with their sound so pure,*
*Tricky twirlers and the rest make sure,*
*That we've got a band, a damned good marching band,*
*That makes Fal con e prou prou prou prou prooow-oud!*

Those "prous" were a "take off" on the way our arranger always seemed to end all his pieces. Again, so silly. But fun.[11]

## J. *"Spartan Bandsman"* newspaper, 1955

*My Two Weeks in a Quandary, and How it Grew,*
or
*The Fable of a Frightened Frail Freshman*

My name is unimportant,
For I'm the lowest of the low.
I'm just a little Freshie,
And here's my tale of woe:

When first I came to campus
With clarinet in hand,
I thought I'd like to join
The MS Marching Band.

A few days later I was in,
We rehearsed a day or two,
And everything was going fine,
Until that whistle blew.

My rank was full of seniors
On the left and on the right.
I heard their voices every day,
And dreamed them every night.
"Lift those feet! Swing that horn!
This is MSU, you know,
And above all else, remember this:
You have to go! Go! GO!"

The sophomores and the juniors
Are on the whole all right,
But those seniors have turned my life
To one of cringing fright.

Someday I'll leave this vale of tears
And pass through the Pearly Gate,
Where no one cares if I pick up my feet.
Or if my rank is straight.
My idea of heaven's bliss,
Whether now or by-and-by,
Would be to play with seniors
Who march worse than I!

~ *Anonymous 1955*[12]

## K. Midwestern Conference on School Vocal and Instrumental Music

January 10, 1958
Hill Auditorium, Ann Arbor, Michigan

| | |
|---|---|
| Fanfare and Allegro | Clifton Williams |
| Toccata | G. Frescobaldi |
| American Overture for Band | Joseph Wilcox Jenkins |
| Three Choral Preludes | William Latham |
| Toccata for Band | Frank Erickson |
| Iphigenia in Aulis | C.W. Gluck |
| March Electric | Creatore-Falcone |
| Dance of the Hours | Amilcare Ponchielli[13] |

## L. College Band Directors National Association

Fourteenth National Conference
February 9, 1967, 9:00 p.m.
Hill Auditorium, Ann Arbor, Michigan

Oberon Overture — C.M. Von Weber

Rondino — James Niblock
*First performance, conducted by composer*

Bells of Rome (Symphonic Prelude) — Andrea Pirazzini
*First Performance*

Sinfonia for Solo Winds and Band — James Slater
*Manuscript selected by the CBDNA Committee on Original Compositions*

Michigan State University Faculty Woodwind Quintet
Finale from Symphony No. 4 — P.I. Tchaikowsky[14]
*Allegro con fuoco*

## M. MSU Shadows

*MSU, we love thy shadows /When twilight silence falls,*
*Flushing deep and softly paling /O'er ivy covered halls;*
*Beneath the pines we'll gather /To give our faith so true,*
*Sing our love for Alma Mater /And thy praises MSU.*

*When from these scenes we wander/ And twilight shadows fade,*
*Our memory still will linger /Where light and shadows played;*
*In the evening oft we'll gather /And pledge our faith anew,*
*Sing our love for Alma Mater /And thy praises MSU.*

## N. Spaghetti Falcone

*Leonard's own recipe, as he wrote it for Gretchen Stansell*

*Pasta:* Make fresh pasta to serve 8-10 people.

*Meat:* Cover the bottom of a heavy kettle with olive oil to depth of ¼." Put several drips (2 tsp. or more) of garlic juice in this olive oil. Brown meat balls (a little larger than golf balls), chicken pieces, or a chuck roast on all sides.

*Sauce:* Prepare in a separate bowl
4 cans tomato paste (Contadina)
4 cans water
2 tsp. salt
1 tsp. pepper
2 tsp. fresh chopped thyme
Mix well.

I just dump in seasonings so I'm guessing as to amounts.

After meat is browned, pour sauce over meat—use a little extra water to clean out bowl. Cover and turn fire on as low as possible. Simmer until meat is cooked. If sauce boils down as it cooks, add a little water. For a more intense flavor make several days ahead and partly cook meat. Let sit in refrigerator with sauce. Day you want to serve it, finish cooking meat and this heats the sauce.

Cook pasta (al dente)

*Buon appetito!*

If serving spaghetti and meatballs, the recipe is complete.

If serving chicken or a roast, serve it as a course separate from the pasta, with the spaghetti simply topped by the meat flavored sauce.

~ *Falcone spaghetti recipe courtesy of Gretchen Stansell*

## O. **Contributors** ***and other voices*****:**

**Aurand, Charles:** clarinet, MSU '55 (BM) and "58 (MM), PhD from the University of Michigan. Aurand was a professor of music and an academic dean for 30 years, and has been a soloist for two International Clarinet Conferences and the host of the 1991 ICS Conference at Flagstaff, Arizona; throughout his career he has performed with numerous chamber music ensembles. A MSU Alumni Band Association member.

***Austin, William:*** *MSC 1933-1937, student president of the MSC Band. Austin later served as superintendent of schools in Muskegon, MI.*

***Bartlett, Dale:*** *Professor Emeritus, Michigan State University School of Music. Earned bachelor's and master's degrees from Michigan State University in 1955 and 1956, and a Ph.D. in Music Education from the University of Kansas in 1969. Taught public school music for seven years, instructed French horn at the University of Kansas for six, and taught for twenty-seven years at MSU, where he also served as Assistant and Associate Director of the School of Music for 13 years.*

**Bates, Jack:** flute, Michigan State Band 1935-1937. A graduate of the University of Michigan School of Dentistry.

**Begian, Harry:** world renowned conductor. Served in the 180th AGS Army Band during World War II, received bachelor's and master's degrees from Wayne State University, and a doctorate from the University of Michigan. Director of Bands at Detroit's Cass Technical High School (1947–1964), Wayne State University (1964–1967), Michigan State University (1967–1970), the University of Illinois (1970–1984). Begian was President of the American Bandmaster's Association, inducted in the NBA Hall of Fame of Distinguished Band Directors, 1994, and Board of Directors of the International Band and Orchestra Clinic in Chicago. He conducted staff and faculty bands at the Blue Lake Fine Arts Camp for many summers.

***Behrend, Roger:** 30 years in the US Navy Band, principal euphonium. Earned a Bachelor of Music Education from Michigan State University, and a master's degree from George Mason University. Behrand, a renowned soloist, has performed throughout the world and is currently teaching at George Mason University in Virginia.*

**Bjerregaard, Carl:** Professor Emeritus, Florida State University. Holds degrees from Western Michigan University and Michigan State University. Directed music programs in Montague and Muskegon, MI, before becoming Director of Bands at Western Michigan University in 1972, and later at Florida State University in 1976. His ensemble recordings have been aired on National Public Radio. He has served as music director of the Blue Lake International Symphony Band and for many summers has also directed the camp's Staff Band, Festival Band, and Festival Orchestra.

**Bloomquist, Kenneth G.:** Emeritus MSU Director of Bands 1970- 1977, Chairperson of the School of Music 1978-1988; past president of the American Bandmasters' Association and the National Band Association; inducted into the National Band Association's Hall of Fame in 2002; recipient of many awards including the American School Band Directors Association Harding Award, the Phi Mu Alpha Sinfonia Orpheus Award, the NBA Citation of Excellence, and the The Midwest Clinic's Medal of Honor. Bloomquist has also written many articles for publications such as *The Instrumentalist, The Getzen Gazette,* and *Bandworld.*

**Bracco, Donato:** Italian immigrant; barber and hairdresser.

**Broka, Thomas:** euphonium. Bachelor's in music education from Central Michigan University 1972, master's from MSU late '70s. Retired music coordinator and band director for Bay City Public Schools. Executive Board of Directors, Leonard Falcone International Euphonium and Tuba Festival, Blue Lake Fine Arts Camp. Longtime member of the Brass Band of Battle Creek and several community bands.

***Brandenburg, Broughton:** port of Naples steerage passenger, 1904.*

***Bronson, Burton:** tuba, MSC Band 1946–1950, 1952–1953.*

***Caldwell, Jack:** silent film organist, 1920s, Palace theater, Dallas.*

***Carter, Gaylord:** silent film organist, 1920s, Paramont Theater, Los Angeles.*

**Church, Jane Gruber:** alto saxophone, MSU 1971-1977, bachelor's and master's degrees. Director of Bands at East Lansing High School for 30 years, retired. State "Band Teacher of the Year," 2004. First female president of the Michigan School Band and Orchestra Association. She serves on the Blue Lake conducting staff.

**Dineen, Mike:** trumpet, MSU 1981-1984. MSU Alumni Band Member. Dineen is an International Release & Classification Trade Specialist for FedEx Trade Networks Customs Brokerage, amateur writer, and extensive world traveler.

**Dobos, Joe:** instrumental music teacher at Oakland Christian High School Lapeer, MI; organist, choir director, at Church of the Immaculate Conception, Lapeer, MI, writer. Graduate of the University of Michigan and past member of the Michigan band.

**Elmore, Fred:** tuba, MSU 1966-1970.

**Erickson, Martin:** tuba, MSU Band 1965-1967; principal/soloist tuba with the US Navy Band in Washington, D.C. for 26 years. Erickson has performed with the Boston Pops, the Smithsonian Masterworks Orchestra, and at Carnegie Hall. Professor of euphonium and tuba at Penn State, Eastern Michigan University, and Lawrence University. A featured jazz and classical performer at international tuba-euphonium conventions; 40 recordings; jazz editor, *ITEA Journal,* MSU Alumni Band.

**Facktor, Pat:** clarinet, MSU 1958- 1962. Danville, Kentucky, Advocate Brass Band. Administrative specialist.

**Falcone, Beryl:** French horn, B.A. and M.A. in music from Western Michigan University and Michigan State University respectively. Past member of the Kalamazoo Symphony Orchestra and the Ft. Wayne Symphony Orchestra. Wife of Leonard, mother of Mary and Cecilia, grandmother of Lisa.

**Falcone, Cecilia:** French horn. Falcone holds two degrees in education from Western Michigan University (Kalamazoo, MI) and currently performs with the MSU Alumni Band as well as with her church orchestra. She has been employed by the United States Postal Service since 1983, and is the daughter of Leonard and Beryl, the sister of Mary, and an aunt to Lisa Fulton.

***Falcone, Nicola:** clarinet virtuoso, brother of Leonard Falcone. Also referred to as "Nick" or "Nicholas." Silent film orchestra director in Ann Arbor theaters until the late 1920's, public school music teacher, and director of the University of Michigan Bands, 1927–1934.*

**Falcone, Susan:** artist, Ann Arbor, Michigan. Great niece of Leonard and Nicola Falcone, and granddaughter of Carmelo Falcone, Leonard's brother.

**Ferrera, Nick:** third cousin of Leonard, Nicola, and Carmelo Falcone.

**Franke, Leonard:** MSC Band 1940-1941.

**Fulton, Lisa:** trumpet. Graduate of East Lansing High School. Formerly with the Honolulu Theater For Youth (Hawaii) and the Intiman Theater (Seattle), currently the Marketing Director for the Milwaukee Repertory Theater; granddaughter of Leonard and Beryl Falcone, daughter of Mary, niece of Cecilia.

**Gillette, Tom:** baritone, MSU band, 1975-1979. An active member of the Michigan State University Alumni Band. Director of the award winning Waukegan (Ill.) Municipal Band and member of the Chicago Brass Band. Gillette served for 8 years in the Navy Music Program and was later managing editor of *Progressions Magazine* and *Music Performance Resources Magazine,* and editor of the *T.U.B.A. Journal.* He has also taught secondary school band, chorus, and general music.

**Goldman, Edwin Franko:** *famous conductor and one of America's most important band composers, Goldman wrote over 150 works, and founded the renowned Goldman Band of New York City, which routinely played in Central Park as well as on radio shows and at the bandstand in Brooklyn's Prospect Park. He ended every concert with an encore, often his most famous march, "On the Mall," which was accompanied by the audience whistling the tune. He founded the American Bandmaster's Association in 1929 and became its second honorary life president, the first being John Philip Sousa. Born 1878, died 1956.*

**Goodrow, Dick:** *MSU band manager, publicity, 1954–1955.*

**Hall, Bob:** *rush participant, Majestic Theater, Ann Arbor, 1920s.*

**Hannah, John:** *twelfth President of Michigan State College/University, for 28 years. Recognized for taking MSC from a regionally known agricultural school to a nationally known and respected research institution, and for increasing enrollment during his tenure from just over 6,000 (1941) to just under 40,000 (1969). He became head of the United States Agency for International Development after his resignation from the university. Hannah married Sarah May Shaw, daughter of Robert Sidney Shaw, eleventh president of MSU.*

**Heger, Avis:** harp. Creator and former director of the Blue Lake Fine Arts Camp harp program.

**Heger, Ted:** former woodwind faculty and member of the Board of Trustees Blue Lake Fine Arts Camp. Oboe teacher at Blue Lake for 25 summers.

**Hemmer, Edward:** *Italian immigrant, 1925.*

***Hickson, Gene:** clarinet, MSC 1951–1954, civil engineering major. Band drum major, 1953.*

***Hoag, Gerald:** silent film theatre manager from 1919, later area manager of Butterfield Theatres, Inc., Ann Arbor, MI.*

***Hodgson, Walter:** Chairman of the MSU Music Department, 1958–1963.*

**Hornstein, Daniel:** MSU band, 1965-68, Bachelor of Music. Hornstein received a master's in orchestra and opera conducting from the Peabody Conservatory, and a doctorate in music education from North Texas State University. Member of the Air Force Band for several years, studied conducting and cello in Munich, Germany, and in Czechoslovakia; featured vocal soloist with the Munich Madrigal Choir; associate principal cellist in the Munich orchestra. Director of the Arts for the Magnet Orchestra program for the Huntsville, AL, City Schools. President of the Alabama Orchestra Association.

**Krive, Kent:** clarinet. Associate Professor of Humanities Emeritus, Ferris State University. Krive holds Bachelor and Master of Music degrees from MSU and is a visiting Assistant Professor and Visiting Adjunct Instructor at Hope College. He is the principal clarinet and featured soloist of the West Shore Symphony Orchestra in Muskegon, MI, a private clarinet teacher and clinician adjudicator, and has performed in the West Michigan Wind Ensemble and served as conductor of Blue Lake's International Symphony, Staff, and Festival Bands.

***Lewis, Ken:** reporter, Pasadena Star News.*

**Lodge, Dick:** snare drum, MSU band 1965-1969; bank investment portfolio manager.

**Louder, Earl:** euphonium, MSU 1955. Louder received his doctoral degree at Florida State University, and for twelve years played with the United States Navy Band in Washington, D.C.. Later, he served as professor of tuba and euphonium and head of the brass department

at Morehead State University in Kentucky, where he is now Professor Emeritus. He is a featured soloist with several bands and spends summers teaching at the Blue Lake Fine Arts Camp.
**Lutz, Merritt:** percussion. Drum line, 1962–1967. Credited with writing MSU's "The Series," along with Joel Leach. Lutz is currently a Senior Advisor at Morgan Stanley Dean Witter and serves as Business Engine's Chairman of the Board. He is the head of Information Technology Strategic Initiatives and the Chairman of MS Technology Holdings, Inc. He is a member of the Alumni Band.

***Marugg, Jim:*** *reporter, Pasadena Star News.*

**McDaniel, John T.:** baritone, MSU 1972-1976. MSU Technology Coordinator late'70s, early '80's.

**Melnik, Mike:** trombone, MSU 1981-1987.

**Meyers, Sr. Robert F.:** MSU Concert and Marching Band, 1957–1959.

***Moffitt, Bill:*** *Assistant Marching Band Director at Michigan State 1960-1969, Marching Band Director at University of Houston 1969-1981, and Director of the Purdue "All-American" Marching Band from 1981 to 1988. Moffitt became Professor Emeritus of the Purdue Band in 1988 and the same year was named Indiana's Music Arranger Laureate by the Indiana General Assembly. At MSU, his famous "Patterns in Motion" featured Spartan band members in constantly changing kaleidoscopic patterns on the field, a style that swept the nation and continues to impact contemporary marching today.*

**Morrill, Denny:** cornet, MSU 1960–'64.

***Murray, Addie:*** *wife of "Smiling Al Renne," owner of the "Old Opry House" theater in Ypsilanti, MI.*

**Nelson, Henry:** flute, sousaphone, string bass, saxophone. MSC Band 1940-43, 1946-47, Michigan teacher of the year in 1978. Nelson led a national championship Lansing VFW Band, was first president of the MSU Alumni Band, and was instrumental in planning the Falcone Alumni Band International tour in spring of 1985. He judged at school band and orchestra festivals until he was 86.

**Niblock, James:** concertmaster of the Lansing Symphony Orchestra and faculty member of the College of Music at Michigan State University where he served as chairman for 15 years, taught theory and composition, and performed in the Beaumont String Quartet. Founding board member, Blue Lake Fine Arts Camp in Twin Lake, Michigan, composer in residence, and principal conductor of the Festival Orchestra. Niblock has published 75 frequently performed compositions. Honored by MSU (2006) with the first ever Distinguished Emeritus Faculty Award for his continuing work in Fine Arts Education.

**Nichols, Jon P.:** MSU '73 and '79; Director Emeritus of Bands at Wyoming Rogers High School in Grand Rapids, 1987-2007.

**Nielsen, Eric W.:** MSU Band, trombone, 1969-1973.

***Notkoff, Pauline:*** *immigrant, 1917.*

**Nye, Harland F.:** MSC band; retired high school band director.

***Palmiero, Angelina:*** *Italian immigrant, 1923.*

**Pearson, Dan:** MSU Band Manager, 1957-1961, business major.

**Piatt, Bob:** sousaphone. MSU band, 1958-1961. Piatt, an insurance adjuster, marketing, and sales manager, has also played in the US Army First Infantry Division Band, the Ann Arbor, MI, Concert Band (32 years), the Scottville, MI, Clown Band and the MSU Alumni Band.

***Platt, Mary:*** *trumpet. MSU 1970–1982. Platt is a writer for the* LA Times *and internet writer and producer for Cox internet. She currently studies piobaireachd (classical bagpipe music). MSU Alumni Band Association member, director of public relations, Chapman University, Orange, CA.*

**Porter, Carol Burt:** saxophone. MSU band, 1957-61.

**Reed, H. Owen:** American composer, conductor, author, professor at Michigan State University, 1939 to 1976. Reed has published eight books concerning musical composition and music theory. His scores, recordings, correspondence, and other papers are stored in the Michigan State University Manuscript Collection, at Michigan State University Libraries.

***Revelli, William D.:*** *world renowned conductor of the University of Michigan Band for 36 years, from 1935-1971. Revelli also was founder of the College Band Directors National Association (CBDNA) in 1941 and served as a President of the National Band Association and the American Bandmasters Association.*

**Rosegart, Eldon:** MSC band drum major, class of 1941.

**Sack, Robert:** clarinet. MSC 1950-1954. Retired and playing in the Birmingham Straw Hat Band and the Birmingham Concert Band; member of MSU Alumni Band Association.

**Salow, Ron:** trumpet. MSC '51. Novi, MI, Community Band and MSU Alumni Band Association member.

***Col. William F. Santelmann:*** *conductor of the US Marine Band, Guest conductor at MSU 1958, NBA Hall of Fame of Distinguished Conductors, 1990, A. Austin Harding Award 1982.*

***Shaw, Robert S.:*** *Michigan State College President, 1928–1941, and father-in-law to John Hannah, his successor. Shaw served briefly as* *interim college president on three prior occasions before he was appointed to the position permanently.*

***Sherwood, Robert:*** *playwright, editor, screenwriter, film critic, an original member of the Algonquin Table when it began in 1919.*

***Stabley, Fred W.:*** *author of* The Spartans, *a book about Michigan State football to 1975.*

**Stansell, Fritz:** baritone. MSC 1950-1954, Purdue 1961. Following service in the 50th Army Band, directed bands and orchestras in the Muskegon area and founded the Blue Lake Fine Arts Camp in 1966.

**Stansell, Gretchen:** violin/French horn. MSC Band 1951-1954, a founding board member of the Blue Lake Fine Arts Camp, and Director of the Blue Lake International Program since its inception in 1969.

**Stansell, Tom:** clarinet, saxophone. An instrument repair technician, and free-lance jazz musician. Son of Fritz and Gretchen.

***Stein, Keith:*** *clarinetist, teacher, once one of the Chicago Symphony's youngest members. Stein earned a Master of Music degree at the University of Michigan where he played in Nicholas Falcone's band. He began his teaching career at Interlochen and MSU, where he remained for 41 years until he retired.*

***Taylor, J.S.:*** *MAC music professor, composer, marching band director, 1919–1922.*

**Thompson, Ted:** clarinet. Member of the MSC and MSU Bands 1949-1953, 1956-1957. Thompson studied with Keith Stein, and earned a masters degree in performance as a woodwind specialist. After graduation and the Army, he taught in the Williamston, Michigan, schools until retirement.

**Underwood, John:** clarinet, MSU band 1946-1950.

**Walters, Bob:** trumpet, MSU band 1968–1971.

***Ward, Alan:*** *sports columnist,* Oakland Tribune.

**Welch, Myron:** clarinet, bassoon. Director of Bands University of Iowa School of Music, and previously at Wright State University in Dayton, Ohio. Recipient of the National Federation of State High School's Outstanding Music Educator Award. Guest conductor for numerous All-State bands, regional honor bands, summer music camps, and community bands. Welch received his bachelor's and master's degrees in music from Michigan State University, and his doctorate in music education from the University of Illinois, where his thesis was a study of the life and work of Leonard Falcone, 1927 to 1967. He conducts the Staff Band, Faculty Band and Orchestra at the Blue Lake Fine Arts Camp.

***Welch, Roseanne:*** *granddaughter of a 1904 Italian immigrant.*

**Welton, A. Roger:** flute, MSU Band 1945-1950. Director of Bands at Pontiac Northern High School, free lance flutist in Detroit area, principal flute with the Pontiac Symphony for 22 years.

**Wisner, Dave:** clarinet, trumpet, MSU band 1956-1959, band president '58-'59. BA in Social Science, 34 years a State Farm Insurance agent; currently plays trumpet daily in 6 ensembles ranging from community bands to big bands.

***Zabrusky, Ed:*** *manager of MSU's News Bureau (now Office of Media Communications) and MSU publicist, from 1956-1994.*

# NOTES

## Chapter 1

1. Zajec, Victor, and Marilea Zajec. "Leonard V. Falcone (1899–1985)." *Memorials and Tributes to Members of the American Bandmasters Association.* American Bandmasters Association. Web. 1 Mar. 2008.

2. Glickman, Ken. "Falcone Memorial Trip." *Lansing State Journal.* 5 Aug. 1985. Print. * *Proud villagers approached several band members to exclaim, "I'm a Falcone, too!"*

3.* *The picture described is half of a snapshot taken of Leonard and Nicholas Falcone during the opening of the National High School Orchestra Camp (now Interlochen Arts Camp) in June, 1928, where the brothers served on the staff. There was no camp uniform that first year; Falcone's attire was of his own choosing.*

4. "Falcone Family Records, Roseto." *Archivio di Stato di Foggia.* Foggia, Italy. E-mail to author. 3 Sept. 2009.
   Bianco, Carla. *The Two Rosetos.* Bloomington and London: Indiana UP, 1974. 11. Print.

5. Bianco, 15.

6.* *See Appendix B for recipe.*

7. Ruggiero, Cesare. E-mail to author. 17 Feb. 2009.

8. Bianco, 16.* *Though by the end of the 18th century the feudal regime had fallen, the Roseto of Leonardo Falcone's day still maintained more than a few traces of its hierarchical social structure. Above all were the Signori (lords), or the old nobility like the Marquis. Beneath them in status were those with more than the usual meager education, particularly workers at the city hall municipio and teachers. Next down on the social ladder were middle class artisans and shopkeepers like the Falcones, and beneath them in class were the* contadini, *those who owned a plot all their own (called a "handkerchief of land") to farm. On the very bottom rung were landless peasant farmers.*

9.* *The concert began with Beryl Falcone, Leonard's wife, giving a brief speech in Italian, followed by a two and one half hour program of music selected by Leonard before his death. It included Verdi and Rosinni along with standard American band fare, plus the national anthems of both countries and Falcone's arrangements of the MSU Fight Song and Alma Mater. At its close, little village girls meandered through the gazebo presenting roses and a souvenir medallion to each band member;* Glickman.

10. Welch, Myron D. *The Life and Work of Leonard Falcone with Emphasis on His Years as Director of Bands at Michigan State University 1927-1967.* Thesis. Michigan State University, 1973. Ann Arbor, Michigan: UMI Dissertation Services, 1973. 28. Print.

11. Falcone, Cecilia. E-mail to author. 6 Jan. 2009.

12. "Roseto Valfortore." Indettaglio.It. 2008. Web. 15 Dec. 2008.

13.* *The Blue Lake Fine Arts Camp, a summer school of arts in Twin Lake, Michigan.*

14. Falcone, Cecilia. Condensed from e-mail to author. 6 Jan. 2009.

15. Puelo, Stephan. *The Boston Italians*. Boston: Beacon P, 2007. 1. Print. Williams, Phyllis. *Southern Italian Folkways in Europe and America: A Handbook for Social Workers, Visiting Nurses, School Teachers, and Physicians.* New Haven: Yale University, 1938. 5. Print.

16. Gladwell, Malcolm. *Outliers: the Story of Success.* New York: Little, Brown, and Company, 2008. 3. Print.

17. Pisarro, Barbara N. "Picture It, Palermo 1900." *The Nucatola Family Tree.* para 5. Web. 5 June 2008.

18. "Roseto Valfortore."

19. Bianco, 13- 14.

20.* *Sometimes referred to as "Nick"or Nicholas" later in the book.*

21.* *Over the course of years, the Falcone family lived in several homes in Roseto. Leonard Falcone believed, but was uncertain, that the house pictured on page 9 was one of them. Falcone family birth records from the Archivio di Stato di Foggia in Foggia, Italy, indicate that at the time of Leonardo's birth, the family was living at an address listed as Course of Popolo n.4; in 1901, when his sister Maria was born, they were domiciled at "Course King d' Italy n.3." These addresses are no longer used in Roseto.*

## Chapter 2

1. McGoldrick, Monica, Joseph Giordano, and Nydia Garcia-Predo, eds. *Ethnicity and FamilyTherapy*. 3rd ed. New York: Guilford Press, 2005. 621. Print.

2. Dobos, Joseph. Falcone Notes #1. "Leonard Falcone Interview with Joseph Dobos and Richard Adler, Jan. 7, 1985." E-mail enclosure to author. 13 Sept. 2008.
   Falcone, Nicholas. *Autobiography of Nicholas D. Falcone and the University of Michigan Bands 1927–1935*. Unpublished manuscript. Print.
3. Dobos, Joseph. Falcone Notes #1.
4. Dobos, Joseph. Falcone Notes #1.
5. Falcone, Beryl. Telephone interview with author. 26 June 2008.
6. Dobos, Joseph. Falcone Notes #1.
7. Falcone, Beryl. Telephone interview with author. 26 June 2008.
8. Falcone, Beryl. Telephone interview with author. 29 Apr. 2009.
9. DelConte, Michele M. *Italian Immigration to Portland, Oregon, 1900-1930.* Thesis. Washington State University. Ann Arbor MI: UMI Dissertation Services, 1995. ProQuest. Dissertations and Theses: Full Text. Houston Public Library, Houston. 172-73. Web. 18 Oct. 2008.
10. Ferrera, Nick. Condensed from e-mails to author. 2 May 2009 and 4 May 2009.
11. McGoldrick, Monica, Joseph Giordano, and Nydia Garcia-Preto, eds. 621.
12. Ruggiero, Cesare. E-mail to the author. 16 Feb. 2011.
13. *Reports of the Immigration Commission: Emigration Conditions in Europe.* "The Dillingham Report." Washington D.C.: Government Printing Office. 1911. 163. Print.
14. DelConte, 172-73.
    Ciongoli, A. Kenneth and Jay Parini. *Passage to Liberty.* Bellvue, Washington: Becker and Meyer, 2002. 16. Print.
15. McGoldrick, Monica, Joseph Giordano, and Nydia Garcia-Preto, eds. 621.
16.* *Italian proberb: "When the husband speaks, the wife must lose her voice."*
17. DelConte, 115, 128.
    McGoldrick, Monica, Joseph Giordano, and Nydia Garcia-Preto, eds. 621.
18. Mangione, Jerre, and Ben Morreale. *La Storia: Five Centuries of the Italian American Experience.* New York: Harper Perennial, 1994. 233-234. Print.
19. Wisner, Dave. E-mail to author. 27 Feb. 2009.
20. Falcone, Beryl. Telephone interview with author. 26 June 2008.
21. Ciongoli, A. Kenneth, and Jay Parini. 16.
22. Falcone, Leonard. Interviewed by Myron Welch. East Lansing, MI. Disc 17 tr. 1. CD-ROM. 22 July 1972.
23. Ferrera, Nick. E-mail to the author. 2 May 2009.
24. Falcone, Beryl. Telephone interview with author. 26 June, 2008.

25. Ferrera, Nick. E-mail to the author. 2 May 2009.

26. Leonard Falcone Papers. Box 1563. Scrapbook 1. Collection UA17.133. Michigan State University Archives and Historical Collections, East Lansing, MI.

27. McGoldrick, Monica, Joseph Giordano, and Nydia Garcia-Preto, eds. 621.

28. Puelo, Stephan. *The Boston Italians.* Boston: Beacon Press, 2007. 50-52. Print.

29.* *A song that some Rosetans still know today refers to this first emigration to South America, the "third part of the world." It begins:*

*I bless Christopher Columbus,*
*Who discovered the third part of the world.*
*He discovered three parts of the world,*
*And we Italians are called to work there.*
*And coffee is all over the land,*
*Long live America and those who are there. . .(refrain);* Bianco, Carla. *The Two Rosetos.* Bloomington and London: Indiana UP, 1974. 35-36. Print.

30. Wepman, Dennis. "The New Immigration: 1881-1918." *Immigration, American Experience.* New York: Facts on File, Inc., 1. American History Online. Web. 14 Aug. 2008.

31. "Falcone Family Records, Roseto." *Archivio di Stato di Foggia.* Foggia, Italy. E-mail to author. 3 Sept. 2009.

32. Dobos, Joseph. Updated Notes.

33.* *During the Dobos/Adler interview, Leonard Falcone states that in 1894 the family moved to South America and lived in Sao Paulo, Brazil, and that in 1898, his mother and brothers, Nicola and Carmen, returned to Italy while his father, Dominico, remained for two more years to work. Leonard was born in 1899, suggesting that Maria may have been pregnant as she took the long journey home with her two young sons;* Dobos, Joseph. Falcone Notes #1.

34. Triner, Gail D. "Review of Anne G. Hanley, Native Capital: Financial Institutions and Economic Development in São Paulo, Brazil, 1850-1920." *Native Capital: Financial Institutions and Economic Development in São Paulo, Brazil, 1850-1920.* EH.Net Economic History Services. Mar. 2006. 1. 9. Web. 21 Jan. 2009.

35. McGoldrick, Monica, Joseph Giordano, and Nydia Garcia-Preto, eds. 621.

36. Falcone, Beryl. Telephone interview with author. 26 June 2008.

37. Dobos, Joseph. Updated Notes.

38. Welch, 30.

39. Falcone, Leonard. Disc 17, tr. 13. CD-ROM. 22 July 1972.

40. Pisarro, Barbara N. "Picture It, Palermo 1900." *The Nucatola Family Tree.* Web. 5 June 2008.

41. Welch, 30.
42. Falcone, Beryl. Telephone interview with author. 26 June 2008.
43.* *Falcone claims in the Dobos/Adler interview that because of the war, he came to America earlier than had been planned*; Dobos, Joseph. Updated Notes.
44. S.S. *Stampalia* Ship Manifest. 23 June-7 July, 1915. "Falcone, Leonardo." 0312-13, line 30. Ellis Island. org Passenger List Database. Web. 5 Sept. 2008.
45. Dobos, Joseph. Updated Notes.
    Welch, 30.
46. Mangione, Jerre, and Ben Morreale. 233-234.
47. Welch, 29.
48. Pisarro.
49. "Banquet to Honor Director's Courage. " Leonard Falcone Papers. Collection UA17.133. Box 1569, Folder 19. Michigan State University Archives and Historical Collections, East Lansing MI.
50. Welch, 29.
51. Falcone, Leonard. CD-ROM. Disc 17, tr. 1. 22 July 1972.
52. Dobos, Joseph. Falcone Notes #1.
53. Gillette, Tom. E-mail to author. 8 Dec. 2008.
54. Welch, 18.
55. Welch, 25.
56. Falcone, Leonard. Disc 17 tr. 4, 8. CD-ROM. 22 July 1972.
57. McGoldrick, Monica, Joseph Giordano, and Nydia Garcia-Preto, eds. 621.
58. Stansell, Fritz. E-mail to author. 1 Mar. 2009.

## Chapter 3

1. Welch, Myron D. *The Life and Work of Leonard Falcone with Emphasis on His Years as Director of Bands at Michigan State University 1927–1967*. Thesis. Michigan State University, 1973. Ann Arbor, MI: UMI Dissertation Services, 1973. 25-28. Print.
2. Falcone, Leonard. Interviewed by Myron Welch. East Lansing, MI. Disc 7 tr. 11-12. CD-ROM. 2 Feb. 1973.
3. Greene, Victor. *A Passion for Polka*. Berkeley: University of California Press. 1992. 35. Print.
4.* *In the Dobos–Adler interview, Falcone stated that the most important part of*

*Roseto's town life was the Municipal Band;* Dobos, Joseph. Updated Notes. *"Leonard Falcone interview, January 7, 1984, with Joseph Dobos and Richard Alder."* E-mail to the author. 14 Sept 2008.

5. Falcone, Leonard. Disc 7, tr. 11-12. CD-ROM. 2 Feb. 1972.

6.* *In his autobiography (p. 1), Nicholas Falcone refers to his study at the "Roseto School of Music" in Roseto Valfortore, a statement which caused Leonard Falcone to chuckle with pleasure when he heard of it. "Donato Donatelli was the Roseto School of Music," he responded.* Dobos, Joseph. Falcone Notes #1. "Leonard Falcone Interview with Joseph Dobos and Richard Adler, Jan. 7, 1985." E-mail enclosure to author. 13 Sept. 2008.

7. Falcone, G. "La Storia del Commune di Roseto Valfortore." *Associazone Pro Loco del Comune di Roseto Valfortore.* 6. Web. 5 Jan. 2009.

8. Welch, 20.

9. Falcone, G, 6. Web. 5 Jan. 2009.

10. Bielinski, Vic. "Falcone Traces Musical Life From Italy to M.S.C." *State News.* 18 May 1934. Print.
Dobos, Joseph. Falcone Notes #1.
Welch, 28.

11. Welch, 29.

12. Welch, 20, 22.

13. Falcone, Leonard. Disc 17 tr. 8. CD-ROM. Summer 1972.

14. Welch, 21.
Dobos, Joseph. Falcone Notes #1. "Leonard Falcone Interview with Joseph Dobos and Richard Adler, Jan. 7 1985." E-mail enclosure to author. 13 Sept. 2008.

15. "Banquet to Honor Director's Courage." Leonard Falcone Papers. Collection UA17.133. Box 1569, folder 19. Michigan State University Archives and Historical Collections, East Lansing MI. **At the turn of the century, young Italian boys were expected to contribute to family income as soon as possible.*

16. Welch, 22.

17. Bielinski.

18. Mayer, Elizabeth. "Personalities at Orchestra Camp." *Record Eagle.* Traverse City. 31 July 1928. Print.

19. Welch, 24.

20. Dobos, Joseph. Falcone Notes #1.

21. Welch, 23-24.

22. Bielinski.
Welch, 25.

23. Dobos, Joseph. Falcone Notes #1.

24. Falcone, Leonard. Disc 17 tr. 9-11. CD-ROM. Summer 1972.

25. Bielinski.

26. Falcone, Leonard. Disc 17, tr. 9-11. CD-ROM Summer 1972.

27. Welch, 28.

28. Falcone, Beryl. Telephone interview with author. 26 June 2008.

29. Falcone, Leonard. Disc 17, tr. 4. CD-ROM. 22 July 1972.

30. Bowman, Brian. "T.U.B.A. Euphonium Profile: Leonard Falcone." *T.U.B.A. Journal 5* (Winter 1978): 3. Print.

31. Welch, 23.

32. Bowman, 3.
Falcone, Beryl. Telephone interview with author. 26 June 2008.

33. Stansell, Fritz. E-mail to the author. 2 Sept. 2009.

## Chapter 4

1. Mangione, Jerre, and Ben Morreale. *La Storia: Five Centuries of the Italian American Experience.* New York: Harper Pereninial. 1994. 233-234. Print.

2.* *The Falcone household would have spoken in an Italian dialect specific to the Italian province of Foggia.*

3.* *Cornhusk mattresses were commonly made during harvest time; after the animals were fed corn, the beaten husks were saved to make mattresses.*

4. Ruggio, Cesare. Email to author, 26 Feb. 2011.

5. *S.S. Stampalia* Ship Manifest. 23 June-7 July1915. "Falcone, Leonardo." 0312-13. Ellis Island. org Passenger List Database. Web. 5 Sept. 2008. Falcone, Leonardo. *Passporto.* Foggia. 18 April 1915. Family newspaper and memento collection. E-mail enclosure to author from Cecilia Falcone. 24 Jan. 2009.

6.* *Beryl Falcone says that upon arrival, Leonard didn't know what he was going to do to make a living but hoped not to be a farm laborer as stated on his manifest;* Falcone, Beryl. Telephone interview with author. 10 July 2008.

7. Bianco, Carla. *The Two Rosetos.* Bloomington and London: Indiana University Press, 1974. 2. Print.

8. Pisarro. 5 June, 2008.

9. "Domani ci Zappa: *Italian Immigration and Ethnicity in Pennsylvania.*" Pennsylvania Folklife 45 (1995): 2. Print.

10.* *Most immigrants packed their bags with two sets of clothes, a blanket, and a* *personal keepsake. According to Pissaro, nearly all wore their very best clothes for the journey to America, and did not change them until they landed.*

11.* *In an early interview, Falcone stated that his original intention was to remain in the US for 5–6 years, further his education, acquire a small sum of money, and return permanently to Roseto;* Bielinski, Vic. "Falcone Traces Musical Life From Italy to MSC" *State News*. 18 May 1934. Print. *Near the end of his life he made reference to this intention by noting that "it was expected that people would leave Roseto, . . . make their fortune, and return home."* Dobos, Joseph. Falcone Notes #1. "Leonard Falcone Interview with Joseph Dobos and Richard Adler, Jan. 7 1985." E-mail enclosure to author. 13 Sept. 2008. *Despite early plans to save enough money to return to Italy and live in the comfort of their homeland village, marriage, children, war, and a faith in their future in America eventually made this idea less attractive to Italian immigrants, and most stayed in the US.*

12. *S.S. Vulcania* Ship Manifest. 24 June 1931. "Falcone, Leonardo." Web. 5 Sept. 2008.
Falcone, Beryl. Telephone interview with author. 26 June 2008 and 10 July 2008.

13.* *To save enough money to return to live in the comfort of the homeland village with their families was a common dream of the Italian immigrant. In reality, of the 4.2 million Italians who emigrated to the US from 1880-1920, only 1 million returned to Italy permanently. Another 1.7 million became "Birds of Passage," an American term for those who traveled back and forth between the two countries, usually during the winter months. A combination of the lack of prospects in Italy and the opportunities offered them in America eventually caused a downward shift in the number of Italians who returned to their homeland permanently, and by 1913, although it may not have been their original intention, most of the 376,000 Italians who immigrated to the US, decided to stay in the United States for good;* Puleo, Stephan. *The Boston Italians*. Boston: Beacon Press. 2007. 53; 91. Print. *That most, Falcone included, did not or were not able to return to their villages should not negate the fact that returning home was not only Falcone's goal, but also the goal of nearly every Italian immigrant;* Bodner, John. 1987. *The Transplanted. A History of Immigrants in Urban America*. Bloomington: Indiana University Press. 53-54. Print. Williams, Phyllis. *Southern Italian Folkways in Europe and America: A Handbook for Workers, Visiting Nurses, School Teachers, and Physicians.* New Haven: Yale University, 1938. Chap. 1. Print.

14.* *It is entirely possible that Leonardo, who was accustomed to carrying food, a knapsack, and his instrument on long walks with the band, made the journey to the train station on foot, with only Antonio as his traveling companion. But as departures for America were momentous events in villagers' lives, and because Leonardo would have been carrying more with him on this journey than when he traveled with the band, it is as likely that Leonardo's father accompanied his youngest son on the ten hour trip to Benevento. If so, Dominico* *would have to have made either a non-stop all night return trip to Roseto, or have napped in the cart some time before morning in a field along the Roseto-Castlefranco Road.*

15.* *The magnificent diurnal red kite, once plentiful, is seldom found in the region now, perhaps because of the modern construction of wind farms.*

16. *Statistical Abstract Supplement, Historical Statistics of the US Colonial Times to 1957.* US Department of Commerce, Bureau of the Census. 42. Print.

17.* *A common sight across Europe as immigrants left their villages was a procession which ". . . resembled both a funeral and a triumph. The women wept over us, reminding us eloquently of the perils of the sea, of the bewilderment of a foreign land, of the torments of homesickness that awaited us."* Antin, Mary. "The Exodus." *The Promised Land.* Boston: Houghton Mifflin Co. 1912. Print.

18.* *G. Capobianco, a local politician, had the Roseto-Castelfranco road designed and built between 1908 and 1920 as the primary outlet of Roseto to Naples;* Falcone, G. "La Storia del Commune di Roseto Valfortore." Associazone Pro Loco del Comune di Roseto Valfortore. Falcone, G.6. Web. 5 Jan. 2009.

19.* *According to Lucilla Parisi, a recent mayor of Roseto Valfortore, and others, it can be safely assumed that the Castle-Franco road to the Benevento station was the most likely route taken by the little entourage and that Leonardo and Antonio did not walk or ride a donkey cart all the way to Naples from Roseto; it should be noted, however, that some few Rosetan emigrants went by horse-cart to Foggia and there caught the train to Naples;* Zizzi, Domenico. E-mail to author. 5 Mar. 2009.

20. LaSorte, Michael. *Images of an Italian Green Experience.* Mar. 31, 1985. Philadelphia: Temple University Press. 12. Print.
Puleo, 61.

21.* *After months of worker strikes, in June of 1914 there was violence in Naples as "anarchist malefactors . . . seized the opportunity to carry out their criminal plans;* "Troops Control Italian Rioters." *The New York Times*, June 13, 1914. ProQuest Historical Newspapers. *The New York Times (1851-2005).* Web. 21 Jan. 2009. *"Troops called in to control rioters fired on the mob, and many were killed." In Naples, "rioters fought with daggers and revolvers, stormed the carabinieri barricades and surrounded a body of artillery, which opened fire with quickfirers";* "Anarchy in Italy; Many are Killed; Warships Ready." *The New York Times*, June 12, 1914. ProQuest Historical Newspapers. *The New York Times (1851-2005).* Web. 21 Jan. 2009. *Then, in February of 1915, just five months before Leonardo left home, 10,000 strikers paraded to city hall to demand that the price of bread be dropped from 10 cents to 7 cents, and "large forces of troops and police were called out to prevent disorder";* "Bread Strike in Naples." *The New York Times.* 25 Feb. 1915. ProQuest Historical Newspapers. *The New York Times (1851-2005).* Web. 21 Jan. 2009.

## Chapter 5

1. “S.S Stampalia” Ship Manifest. 23 June-7 July. “Falcone, Leonardo.” 0312-13. Ellis Island. org Passenger List Database. Web. 5 Sept. 2008.
2. LaSorte, Michael. *Images of an Italian Green Experience*. Mar. 31, 1985. Philadelphia: Temple University Press. 13. Print.
3. Puleo, Stephan. *The Boston Italians*. Boston: Beacon Press. 2007. 60-61. Print.
4. Brandenburg, Broughton. *Imported Americans*. New York: Frederick A. Stokes Co. Publishers. 1904. 144-145. Print.
5.* *In ancient times, the city was called “Parthenope,” the name of the sweetly singing siren who, along with her sisters, dwelt on a rock in the bay and lured sailors to their destruction.*
6. *The New International Encyclopedia*. Second Edition. Volume XIV. New York: Dodd, Mead and Co. 556. 1916. Print.
7. “Eruption of Vesuvius Felt at San Francisco.” *Los Angeles Times*. Nov. 9, 1914. ProQuest Historical Newspapers. Los Angeles Times (1881–1986). 11. Web. 1 Aug. 2008.
8. “Vesuvius Very Active. Fiery Lava Can Be Seen From Naples—Earthquake Shocks Near Volcano.” *The New York Times*. 9 Oct. 1915. Print.
9. Holmes, Burton, and Schlesinger. *The World 100 Years Ago. Southern Italy.* 37. Philadelphia: Chelsea House Publishers, 1998. Print.
10. Holmes, Burton, and Schlesinger, 44.
11. “Italians Coming in Great Numbers.” *The New York Times Archives*. 17 Apr. 1921. Web. 1 Aug. 2008.
12. “Florence and Naples in Contrast.” *Christian Science Monitor*. 1908; Apr 23, 1914; Proquest Historical Newspapers Christian Science Monitor, 9. Web. 1 Aug. 2008.
13. “Italians Coming”
14. Holmes, Burton, and Schlesinger, 44, 56.
15. *The New International Encyclopedia*, 557.
16. “Italians Coming”
17. “Italians Coming”
18. Holmes, Burton, and Schlesinger, 52.
19. *The New International Encyclopedia*, 556.
20. “Naples and Vesuvius.” *Old and Sold*. Web. 5 Sept. 2009.
21.* *Though traditionally Neopolitan songs were written anonymously, the com-*

*posers of the enduring "O Sole Mio" are known to be an impoverished trio of Neopolitans named Giovanni Capurro (1859-1929), Alfredo Mazzucchi (1878-1972), and Eduardo di Capua (1865-1917).*

22. Holmes, Burton, and Schlesinger, 46.

23. "Florence and Naples in Contrast."

24. "Italians Coming "

25. Holmes, Burton, and Schlesinger, 52.

26. "Florence and Naples in Contrast."

27. *Reports of the Immigration Commission: Emigration Conditions in Europe.* "The Dillingham Report." Washington D.C. : Government Printing Office, 1911. Vol. 4: 147. Print.

28.* *On August 17th, 1916, just one year after Leonard Falcone set foot in the United States, the Stampalia was torpedoed by a German submarine and sunk to the bottom of the Aegean Sea. Fortunately, just two weeks prior to this event she had been "requisitioned by the Italian government and. . . her future sailing canceled." Thus, she was not carrying any passengers;* "Stampalia Stuck in the War Zone." *The New York Times*. 1857–Current: Aug. 20, 1916. ProQuest Historical Newspapers. *The New York Times (1851–2004)*, 2. Web. 10 Mar. 2008.

29. "Stampalia." Ellis Island. org . Web. 23 Sept. 2008.

30.* *Any ship passenger found at Ellis Island to have a communicable disease was returned to Italy and became the responsibility of the ship company--which then had to pay a $100 fine and reimburse the emigrant for his or her journey;* Pisarro, Barbara N. "Picture It, Palermo 1900." *The Nucatola Family Tree.* para 47. Web. 5 June 2008.

31.* *First and second class passengers were not examined by US officers in Naples, but instead were seen in their cabins by physicians who were employed by the steamship company and under the supervision of the Italian Emigration Commission; Reports*, 115–117.

32. "S.S Stampalia" Ship Manifest. 23 June-7 July, 1915. "Falcone, Leonardo." 0312-13. Ellis Island. org Passenger List Database. Web. 5 Sept. 2008.

33.* *Nicola, who was older than Leonardo when he left Italy for the United States and came well before America's entry in WWI, felt comfortable in telling the authorities that he was emigrating to be a "barber," like his father. He, too, hoped to be a musician in the United States;* "Nocsla [sic] Falcone." Duca D Aosta Ship Manifest. Nov. 21–Dec. 3 1912. 0890 l. 3. Ellis Island. org Passenger List Database. Web. 5 Sept. 2008.

34. "American Money Sent to Europe." *Wall Street Journal*. Apr. 12, 1912. ProQuest Historical Newspapers: *The Wall Street Journal (1889–1985)* 6. Web. 2 Feb 2009.

35.* *Thus, for example, they might become a member of group H, number 17.*

36. Grose, Howard B. "Aliens or Americans?" Young People's Missionary Movement: New York. 1906. Gjenvick-Gjonvik Archives. Web. 23 Sept. 2009.

37* *An inspector's report: "The supplemental inspection at the gangplank was begun after a steamer landed in New York with ten cases of acute trachoma aboard. It was clear that the passengers had never passed the inspections at Naples at all, and that there had been substitutions. The method of substitution was that a healthy person who had no intention of emigrating to the United States at all would pass through all the medical inspections on the shore, ultimately receiving a stamped inspection card which allowed him or her to board the steamer. On the quay outside the Capitaneria del Porto, the card would be passed to the diseased person, who would then pay the substitute a fee and board the ship"; Reports,* 115–116.

38.* *Young Leonardo, a mere 4'9" at the time of his emigration, looked much younger than 16.*

39. *Reports,* 148.

40. De Crescenzo, Luciano. "The Ball of Yarn" *Immigration: Ellis Island Virtual Tour.* Web. 11 Oct. 2009.

41.* *The* Stampalia *on this day may have instead sailed past Capri.*

42. "Ischia, in the Bay of Naples." *Christian Science Monitor* (1908-Current file). 11 Apr. 1914. Proquest Historical Newspapers Christian Science Monitor 1908, p. 31). Web. 4 Aug. 2009.

## Chapter 6

1. Bowman, Brian. "T.U.B.A. Euphonium Profile: Leonard Falcone." *T.U.B.A. Journal* 5, no. 2 (winter 1978). 2. Print.

2. "Steerage Conditions." *A Report of the Immigration Commission 1911*. Gjenvick-Gjonvik Archives. Web. 19 Oct. 2009.

3. Puleo, Stephan. *The Boston Italians.* Boston: Beacon Press. 2007. 43. Print.

4. Bernardy, Amy A. *Italiarandagia Attraverso gli Stati Uniti. Torino:* Fratelli Bocca, 1913. p. 13. Print.

5.* *Most likely there was a seasickness "curative" in his bag, alongside articles of clothing. According to one immigrant, "nearly everyone seemed to be provided with a specific for seasickness. One man had apples, another a patent medicine, a third carried a pocketful of lime-drops, and yet another had pinned his faith upon raw onions. It may perhaps be interesting to intending voyagers to know that not one of these preventives had the slightest effect. I was an unwilling witness of their non-efficacy afterward";* Whitmarsh, H.

Phelps. "The Steerage of Today - A Personal Experience" *Century Magazine.* Vol. LV, Number 67. 1898. 528-543. Gjenvick-Gjonvik Archives. Web. 19 Oct. 2009.

6. "Steerage Conditions."

7.* *Greasy plates and bowls were a primary cause of seasickness, which kept many passengers confined to their berths for the entire passage.* "Steerage Conditions." *Many carried their cups/plates/bowls on a string around their neck to prevent theft. Because washing facilities in steerage were inadequate, there was little effort made to wash dishes;* LaSorte, Michael. *La Merica: Images of Italian Greenhorn Experience.* 31 Mar. 1985. Philadelphia: Temple University Press. 26. Print.

8. Pisarro, Barbara N. "Picture It, Palermo 1900." *The Nucatola Family Tree.* para 5. Web. 5 June 2008.

9. "Steerage Conditions."

10.* *In his memoir, one 1906 steerage passenger on a ship traveling to Naples wrote "The food was poor. We had to pick our way through the porridge to avoid unwelcome strangers";* Taylor, Richard Herbert. "Memoirs of Richard Herbert Taylor 15 Dec. 1884–16 May 1976." Web. 10 Jan. 2009.

11.* *Excepting during medical inspections, many ships did not allow women on deck until the boat was pulling into New York Harbor.*

12. "Steerage Conditions."

13.* *From Keats's "A Valediction Forbidding Mourning."*

14. LaSorte, 26.

15. Whitmarsh, 528-543.

16. LaSorte, 29.

17.* *Most anti-Italian discrimination in the United States was aimed at Southern Italians, who were viewed by Americans in general and the US Bureau of Immigration specifically as a different race entirely from the Northern Italians, most likely because they were darker, poorer, and less literate than their northern countrymen, and because Northern Italians had come to the US first, and had already established themselves;* Puleo, 81.

18. Powell, John. "Ellis Island." *Encyclopedia of North American Immigration.* New York: Facts on File, Inc. 2005. 87. Print.
LaSorte, 29-30.

19. Coan, Peter M. "Edward Hemmer." *Ellis Island Interviews.* Barnes and Noble Books, 2004. 70. Print.

20. Coan. "Angelina Palmiero." 49.

21. Coan. "Nina Hemmer." 70.

22. Powell, 87.

23* *Passengers underwent three sets of medical examinations: first, at home upon application for passage; second, on board the vessel, and third, upon arrival in the United States. Since an ill first or second class passenger had a much better chance of slipping through the inspections than a steerage passenger, any immigrant who could purchase the more expensive ticket did so. This became known as the "second-class scam." But when in 1905 physicians found an invalid immigrant named Henry Hayon had previously arrived in the steerage of a French liner and been deported on account of physical disabilities, and then, by returning in a saloon cabin, was able to dodge the health examination, it "opened the eyes of the immigration officials." Subsequently, authorities determined that beginning November 1, 1905, upon arrival at New York, saloon and second cabin passengers had to undergo inspection by Federal doctors just as steerage passengers did, though their exams were done in the comfort of their cabins; "Cabin Passengers to be Inspected, Too." The New York Times.* 1 Nov. 1905. Print.

24.* *The New York Times reported that on the Stampalia's return trip on July 10, 1915, "Extraordinary precautions were taken. . . before the departure to see that no bombs had been smuggled on board. Every piece of baggage belonging to the seventy cabin passengers was searched on the pier, and revolvers, daggers, and knives were taken away, as well as razors, carried by passengers. The baggage of the 800 steerage passengers, of whom 500 were reservists going to join the colors, was examined in the same manner. Weapons of all descriptions, from cavalry sabers and pearl handled dueling pistols to sardine can openers were carefully tagged and put in charge of the purser to be returned to the owners in Naples. Three hundred steerage passengers were turned away at the pier because there were no accommodations for them . . . After leaving her pier, the Stampalia steamed down the harbor to the Statue of Liberty, where she anchored for five hours to embark 250 cavalry horses. There was not an American citizen among the 870 passengers";* "Search Liner for Bombs." *The New York Times.* 11 July, 1915. Print.

25. "Roseanne Welch." *Immigration: Ellis Island Virtual Tour.* Web. 11 Oct. 2009.

26.* *The first major translation event for Italian immigrants occurred at Ellis Island where legions of interpreters, working the floors assisting inspectors and immigrants alike, were employed to translate the various languages of the newcomers.;* Carnevale, Nancy C. *Living in Translation: Language and the Italian Immigrants in the United States, 1890–1945.* Thesis. Rutgers The State University of New Jersey. New Brunswick, 2000. p. 83. Dissertations and Theses: *Full Text. ProQuest.* Houston Public Library, Houston, Texas. Web. 18 Oct. 2008.

27. Brownestone, David M., Irene M. Frank, Douglas L. Brownestone. *Island of Hope Island of Tears.* Barnes and Noble, 2000. 239; 244. Print.

28.* *Ellis Island was known by immigrants not only as "The Island of Hope," but also "The Island of Tears," the latter term because of the 9 percent who* *were sent to the detention pens for further examination and possible deportation, and the 2 percent who were found lacking in some way and sent back to their homeland;* Berman, 92; 53.

29.* *Deported sick children under the age of 12 had to be accompanied by a parent.*

30. Berman, 92; 54.

31. "Pauline Notkiff." *Immigration: Ellis Island Virtual Tour.* Web. 11 Oct. 2009.

32. Dobos, Joseph. Falcone Notes #1. "Leonard Falcone Interview with Joseph Dobos and Richard Adler, Jan. 7, 1985." E-mail enclosure to author. 13 Sept. 2008.

33. Falcone, Beryl. Telephone interview with author. 26 June 2008.

34. *S.S Stampalia* Ship Manifest. 23 June–7 July 1915. "Falcone, Leonardo." 0308-09. Ellis Island. org. Passenger List Database. Web. 5 Sept. 2008.

35. Falcone, Beryl. Telephone interview. 26 June 2008.

36. Brownestone, Frank, and Brownestone. 185.

37. Berman, 84.

38. Puleo, 67.

39.* *Leonardo Falcone was one of 49,688 Italians to enter the US in 1915;* "A Statistical Abstract Supplement, Historical Statistics of the US Colonial Times to 1957." US Department of Commerce, Bureau of the Census. 42. Print.

40. Brownestone, Frank, and Brownestone. 157.

41. *S.S Stampalia* Ship Manifest. 23 June-7 July 1915. "Romano, Antonio." 0308-09. Ellis Island. org Passenger List Database. Web. 5 Sept. 2008.

42.* *Italians began immigrating to Michigan's copper country in the 1860s, but did not appear in large numbers there until the 1890s. By 1900, the Italian Immigrant community in Houghton County accounted for 25 percent of the entire foreign-born Italian population in Michigan.and was the state's largest Italian community;*Twelfth Census of the United States, 1900, Census Reports, Vol. I, Part I, Washington, D.C.: United States Census Office, 1901. *Fourteenth Census of the United States, Vol. III*: Population 1920, Washington, D.C.: Government Printing Office, 1922.

43. Falcone, Beryl. Telephone interview. 26 June 2008.

44.* *Based on statements made by Leonard Falcone himself concerning seeing the Hudson River, Niagara Falls, and changing trains in Buffalo, his train journey would have followed the "New York Central/ Water Level Route" to Detroit;* Falcone, Beryl. Telephone interview with author. 26 June 2008. Lester, John E. *The Atlantic to the Pacific: What to See and How to See It.* London: Longmans, Green, and Co. 1873. 3-4. Print.

45. Dobos, Joseph. Falcone Notes #1. **20 or 25 cents was the usual tip at the time.*

46. Hammond, Susan. *Tchaikovsky Discovers America.* Douglas Cowling. Pickering, Ontario, Can-ada: The Children's Group, Inc., 1998. 36. Print.
47. Dobos, Joseph. Falcone Notes #1.
48. Falcone, Leonard. Interviewed by Myron Welch. East Lansing, MI. Disc 18, tr. 8. CD-ROM. 22 July 1972.
49. Dobos, Joseph. Telephone interview with author. 7 Nov. 2008.
50.* *The Ypsi-Ann was extended to Detroit in 1898 and by 1899, averaged 4,000 passengers daily. An interurban, it brought people to the center of the town, leaving them off at a convenient location. The fare was 1 cent a mile;* Duff, Lela. *Ann Arbor Yesterdays.* Ann Arbor: Friends of the Ann Arbor Public Library. 1962. 180. Print. McLaughlin, Marilyn S. *Ann Arbor, Michigan. A Pictorial History.* St. Louis: G. Bradley Publishing, Inc. 1995. 53. Print.

## Chapter 7

1.* *Record temperatures were reported throughout the eastern portion of the nation the week of July 19, 1915.*
2. Hoag, Gerald H. Papers, 1918-1978. Folder 6703. *Ann Arbor News.* 8 Dec. 1964. Bentley Historical Library. Ann Arbor: University of Michigan. Print.
3. Greene, Victor. *A Passion for Polka.* Berkeley: University of California Press. 1992. 38, 40. Print.
4. **Which is not to say that Italian musicians didn't encounter bias. John Phillip Sousa himself got a taste of it in late 1892 when, against his wishes, he was booked for a Sunday concert in Lima, Ohio. Local clergy, outraged that a concert would be played on a Sunday and incorrectly assuming Sousa was Italian, stated that they "didn't want any dago and his band here";* Bierley, Paul E. *The Incredible Band of John Phillip Sousa.* University of Illinois Press. 34. Print.
5.* *Michelangelo Donatelli directed the Roseto, PA, band for some time, and was band conductor at the feast of Our Lady of Mount Caramel on 16 July 1915. He also conducted his band in New York and in Philadelphia;* "Benvenuti nel Sito dell'Associazione Pro Loco del Comune di Roseto Valfortore ." 7. Web. 23 Sept. 2009.
6. Greene, 32, 33. 35.
7.* *Music was considered essential to providing mood and emotional effect to film. In their heyday, movie theaters offered the largest single source of employment to instrumental musicians and often, particularly in large cities, had sizeable and accomplished theater orchestras. William Revelli's first job was playing violin in an orchestra pit in Chicago. Eugene Ormandy, who had been concertmaster of an 85 piece orchestra at the Capitol in New York City, com-*

*mented at his debut as conductor of the Philadelphia Orchestra that when he was called upon to conduct Richard Strauss's "Till Eulenspiegel" on short notice, it had not presented a problem. "Of course I knew 'Till Eulenspiegel' very well," he said. "We played it at the Capitol"*; Eyman, Scott. *The Speed of Sound: Hollywood and the Talkie Revolution, 1926-1930.* New York: Simon and Schuster, 1997. 39. Print.

8. Dobos, Joseph. *"That Michigan Band:" A History of the University of Michigan Bands.* Unpublished manuscript. E-mail attachment to author. 14 Sept. 2008.

9. Sergent, Porter. *A Handbook of American Private Schools.* Boston: Porter Sergent. 1915. 181. Print.

10. Falcone, Nicholas. *Autobiography of Nicholas D. Falcone and the University of Michigan Bands 1927-1935.* Unpublished manuscript. 1. Print.
Welch, Myron D. *The Life and Work of Leonard Falcone with Emphasis on His Years as Director of Bands at Michigan State University 1927-1967.* Thesis. Michigan State University, 1973. Ann Arbor, MI: UMI Dissertation Services, 1973. 31. Print.

11.* *The bands were sponsored by businesses, families, and churches. One particularly popular band, Otto's Knights Templar Band (formerly the "Washenaw Times Band") was the first to play U of M's fight song, "The Victors"*; Shackman, Grace. "Otto's Band." *Ann Arbor Observer: Then and Now.* Oct. 2001.

12. Dobos, Joseph. "That Michigan Band."

13. Falcone, Leonard. Interviewed by Myron Welch. Disc 17, tr. 14. CD-ROM. 22 July 1972.

14. Upton, Lee. "Falcone's Fifty Years: Still Making Beautiful Music."*Lansing State Journal.* 1 June 1978.

15. "Queen Anne Soap Revives Memory of Old Ypsilanti." *Ypsilanti Gleanings,* March 1997. Web. Oct. 10, 2008.

16. Falcone, Leonard. Disc 17 tr. 14. CD-ROM. 22 July 1972.

17. "Queen Anne Soap."

18. Falcone, Leonard. Disc 17 tr. 14. CD-ROM. 22 July 1972.

19.* *According to Falcone, the girls on the interurban piqued the then sixteen year old boy's interest in learning English. He soon learned enough words to know what they were talking and laughing about, and then he could enjoy their conversation. As for the attractive woman, he purchased the book he saw her reading and "taught himself to read it" so he would be able to chat about it with her;* Dobos, Joseph. Telephone interview with author. 7 Nov. 2008.

20. Leonard Falcone Papers. Box 1583 Folder 2. 1934 *State News* May 18. Collection UA17.133. Michigan State University Archives and Historical Collections, East Lansing MI.

21. Bracco, Donato. Personal interview. 17 Nov. 2009.

22. Upton.

23. Welch, 31–32.

24.* *There is a connection between language and the mother. Mothers maintain a very strong symbolic position in Italian culture, as they are the heart of the family. While speaking the "mother tongue" is a powerful way to connect to the mother, adopting a foreign language is just as powerful a way to separate from her;* Grinberg, Leon, MD, and Rebecca Grenberg, MD. *Psychoanalytic Perspective on Migration and Exile.* New Haven: Yale University Press. 1989. 109. Print.

25.* *For the Southern Italian, hand and body gestures add meaning and nuance to speech and are a very important accompaniment to oral communication. Americans, who tended to have little appreciation for such gesticulations, often disdained them. The result was that nearly all Southern Italians deliberately learned to reduce conversational gestures.*

26.* *Italian immigrants were known for their frugality and extraordinary saving, keeping their basic needs to an absolute minimum so they could save a few pennies to buy property in the U.S. or Italy, pay for passage for another family member to come over, and/or to care for their families back home. Though they were the lowest paid workers in America, in 1914 alone they managed to send an astonishing sixty six million dollars back to Italy;* DelConte, Michele M. Italian *Immigration to Portland, Oregon, 1900-1930.* Thesis. Washington State University. Ann Arbor MI: UMI Dissertation Services, 1995. *ProQuest. Dissertations and Theses: Full Text.* Houston Public Library, Houston. 92, 94. Web. 18 Oct. 2008.

27. Falcone, Leonard. Disc 17 tr. 15. CD-ROM. Summer, 1972.

28. Welch, 32.

29. Falcone, Beryl. Telephone interview with author. 16 June, 2008.

30. Falcone, Leonard. Disc 17, tr. 15. CD-ROM. Summer, 1972.

31.* *The University School of Music was separate from the University of Michigan. Credits were transferable between the two schools, but only the University of Michigan granted degrees in music.*

32. Welch, 35.

33. Falcone, Leonard. Disc 18, tr. 3. CD-ROM. 22 July 1972.

34.* *One example among others: Leonard could hear and write melodic phrases so well that he was excused from an entire semester of classes in melodic dictation;* Welch, 36.

35. Welch, 37.

36. Dobos, Joseph. Falcone Notes #1.

37. "Falcone Traced Musical Life from Italy to M.S.C." Leonard Falcone Pa-

pers. *Lansing State Journal.* May 18 1934. Box 1583 Folder 2. Collection UA17.133. Michigan State University Archives and Historical Collections, East Lansing MI.

38. Falcone, Leonard. Disc 18, tr. 4. CD-ROM. 22 July 1972.

39. Falcone, Leonard. Disc 18 tr. 4.

40. Falcone, Leonard. Disc 18 tr. 1.

41. Falcone, Leonard. Disc 18 tr. 7.

42. Falcone, Beryl. Telephone interview with author. 16 June, 2008.

43. Nielsen, Erik W., MD. E-mail to CeCe Falcone. Forwarded to author 14 Apr. 2008.

44.* *Leonard later doubled in bands as a baritone player, an instrument he preferred because, as he once said, it requires more involvement—in addition to intellect, emotion, and technique, the player must also control breath. Years later, he told former student Earle Louder that baritone players use every faculty and sense they have in their performance, whereas violinists or pianists use only their fingers and minds;* Good, Richard. *A Biography of Earle L. Louder: Euphonium Performer and Educator.* Thesis. Arizona State University, 1996. Ann Arbor: UMI, 1997. 33. Print.

45.* *A diploma comparable to one in applied music; see Appendix C for the program.*

46. "Carmelo Falcone." US Customs Service. Passenger and Crew Lists of Vessels Arriving at New York, New York, 1925; (National Archives Microfilm Serial T715; Microfilm roll: T715_3655; Line:11).

47. "A Statistical Abstract Supplement, Historical Statistics of the US Colonial Times to 1957." US Department of Commerce, Bureau of the Census. 56-57. Print.

48. Falcone, Susan. E-mail to author. 24 Feb. 2009.

49. "Carmela Bruno Falcone." US Customs Service. Passenger and Crew Lists of Vessels Arriving at New York, New York, 1928; (National Archives Microfilm Serial T715; Microfilm roll T715_4263; Line:28).

50. Dobos, Joseph. Telephone interview with author . 7 Nov 2008.

51.* *The Wuerth, which was reached through a skylighted arcade to the north of owner Fred Wuerth's clothing store, was situated perpendicular to the Orpheum, another of Ann Arbor's theaters; carefully positioned between the two so that it could be heard equally well in boththeaters was a Hope-Jones organ.*

52.* *Leonard states in the Welch interview that the year he and his brother first played at the new Wuerth Theater was 1918, but Nicholas writes in his autobiography that it was 1920. Since Ann Arbor's Wuerth was built in 1918, and Nicholas was asked to start up its orchestra, Leonard's memory of the 1918 date is likely the correct one;* Welch, 34. Falcone, Nicholas, 2.

53.* *The Arcade, which dominated the corner of N. University and Thayer Streets, was destroyed by fire in late December of 1928. Hoards of students watched and cheered as flames licked advertising posters, one featuring Charlie Chaplin in the "Circus." When a few hours later the nearby Parrot Restaurant also caught fire, students ran from one fire to the next cheering;* Hoag.

54. Shackman, Grace. "The Rise, Fall, and Revival of Ann Arbor's Downtown Theaters." *Ann Arbor Observer.* September 2003. Web. May, 2008.

55. Dobos, Joseph. E-mail to author. 2 Dec. 2009.

56. Eyman, 39–40.

57. Eyman, 39–40. **See Appendix D.*

58. Welch, 34.

59. Welch, 34-35.

60. Hoag, Folder 6703, *Ann Arbor News.*

61. Leonard Falcone Papers. Box 1583. Folder 2.

62. Hoag, Folder 6703.

63.* *Leonard Falcone became a naturalized citizen on 6 February, 1924, in Ann Arbor.*

64. Eyman, 39-40.

65. Bloomquist, Kenneth G. "A Tribute to Dr. Leonard V. Falcone Who Passed Away on Thursday, May 2, 1985." Letter to Michigan State University School of Music. 8 May 1985. East Lansing, MI. Print.

66. DelConte, 126.

67.* *May evening Cap Nights featured stories and sentimental college songs, and culminated in the flimsy felt "pots" worn by the "frosh" being flung into a bonfire, signifying their elevation to sophomore status. According to Hoag, the worst theater rush he ever had was after a Cap Night. In winter, the freshmen traded their "pots" for stocking caps, which were worn by everyone: freshmen, grey; sophomores, red; juniors, blue; and seniors, white.*

68. Hoag, Gerald H. Papers. 1918-1978. Folder 6703. *Ann Arbor News.* 8 Dec. 1964.

69.* *A wise response. At the theater riot at the Whitney in the early 1920s, students used utility poles to be installed on Ann St. to batter open exit doors, filled all the seats, and refused to budge despite fervent pleas from university officials. The show, a musical called "Up in the Clouds," opened two hours late with a very nervous cast and crew—but there were no more problems, and ticketholders received a refund. And in every theater manager's mind was the very serious rush, the Star Theater riot of 1908, when thousands of students filled E. Washtenaw from S. Fifth to S. Main with the intention of destroying the theater to avenge a rumored insult to one of its student patrons. The air turned thick with bricks, cobblestones, baseball bats, and hitching posts,* *students were bloodied, and President Angell appeared to plead with the participants to stop. The affair was soon smoothed over, and a week later the Star reopened;* Hoag, Folder 6703. "History of Old Whitney Filled with Great Names." *Ann Arbor News*. 1 Oct. 1954.

70.* *Students snake-danced their way through the streets from Ferry Field to the theater;* Hoag, Folder 6703. *Ann Arbor News*. 5 Oct. 1969. 7.

71. Hoag, Folder 6703. *Ann Arbor News*. 5 Oct. 1969. 7.

72. Shackman, Grace. "Cinema's First Century—the Rise, Fall, and Revival of Ann Arbor's Down-town Theaters." *Ann Arbor Observer Then & Now*. Web. 23 Oct. 2008.

73. Hoag, Folder 6703. **See Appendix E.*

74. Leonard Falcone Papers. "McCarrell-Falcone Interview." Box 1563. Scrapbook 1, 1969.
Falcone, Leonard. "Great Moments in the History of the College Bands." Paper Prepared for the Biennial Meeting of the College Band Directors National Association. 13 Jan. 1973. Urbana, IL. Print.

75. Falcone, Leonard. Disc 18, tr. 7.CD-ROM. 22 July 1972. **Not all in the group were "fellows." A 1926 picture shows the entire ensemble standing on the sidewalk outside the theater. Six are men, and one of them, the young Leonard Falcone, his neatly coiffed thatch of hair shining in the sun, is smirking and smoking a cigarette. Standing next to him is a seventh person, an attractive female who, in a cloche, low waisted white blouse, and dark skirt and sweater, smiles fetchingly at the camera. See p. 83. Could she be Helen Snyder?* Leonard Falcone Papers. Box 1563. Scrapbook 1.

76.* *Ann Arbor theaters hosted, among other, such vaudeville greats as then stilt walker Cary Grant, comedians Jack Benny, the Marx Brothers, and Buster Keaton, and musicians Bing Crosby and Fred Waring and his Pennsylvanians. Other stage shows Leonard would have seen featured amateur nights, fiddling contests, and country store nights, all with prizes.* Hoag, *Ann Arbor News*. 8 Dec. 1964.

77. Bowman, 9.

78.* *See Appendix F.*

79. Welch, 257.

80. Eyman, 287; 286.

81. Dobos, Joseph. Updated Notes. "Leonard Falcone Interview with Joseph Dobos and Richard Adler, Jan. 7 1985." E-mail to the author. 14 Sept. 2008.

## Chapter 8

1. Falcone, Cecilia. Family newspaper and memento collection. E-mail enclosure to author. 24 Jan. 2009.

2. Falcone, Nicholas. *Autobiography of Nicholas D. Falcone and the University of Michigan Bands 1927–1935*. Unpublished manuscript. Print.

3. Dobos, Joseph. Telephone interview with author. 7 Nov. 2008.

4.* *The June date is corroborated by Nick in his family held unpublished autobiography, "Autobiography of Nicholas D. Falcone and the University of Michigan Bands 1927–1935," and in a June 1927 letter from U of M's president congratulating Nick on his appointment;* Falcone, Nicholas. Dobos, Joseph. E-mail to author. 14 Nov. 2010.

5. Gebring, Carl E. "Falcone Brothers to Direct U. of M. and Michigan State Bands." Box 1583 Folder 2, pp. 4-5. Collection UA17.133. Michigan State University Archives and Historical Collections, East Lansing, MI.

6.* *Leonard often said that he and Nicholas were both offered the positions and decided that since Nick was already established in Ann Arbor with a family while he, Leonard, was a bachelor, that Nick should stay where he was.*

7. Kuhn, Madison. *Michigan State: The First Hundred Years. 1855–1955*. East Lansing. MI: State University Press, 1955. 306–307; 37. Print.

8.* *Farwell was the first conductor of the hymns in "Canticle of Praise," which was first presented to an audience of over 8,000 people on Dec. 4, 1918*; Bynner, Witter. *A Canticle of Pan and Other Poems*. New York: Alfred Knopf, Inc. 1920. p. vii.

9. Kuhn, 296; 342; 297; 343.

10. Welch, Myron D. *The Life and Work of Leonard Falcone with Emphasis on His Years as Director of Bands at Michigan State University 1927–1967*. Thesis. Michigan State University, 1973. Ann Arbor, MI: UMI Dissertation Services, 1973. 41–42. Print.

11. Kuhn, 361.

12. Kuhn, 319.

13. "MSU Sesquicentennial" Web. 19 Feb. 2010.

14. Kuhn, 352.

15.* *Beaumont Tower was built on the site of the old College Hall, the first building on campus; it is pictured in the center of Michigan State's official seal.*

16. Falcone, Leonard. Interviewed by Myron Welch. East Lansing, MI. Disc 9 tr. 5. CD-ROM. 2 Feb. 1973.

17. Kuhn, 306. **See Appendix G.*

18. Kuhn, 326.

19.* *On July 2, 1862, President Abraham Lincoln signed The Morrill Act into law. The purpose was "without excluding other scientific and classical studies and including military tactic, to teach such branches of learning as are related to agriculture and the mechanic arts, in such manner as the legislatures of the*

*States may respectively prescribe, in order to promote the liberal and practical education of the industrial classes in the several pursuits and professions in life"* Act of July 2, 1862 (Morrill Act), ch. 130, 12 Stat. 503, Title 7 US Code sec. 301. Office of the Law Revision Counsel of the House of Representatives. Web. 10 Mar. 2010. *By 1890, the act required each state to show that race was not an admissions requirement, or else to designate a separate land-grant institution for persons of color. The result was that 70 colleges and universities were established to serve the African-American population;* Act of Aug. 30, 1890 (Second Morrill Act) ch. 841, 26 Stat. 417, Title 7 US Code sec. 323. Office of the Law Revision Counsel of the House of Representatives. Web. 10 Mar. 2010.

20. Kuhn, 117.
21. "History." Spartanband.net. Web. 23 Sept. 2009.
22. Kuhn, 202-203.
23. "Music for the Michigan Aggies." Leonard Falcone Papers Box 1583, folder 2, p. 19, Book 11.
24. Kuhn, 202.
25. "Music for Michigan Aggies."
26. Welch, 47.
27. Kuhn, 247.
28. Welch, 51.
29. "History." Spartanband.net. Web. 3 Feb. 2010.
30. Kuhn, 247.
31. *Fifty-ninth Annual Report of the Secretary of the State Board of Agriculture of the State of Michigan.* East Lansing: The Agricultural College, 1920. 122. Print.
32. Welch, 52- 54.
33. Welch, 64.
34. Falcone, Leonard. Disc 18 tr. 11. CD-ROM. Summer 1972.
35. Falcone, Leonard. Disc 18 tr. 10. CD-ROM. Summer 1972.
36. Welch, 63.
37. Falcone, Leonard. Disc 18 tr. 10. CD-ROM. Summer 1972.
38. Falcone, Leonard. Disc 18 tr. 10. CD-ROM. Summer 1972.
39.* *Lewis Richard's 1928 Report mentions that the Military Band made 39 public appearances during Falcone's first year;* Welch, 50.
40. Falcone, Leonard. Disc 18 tr. 9. CD-ROM. Summer 1972.
41.* *The only parade experience he'd had was as a boy in Italy, when he participated in the Roseto band's style of "lackadaisical marching," which was no more than a leisurely group stroll through the streets;* Welch, 66.

42. Falcone, Leonard. Disc 18, tr. 11, 12. CD-ROM. Summer 1972.

43. Leonard Falcone Papers, Box 1583, folder 2. Collection UA 17.133. Michigan State University Archives and Historical Collections, East Lansing, MI.

44.* *From the beginning of his career, Leonard showed by his words and actions that he believed that one of the most important jobs of a college or university band is to reflect the quality and dignity of the school itself.*

45. Falcone, Leonard. Disc 18 tr. 11. CD-ROM. Summer 1972.

46. Falcone, Leonard. Disc 18 tr. 11. CD-ROM. Summer 1972.

47. Falcone, Leonard. Disc 18 tr. 9. CD-ROM. Summer 1972.

48. Kuhn, 320.

49. Welch, 64–65.

50. Welch, 65.

51. Leonard Falcone Papers, Box 1583, folder 2.

52. Welch, 65.

53.* *Now called "Agriculture and Natural Resources Week," an event that continues today as one of the nation's largest events of its kind.*

54. Kuhn, 306.

55. Welch, 67.

56. Browning, Norma Lee. *Music Educators Journal.* Apr–May 1953. Vol. 39, No. 5. 38-39. **Interlochen was not, however, the nation's first music camp. The MacDowell Colony in New Hampshire, founded in 1907, is the oldest artists' colony in the United States. The Arens Art Colony, a co-ed summer music camp founded in 1922 in Wisconsin, preceded Interlochen by five years.*

57. Welch, 57.

58. "History." Interlochen Center for the Arts. Web. 28 Feb. 2010.

59. Mayer, Elizabeth. "Personalities at Orchestra Camp." *Record Eagle.* Traverse City. 31 July 1928. Print.

60.* *Falcone claimed his most memorable performances were at Interlochen in 1928, 1930, 1958, and 1963; the National High School Band Contest, Flint, Michigan, 1929; the University of Illinois, 1931; Pontiac High School, 1958; and the Mid-Eastern Instrumental Music Conference, Pittsburg, Pennsylvania;* Welch, 245.

61. Falcone, Leonard. Disc 11 tr. 1. CD-ROM. 3 Feb. 1973.

62. "A Military Band?" Leonard Falcone Papers, Box 1583, folder 2.

63. Leonard Falcone Papers, Box 1583, folder 2.

64. "An Improved Band." *Michigan State News*, fall 1928. Leonard Falcone Papers, Box 1583, folder 2.

65. Sack, Robert. Telephone interview with author. 25 June 2009.

66. Welch, 71–72.
67. "Leonard Falcone on Hearing the Sousa Band." Letter to David Whitwell. East Lansing, MI, Aug. 26, 1980. Web. 3 May 2009.
68. Falcone, Leonard. Disc 11 tr. 1. CD-ROM. 3 Feb. 1973.
69. "Midnight Solo Falcone Engagement." Leonard Falcone Papers, Box 1583, folder 2. Print.
70. Welch, 71.
71. "Goldman to Direct MSC Band. *Lansing State Journal*, 20 Feb. 1955. Leonard Falcone Papers, Box 1569, folder 21. Print.
72. Welch, 75.
73. Welch, 121–122.
74. "Goldman Set for Concert" 4 Mar. 1955. Leonard Falcone Papers, Box 1587, folder 27. 1955. **Others were "March, Michigan," "March for Brasses," "Bluejackets on Parade," and "Anniversary March."*
75. *State Journal*, Lansing, MI. March 7, 1955. Leonard Falcone Papers, Box 1587, folder 27, 1955.
76. Falcone, Beryl. Telephone interview with author. 26 June 2008.
77. Snider, Louis D. ed. 1928 -1929. Wolverine yearbook. East Lansing, MI: Students of Michigan State College. 196. Print.
78. "Aug. 9, 1929, Traverse City." Leonard Falcone Papers, Box 1583, folder 2.
79. Welch, 72-73.
80. "Spartan Band Begins Practice." *Michigan State News*. 25 Sept. 1929.
81. Bowman, Brian. "T.U.B.A. Euphonium Profile: Leonard Falcone." *T.U.B.A. Journal* 5, no. 2 (winter 1978): 3. Print.
82. Welch, 77.

## Chapter 9

1. Brubacher, John S. and Willis Rudy. *Higher Education in Transition: A History of American Colleges and Universities*. New Brunswick, NJ: Harper and Row, Inc. 380. Print.
2. "Life Expectancy at Birth by Race and Sex, 1930–2005 — Infoplease.com." Web. 1 Nov. 2010.
3. Meno, Harlow B., ed. *Wolverine Yearbook*. 357. Print.
4.* *One Flint paper noted that when the band marched down the center of the field headed by a high stepping drum major and playing a rousing march,*

*15,000 men, women, and children jumped to their feet in the grandstand with thunderous applause;* "Band Gets Ovation." Leonard Falcone Papers, Box 1583, folder 2. Collection UA 17.133. Michigan State University Archives and Historical Collections, East Lansing, MI. Print.

5. "Michigan State College Band Wins High Honors During Past Year" 1930 Box 1583, folder 2.

6. Welch, Myron D. *The Life and Work of Leonard Falcone with Emphasis on His Years as Director of Bands at Michigan State University 1927-1967*. Thesis. Michigan State University, 1973. Ann Arbor, MI: UMI Dissertation Services, 1973. 73. Print.

7. "Four Weekly Concerts to be Given on Campus During Month of May." Leonard Falcone Papers, Box 1583, folder 2, 1930. Print.

8. "Over 500 Attend Band Concert" *Michigan State News*. Leonard Falcone Papers, Box 1583 folder 2, 1930. Print.

9. "Announces Series of Band Concerts" *State Journal*. Lansing, MI. May. Leonard Falcone Papers, Box 1583 folder 2, 1930. Print.

10.* *He had no shortage of candidates to choose from. The October 1931 edition of the Michigan State News reported that band tryouts that year drew 80 freshmen.*

11.* *"A tie score is as dull as kissing your sister," Coach Duffy Daugherty famously said many years later. Though that may be true in most cases, in 1930 the 0–0 MSC–U of M tie, in the eyes of Spartan fans, was nearly as thrilling as a victory. Before then, State had lost the previous fourteen straight games to the Wolverines and had been humiliated by a 392 to nine point spread in same time period. Their moral victory may have occurred in part because of star center Harold Smead, who had been seriously injured in a motorcycle accident in Massachusetts that summer and was in a Boston hospital up until a few days before the game. Coach Jim Crowley had him flown to Ann Arbor and seated on game day on the sidelines in his wheel chair. As the Spartan team took the field, Smead shook each player's hand and gave him words of encouragement. It was a kind move on Crowley's part, and it surely boosted team morale;* Stabley, Fred. *The Spartans*. Huntsville, AL: The Strode Publishers. 1975. 70–71. Print.

12. "Michigan State College Band Has Its Most Successful Season During Past Year; Plays for President Hoover." *State Journal,* Lansing, MI. 1 Jan. 1931. Falcone Archives, Box 1583, folder 2. Print.

13. "News Begins Campaign to Stress 'Fight Song.'" *Michigan State News,* Oct. 1931. Print.

14. Welch, 75.

15. "Michigan State College Band Has Its Most Successful Season"

16. "Spartan Special Attracts Many on Eastern Trip" *The Michigan State Col-*

*lege Record.* Leonard Falcone Papers, Box 1583, folder 2. Nov. 1930. 5. Print. **Now "MSU Shadows." The words were written in 1927 by Bernard Traynor, an MSC football and basketball coach who later became an attorney in Chicago. It is sung to the "Lucia Sextet" melody from the end of Act 2 of Donazetti's opera Lucia di Lammermoor.*

17. Gillette, Tom. E-mail to author. 3 Nov. 2008.

18. "Spartan Special"

19. "Spartan Special"

20. Welch, 77.

21.* *He also held professional performers and conductors as a standard, often attending the University's Lecture Concert Series or driving to Ann Arbor, Detroit, or Chicago to hear major symphony orchestras.*

22. Falcone, Leonard. Interviewed by Myron Welch. East Lansing, MI. Disc 1 tr. 7. CD-ROM. 26 Jan. 1973.

23. **He returned on the "Empress of Britain," sailing from Southhampton, England to the Port of Quebec, on August 31st; Empress of Britain* Ship Manifest. 26 Aug.–31 Aug. 1939. "Falcone, Leonard." Records of the Immigration and Naturalization Service. RG 85. Washington D.C.: National Archives and Records Administration.

24. Leonard Falcone Papers. Box 1583, scrapbook 2. Collection UA 178.133. Michigan State Uni-versity Archives and Historical Collections, East Lansing, MI. Print.

25. Falcone, Beryl. Telephone interview with author. 10 July 2008. **Beryl Falcone: "Leonard's father passed away before Labor Day in 1948, before we got married. His mother passed away earlier—he never saw her again after he came here at 16 years of age."*

26. "Music Better in US Says Falcone." *The State Journal.* Lansing, MI. Oct. 1931. Falcone Archives, Box 1583, folder 2, 1932. Print.

27. Cascioli, Giovanni. "Roseto Valfortore." *La Stella.* Roseto, PA. July 20, 1931. Falcone Archives, Box 1583, folder 2, 1932. Print.

28. Leonard Falcone Papers, Box 1583, folder 2. Print.

29. Leonard Falcone Papers, Box 1583, folder 2. Print.

30. "Music Better in US"

31. Welch, 77–78.

32. "1812 Overture Ends Band Series." *Michigan State News*, 2 June 1932. Print.

33. Leonard Falcone Testimionial Dinner, 21 May, 1967. Tape.

34. Kuhn, Madison. *Michigan State: The First Hundred Years, 1855–1955. East Lansing, MI: State University Press, 1955.* 341–344. Print.

35. Kuhn, 343.

36.* *The Institute survived in the form of the Wilde Conservatory of Music and Dance in Lansing, an organization formed by private area businessmen.*

37. Welch, 79.

38. Kuhn, 344.

39. Kuhn, 344.

40. Welch, 80.

41.* *See Appendix H.*

42. Welch, 80. *State News.* 6 Oct. 1932.

43. Welch, 80-81.

44. Sheir, Theresa, "Band and Weather at Best for Concert Wednesday Night." *The State Journal* Lansing MI. 1 June 1933. Print.

45. Stabley, 86.

46. "Falcone Brothers Rivals for Seventh Time as Bands Meet." *The Michigan Daily.* 6 Oct. 1933. Print.

47. Welch, 83.

48. Falcone, Nicholas. *Autobiography of Nicholas D. Falcone and the University of Michigan Bands 1927–1935.* Unpublished manuscript. Print.

49. "Band Holds Daily Drills in Preparing for Parades." *Michigan State News,* Lansing MI. 7 Apr. 1934. Print.

50. Falcone, Leonard. Disc 11 tr. 6. CD-ROM. 3 Feb. 1973.

51.* *In the final outdoor concert of the season, held on Wednesday, May 23rd, Falcone appeared as the "artist soloist" with his "well trained band" in front of a crowd of 3,000 people. Michael Press, head of the violin department, conducted. His solo selection was the "Fantaisie Original" by Picchi, a number which he had arranged for baritone himself. His encore, the plaintive "Flower Song" from Carmen, "captured the hearts of the audience";* Shier, Theresa, "Final Concert of M.S.C. Band's Series Most Successful of Year" May 24 1934 *The State Journal*, Lansing, MI. Print.

52. Bielinski, Vic, "Falcone Traces Musical Life from Italy to M.S.C." *State News:* Lansing, MI. 18 May 1934. Print.

53. Falcone, Leonard. Disc 2 tr. 1. CD-ROM. 26 Jan. 1973.

54. Falcone, Leonard. Disc 9 tr. 2-3. CD-ROM. 2 Feb. 1973.

55. Falcone, Nicholas. *Autobiography of Nicholas D. Falcone.*

56. Dobos, Joseph. Telephone interview with author. 7 Nov. 2008.

57. Falcone, Beryl. Telephone interview with author. Condensed. 10 July 2008.

58. Falcone, Leonard. Disc 11 tr. 5- 6. CD-ROM. 3 Feb. 1973.

59. Falcone, Leonard. Disc 11 tr. 6. CD-ROM. 3 Feb. 1973.

60. Welch, 88.

61. "Duties of Band Call for Increase in Membership." *State News*. 24 Apr. 1934. Print.

62. Welch, 89.

63. Bates, Jack. Condensed from e-mails to author. 2 Mar. 2009.

64. Bates, Jack. Condensed from e-mail to author. 2 Mar. 2009 and 10 June 2010.

65. Falcone, Beryl. Telephone interview with author. 10 July 2008.

66. Falcone, Leonard. Disc 11 tr. 6. CD-ROM. 3 Feb. 1973.

67. "Falcone- University of Michigan Marching Band." Web. 10 July 2009.

68. Bates, Jack. E-mail to author. 2 Mar. 2009.

69. Falcone, Beryl. Telephone interviews with author. Condensed. 26 June 2008 and 10 July 2008.

70. *State News*. East Lansing, Michigan State College. 1 Oct. 1935. Print.

71. Welch, 89-90.

72. Bates, Jack. Condensed from e-mails to author. 2 Mar. 2009 and 9 June 2010.

73. "Spartans Find Music and Football Don't Mix" *The Washington Post*, 28 Sept. 1937. 19. Print.

74.* *Falcone's many band arrangements of classical orchestral and operatic music, as well as his adaptations of military marches from cultures around the world to Western band instrumentation and character, are an important part of his legacy to the American Band Movement.*

75. Welch, 91–92.

76. "Fine Program, Large Audience help Dedicate M.S.C Band Shell." *State Journal*. Leonard Falcone Papers, Box 1584, folder 11. Print.

77.* *Though it occurred some 70 years ago, one former student still recalls making a rare—but loud—mistake during one of the concerts held there.* Eldon Rosegart, drum major, MSC '41: "*One number on the program was a delightful Pastoral, and of course we played some marches. Whatever we played was passed back to me, and I was playing cymbals at the time. Somehow the titles were changed before word reached me, and instead of a serene Pastoral, I had a march in front of me. Leonard gave a gentle down beat and I crashed the cymbals loud enough to be heard in downtown Lansing. I'll never forget the scowl I received from Leonard. It's a good thing he wasn't armed or he would have shot me on the spot*"; Tellenger, Tammy. E-mail forwarded to author by Cecilia Falcone. 22 May 2008.

78. "School Music Well Developed Here, He Says" *The State Journal*. 28 May 1939. Leonard Falcone Papers, Box 1584, folder 11. Print.
79. "School Music"
80. "School Music"

## Chapter 10

1. "No Excuse." Leonard Falcone Papers. Box 1584. Folder 11. Collection UA17.133. Michigan State University Archives and Historical Collections, East Lansing, MI.
2. Welch, Myron D. *The Life and Work of Leonard Falcone with Emphasis on His Years as Director of Bands at Michigan State University 1927–1967*. Thesis. Michigan State University, 1973. Ann Arbor, MI: UMI Dissertation Services, 1973. 94. Print.
3. Falcone, Leonard. Interviewed by Myron Welch. East Lansing, MI. Disc 5 tr. 1. CD-ROM. 27 Jan. 1973.
4. Broka, Tom. E-mails to author. 1 Sept. 2008 and 15 Nov. 2010.
5.* *The music department was the first in liberal arts to move into a building specifically designed for its own needs. It was located, along with Cowles House, as the western anchor of an area surrounded by West Circle Drive, which has remained intact since the school's founding, the "sacred space," an "oak opening" where Michigan State first began. It is there where Robert Burcham's log cabin and small fields, hugged by a dense surrounding forest, once stood, and where Indians who camped on the banks of the nearby Red Cedar, fishing, boiling maple sap, and hunting, came in the early 1850s to trade beadwork and baskets with him for flour and vegetables. Later, the college's students, who from 1857 were required by the school's curriculum to provide 3 hours a day of labor, removed stumps, plowed, harrowed, and weeded the area so that they could plant vegetables and harvest them in the fall for the boarding hall kitchen.* Kuhn, Madison. *Michigan State The First Hundred Years. 1855–1955*. East Lansing. MI: State University Press, 1955. 12; 37. Print.
6.* *One of its features was its big green curtains, which (remarkably) exist today, that open and close to adjust acoustics, and good sized windows with pleasant views of the trees outside.*
7. Kuhn, 297; 396.
8. Heineman, Kenneth. *Campus Wars: The Peace Movement at American State Universities in the Viet Nam Era*. New York: New York University Press. 1993. 21. Print.
9.* *Today, the event continues as thousands of Michigan schools and students are adjudicated by expert musicians and music directors each year at district and*

*then, if deemed eligible, state levels in concert band, marching band, orchestra, and solo and ensemble festivals.*

10. "M.S.C. Band to Open Season Wednesday." *Lansing State Journal,* 11 May 1941. Falcone Papers 1569 folder 15. 1941 and 1944. Print.
11. Stein, Keith. Interviewed by Myron Welch. East Lansing, MI. Disc 22 tr 2. CD-ROM. 8 Feb. 1973.
12. Sexton, Ethelyn."Ex-M.S.C. Music Head Ready to Enter Army." Box 1567 folder 15 1942. Print.
13. "Director Who Made MSC Band Crack Marching Unit is Drafted," *The State Journal,* 25 Sept. 1942. Falcone Family papers. Print.
14. Hodgson, Walter. Interviewed by Myron Welch. East Lansing, MI. Disc 19 tr. 7. CD-ROM. 14 May 1973.
15. Welch, 98.
16.* *Inexplicably, Falcone's army enlistment papers lists his occupation as "Blacksmith or band or orchestra leader or Musician, Instrumental." Perhaps he was thinking of giving up the conducting gig and becoming a blacksmith? Teaching can do that to a person;* "Leonard Falcone." US World War II Army Enlistment Record 1938–1946. US World War II Army Enlistment Records, 1938–1946 Ancestry. Library Edition. Web. 22 Apr. 2008.
17.* *Though Leonard's army posting turned out to be"not a happy assignment," it beat the one his father-in law, also musician, received in an earlier war. "My father was in WWI," explained Beryl Falcone, "and he played in a band. The job he and the others had, other than to make music, was to go out to pick up the bodies after a battle. That was what the band members had to do."* Falcone, Beryl. Telephone interview with author. 26 June 2008.
18. Falcone, Beryl. Telephone interview with author. 5 Nov. 2008.
19. Welch, 98-99.
20. Welch, 102.
21. Welch, 103.
22. Falcone, Leonard. Disc 11 tr. 9. CD-ROM. 2 Mar. 1973.
23. Welch, 103-104.
24. Kuhn, 312.
25.* *In September, 1946, James Donovan ("Don") Jackson became trumpet instructor and assistant director of bands and Douglas Campbell relieved Falcone of his French horn students. Jackson's Varsity Band, which played for various athletic and other college events, attracted 36 male and female students whose schedules or qualifications did not allow them an immediate enrollment in the concert band.* Welch, 108–109.
26. Welch, 110. *Ann Arbor News.* 18 Sept. 1946.

27. "GI Aversion to Marching Puts MSC Band in a Fix." *Detroit Free Press*. Sept. 18, 1946. Leonard Falcone Papers, Box 1569 Folder 16 1946. Print.
28. Welch, 110. *Lansing State Journal*. 3 Oct. 1946.
29. Welch, 110.
30. Welton, A. Roger. Letter to Beryl Falcone. 2008.
31. Welch, 103.
32. Falcone, Leonard. Disc 11 tr. 9. CD-ROM. 3 Feb. 1973.
33. Welch, 109.
34. "M.S.C. Band in Concert." *Lansing State Journal*. 18 May 1947. Print.
35.* *Concert Band boasted a record 115 players that year, and the Spartan Marching Band grew to 108;* Welch, 111.
36.* *Because of his crushing loss to Michigan during his debut performance as State's football coach, Biggie Munn vowed to get even. Though he turned the team around so that the season ended 7-2, for the rest of his time at MSU he never forgot that first loss and used it to "fire himself into a frenzy as each Michigan game approached, and to goad his athletes into stupendous effort toward revenge";* Stabley, Fred. *The Spartans*. The Strode Publishers: Huntsville, AL, 1975. 121. Print. *Always a superstitious man, he even changed the new white leather helmets with a green wing design the team wore at the disastrous game for plastic Ridell green suspension shells with a white one-inch center stripe down the center. They were a huge hit, and Munn's helmet design would appear on his players' heads for the rest of his career.*
37.* *He was replaced by Robert E. Dahnert.*
38. Carver, Carlisle, "M.S.C. Band Stages Campaign Skit" *Lansing State Journal*. Box 1569 folder 17. Print.
39.* *In December, 1948, with competition to begin in the fall of 1953.*
40.* *Its lyrics were written by former Spartan coach" Barney" Traynor, to a tune from Donizetti's "Lucia de Lammermoor," and it was arranged by Dr. H.Owen Reed of the music department. Falcone and the Marching Band introduced "MSC Shadows" at the first home game of 1949, and it soon became a prized Falcone band tradition, so much so that band members serenaded Leonard with the tune just hours before his death.*
41.* *Falcone was relieved of applied trombone instruction with the appointment of Michigan State's first trombone specialist, Merrill Sherburn, in 1957;* Welch, 108.

## Chapter 11

1. Ferrera, Nick. Condensed from E-mail to author. 4 May 2009.

2. "Prof. Leonard Falcone of MSC is Wed to Sturgis Woman Sunday." *Lansing State Journal*, Dec. 20, 1948, East Lansing MI. 13. Box 1568, folder 2. 1948. Collection UA17.133. Michigan State University Archives and Historical Collections, East Lansing MI.
3. Falcone, Beryl. Telephone interview with author. 26 June, 2008.
4. Tellinger, Tammy. E-mail to author. 18 Dec. 2008.
5.* *In an embarrassment eerily reminiscent of her mother's, Cece Falcone broke a string on her French horn during a performance in Köln, Germany. "While I was effecting repairs (probably the longest minutes of my life, fingers shaking, the whole nine yards), my father stood on the podium facing the band and patiently waiting. I knew he was mortified with this lapse on my part, but I don't remember his saying anything about it to me. That non-matching color string is still on my horn. I've never had another string break, ever."* Falcone, Cecilia. E-mail to author. 5 Dec. 2008.
6. Falcone, Beryl. Condensed telephone interviews with author. 26 June and 10 July 2008.
7. Welch, Myron D. *The Life and Work of Leonard Falcone with Emphasis on His Years as Director of Bands at Michigan State University 1927–1967*. Thesis. Michigan State University, 1973. Ann Arbor, Michigan: UMI Dissertation Services, 1973. 177. Print.
8.* *"P.S. It's a girl!" read the bottom of Falcone's letter announcing Mary's birth to his bandsmen prior to the 1950 band camp; Welch, 113. According to Beryl Falcone, Leonard thought August was a good time for Mary to be born and, thinking ahead to future births, said, "We can't ever have any children during football season!"* Falcone, Beryl. Telephone interview with author. 5 Nov. 2008.
9.* *Cecilia (Cece) Falcone was named for St. Cecilia, the patron saint of music. The middle name "Yolanda" was added two weeks after her birth when Leonard went to the courthouse and had it placed on her birth certificate as a middle name because he liked it so much.* Falcone, Beryl. Telephone interview with author. 5 Nov. 2008.
10. Hodgson, Walter. Interviewed by Myron Welch. East Lansing, MI. Disc 19 tr. 16. CD-ROM. 14 May 1973.
11. Falcone, Beryl. Telephone interview with author. 5 Nov. 2008.
12. Falcone, Susan. E-mail to author. 29 July 2010.

## Chapter 12

1. Welch, Myron D. *The Life and Work of Leonard Falcone with Emphasis on His Years as Director of Bands at Michigan State University 1927–1967*. The-

sis. Michigan State University, 1973. Ann Arbor, MI: UMI Dissertation Services, 1973. 115. Print.

2. Welch, 114.

3.* *Three professional organizations—the American Bandmasters Association, which is a select and prestigious group of professional and collegiate bandmasters, the College Band Directors National Association, and the Michigan School Band and Orchestra Association, were influential in Falcone's career for a number of reasons, not the least of which was that he developed personal and professional relationships with colleagues, and through discussion, studying one another's work, and hearing one another's bands perform, he was able to contribute to as well as keep abreast of the American Band Movement.*

4. Welch, 153; 115.

5. Stein, Keith. Interviewed by Myron Welch. East Lansing, MI. Disc 22 tr. 12. CD-ROM. 8 Feb. 1973.

6. Geissler, Janet. "Hundreds Pay Respect to MSU Music Man." *Lansing State Journal.* 10 May 1985. Print.

7. Sack, Robert. Telephone interview with author. 25 June 2009.

8.* *During the summer of his 81st year, Leonard read a biography about MacArthur and, in a paraphrase of one of the general's most famous lines, commented to a reporter that "Band leaders should never die, just fade away";* Harrison, Susan. "The Stories Can Wait for Leonard Falcone." *Grand Rapids Press.* 17 Aug. 1980.

9. Stansell, Fritz. Condensed from e-mails to author. 9 Oct. 2008, 20 Nov. 2008, 1 Dec. 2008.

10. "Banquet to Honor Director's Courage." Leonard Falcone Papers, Box 1569 Folder 19.

11. Welch, 120.

12. "Leonard Falcone Twenty-fifth Anniversary Testimonial Dinner." 17 Jan. 1953. Tape.

13. "Leonard Falcone Twenty fifth"

14. Welch, 122.

15.* *The first loss after the Maryland game came Sack's senior year, when in fall of 1953 Purdue broke the 28 game winning streak (score: State 0, Purdue 6.) State went on to win the rest of the season, and finished with a record of 9 wins, 1 loss, 0 ties;* Stabley, Fred. *The Spartans.* Huntsville. AL: Strode Publishers, Inc. 1975. 287.

16. Sack.

17. Stansell, Fritz. E-mails to author. 19 Nov. 2008, 26 Jan. 2009.

18. Louder, Earl. Telephone interview with author. 14 Nov. 2008.

19. Niblock, James. E-mail to author. 23 Feb. 2010.
20. Franke, Leonard. Telephone interview with author. 24 Feb. 2009.
21. Niblock.
22. Welch, 118.
23. Falcone, Leonard. Interviewed by Myron Welch. East Lansing, MI. Disc 13 tr. 8-9, condensed. CD-ROM. 3 Feb. 1973.
24. Falcone, Leonard. Disc 13 tr 8-9, condensed. CD-ROM. 3 Feb. 1973.
25. Falcone, Beryl. Telephone interview with author. 10 July 2008.
26. Thompson, Ted. E-mail to author. 13 Dec. 2008.
27. Underwood, John. E-mail forward to author by Cecilia Falcone 15 Aug. 2008.
28. Stansell, Fritz. E-mail to author. 19 Nov. 2009.
29. Dobos, Joseph. Telephone interview with author. 7 Nov. 2008.
30. "1950–1953 Oldsmobile Rocket Origins." *How Stuff Works*. 22 Sept.2007. Web. 19 Nov. 2008.
31. Falcone, Beryl. Telephone interview with author. 10 July 2008.
32.* *Walter Hodgson, later head of MSU's Music Department, explained that Hannah "realized that if we were going to go from a cow college against a full fledged member of the Big 10, especially against the will of the U of M—and the U of M did everything they could to keep us from getting in—then when we finally got in, we couldn't be a doormat or a laughing stock. He decided if we were going to be playing football against them then we would have to win big, and of course we did . . . He saw that the band was part of that, and that's the reason. . . if it was something of an all-university project with the band, he was there;* Hodgson, Walter. Interviewed by Myron Welch. East Lansing, MI. Disc 19. tr.6. CD-ROM. 14 May 1973.
33. Falcone, Leonard. Disc 15 tr. 9, condensed. CD-ROM. 4 Feb. 1973.
34. Welch, 125; 124.
35. Falcone, Leonard. Disc 15 tr. 9, condensed.. CD-ROM. 4 Feb. 1973.
36.* *Except for occasional marching appearances at small universities, until 1954 the band was virtually unknown except to Michigan audiences.*
37. Stansell, Fritz. E-mail to author. 2 June 2008.
38. Falcone, Leonard. Disc 15 tr. 10. CD-ROM. 4 Feb. 1973.
39. Stansell, Fritz. E-mail to author. 2 June 2008.
40. Sack.
41. Thompson.
42.* *MSC's admittance to the Big 10 angered countless University of Michigan*

*students and alumni, many of whom enjoyed calling the college pejorative names. The fact that MSC had a better football team than Michigan's only made the disdain worse.*

43. Marugg, Jim. "Rose Bowl Predictions: UCLA to Win Card Tricks Spartans Have Best Band": *Pasadena Star News* Tues. 22 Dec. 1953.

44. Stansell, Fritz. E-mail to author. 2 June 2008.

45. "Praise of Band Still Echoing." Qtd. In *Kansas City Times*. Leonard Falcone Papers, Box 1586, folder 23. Collection UA 17.133. Michigan State University Archives and Historical Collections, East Lansing, MI. Print.

46. "Michigan State College Band Marches in E.P." Leonard Falcone Papers, Box 1586, folder 23.

47. "Small Rally Welcomes Band at End of Tour." Leonard Falcone Papers, Box 1586, folder 23, 1954.

48. Welch, 127.

49. "Small Rally"

50. Welch, 125.

51. "Rose Bowl Preparations Become Big Production." *State Journal*. Leonard Falcone Papers, Box 1586 Folder 23.

52.* I*n addition to having two young children at home, Falcone was maintaining an exhausting schedule working seven days a week with the marching and concert bands, teaching classes, giving lessons, making guest conducting appearances, adjudicating, performing, consulting, and contributing time to national professional organizations. An additional load was added to his situation when the Michigan State Marching Band made the transition from a military to a modern college band, since for the first time in more than 40 years it did not have an assigned drillmaster. In a March 4, 1953, letter to Mr. Underwood, Falcone expressed concern over this state of affairs, claiming that all major colleges had assistant band directors to help with the marching band and that his doctors had advised him to avoid the loss of sleep and strenuous physical exertion that training a marching band by himself entailed. Subsequently, Stover was hired on July 1, 1953, with his primary responsibilities being the Marching Band and teaching applied percussion classes. At the same time, as part of a personnel shuffle, Don Jackson transferred from director of Varsity Band to coordinator of special courses and music conferences, Byron Autry was hired as a trumpet instructor, and Stover took over the Varsity Band, soon after called the "Activity Band";* Welch, 122–124.

53. "Rose Bowl Preparations" Nouse, Dale. "The Band Also Works Hard for Saturday." *Detroit Free Press*. Sunday 30 Sept. 1953.

54. "Rose Bowl Preparations"

55. Louder.

56. Deeb, Edward, "Dean of the Nation's Bandmasters." Family newspaper and memento collection. E-mail enclosure to author from Cecilia Falcone. 24 Jan. 2009.
57. Marugg.
58. Mainville, Frank. "MSC Band Returns Home, Receives Warm Welcome." Leonard Falcone Papers, Box 1536, Folder 23.
59. Thompson.
60. Sack.
61. Whitmore, Seth. "Praise of Band Still Echoing." *Lansing State Journal.* Leonard Falcone Papers, Box 1586 folder 23.
62. "Michigan Rose Parade Float Features 100 dozen Tulips." *State Journal.* 24 Dec. 1953.
63. Sack.
64. Whitmore.
65. Stansell, Fritz. E-mail to author. 2 June 2008.
66. H. Owen Reed. E-mail forwarded to the author by Fritz Stansell. 6 Jan. 2008.
67. Leonard Falcone Papers, Box 1586 Folder 23. 2 Jan. 1954.
68. Whitmore.
69. Whitmore.
70. "MSC Band Returns Home, Receives Warm Welcome." Leonard Falcone Papers. Box 1586 Folder 23.
    "Small Rally"
71.* *One news article quoted the Munn family as saying it was "mighty proud of the Michigan State band";* "Trip, Rogers Swell." Leonard Falcone Papers, Box 1586 Folder 23.
72. Thompson.
73. Whitmore.
74. Mainville.
75.* *Other guest conductors to work with Falcone's bands were Col. William F. Santelmann, Conductor of the US Marine Band, on March 2, 1958, two Michigan State's composers, Dr. H. Owen Reed on March 1, 1959, and Dr. James Niblock on March 6, 1960, and Don Gillis, noted American composer, on March 5, 1961. After his appearance, Santelmann remarked "This has been one of my most inspiring concerts as a guest conductor of one of the nation's finest concert bands";* Welch, 129.
76. Falcone, Leonard. Disc 9 tr 6-7. CD-ROM. 2 Feb. 1973.
77. "First Michigan State Rooters Roll in for Tilt." *LA Times.* 29 Dec. 1955. A1.
78. *Instrumentalist Magazine.* Mar. 2004.

79. Falcone, Leonard. Disc 1 tr. 10, condensed. CD-ROM. 26 Jan. 1973.

80. Falcone, Leonard. Disc 9 tr. 3. CD-ROM. 3 Feb. 1973.

81. Welch, 132. **See Appendix K.*

82. Falcone, Leonard. Disc 1 tr. 11. CD-ROM. 26 Jan. 1973.

83.* *Falcone programmed his concerts to open with a "big work" and climax with a "brilliant piece of music." Sandwiched between were symphonies, suites, overtures, dances, and concert pieces of varied styles and periods. Soloists often appeared, and sometimes sections were featured, especially on light outdoor concerts or tour programs. Transcriptions and contemporary music were an important aspect of his band programming as well, offering variety, audience appeal, and opportunity to perform the "outstanding literature of yesterday" as well as the new works of today;* Welch, 267.

84. Welch, 130.

85. Welch, 131.

86. Welch, 134.

87. Welch, 134.

88. "MSU Band Director Honored Tonight." *Lansing Journal.* 4 Mar. 1984.

## Chapter 13

1. Falcone, Leonard. Interviewed by Myron Welch. East Lansing, MI. Disc 9 tr 6-7, condensed. CD-ROM. 2 Feb. 1973.

2. Gillette, Tom. E-mail to author. 14 Oct. 2008.

3. "When the College Band Plays." Leonard Falcone Papers, Box 1583, folder 2. Collection UA 17.133. Michigan State University Archives and Historical Collections, East Lansing, MI. Print.

4. Welch, Myron D. *The Life and Work of Leonard Falcone with Emphasis on His Years as Director of Bands at Michigan State University 1927–1967.* Thesis. Michigan State University, 1973. Ann Arbor, MI: UMI Dissertation Services, 1973. 137. Print.

5. Falcone, Leonard. Disc 4 tr. 3. CD-ROM. 26 Jan. 1973.

6. Hodgson, Walter. Interviewed by Myron Welch. East Lansing, MI. Disc 19. tr. 6. CD-ROM. 14 May 1973.

7. Falcone, Cecilia. E-mail to author. 25 Apr. 2008.

8. Falcone, Beryl. Telephone interview with author. 26 June 2008.

9. Welch, 138-139.

10. Brill, Ed. *Michigan State News.* 15 Oct. 1965.

11. "Michigan Day at NY Fair Big Success." *The State Journal.* Lansing. 19 May 1964. A2. Print.

12. Lutz, Merritt. Telephone interview with author. 10 Dec. 2009.

13. Stansell, Fritz. E-mail to author. 11 Dec. 2008.

14.* *The "Series," written by Joel Leach from 1960 to 1963 and Merritt Lutz from 1964 to 1966, is an intricate four minute succession of seven different cadences, each requiring a unique set of maneuvers specific to each instrumental section in the band. The MSU drum line has been playing "The Series," largely in its original form since 1966, when Leonard Falcone gave the order to stop extensions. Because the Series was frozen in the same form from that time, it has allowed each subsequent generation of MSU drummers to use it as common ground in relating to each other across the years (today's alumni band drummers range from the early 1960s to last years' graduating class, and all are able to play the Series together) and to support, recruit, and finance new generations of MSU drumlines.*

15. Lutz.

16. Bateman, Hal. "State Marching Band Expects no Trouble." Leonard Falcone Papers, Box 1591, Folder 47.

17. Lutz.

18. "New Recordings." *The Instrumentalist.* XIV Jan 1960. 26. Print.
"New Recordings. "*The Instrumentalist.* XX Jan, 1966. 31. Print.

19.* *To hear, visit http://onthebanks.msu.edu/Search/ Keyword: "Falcone." Copyright to this resource is held by Michigan State University and is provided here for educational purposes only.*

20. Welch, 251.

21. Piatt, Bob. E-mail forwarded to author by Cecilia Falcone. 9 Aug. 2008.

22. "MSU Band Makes Hit in Inaugural Parade." Falcone. Leonard Falcone Papers, Collection UA 17.133 Box 1583, folder 9 1965. Michigan State University Archives and Historical Collections, East Lansing, MI.

23. Lutz.

24. Stansell, Fritz. E-mail to author. 11 Nov. 2008.

25. Krive, Kent. E-mail forwarded to author by Cecilia Falcone. Condensed. 24 July 2008.

26. Stabley, Fred. *The Spartans.* Huntsville, AL: The Strode Publishers. 1975. 231. Print.

27.* *60 floats and 2,500 musicians took part in the parade, which had the theme "It's a Small World"; the Grand Marshall was Walt Disney.*

28. Stabley, 231.

29. "Musical Extravaganza by MSU Band at H.S. Fabulous Entertainment." "Town Talk." *The News Daily.* 24 Mar. 1966.

30. Lutz.

31. Lodge, Dick. E-mail to author. 3 Mar. 2009.

32. Falcone, Cecilia. Family newspaper and memento collection. E-mail enclosure to author. 24 Jan. 2009.

33. Welch, 142.

34. Begian, Harry. Telephone interview with author 10 Dec. 2009.

35.* *The title is reserved for the Big Ten band director with the longest tenure at his school; Leonard received it in 1959.*

36. Lutz.

37. Welch, 143.

38.* *Leonard's friends and family were well aware of his deep embarrassment when publically praised. In a speech made after he was inducted into the NBA's Hall of Fame, he remarked "Praise . . . makes me rather uncomfortable. I guess I'm not of the right nature. I have been unable through my life to be on the receiving end of praises and feel comfortable with it."* Falcone, Leonard. Sound clip. 4 Mar. 1984. E-mail enclosure to author from Tom Gillette. 15 Nov. 2008.

39.* *Falcone's characteristic hand movements were dubbed "magic circles" by his students; he would use his entire arm (bent at the elbow with the forearm in front of him) to make a circular motion as he smiled or nodded, always with noticeably curious eyes.*

40. Louder, Earle Telephone interview with author. 14 Nov. 2008.

41. Welch, 141.

42. Welch, 141, 144.

43. Welch, 144.

44. Gillette, Tom. E-mail to author. 25 Oct. 2008. **See Appendix L.*

45. Welch, 144, 148.

46. Falcone, Leonard. Disc 4, tr. 8. CD- ROM. 27 Jan. 1973.

47. Louder, Earl. Telephone interview with author. 14 Nov. 2008.

48. Digby, Dora. "Falcone Winds Up Director's Career." *The State Journal.* Lansing, MI. 22 May 1967. Print.

## Chapter 14

1. Falcone, Leonard. Interviewed by Myron Welch. East Lansing, MI. Disc 18 tr. 5. CD-ROM. 2 Feb. 1973.

2. Fulton, Lisa. Telephone interview with author. 5 Dec. 2008.

3. Gillette, Tom. E-mail forwarded to author from Cecilia Falcone. 16 July 2008.
4. Gillette, Tom. E-mail to author. ND.
5. Gillette.
6. Piatt, Bob. Forwarded to author by Cecilia Falcone. 9 Aug. 2008.
7. Dobos, Joseph. Telephone interview with author. 7 Nov. 2008.
8. Glickman, Ken. "Leonard Falcone: A Remembrance" *Lansing State Journal.* 7 May 1985. Capitol Area District Library. Lansing, MI.
9. Stansell, Tom. E-mail to author. 11 Nov. 2008.
10. Stansell, Fritz. E-mail to author. 11 Nov. 2008.
11. Bloomquist, Kenneth. E-mail to author. 19 Oct. 2009.
12. Walters, Bob. Forwarded to author by Cecilia Falcone. 14 Apr. 2008.
13. Gillette, Tom. E-mail to author. 15 Nov. 2010.
14. Stansell, Fritz. E-mail to author. 19 Nov. 2008.
15. Church, Jane. From "Notes from Northfield." *The Instrumentalist,* Mar. 2004, and e-mail to author, 8 Aug. 2010.
16. Heger, Avis. Letter to Beryl Falcone. 11 June 2008.
17. Erickson, Marty. E-mail forwarded to author by Cecilia Falcone. 16 June 2008.
18.* *Henry Nelson, Seymour Okun, Eldon Rosegart, and Fritz Stansell.*
19.* *In 1980, Leonard Falcone was the first to receive this group's prestigious A. Austin Harding Award for exceptional personal contribution to the School Band Movement.*
20. Harrison, Susan E. "The Stories Can Wait for Leonard Falcone." *Grand Rapids Press.* 17 Aug. 1980.
21. Bloomquist, Kenneth. E-mail to author. 19 Oct. 2008.
22. Denery, Jim "Band Hall of Fame Adds Falcone, Wiley to List" *The Troy Messenger,* Troy, Alabama. 5 Feb. 1984.
23. Denery.
24. Dobos, Joseph. E-mail to author. 12 Sept. 2008.
25. Fulton.
26. Fulton.
27. Falcone, Cecilia. E-mail to author. 13 Oct. 2008.
28. Nichols, Sue. "Purdue Band gives Falcone Home Concert." *Lansing State Journal.* 30 Sept. 1984.
29. Ball, Zachere. "Spartans' Band Leader for 40 Years is Dead." *Detroit Free*

*Press*. 4 May 1985.

30. Falcone, Cecilia. E-mail to author. 13 Oct. 2008.

31. Nichols.

32. Bloomquist, Kenneth. Telephone interview with author. 17 Mar. 2009.

33.* *Leonard, lifted to the podium in his wheelchair, conducted the "Falcone Italian Tour Alumni Band" in a rehearsal of the "Michigan State Fight Song" in the band room at MSU in the spring of 1985. Characteristically, he began with a downbeat which he quickly cut off when he didn't like the group's attack. By the end of the march, there were few dry eyes in the room;* Stansell, Fritz. Telephone interview with author. 30 Nov. 2010.

34. Louder, Earl. Telephone interview with author. 14 Nov. 2008.

## Chapter 15

1. Falcone, Beryl. Telephone interview with author. 5 Dec. 2008.

2. Fulton, Lisa. Telephone interview with author. 5 Dec. 2008.

3. Albright, John B. *Lansing State Journal* "Leonard Falcone, Father of MSU Bands, Dies at 86." 4 May 1985.

4. Bloomquist, Kenneth. Telephone interview with author. 17 Mar. 2009.

5. Hall, Lori A. "Former "U" Band Director Dies." *Lansing State News*. 6 May, 1985. Print.

6.* *This fact, and others made in tribute to Leonard Falcone's contributions to the Michigan State Band, was read into the Congressional Record on the 130th anniversary of the Spartan Marching Band on October 10, 2000, pp. 21884–21885. See Appendix M.*

7. Falcone, Cecilia. E-mails to author. 18 Jan. 2009.

8.* *Behrend also appeared as a soloist at the MSU Wind Ensemble's performance of the Willson Suite by Robert W. Smith honoring the 100th anniversary of Leonard's birth. It can be heard on Youtube.com.*

9. Geissler, Janet. "Hundreds Pay Respect to MSU Music Man." *Lansing State Journal*. 10 May 1985. Print.

10.* *Falcone (no doubt conservatively) estimated months before he died that 500 of his former students were professional musicians and figured that many more still played the instruments they learned under his baton. At the time of his death, the MSU Band Association, had 1,400 members, nearly all of whom had played under his direction;* Dzwonkowski, Ron. "Strike Up the Band." Falcone family newspaper and memento collection. E-mail enclosure to author from Cecilia Falcone. 24 Jan. 2009.

11. Geissler.

12. Geissler.

13. Sack, Robert. Telephone interview with author. 25 June 2009.

14. Stein, Keith. Interviewed by Myron Welch. East Lansing, MI. Disc 22 tr. 12. CD-ROM. 8 Feb. 1973.

15. Nelson, Henry. Letter to Beryl Falcone. 2008.

16. Hall.

17. Niblock, James. From e-mails to author, 23 Feb. 2010, and forward to author from Fritz Stansell 1 June 2008.

18. Begian, Harry. Telephone interview with author. 10 Dec. 2009.

19. Stansell, Fritz. Telephone interview with author. 7 Oct. 2010. **Leonard was twice honored by MSBOA for his assistance and cooperation to the association and the youth of the State.*

20. Hall.

21. Falcone, Cecilia. E-mail to author. 17 Jan. 2009.

## Chapter 16

1. Nelson, Henry. Letter to Beryl Falcone. 2008.

2. Welch, Myron D. *The Life and Work of Leonard Falcone with Emphasis on His Years as Director of Bands at Michigan State University 1927–1967*. Thesis. Michigan State University, 1973. Ann Arbor, MI: UMI Dissertation Services, 1973. 273. Print.

3. "Gillette, Tom. Forwarded from Cecilia Falcone to author 19 Jan. 2009.

4. Krive, Kent. Forwarded to author by Cecilia Falcone. 24 July 2008.

5. Lutz, Merritt, Telephone interview with author. 10 Dec. 2009.

6. Stansell, Fritz. E-mail to author. 1 Mar. 2009.

7. Condensed from Pat Facktor to author. 26 Feb. 2009.

8. Sack, Robert. Telephone interview with author. 25 June 2009.

9. Pearson, Dan. Telephone interview with author. 9 Mar. 2009.

10. Bloomquist, Kenneth. E-mail to author. 19 Oct. 2009.

11. Louder, Earl. Telephone interview with author. 14 Nov. 2008.

12. Gillette, Tom. E-mail to author forwarded by Cecilia Falcone. 19 Jan. 2009.

13. Erickson, Marty. E-mail to author forwarded by Cecilia Falcone 16 June 2008.

14. Thompson, Ted. E-mail to author. 12 Dec. 2008.

15. Begian, Harry. Telephone interview with author. 10 Dec. 2009.

16. Falcone, Cecilia. E-mail to author. 8 Nov. 2008.

17. Fulton, Lisa. Telephone interview with author. 5 Dec. 2008. **see Appendix N for recipe.*
18. Falcone, Beryl. Telephone interview with author. 19 Nov. 2008.
19. Hodgson, Walter. Interviewed by Myron Welch. East Lansing, MI. Disc 19. CD-ROM. 14 May 1973.
20. Louder.
21. Falcone, Beryl. Telephone interview with author. 26 June 2008.
22. Falcone, Cecilia. E-mail to author. 23 Jan. 2009.
23. Fulton.
24. Gillette, Tom. E-mail to author. 25 Oct. 2008.
25. McDaniel, John T. Forwarded by Cecilia Falcone to author. 3 Sept. 2008.
26. Falcone, Cecilia. E-mail to author. 4 Sept. 2008.
27. Fulton.
28. Falcone, Beryl. Condensed telephone interviews. 5 Nov. 2008 and 10 July 2008.
29. Nelson.
30. Gillette, Tom. E-mail to author. 5 Dec. 2008.
31. Fulton.
32. Gillette, Tom. E-mail to author. 5 Dec. 2008.
33. Louder.
34. Erickson.
35. Krive.
36. Falcone, Cecilia. E-mail to author. 8 Oct. 2008.
37. Dineen, Mike. E-mail to author. 1 Feb. 2010.
38. Falcone, Cecilia. E-mail to author. 3 Aug. 2010.
39. Stansell, Fritz. E-mail to author. 27 Apr. 2008.
40. Falcone, Cecilia. E-mail to author. 26 Apr. 2008.
41. Falcone, Beryl. Telephone interview with author. 10 July 2008.
42. Gillette, Tom. E-mail to author. 4 Mar. 2009.
43. Fulton.
44. Falcone, Beryl. Telephone interview with author. 5 Dec. 2008.
45. Stansell, Fritz. E-mail to author. 10 Dec. 2008.
46. Anonymous. E-mail to author. 6 Feb. 2009.
47. Lutz.
48. Gillette, Tom. E-mail to author. 25 Nov. 2008.

49. Louder.
50. Stansell, Fritz. E-mail to author. 9 Oct. 2008.
51. Falcone, Cecilia. Condensed from e-mail to author. 12 Sept. 2008.
52. Bjerregaard, Carl. E-mail forwarded to author by Cecilia Falcone. 4 June 2008.
53. Nye, Harland. Letter to Beryl Falcone. 2008.
54. Nichols, Jon. E-mail forwarded to author by Cecilia Falcone. 14 Apr. 2008.
55. Begian.
56. Fulton.
57. Falcone, Beryl. Telephone interview with author. 26 June 2008.
58. Underwood, John. E-mail forwarded to author by Cecilia Falcone. 13 Aug. 2008.
59. Stansell, Fritz. E-mail to author. 9 Oct. 2008.
60. Louder.
61. Fulton.
62. Stansell, Fritz. E-mail to author. 1 Dec. 2008.
63. Lutz.
64. Dobos, Joseph. Telephone interview with author. 7 Nov. 2008.
65. Gillette, Tom. E-mail to author. 25 Oct. 2008.
66. Falcone, Beryl. Telephone interview with author. 5 Nov. 2008.
67. Gillette, Tom. E-mail to author. 25 Oct. 2008.
68. Falcone, Beryl. Telephone interview with author. 5 Nov. 2008.
69. Dobos.
70. Bjerregaard.
71. Porter, Carol. Forwarded to author by Cecilia Falcone. 19 July 2008.
72. Krive.
73. Louder.
74. Falcone, Beryl. Telephone interview with author. 5 Nov. 2008.
75. Salow, Ron. Letter to Beryl Falcone. 2008.
76. Franke, Leonard. Telephone interview with author. 24 Feb. 2009.
77. Bloomquist, Kenneth. Telephone interview with author. 17 Mar. 2009.
78. Nye.
79. Bjerregaard.
80. Begian.

81. Nye.
82. Gillette, Tom. E-mail to author. 3 Dec. 2008.
83. Meyers, Robert F. E-mail to author. 27 Feb. 2009.
84. Falcone, Cecilia. E-mail to author. 25 Feb. 2009.
85. Bloomquist, Kenneth. Condensed from e-mail to author 19 Oct. 2009 and telephone interview 17 Mar. 2009.
86. Pearson.
87. Dobos.
88. Stansell, Fritz. E-mail to author. 9 Oct. 2008.
89. Falcone, Beryl. Telephone interview with author. 26 June 2008.
90. Louder.
91. Meyers.
92. Good, Richard D. *A Biography of Earle L. Louder: Euphonium Performer and Educator.* Diss. Arizona State University, 1996. Ann Arbor: UMI, 1997. 30. Print.
93. Morrill, Denny. E-mail to author. 27 Feb. 2009.
94. Durand, Charles. E-mail to author. 11 July 2008.
95. Elmore, Fred. E-mail to author. 27 Feb. 2009.
96. Stansell, Fritz. E-mail to author. 7 Nov. 2008.
97. Bloomquist, Kenneth G. Telephone interview with author. 17 Mar. 2009.
98. Falcone, Beryl. Telephone interview with author. 5 Nov. 2008.
99. Louder.
100. Begian.
101. Nelson.
102. Falcone, Cecilia. E-mail to author. 24 Jan. 2009.
103. Nelson.
104. Louder.
105. Sack, Robert. Telephone interview with author. Condensed. 25 June 2009. Porter, Carol. Condensed e-mail forwarded to author by Cecilia Facone.19 July 2008.
106. Stansell, Fritz. E-mail to author. 10 Dec. 2008.
107. Krive.
108. Heger, Ted. Letter to Beryl Falcone. 11 June 2008.
109. Pearson.
110. Dobos.

111. Gillette, Tom. E-mail to author. 25 Sept. 2008.
112. Dobos.
113. Franke, Leonard. Telephone interview with author. 24 Feb. 2009.
114. Hornstein, Daniel. E-mail forwarded to author by Cecilia Falcone 18 Apr. 2008.
115. Nye.
116. Pearson, Dan. Telephone interview with author. 9 Mar. 2009.
117. Myers.
118. Stansell, Fritz. Forwarded to author by Sandy Sheroky. 27 Jan. 2009.
119. Fulton.
120. Falcone, Cecilia. Condensed from e-mail to author. 25 Feb. 2009.
121. Gillette, Tom. E-mail to author. 25 Oct. 2008.
122. Falcone, Beryl. Telephone interview with author. 5 Nov. 2008.
123. Gillette, Tom. Condensed from e-mail to author. 25 Oct. 2008.
124. Begian.
125. Anonymous. E-mail to author. 10 Feb. 2010.
126. Begian.
127. Pearson.
128. Wisner, Dave. E-mail to author. 11 Mar. 2009.
129. Falcone, Leonard. Interviewed by Myron Welch. East Lansing, MI. Disc 4 tr. 5–6. CD-ROM. 26 Jan. 1973.
130. Falcone, Beryl. Telephone interview with author. 5 Nov. 2008.
131. Louder.
132. Stansell, Gretchen. Telephone interview with author. 7 Sept. 2010.
133. Stansell, Fritz. E-mail to author forwarded by Sandy Sheroky. 19 Nov. 2008.
134. Anonymous. E-mail to author. 10 Feb. 2010.
135. Dobos, Joseph. Telephone interview with author. 7 Nov. 2008.
136. Falcone, Leonard. Disc 4 tr. 5-6. CD-ROM. 26 Jan. 1973.
137. Gillette, Tom. E-mail to author. 3 Dec. 2008.
138. Bloomquist, Kenneth G. E-mail to author. 13 Mar. 2009.
139. Gillette, Tom. E-mail to author. 3 Dec. 2008.
140. Bloomquist, Kenneth G. E-mail to author. 13 Mar. 2009.
141. Stein, Keith. Interviewed by Myron Welch. East Lansing, MI. CD-ROM. 8 Feb. 1973. Disc 22 tr. 2.
142. Gillette, Tom. E-mail to author. 9 Dec. 2008.

143. Louder.
144. Louder.
145. Nelson.
146. Falcone, Beryl. Telephone interview with author. 26 June 2008.
147. Stansell, Gretchen. E-mail to author. 17 Nov. 2010. **Heidi is Fritz and Gretchen Stansell's daughter. Fr. Marek, now deceased, was a founding board member of Blue Lake Fine Arts Camp and served as its treasurer. Beryl and Lisa are, of course, Leonard's wife and granddaughter.*
148. Pearson.
149. Bates, Jack. E-mail to author. 2 Mar. 2009.
150. Wisner, Dan. E-mail to author. 27 Feb. 2009.
151. Bloomquist, Kenneth G. E-mail to author. 13 Mar. 2009.
152. Hodgson, Walter. Disc 19 tr. 16.CD-ROM. 14 May 1973.
153. Lutz.
154. Louder.
155. Pearson.
156. Lodge, Dick. E-mail to author. 3 Mar. 2009.
157. Louder.

## Appendices

1. Falcone, Leonard. Interviewed by Myron Welch. East Lansing, MI. 3 Feb. 1973. CD-ROM. Disc 10, tr. 1-12.
2. Welch, Myron D. *The Life and Work of Leonard Falcone with Emphasis on His Years as Director of Bands at Michigan State University 1927–1967*. Thesis. Michigan State University, 1973. Ann Arbor, MI: UMI Dissertation Services, 1973. 40. Print.
3. Hoag, Gerald H. Papers.1918-1978. Folder 6703. Bentley Historical Library. Ann Arbor: University of Michigan. Print.
4. Hoag, Folder 6703. Ann Arbor News, 8 Dec. 1964.
5. Welch, 157.
6. "MSU Band Conductor Honored Tonight." *Lansing State Journal.* 4 Mar. 1984. p. 1D. Print.
7. Bowman, Brian. "T.U.B.A. Euphonium Profile: Leonard Falcone." T.U.B.A. Journal 5 (Winter 1978): 2. Print.
8. Kuhn, 306.

9. "History." Spartanband.net. Web. 23 Sept. 2009.

10. Welch, 183.

11. Wisner, Dave. E-mail to author. 11 Mar. 2009.

12. Leonard Falcone Papers, Collection UA 17.133. Michigan State University Archives and Historical Collections, East Lansing, MI.

13. Welch, 282.

14. Welch, 283.

*The approach to Roseto Valfortore from Foggia*
*~ courtesy of Cesare Ruggiero*

All proceeds from the sale of *Solid Brass: The Leonard Falcone Story* will be donated to the Leonard Falcone Endowment Fund at Blue Lake Fine Arts Camp.

To learn more about Leonard Falcone or make a contribution to the Leonard Falcone Endowment Fund, log on to *bluelakepress.org*.